Episode 1: "Bad Luck Still Brings Bad Luck"

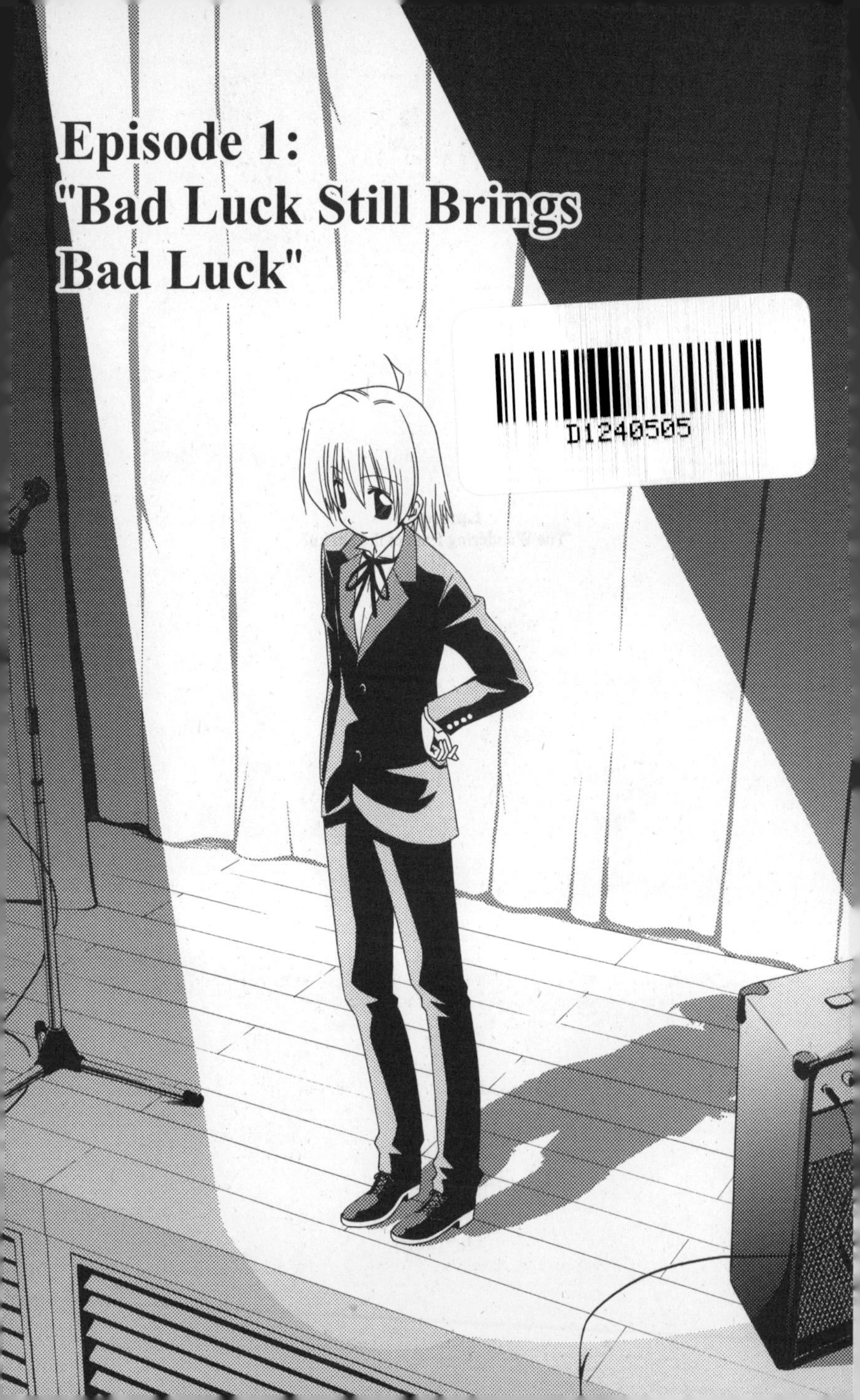

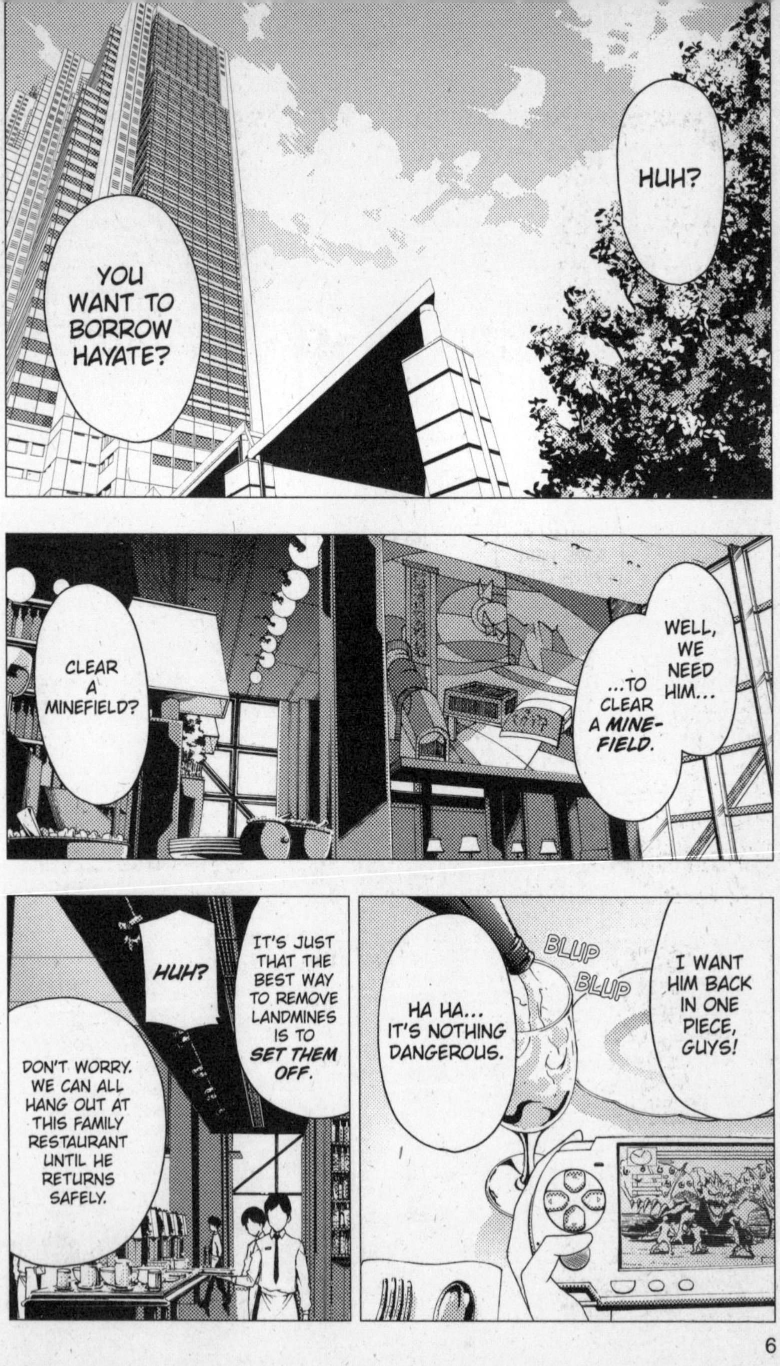
HUH?
YOU WANT TO BORROW HAYATE?
WELL, WE NEED HIM...
...TO CLEAR A *MINEFIELD*.
CLEAR A MINEFIELD?
I WANT HIM BACK IN ONE PIECE, GUYS!
BLUP
BLUP
HA HA... IT'S NOTHING DANGEROUS.
IT'S JUST THAT THE BEST WAY TO REMOVE LANDMINES IS TO *SET THEM OFF*.
HUH?
DON'T WORRY. WE CAN ALL HANG OUT AT THIS FAMILY RESTAURANT UNTIL HE RETURNS SAFELY.

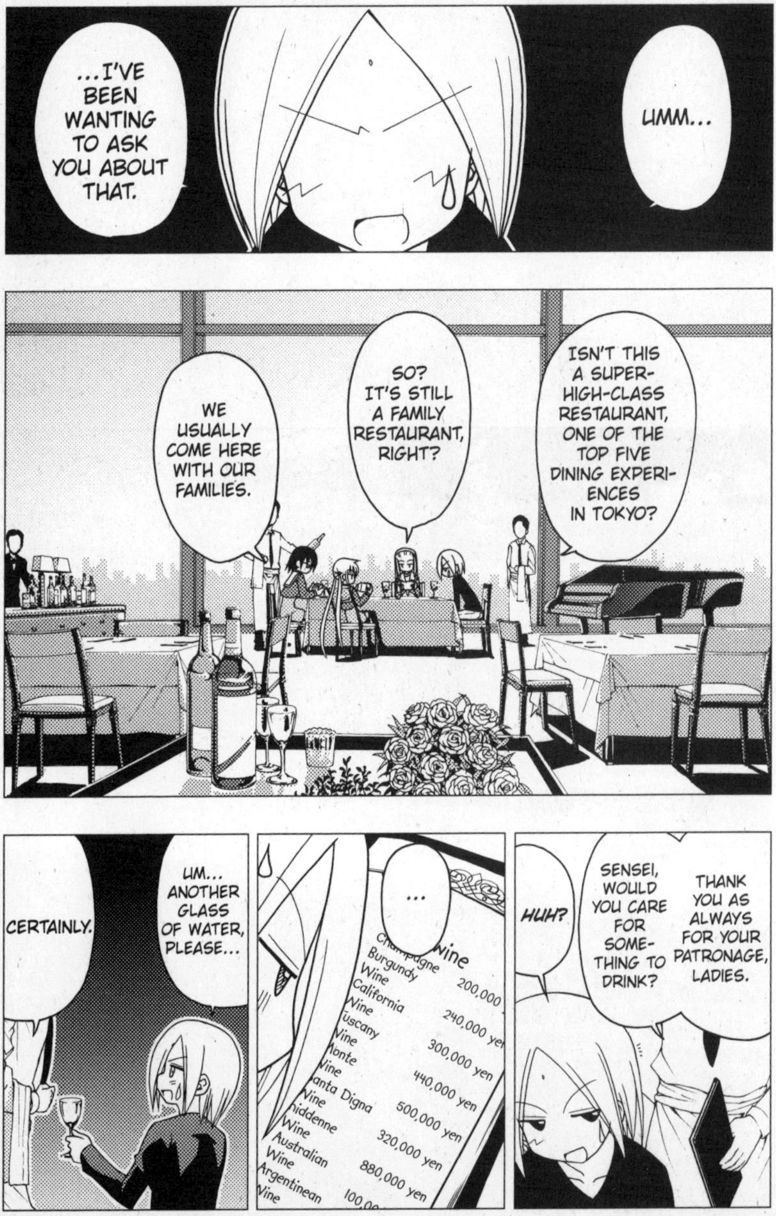
UMM...
...I'VE BEEN WANTING TO ASK YOU ABOUT THAT.
ISN'T THIS A SUPER-HIGH-CLASS RESTAURANT, ONE OF THE TOP FIVE DINING EXPERIENCES IN TOKYO?
SO? IT'S STILL A FAMILY RESTAURANT, RIGHT?
WE USUALLY COME HERE WITH OUR FAMILIES.
THANK YOU AS ALWAYS FOR YOUR PATRONAGE, LADIES.
SENSEI, WOULD YOU CARE FOR SOMETHING TO DRINK?
HUH?
...
Wine
Champagne 200,000
Burgundy Wine 240,000 yen
California Wine 300,000 yen
Tuscany Wine 440,000 yen
Monte Wine 500,000 yen
Wine 320,000 yen
Wine 880,000 yen
Australian Wine
Argentinean Wine
UM... ANOTHER GLASS OF WATER, PLEASE...
CERTAINLY.

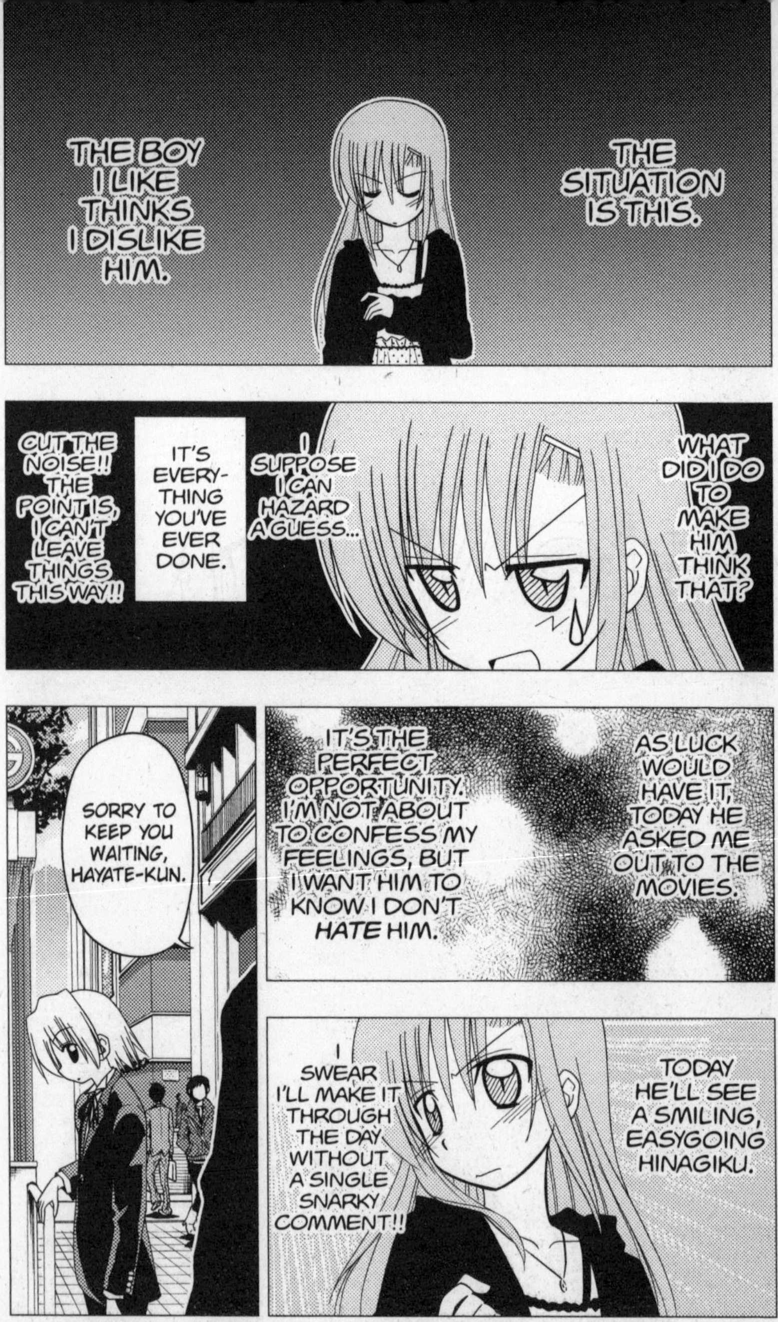
THE SITUATION IS THIS.
THE BOY I LIKE THINKS I DISLIKE HIM.
WHAT DID I DO TO MAKE HIM THINK THAT?
I SUPPOSE I CAN HAZARD A GUESS...
IT'S EVERY-THING YOU'VE EVER DONE.
CUT THE NOISE!! THE POINT IS, I CAN'T LEAVE THINGS THIS WAY!!
AS LUCK WOULD HAVE IT, TODAY HE ASKED ME OUT TO THE MOVIES.
IT'S THE PERFECT OPPORTUNITY. I'M NOT ABOUT TO CONFESS MY FEELINGS, BUT I WANT HIM TO KNOW I DON'T *HATE* HIM.
TODAY HE'LL SEE A SMILING, EASYGOING HINAGIKU.
I SWEAR I'LL MAKE IT THROUGH THE DAY WITHOUT A SINGLE SNARKY COMMENT!!
SORRY TO KEEP YOU WAITING, HAYATE-KUN.

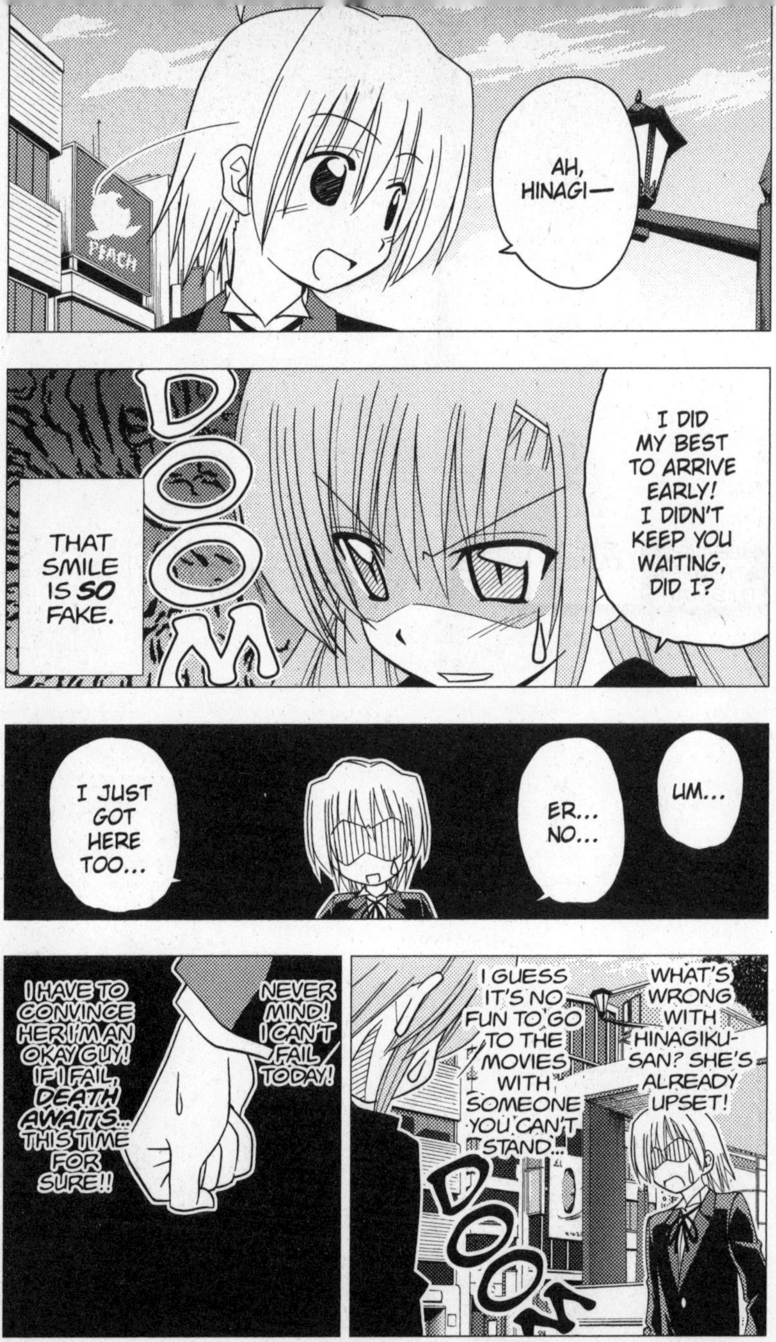
AH, HINAGI—
I DID MY BEST TO ARRIVE EARLY! I DIDN'T KEEP YOU WAITING, DID I?
THAT SMILE IS SO FAKE.
DOOM
UM...
ER... NO...
I JUST GOT HERE TOO...
WHAT'S WRONG WITH HINAGIKU-SAN? SHE'S ALREADY UPSET!
I GUESS IT'S NO FUN TO GO TO THE MOVIES WITH SOMEONE YOU CAN'T STAND...
DOOM
NEVER MIND! I CAN'T FAIL TODAY!
I HAVE TO CONVINCE HER I'M AN OKAY GUY! IF I FAIL, DEATH AWAITS... THIS TIME FOR SURE!!

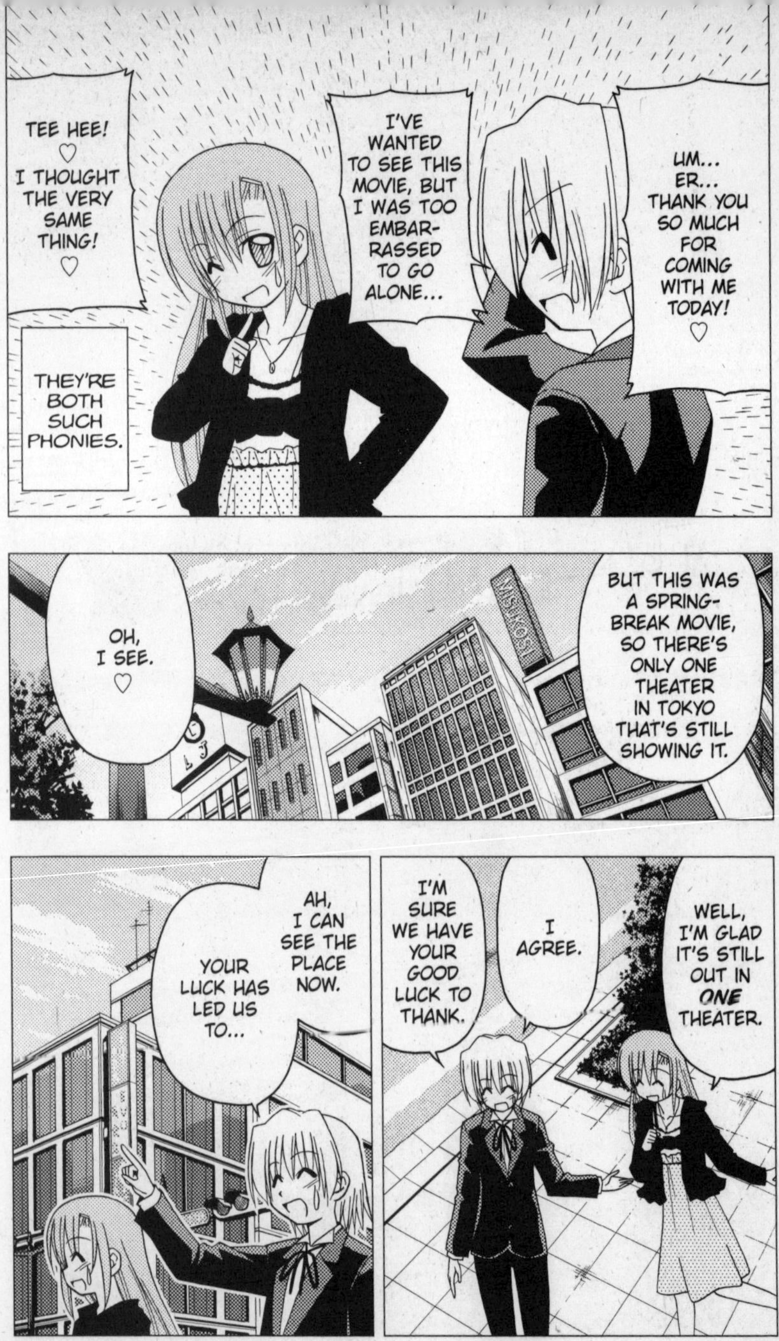
UM... ER... THANK YOU SO MUCH FOR COMING WITH ME TODAY! ♡
I'VE WANTED TO SEE THIS MOVIE, BUT I WAS TOO EMBARRASSED TO GO ALONE...
TEE HEE! ♡ I THOUGHT THE VERY SAME THING! ♡
THEY'RE BOTH SUCH PHONIES.
BUT THIS WAS A SPRING-BREAK MOVIE, SO THERE'S ONLY ONE THEATER IN TOKYO THAT'S STILL SHOWING IT.
OH, I SEE. ♡
WELL, I'M GLAD IT'S STILL OUT IN *ONE* THEATER.
I AGREE.
I'M SURE WE HAVE YOUR GOOD LUCK TO THANK.
AH, I CAN SEE THE PLACE NOW.
YOUR LUCK HAS LED US TO...

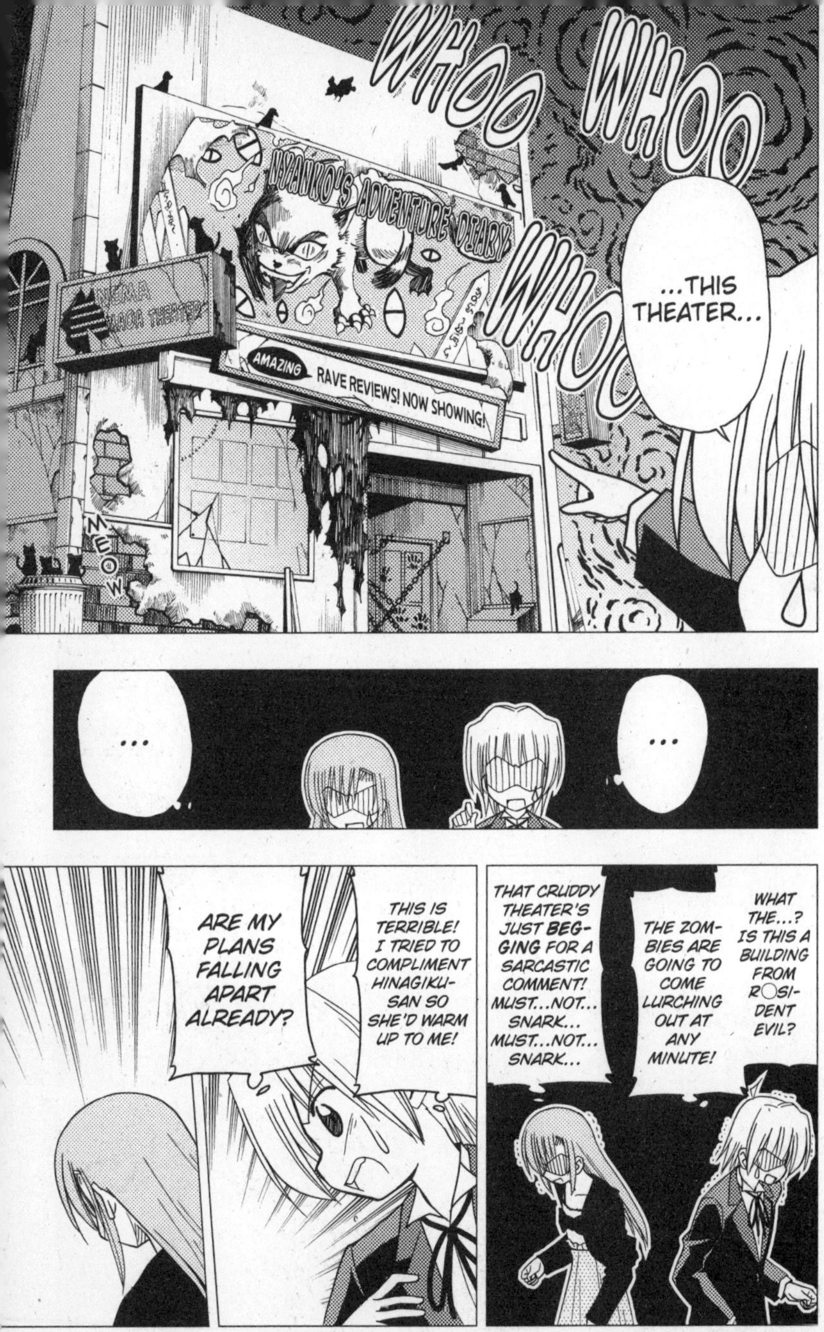
WHOO WHOO WHOO
...THIS THEATER...
NYANKO'S ADVENTURE DIARY
AMAZING RAVE REVIEWS! NOW SHOWING!
MEOW
...
...
WHAT THE...? IS THIS A BUILDING FROM R○SIDENT EVIL?
THE ZOMBIES ARE GOING TO COME LURCHING OUT AT ANY MINUTE!
THAT CRUDDY THEATER'S JUST **BEGGING** FOR A SARCASTIC COMMENT! MUST...NOT... SNARK... MUST...NOT... SNARK...
THIS IS TERRIBLE! I TRIED TO COMPLIMENT HINAGIKU-SAN SO SHE'D WARM UP TO ME!
ARE MY PLANS FALLING APART ALREADY?

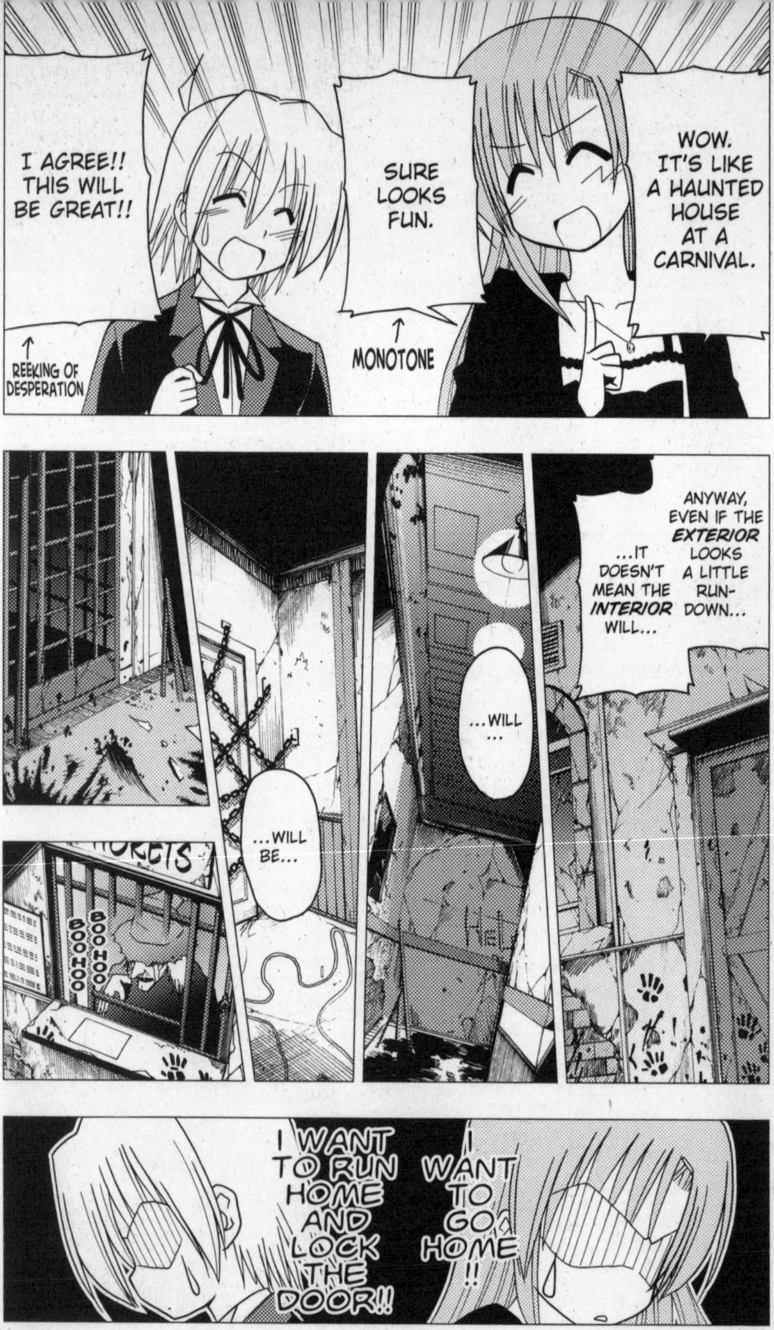
WOW. IT'S LIKE A HAUNTED HOUSE AT A CARNIVAL.
SURE LOOKS FUN.
MONOTONE
I AGREE!! THIS WILL BE GREAT!!
REEKING OF DESPERATION
ANYWAY, EVEN IF THE *EXTERIOR* LOOKS A LITTLE RUN-DOWN...
...IT DOESN'T MEAN THE *INTERIOR* WILL...
...WILL ...
...WILL BE...
BOO HOO
BOO HOO
I WANT TO GO HOME!!
I WANT TO RUN HOME AND LOCK THE DOOR!!

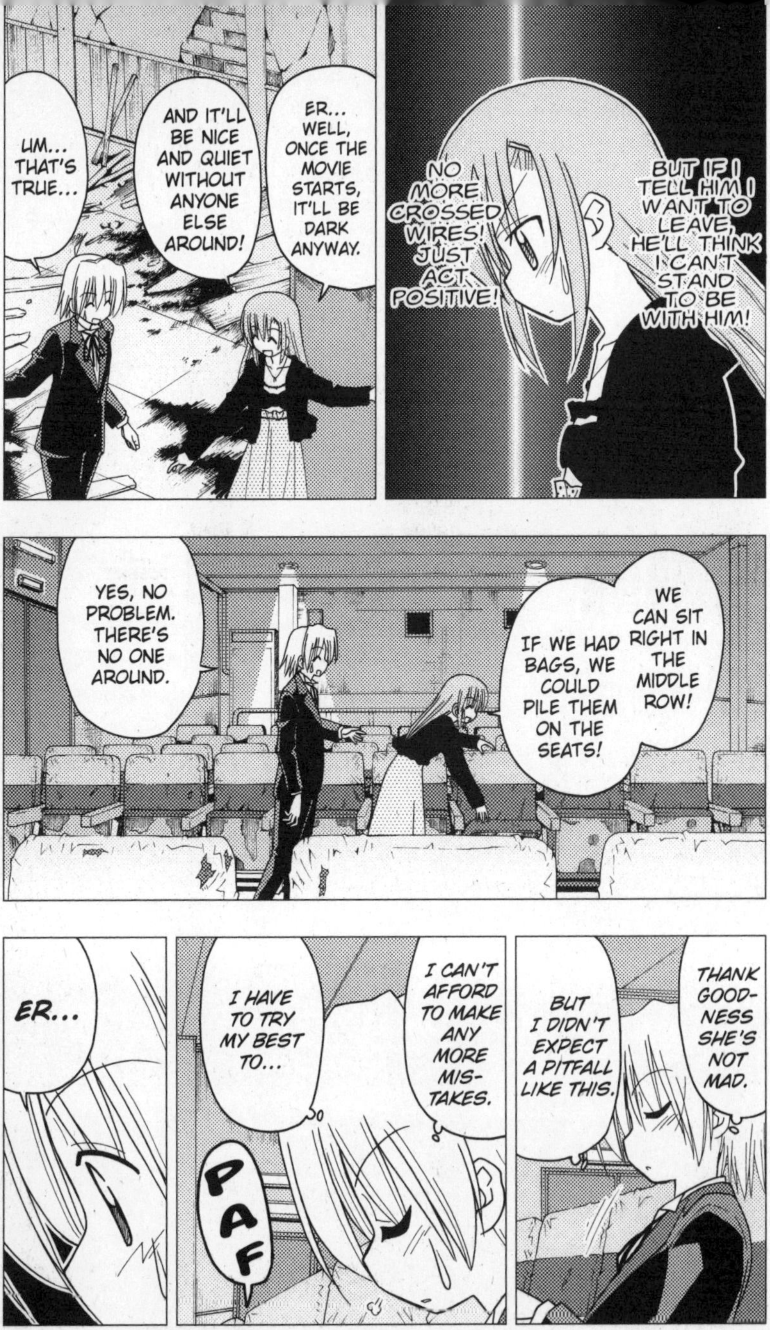
BUT IF I TELL HIM I WANT TO LEAVE, HE'LL THINK I CAN'T STAND TO BE WITH HIM!
NO MORE CROSSED WIRES! JUST ACT POSITIVE!
ER... WELL, ONCE THE MOVIE STARTS, IT'LL BE DARK ANYWAY.
AND IT'LL BE NICE AND QUIET WITHOUT ANYONE ELSE AROUND!
UM... THAT'S TRUE...
WE CAN SIT RIGHT IN THE MIDDLE ROW!
IF WE HAD BAGS, WE COULD PILE THEM ON THE SEATS!
YES, NO PROBLEM. THERE'S NO ONE AROUND.
THANK GOODNESS SHE'S NOT MAD.
BUT I DIDN'T EXPECT A PITFALL LIKE THIS.
I CAN'T AFFORD TO MAKE ANY MORE MISTAKES.
I HAVE TO TRY MY BEST TO...
PAF
ER...

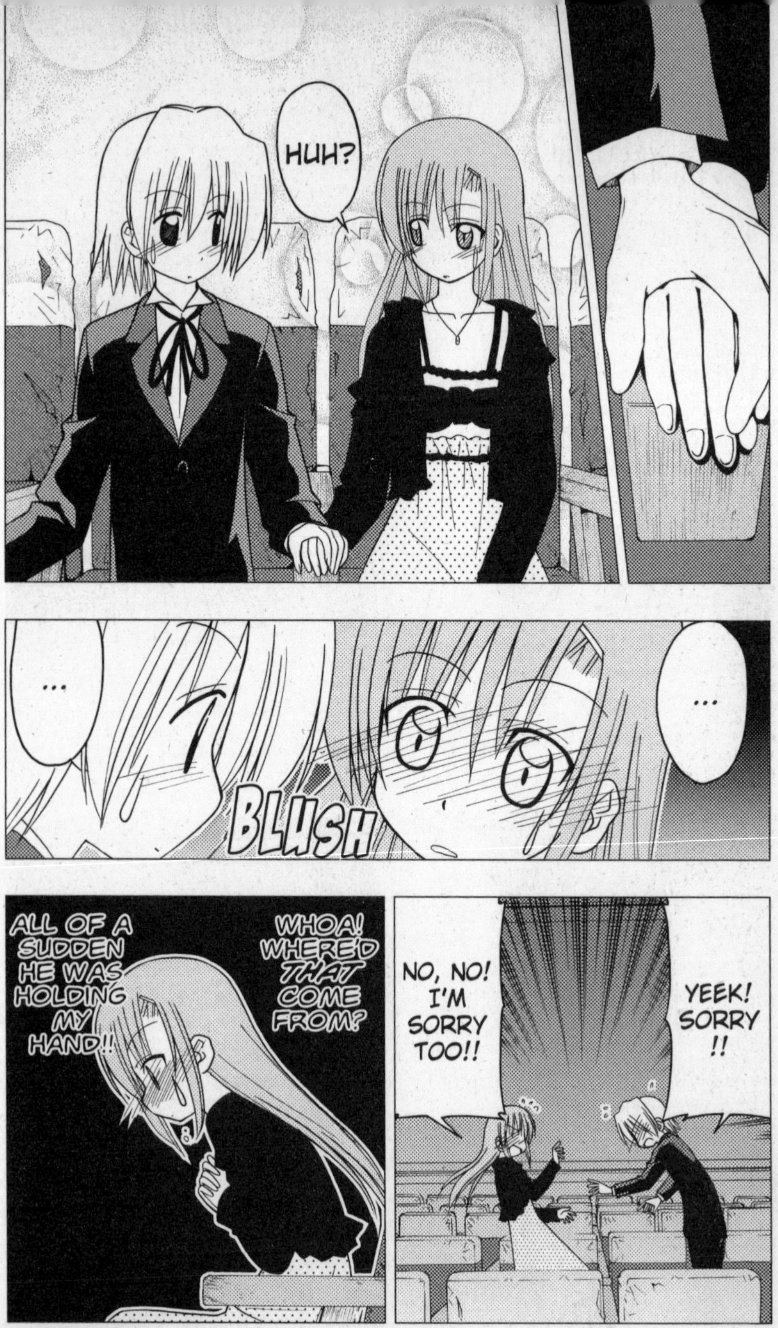
HUH?
...
...
BLUSH
YEEK! SORRY !!
NO, NO! I'M SORRY TOO!!
WHOA! WHERE'D THAT COME FROM?
ALL OF A SUDDEN HE WAS HOLDING MY HAND!!

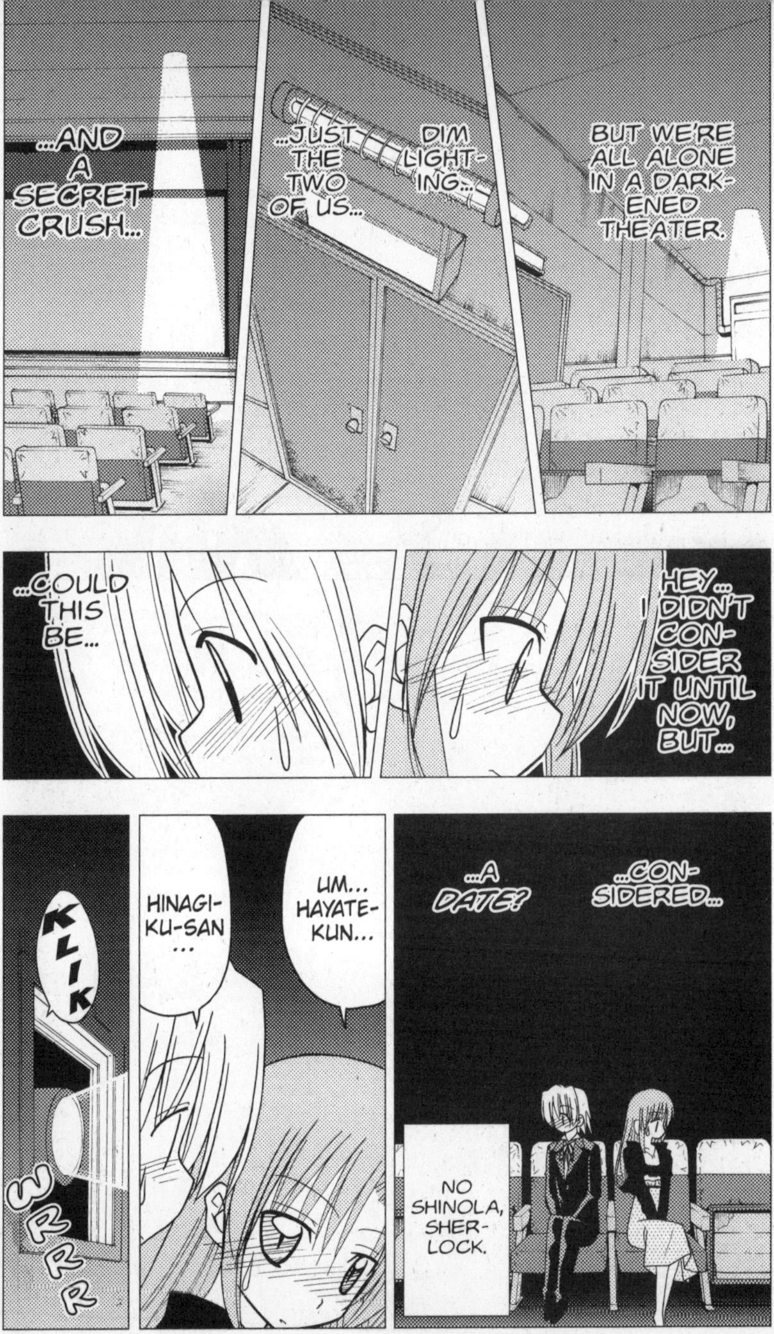
BUT WE'RE ALL ALONE IN A DARKENED THEATER.
DIM LIGHTING...
...JUST THE TWO OF US...
...AND A SECRET CRUSH...
HEY... I DIDN'T CONSIDER IT UNTIL NOW, BUT...
...COULD THIS BE...
...CONSIDERED...
...A DATE?
NO SHINOLA, SHERLOCK.
UM... HAYATE-KUN...
HINAGIKU-SAN...
KLIK
WRRR

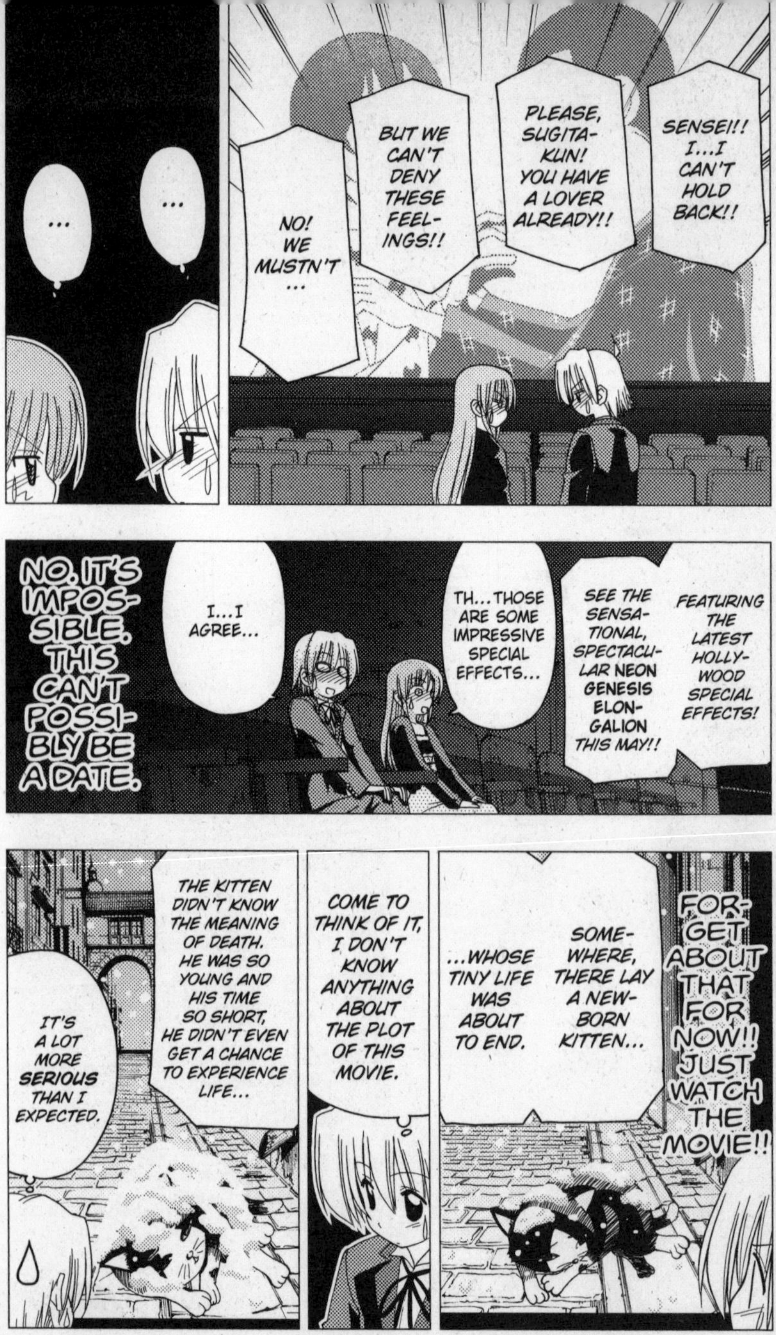
SENSEI!! I...I CAN'T HOLD BACK!!
PLEASE, SUGITA-KUN! YOU HAVE A LOVER ALREADY!!
BUT WE CAN'T DENY THESE FEELINGS!!
NO! WE MUSTN'T...
...
...
FEATURING THE LATEST HOLLYWOOD SPECIAL EFFECTS!
SEE THE SENSATIONAL, SPECTACULAR NEON GENESIS ELONGALION THIS MAY!!
TH...THOSE ARE SOME IMPRESSIVE SPECIAL EFFECTS...
I...I AGREE...
NO. IT'S IMPOSSIBLE. THIS CAN'T POSSIBLY BE A DATE.
FORGET ABOUT THAT FOR NOW!! JUST WATCH THE MOVIE!!
SOMEWHERE, THERE LAY A NEWBORN KITTEN...
...WHOSE TINY LIFE WAS ABOUT TO END.
COME TO THINK OF IT, I DON'T KNOW ANYTHING ABOUT THE PLOT OF THIS MOVIE.
THE KITTEN DIDN'T KNOW THE MEANING OF DEATH. HE WAS SO YOUNG AND HIS TIME SO SHORT, HE DIDN'T EVEN GET A CHANCE TO EXPERIENCE LIFE...
IT'S A LOT MORE SERIOUS THAN I EXPECTED.

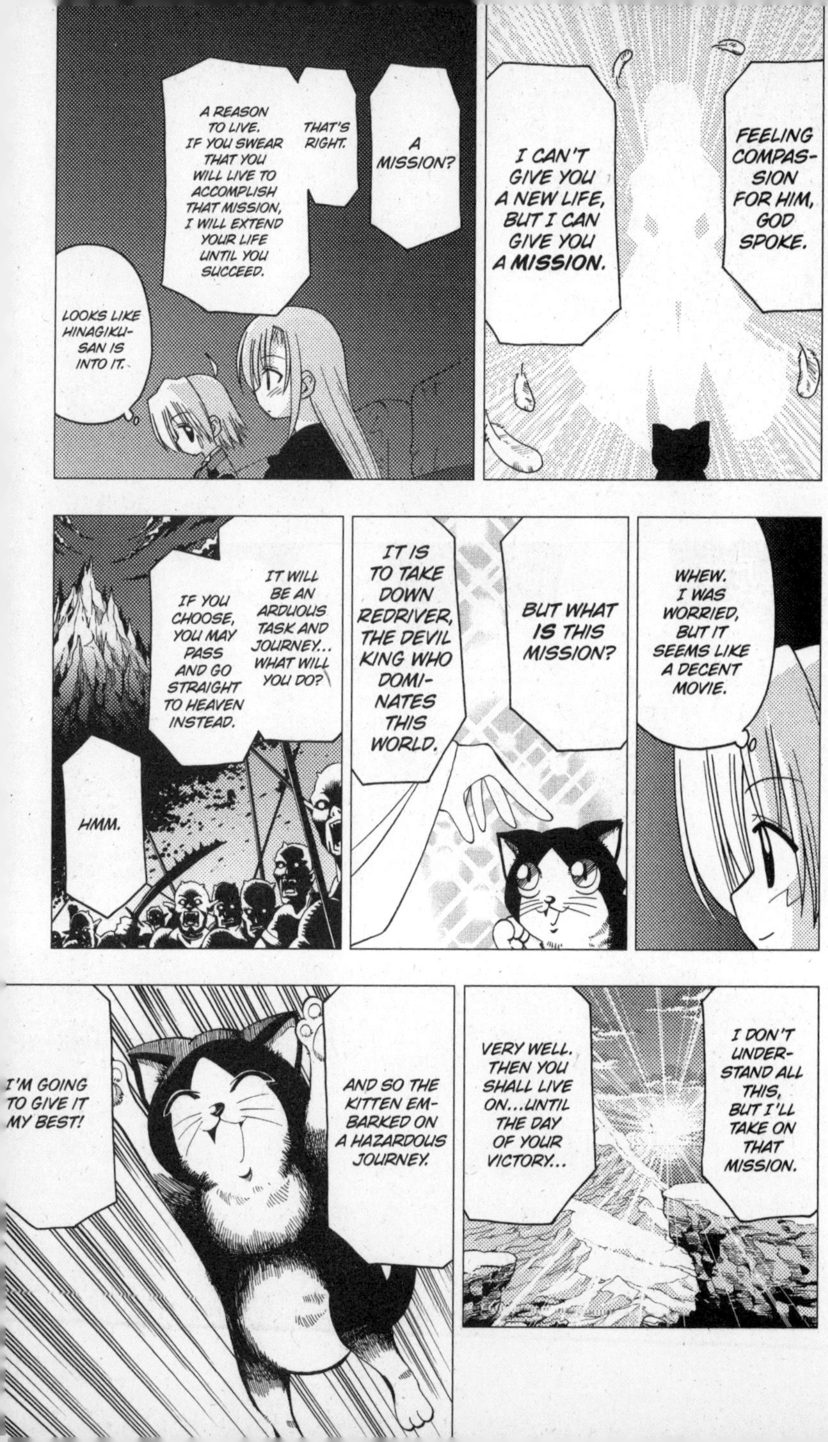
FEELING COMPASSION FOR HIM, GOD SPOKE.
I CAN'T GIVE YOU A NEW LIFE, BUT I CAN GIVE YOU A MISSION.
A MISSION?
THAT'S RIGHT.
A REASON TO LIVE. IF YOU SWEAR THAT YOU WILL LIVE TO ACCOMPLISH THAT MISSION, I WILL EXTEND YOUR LIFE UNTIL YOU SUCCEED.
LOOKS LIKE HINAGIKU-SAN IS INTO IT.
WHEW. I WAS WORRIED, BUT IT SEEMS LIKE A DECENT MOVIE.
BUT WHAT IS THIS MISSION?
IT IS TO TAKE DOWN REDRIVER, THE DEVIL KING WHO DOMINATES THIS WORLD.
IT WILL BE AN ARDUOUS TASK AND JOURNEY... WHAT WILL YOU DO?
IF YOU CHOOSE, YOU MAY PASS AND GO STRAIGHT TO HEAVEN INSTEAD.
HMM.
I DON'T UNDERSTAND ALL THIS, BUT I'LL TAKE ON THAT MISSION.
VERY WELL. THEN YOU SHALL LIVE ON...UNTIL THE DAY OF YOUR VICTORY...
AND SO THE KITTEN EMBARKED ON A HAZARDOUS JOURNEY.
I'M GOING TO GIVE IT MY BEST!

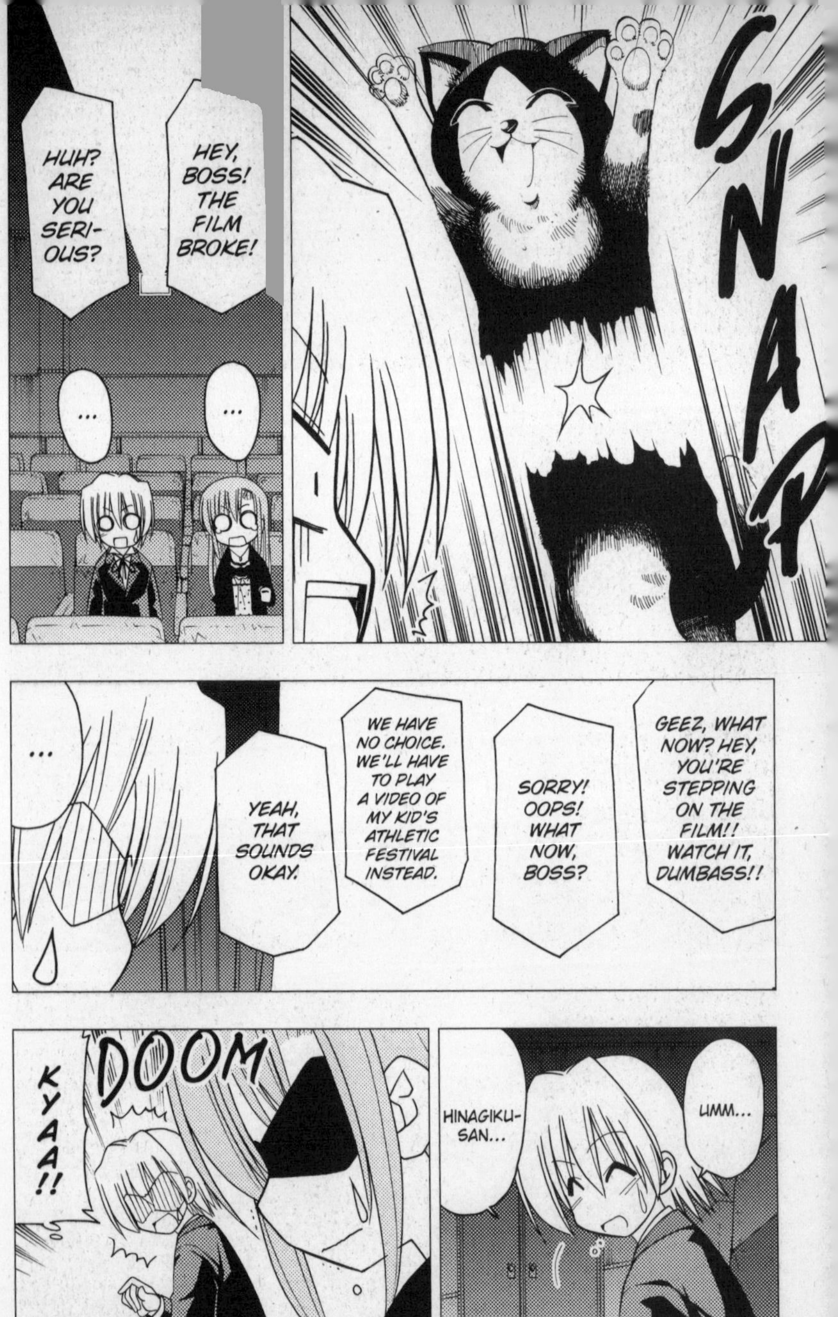
SNAP
HEY, BOSS! THE FILM BROKE!
HUH? ARE YOU SERI-OUS?
...
...
GEEZ, WHAT NOW? HEY, YOU'RE STEPPING ON THE FILM!! WATCH IT, DUMBASS!!
SORRY! OOPS! WHAT NOW, BOSS?
WE HAVE NO CHOICE. WE'LL HAVE TO PLAY A VIDEO OF MY KID'S ATHLETIC FESTIVAL INSTEAD.
YEAH, THAT SOUNDS OKAY.
...
UMM...
HINAGIKU-SAN...
DOOM
KYAA!!

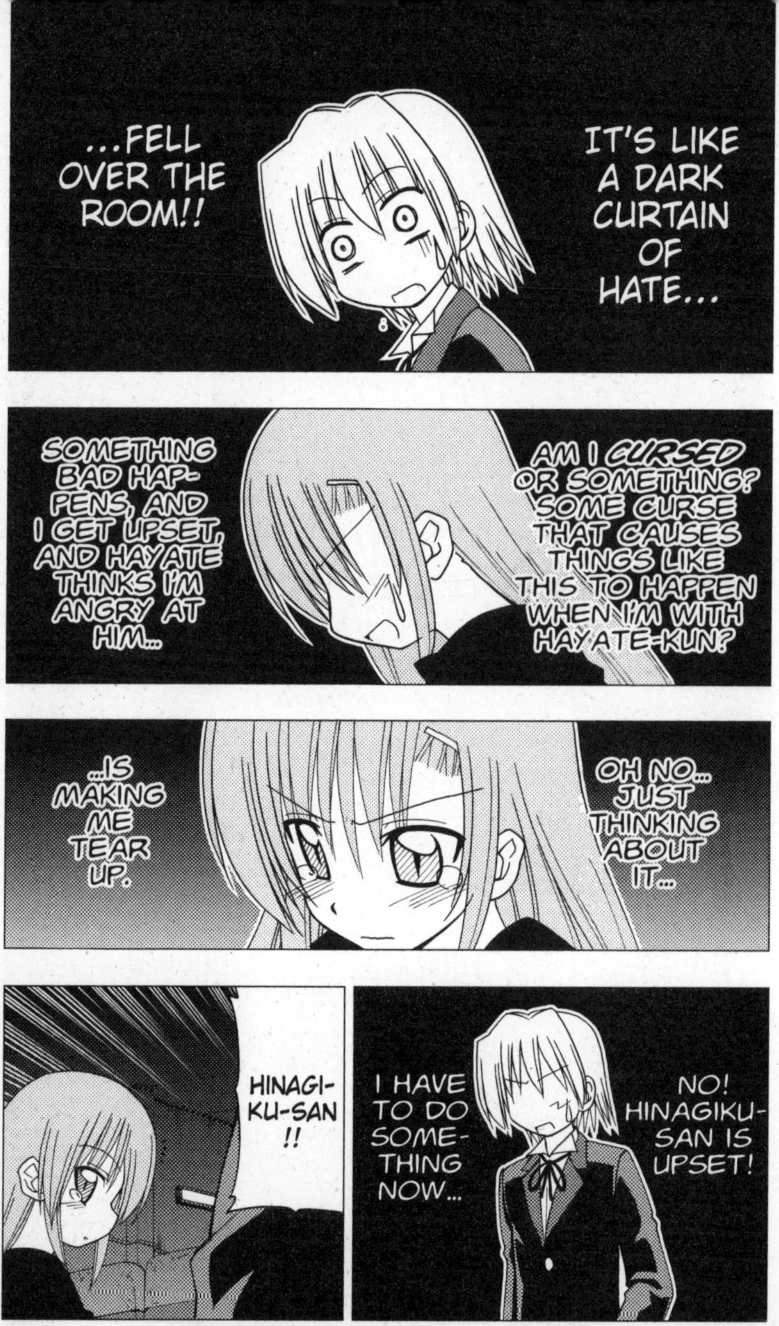
IT'S LIKE A DARK CURTAIN OF HATE...
...FELL OVER THE ROOM!!
AM I *CURSED* OR SOMETHING? SOME CURSE THAT CAUSES THINGS LIKE THIS TO HAPPEN WHEN I'M WITH HAYATE-KUN?
SOMETHING BAD HAP-PENS, AND I GET UPSET, AND HAYATE THINKS I'M ANGRY AT HIM...
OH NO... JUST THINKING ABOUT IT...
...IS MAKING ME TEAR UP.
NO! HINAGIKU-SAN IS UPSET!
I HAVE TO DO SOME-THING NOW...
HINAGI-KU-SAN!!

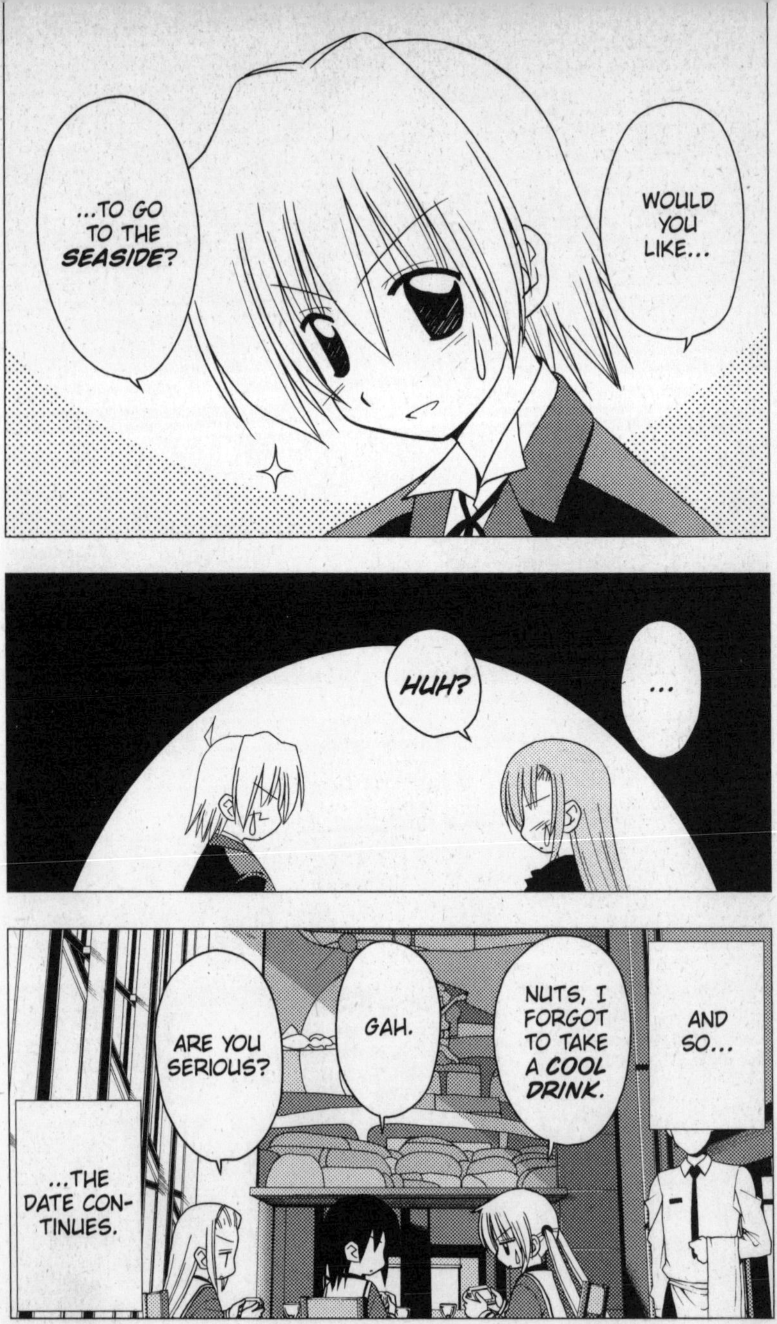
WOULD YOU LIKE...
...TO GO TO THE SEASIDE?
...
HUH?
AND SO...
NUTS, I FORGOT TO TAKE A COOL DRINK.
GAH.
ARE YOU SERIOUS?
...THE DATE CONTINUES.

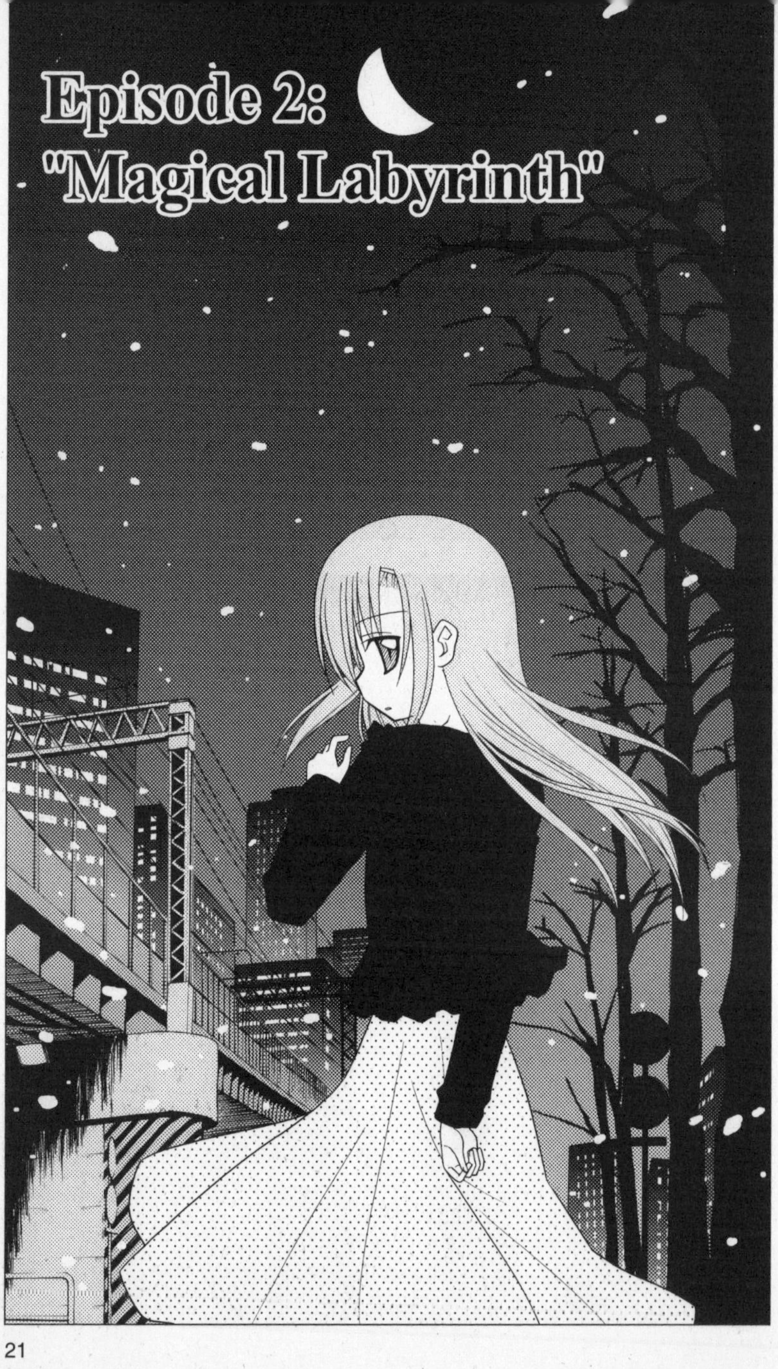
Episode 2:
"Magical Labyrinth"

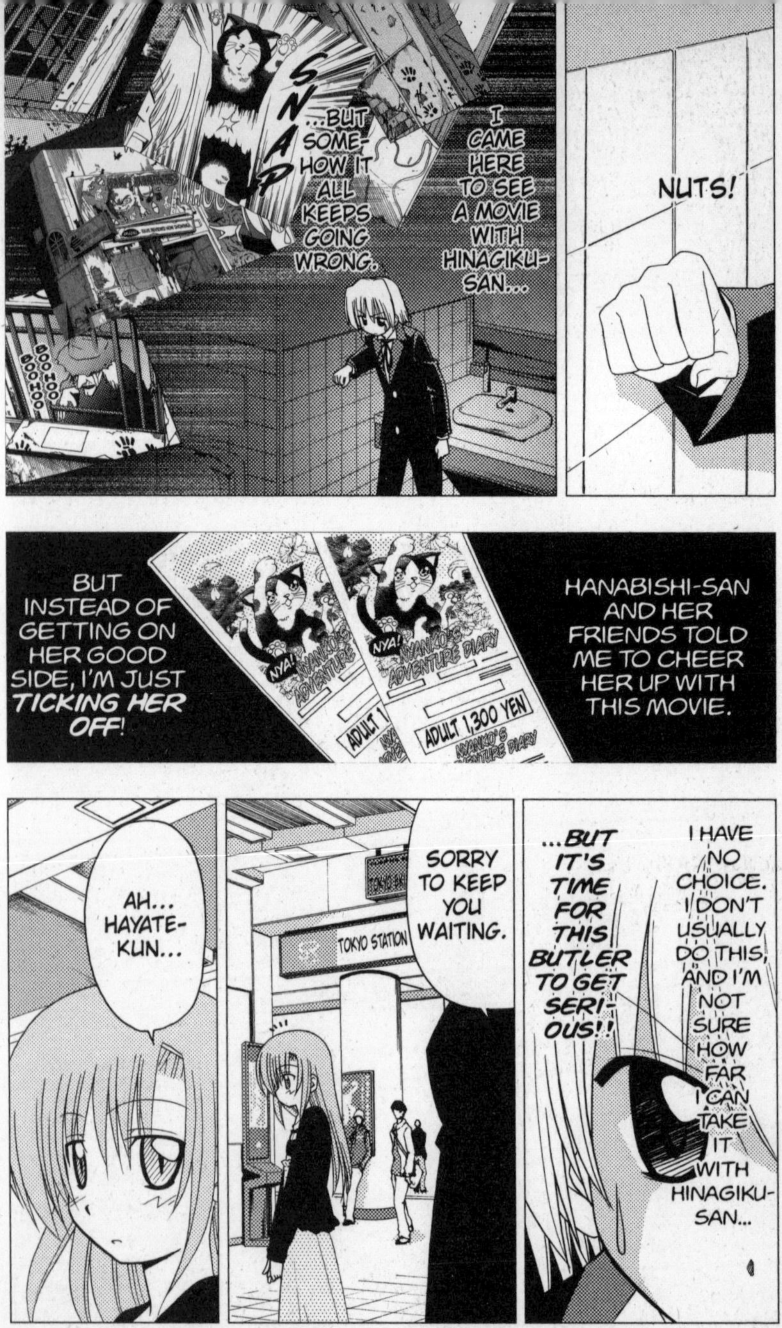
NUTS!
I CAME HERE TO SEE A MOVIE WITH HINAGIKU-SAN...
SNAP
...BUT SOMEHOW IT ALL KEEPS GOING WRONG.
BOO HOO BOO HOO
HANABISHI-SAN AND HER FRIENDS TOLD ME TO CHEER HER UP WITH THIS MOVIE.
NYA!
NYANKO'S ADVENTURE DIARY
ADULT 1,300 YEN
NYANKO'S ADVENTURE DIARY
NYA!
NYANKO'S ADVENTURE
ADULT 1
BUT INSTEAD OF GETTING ON HER GOOD SIDE, I'M JUST *TICKING HER OFF*!
I HAVE NO CHOICE. I DON'T USUALLY DO THIS, AND I'M NOT SURE HOW FAR I CAN TAKE IT WITH HINAGIKU-SAN...
...BUT IT'S TIME FOR THIS BUTLER TO GET SERIOUS!!
SORRY TO KEEP YOU WAITING.
TOKYO STATION
AH... HAYATE-KUN...

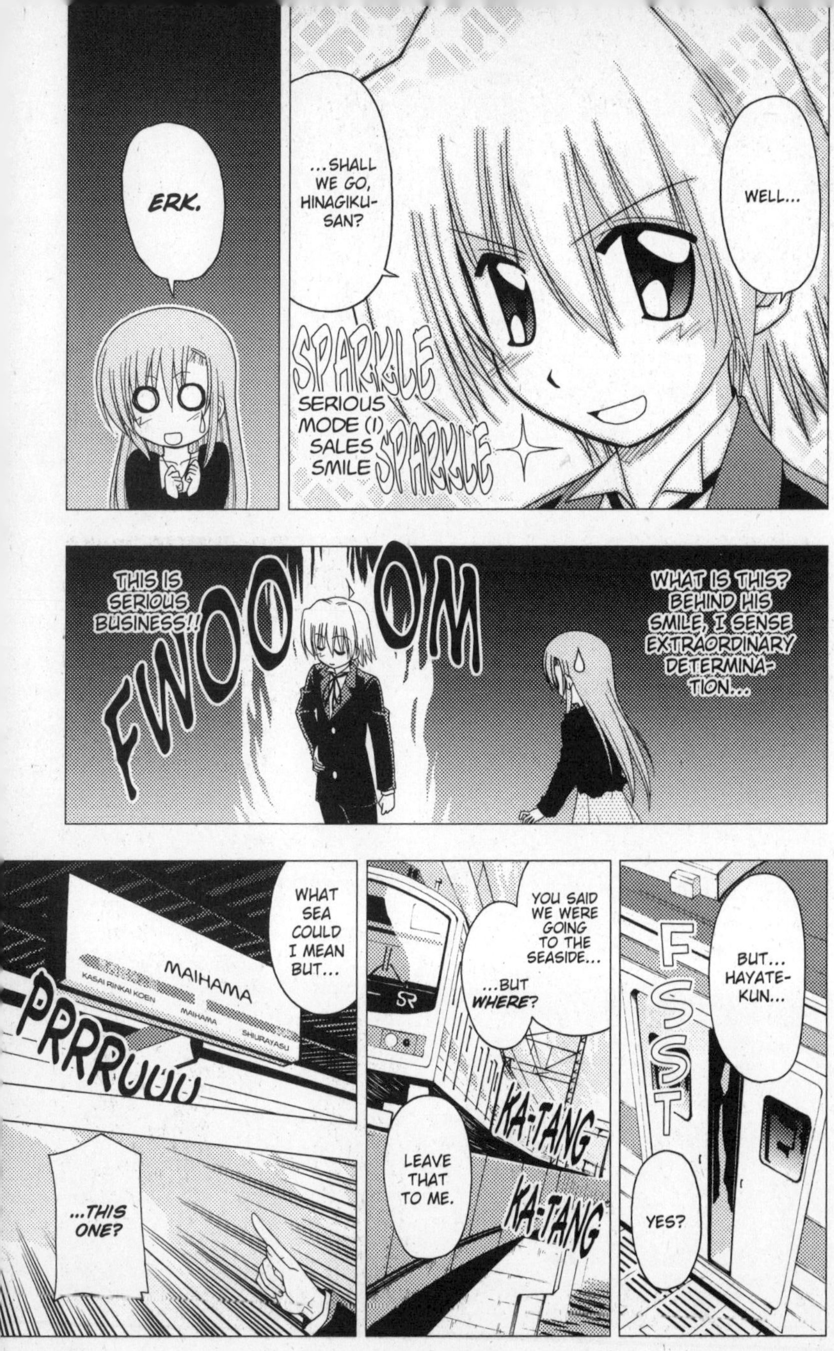

WELL...
...SHALL WE GO, HINAGIKU-SAN?
SPARKLE
SERIOUS MODE (1) SALES SMILE
SPARKLE
ERK.
WHAT IS THIS? BEHIND HIS SMILE, I SENSE EXTRAORDINARY DETERMINATION...
FWOOOM
THIS IS SERIOUS BUSINESS!!
FSST
BUT... HAYATE-KUN...
YES?
YOU SAID WE WERE GOING TO THE SEASIDE...
...BUT WHERE?
LEAVE THAT TO ME.
KA-TANG
KA-TANG
WHAT SEA COULD I MEAN BUT...
MAIHAMA
KASAI RINKAI KOEN
MAIHAMA
SHIURAYASU
PRRRUUUU
...THIS ONE?

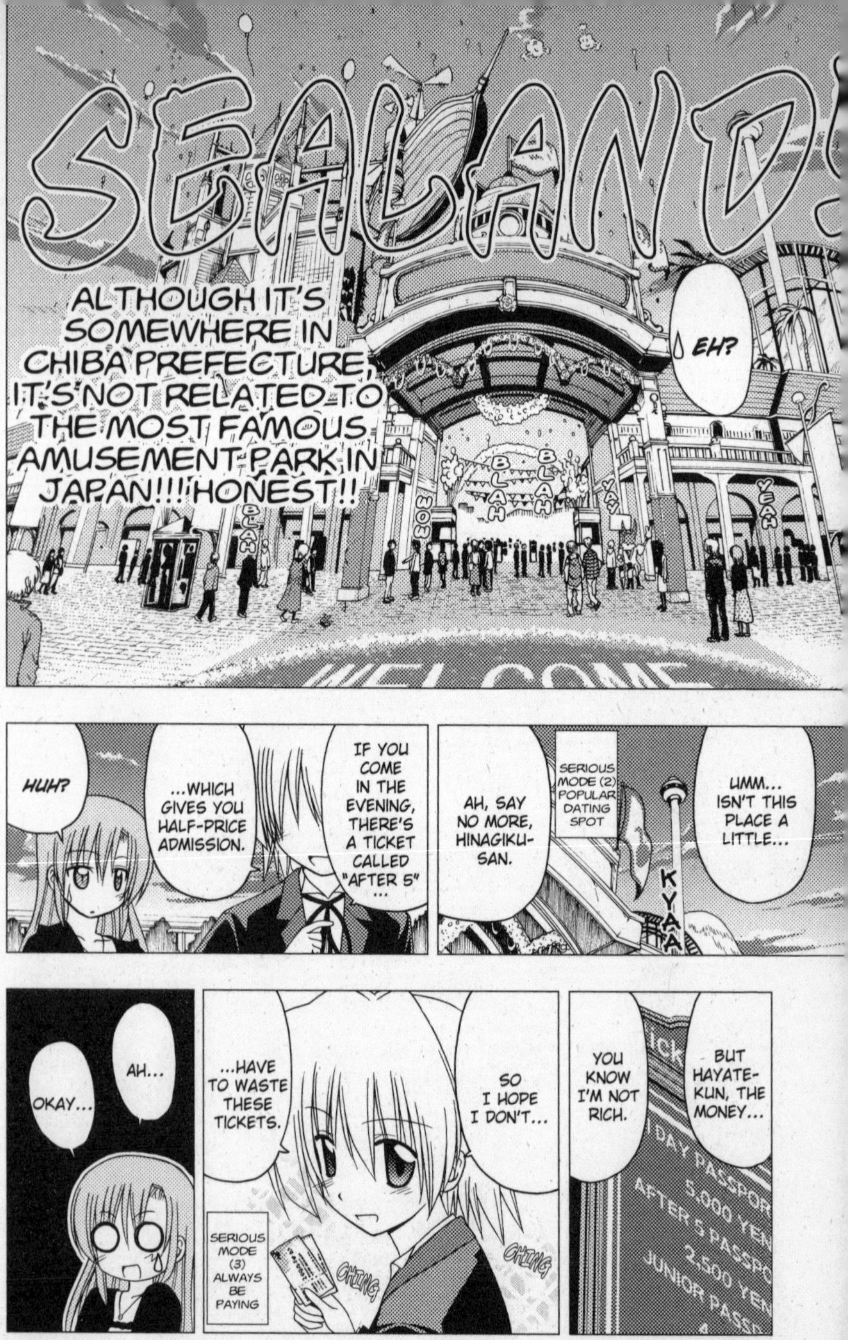
SEALAND!
EH?
ALTHOUGH IT'S SOMEWHERE IN CHIBA PREFECTURE, IT'S NOT RELATED TO THE MOST FAMOUS AMUSEMENT PARK IN JAPAN!!! HONEST!!
YEAH
BLAH
BLAH
YAY
WOW
BLAH
UMM... ISN'T THIS PLACE A LITTLE...
KYAA
SERIOUS MODE (2) POPULAR DATING SPOT
AH, SAY NO MORE, HINAGIKU-SAN.
IF YOU COME IN THE EVENING, THERE'S A TICKET CALLED "AFTER 5"...
...WHICH GIVES YOU HALF-PRICE ADMISSION.
HUH?
BUT HAYATE-KUN, THE MONEY...
YOU KNOW I'M NOT RICH.
SO I HOPE I DON'T...
...HAVE TO WASTE THESE TICKETS.
CHING
CHING
SERIOUS MODE (3) ALWAYS BE PAYING
AH...
OKAY...

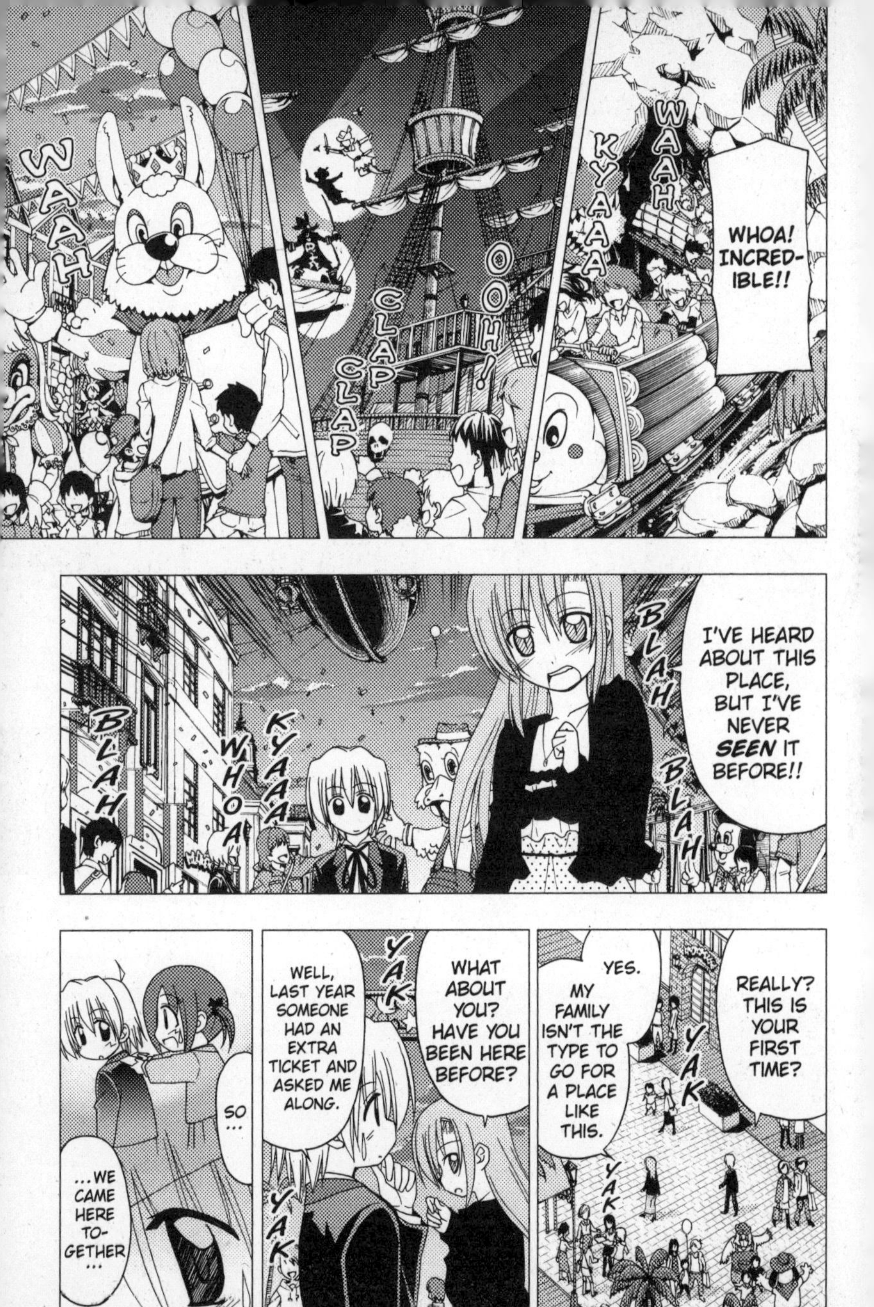
WAAH
KYAAAA
WHOA! INCRED-IBLE!!
OOOH!
CLAP CLAP CLAP
WAAAH
BLAH BLAH
I'VE HEARD ABOUT THIS PLACE, BUT I'VE NEVER ***SEEN*** IT BEFORE!!
BLAH BLAH
KYAAAA
WHOA
BLAH
REALLY? THIS IS YOUR FIRST TIME?
YES.
MY FAMILY ISN'T THE TYPE TO GO FOR A PLACE LIKE THIS.
YAK YAK
YAK
WHAT ABOUT YOU? HAVE YOU BEEN HERE BEFORE?
YAK
WELL, LAST YEAR SOMEONE HAD AN EXTRA TICKET AND ASKED ME ALONG.
YAK YAK
SO...
...WE CAME HERE TO-GETHER...

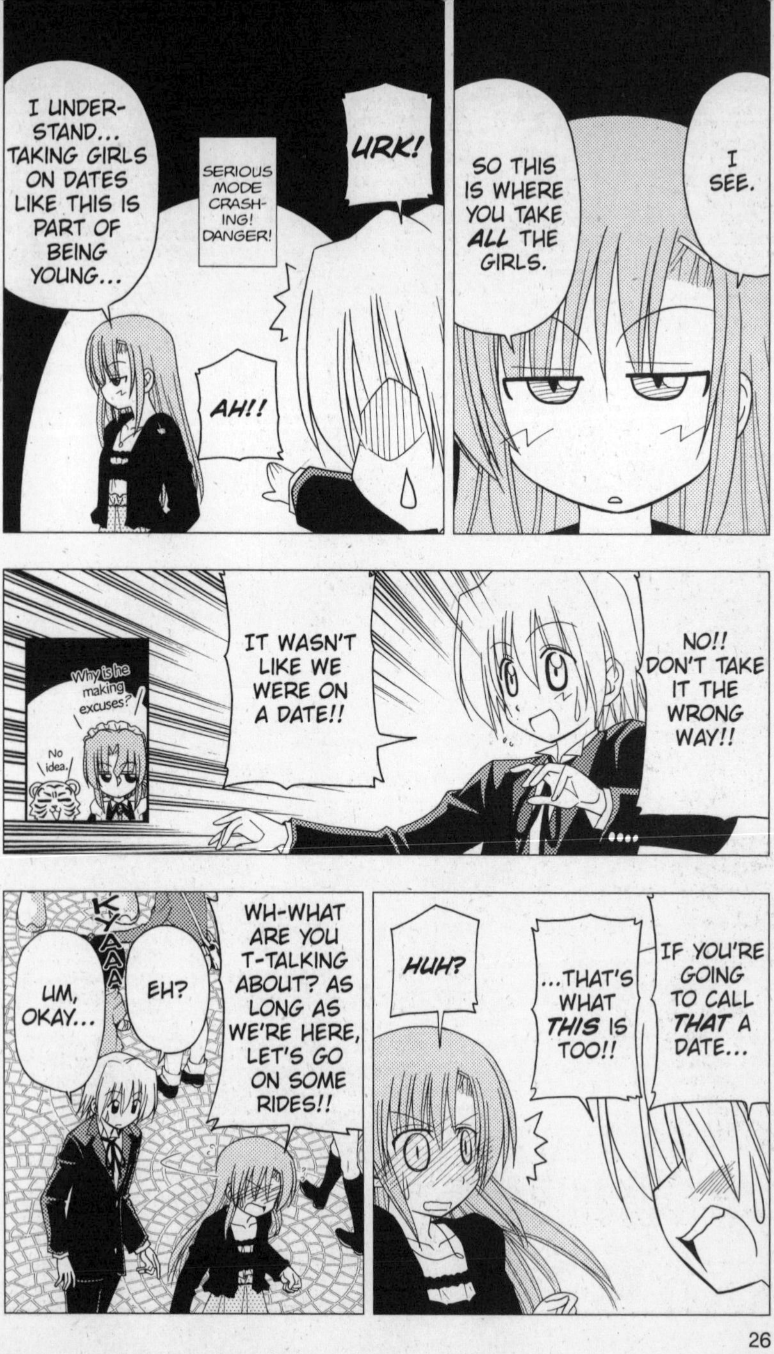
I SEE.
SO THIS IS WHERE YOU TAKE ALL THE GIRLS.
URK!
SERIOUS MODE CRASHING! DANGER!
I UNDERSTAND... TAKING GIRLS ON DATES LIKE THIS IS PART OF BEING YOUNG...
AH!!
NO!! DON'T TAKE IT THE WRONG WAY!!
IT WASN'T LIKE WE WERE ON A DATE!!
Why is he making excuses?
No idea.
IF YOU'RE GOING TO CALL THAT A DATE...
...THAT'S WHAT THIS IS TOO!!
HUH?
WH-WHAT ARE YOU T-TALKING ABOUT? AS LONG AS WE'RE HERE, LET'S GO ON SOME RIDES!!
KYAAA
EH?
UM, OKAY...

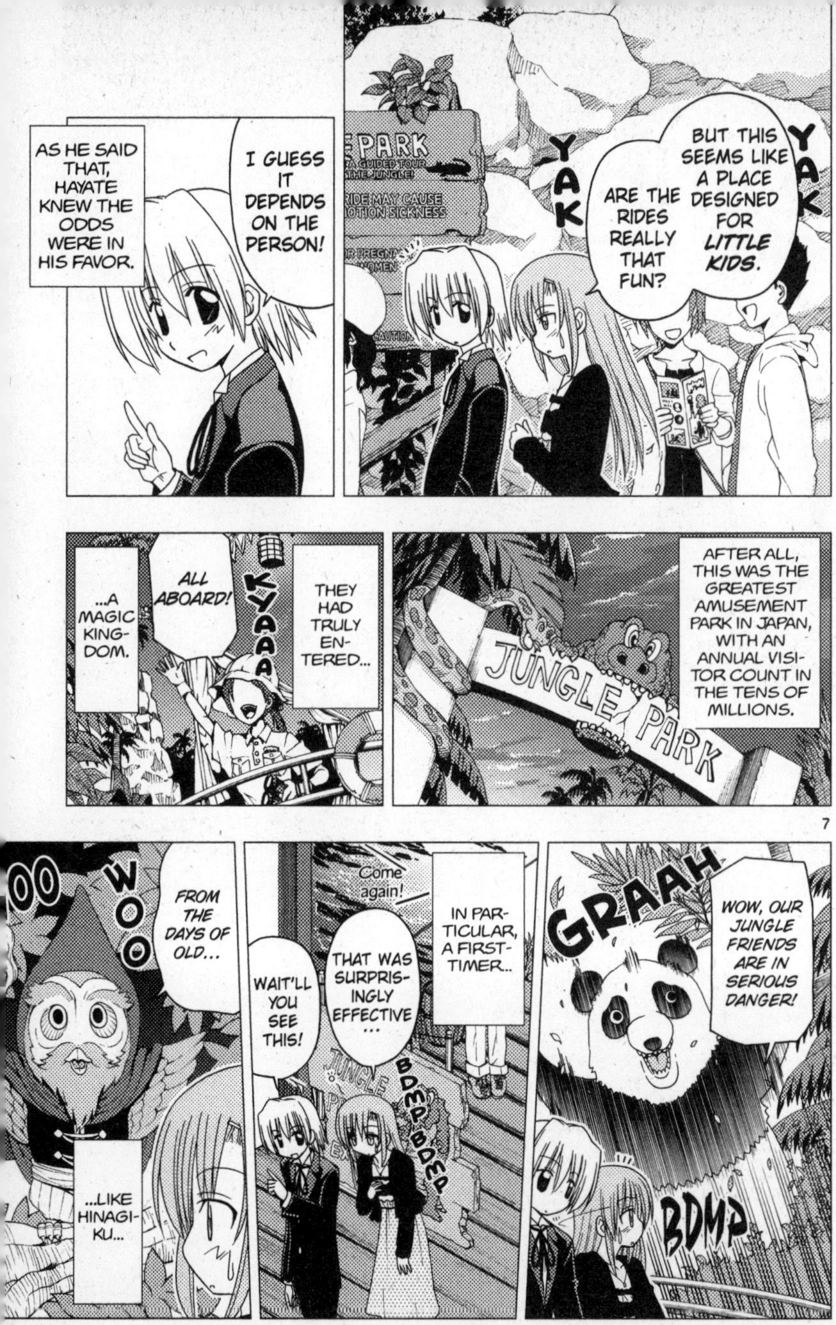
YAK
YAK
BUT THIS SEEMS LIKE A PLACE DESIGNED FOR *LITTLE KIDS.*
ARE THE RIDES REALLY THAT FUN?
PARK
RIDE MAY CAUSE MOTION SICKNESS
CAUTION
I GUESS IT DEPENDS ON THE PERSON!
AS HE SAID THAT, HAYATE KNEW THE ODDS WERE IN HIS FAVOR.
AFTER ALL, THIS WAS THE GREATEST AMUSEMENT PARK IN JAPAN, WITH AN ANNUAL VISITOR COUNT IN THE TENS OF MILLIONS.
JUNGLE PARK
THEY HAD TRULY ENTERED...
KYAAA
ALL ABOARD!
...A MAGIC KINGDOM.
GRAAH
WOW, OUR JUNGLE FRIENDS ARE IN SERIOUS DANGER!
BDMP
IN PARTICULAR, A FIRST-TIMER...
Come again!
THAT WAS SURPRISINGLY EFFECTIVE...
WAIT'LL YOU SEE THIS!
BDMP BDMP
WOO
WOO
FROM THE DAYS OF OLD...
...LIKE HINAGIKU...

7

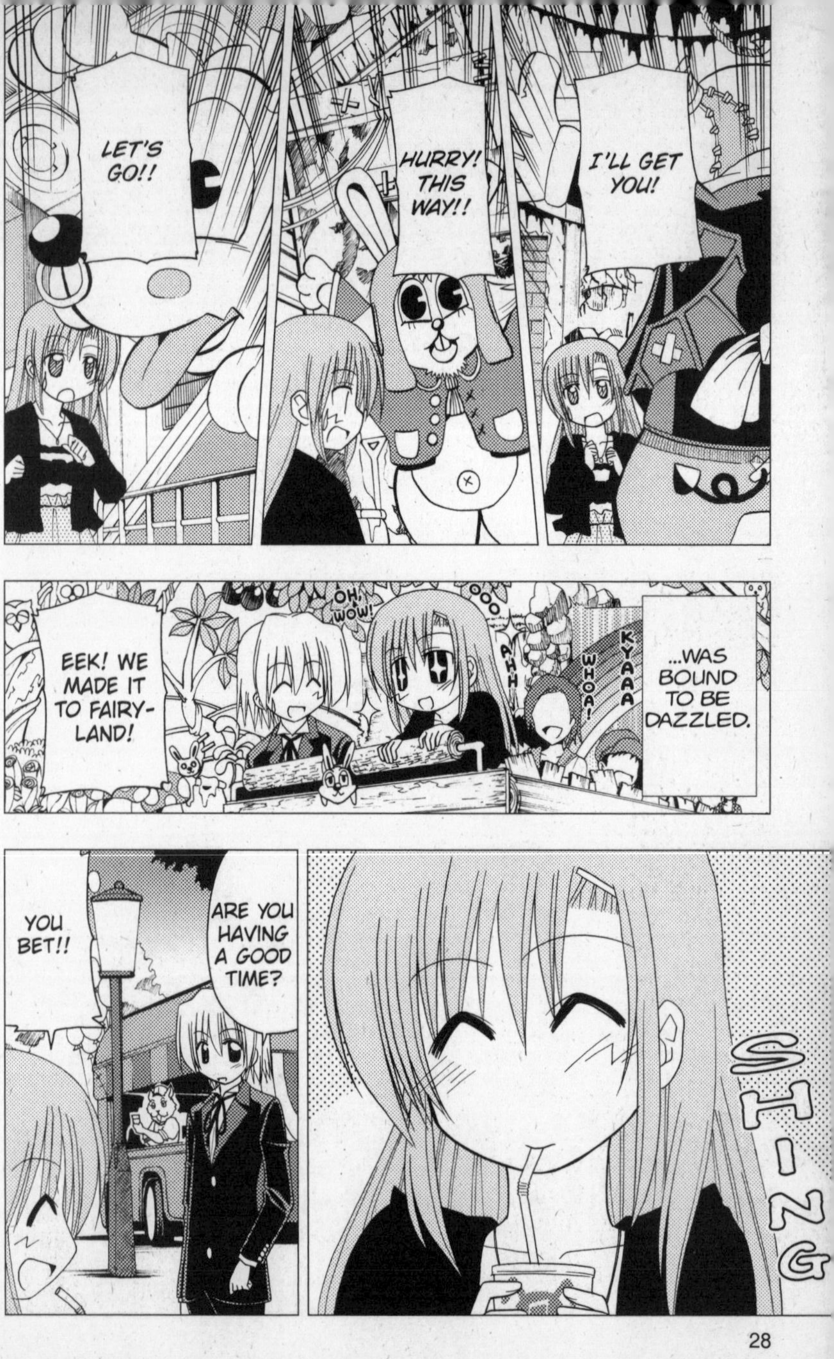
I'LL GET YOU!
HURRY! THIS WAY!!
LET'S GO!!
...WAS BOUND TO BE DAZZLED.
KYAAA
WHOA!
AHH
OOO
OH, WOW!
EEK! WE MADE IT TO FAIRY-LAND!
SHING
ARE YOU HAVING A GOOD TIME?
YOU BET!!

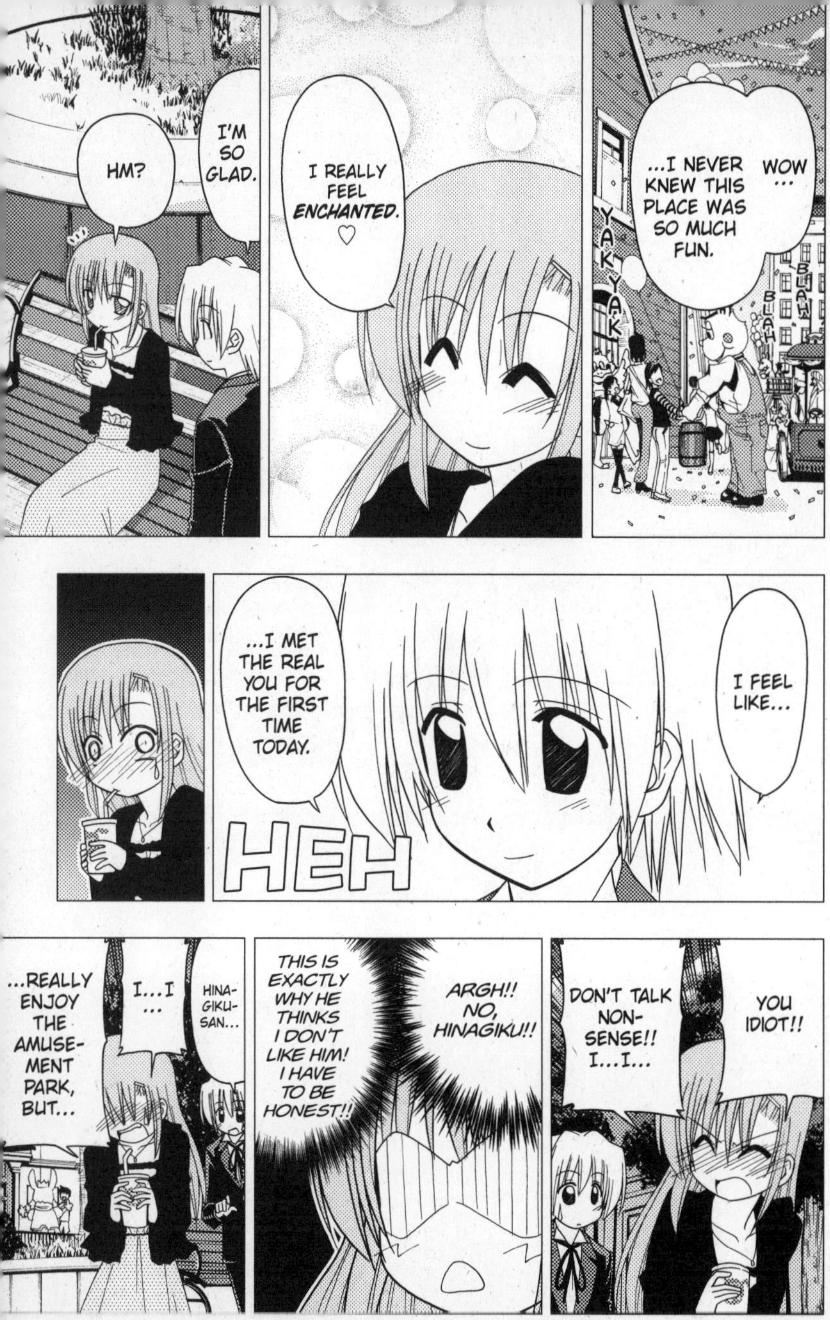
WOW...
...I NEVER KNEW THIS PLACE WAS SO MUCH FUN.
YAK YAK
BLAH BLAH
I REALLY FEEL ENCHANTED. ♡
I'M SO GLAD.
HM?
I FEEL LIKE...
...I MET THE REAL YOU FOR THE FIRST TIME TODAY.
HEH
YOU IDIOT!!
DON'T TALK NONSENSE!! I...I...
ARGH!! NO, HINAGIKU!!
THIS IS EXACTLY WHY HE THINKS I DON'T LIKE HIM! I HAVE TO BE HONEST!!
HINAGIKU-SAN...
I...I...
...REALLY ENJOY THE AMUSEMENT PARK, BUT...

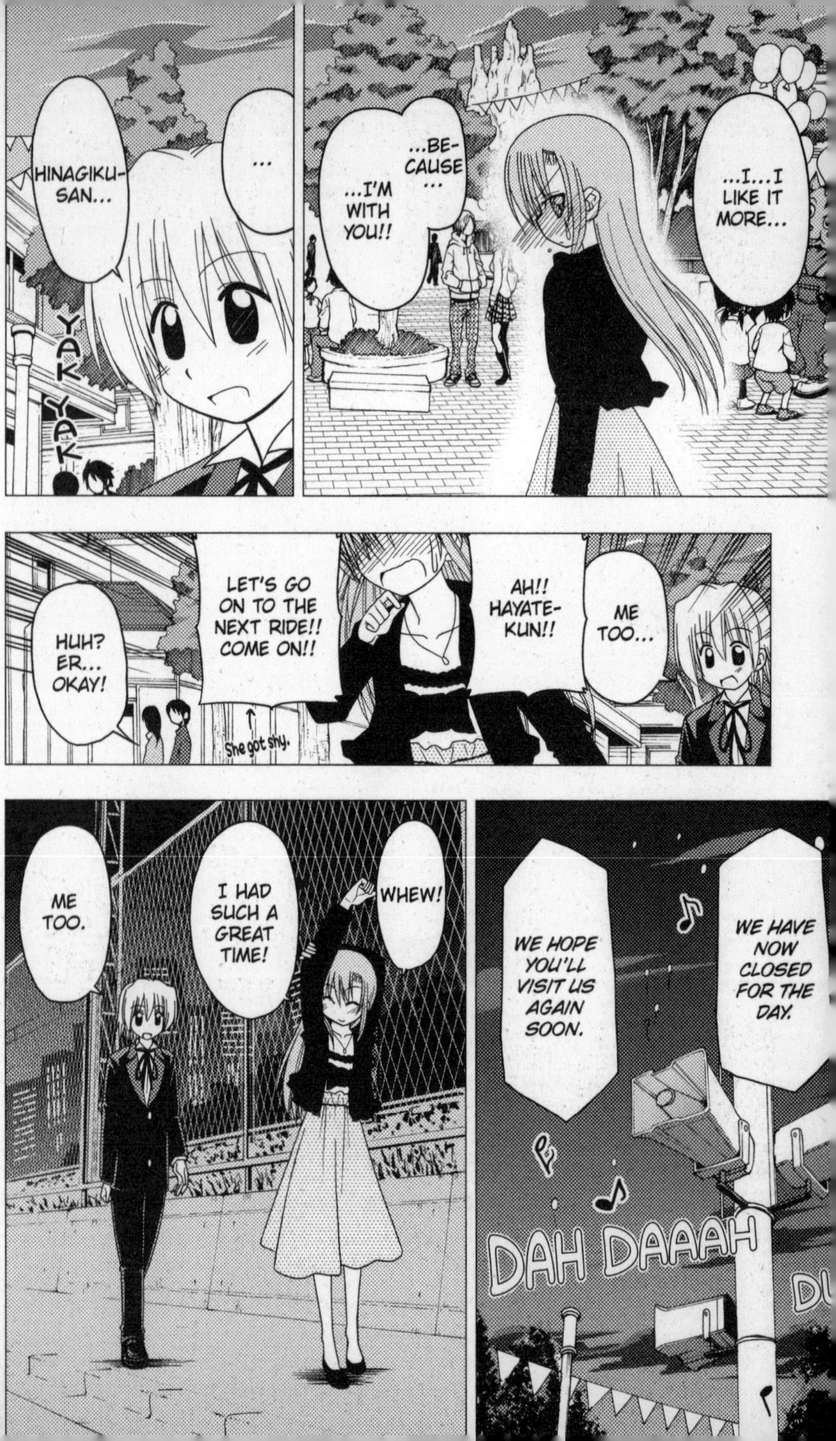
...I...I LIKE IT MORE...
...BE-CAUSE...
...I'M WITH YOU!!
...
HINAGIKU-SAN...
YAK YAK
ME TOO...
AH!! HAYATE-KUN!!
LET'S GO ON TO THE NEXT RIDE!! COME ON!!
She got shy.
HUH? ER... OKAY!
WE HAVE NOW CLOSED FOR THE DAY.
WE HOPE YOU'LL VISIT US AGAIN SOON.
DAH DAAAH DU
WHEW!
I HAD SUCH A GREAT TIME!
ME TOO.

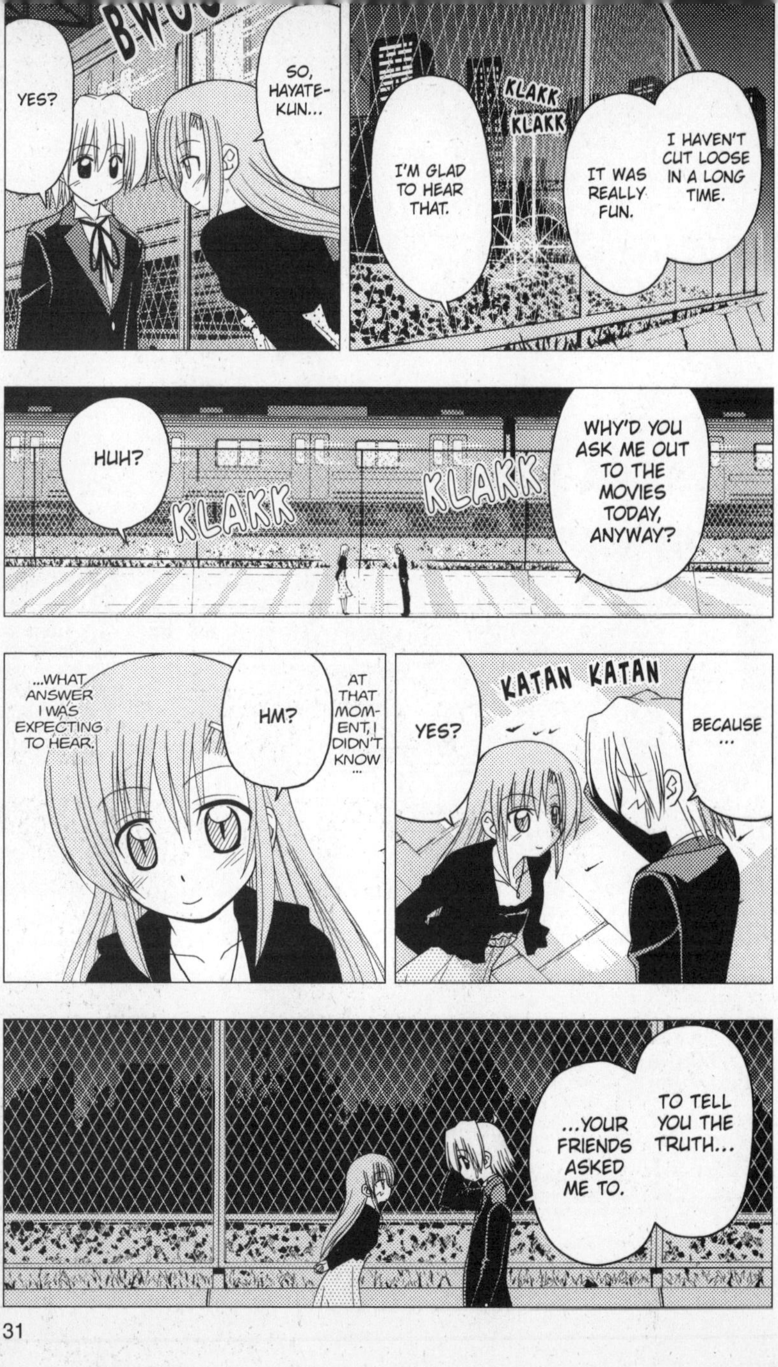
KLAKK
KLAKK
I HAVEN'T CUT LOOSE IN A LONG TIME.
IT WAS REALLY FUN.
I'M GLAD TO HEAR THAT.
SO, HAYATE-KUN...
YES?
WHY'D YOU ASK ME OUT TO THE MOVIES TODAY, ANYWAY?
KLAKK
KLAKK
HUH?
KATAN KATAN
BECAUSE...
YES?
AT THAT MOMENT, I DIDN'T KNOW...
HM?
...WHAT ANSWER I WAS EXPECTING TO HEAR.
TO TELL YOU THE TRUTH...
...YOUR FRIENDS ASKED ME TO.

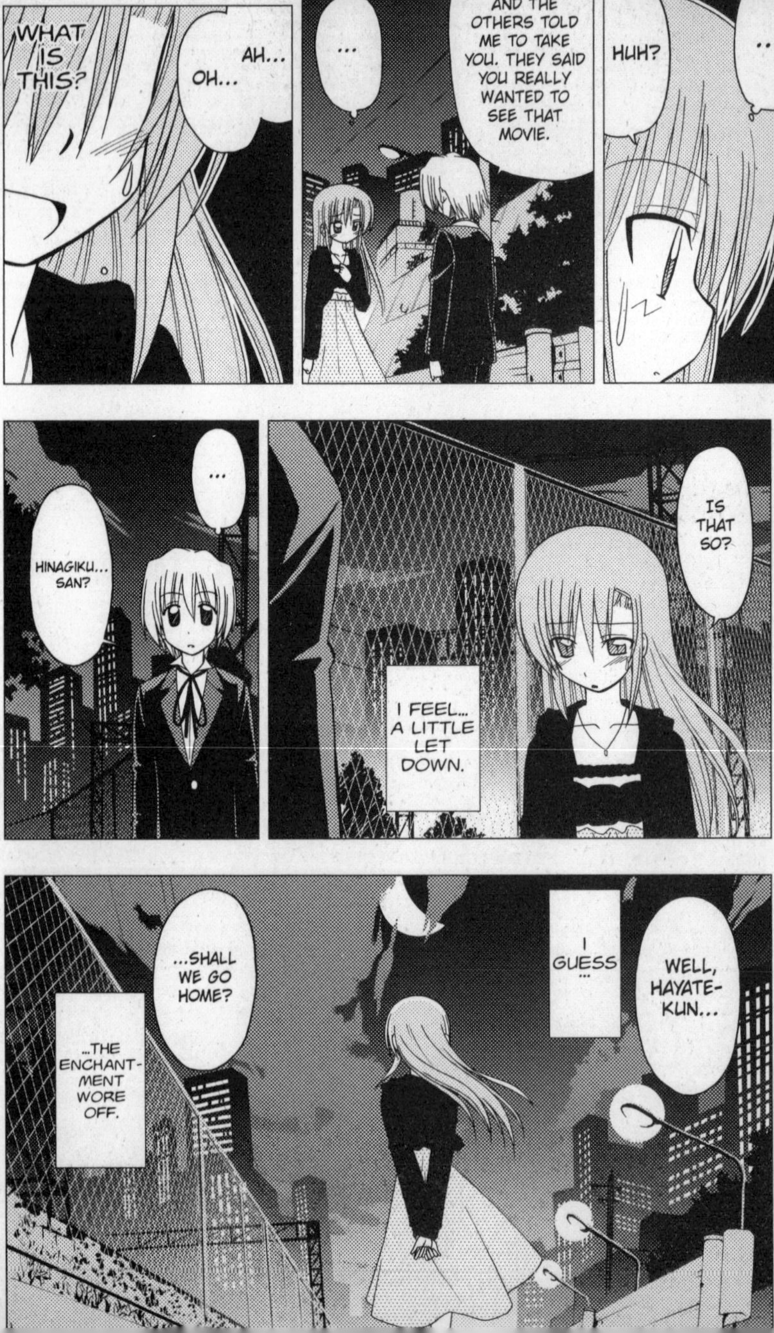
...
HUH?
HANABISHI-SAN AND THE OTHERS TOLD ME TO TAKE YOU. THEY SAID YOU REALLY WANTED TO SEE THAT MOVIE.
...
AH... OH...
WHAT IS THIS?
IS THAT SO?
I FEEL... A LITTLE LET DOWN.
...
HINAGIKU... SAN?
WELL, HAYATE-KUN...
I GUESS...
...SHALL WE GO HOME?
...THE ENCHANTMENT WORE OFF.

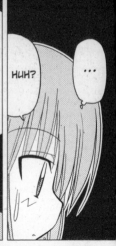

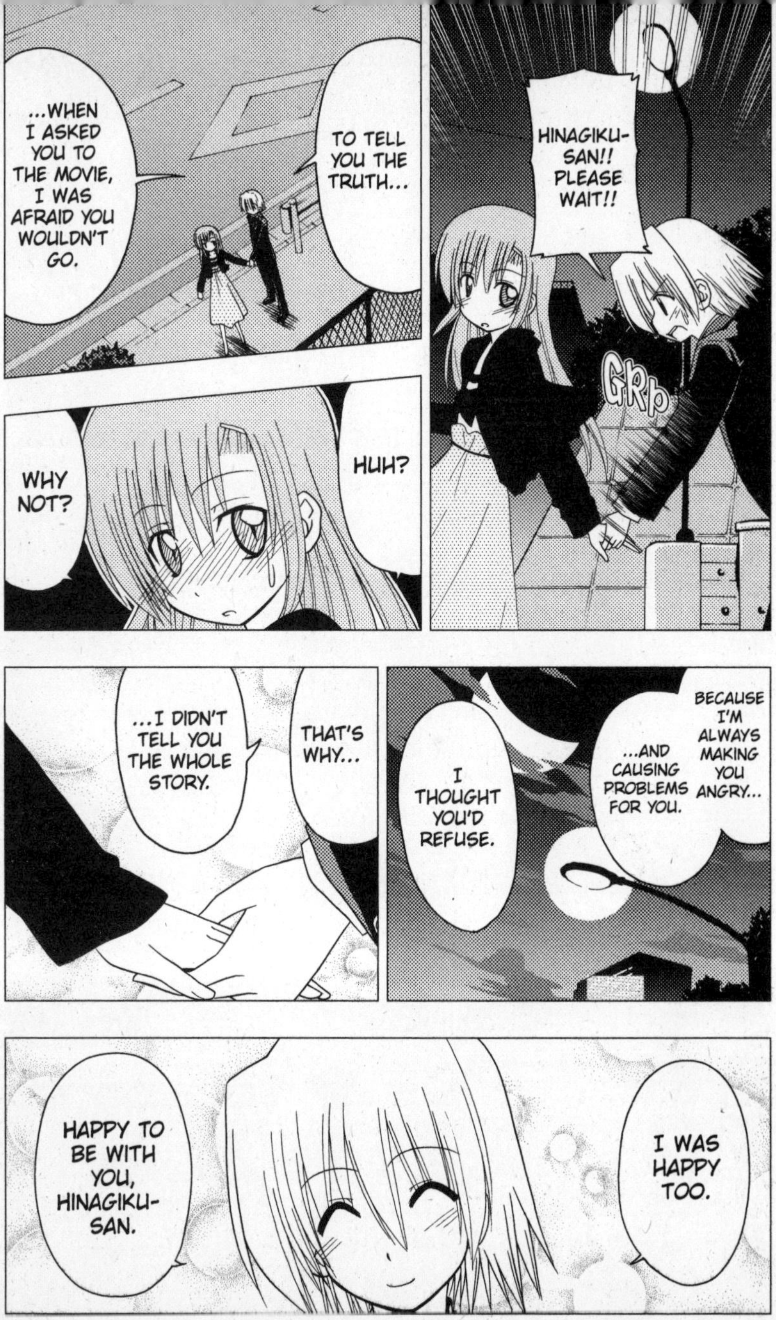
HINAGIKU-SAN!! PLEASE WAIT!!
GRP
TO TELL YOU THE TRUTH...
...WHEN I ASKED YOU TO THE MOVIE, I WAS AFRAID YOU WOULDN'T GO.
HUH?
WHY NOT?
BECAUSE I'M ALWAYS MAKING YOU ANGRY...
...AND CAUSING PROBLEMS FOR YOU.
I THOUGHT YOU'D REFUSE.
THAT'S WHY...
...I DIDN'T TELL YOU THE WHOLE STORY.
I WAS HAPPY TOO.
HAPPY TO BE WITH YOU, HINAGIKU-SAN.

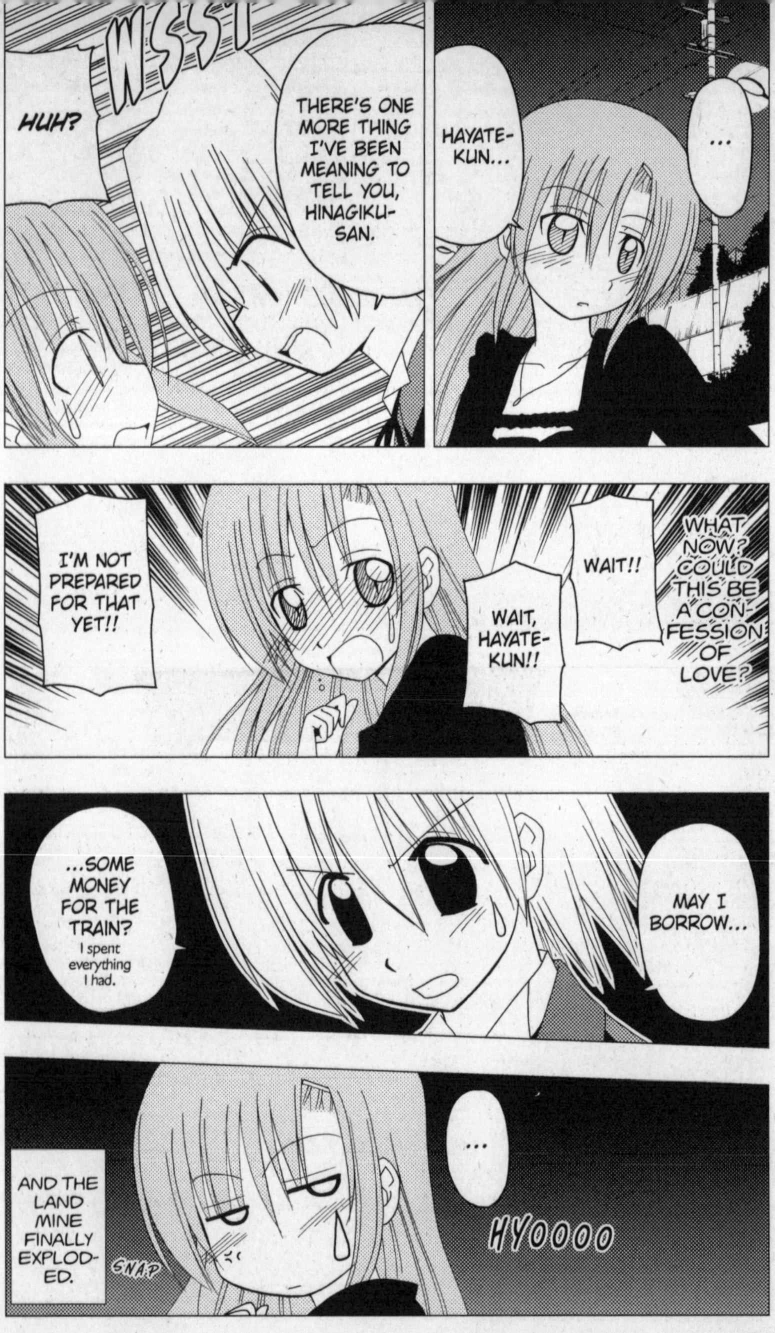
...
HAYATE-KUN...
WSSST
THERE'S ONE MORE THING I'VE BEEN MEANING TO TELL YOU, HINAGIKU-SAN.
HUH?
WHAT NOW? COULD THIS BE A CONFESSION OF LOVE?
WAIT!!
WAIT, HAYATE-KUN!!
I'M NOT PREPARED FOR THAT YET!!
MAY I BORROW...
...SOME MONEY FOR THE TRAIN? I spent everything I had.
...
HYOOOO
SNAP
AND THE LAND MINE FINALLY EXPLODED.

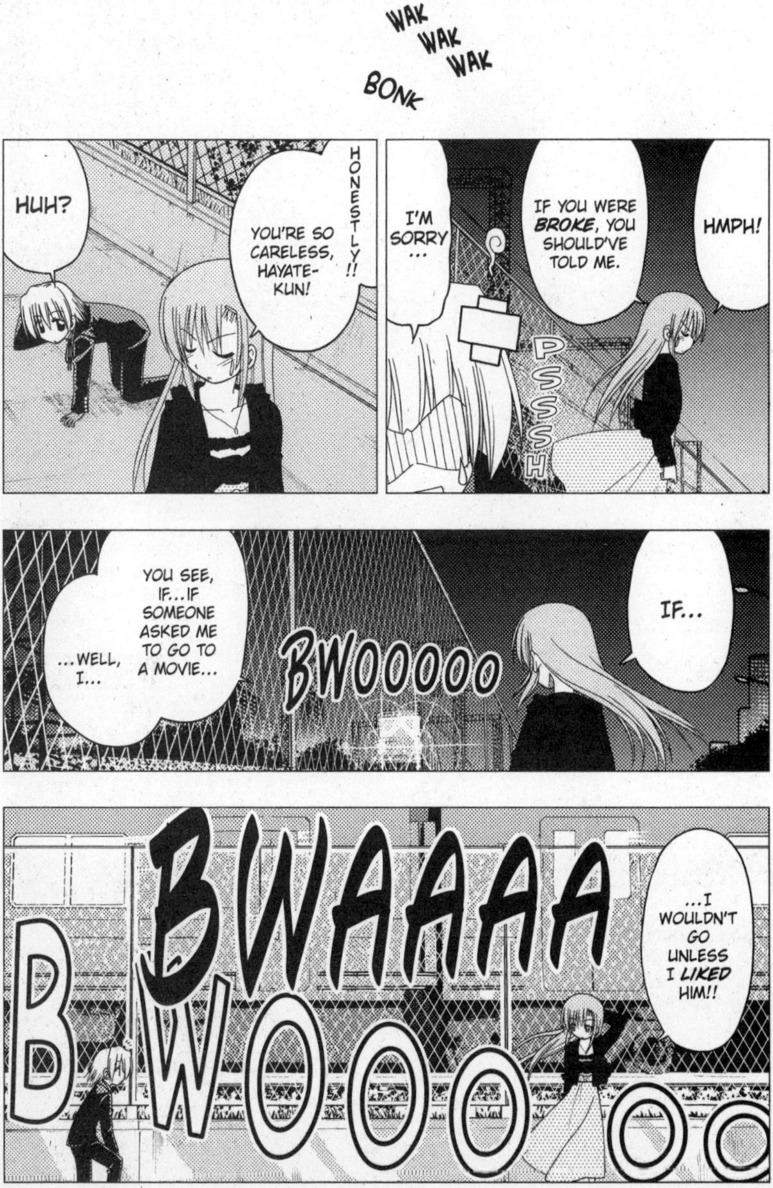
WAK WAK WAK
BONK
HMPH!
IF YOU WERE BROKE, YOU SHOULD'VE TOLD ME.
I'M SORRY...
PSSSH
HONESTLY!!
YOU'RE SO CARELESS, HAYATE-KUN!
HUH?
IF...
BWOOOOO
YOU SEE, IF...IF SOMEONE ASKED ME TO GO TO A MOVIE...
...WELL, I...
...I WOULDN'T GO UNLESS I LIKED HIM!!
BWAAAA
BWOOOOOO

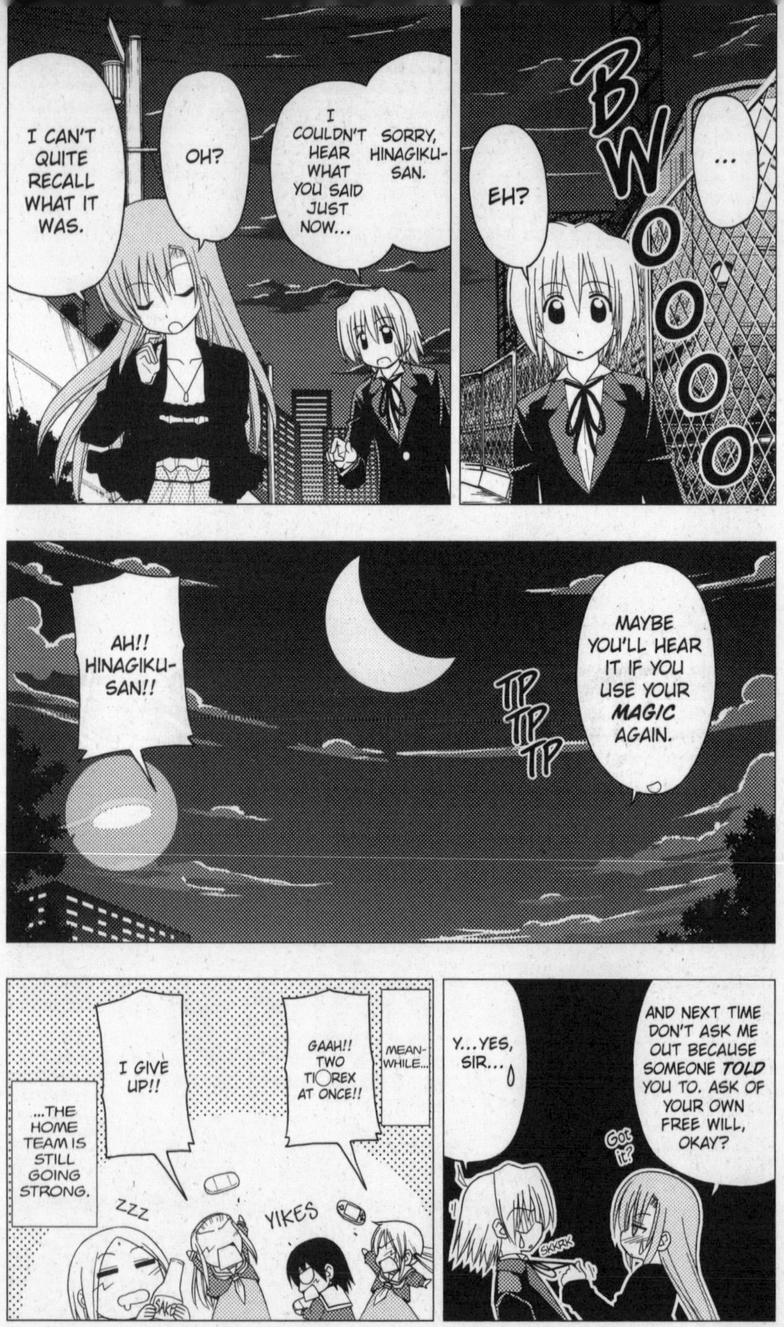
...
BWOOOOO
EH?
SORRY, HINAGIKU-SAN.
I COULDN'T HEAR WHAT YOU SAID JUST NOW...
OH?
I CAN'T QUITE RECALL WHAT IT WAS.
MAYBE YOU'LL HEAR IT IF YOU USE YOUR ***MAGIC*** AGAIN.
TP TP TP
AH!! HINAGIKU-SAN!!
AND NEXT TIME DON'T ASK ME OUT BECAUSE SOMEONE ***TOLD*** YOU TO. ASK OF YOUR OWN FREE WILL, OKAY?
Got it?
Y...YES, SIR...
SKKRK
MEAN-WHILE...
GAAH!! TWO TI◯REX AT ONCE!!
I GIVE UP!!
YIKES
ZZZ
...THE HOME TEAM IS STILL GOING STRONG.
SAKE

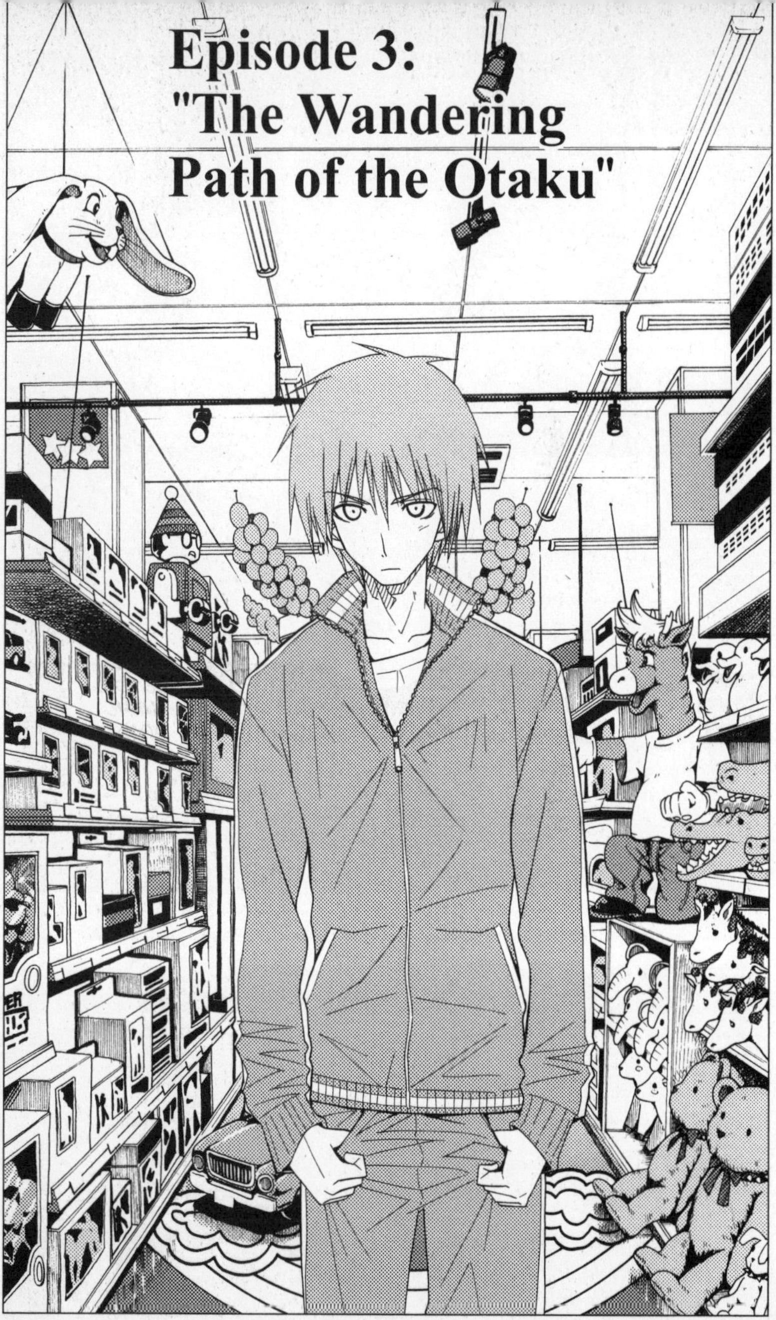
Episode 3:
"The Wandering
Path of the Otaku"

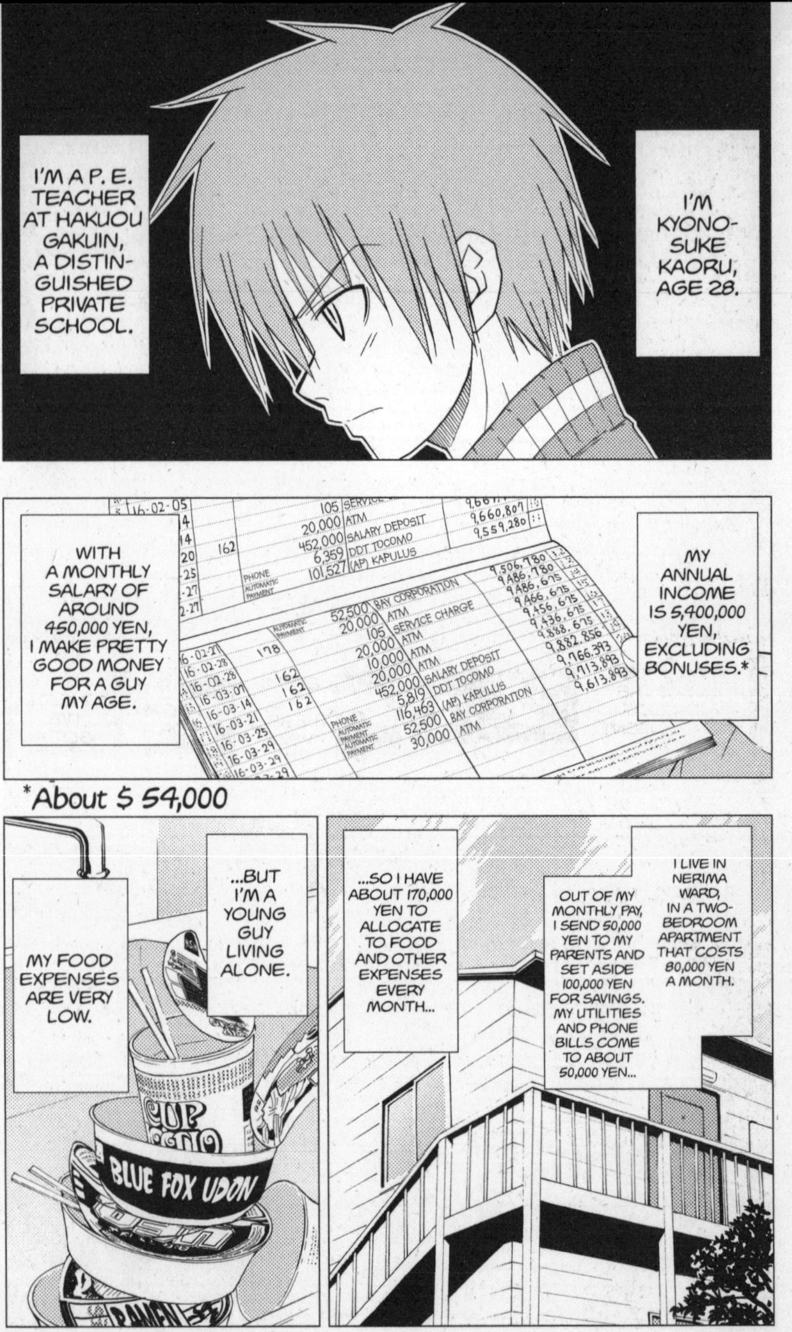
I'M KYONOSUKE KAORU, AGE 28.
I'M A P. E. TEACHER AT HAKUOU GAKUIN, A DISTINGUISHED PRIVATE SCHOOL.
MY ANNUAL INCOME IS 5,400,000 YEN, EXCLUDING BONUSES.*
WITH A MONTHLY SALARY OF AROUND 450,000 YEN, I MAKE PRETTY GOOD MONEY FOR A GUY MY AGE.
I LIVE IN NERIMA WARD, IN A TWO-BEDROOM APARTMENT THAT COSTS 80,000 YEN A MONTH.
OUT OF MY MONTHLY PAY, I SEND 50,000 YEN TO MY PARENTS AND SET ASIDE 100,000 YEN FOR SAVINGS. MY UTILITIES AND PHONE BILLS COME TO ABOUT 50,000 YEN...
...SO I HAVE ABOUT 170,000 YEN TO ALLOCATE TO FOOD AND OTHER EXPENSES EVERY MONTH...
...BUT I'M A YOUNG GUY LIVING ALONE.
MY FOOD EXPENSES ARE VERY LOW.
BLUE FOX UDON

*About $ 54,000

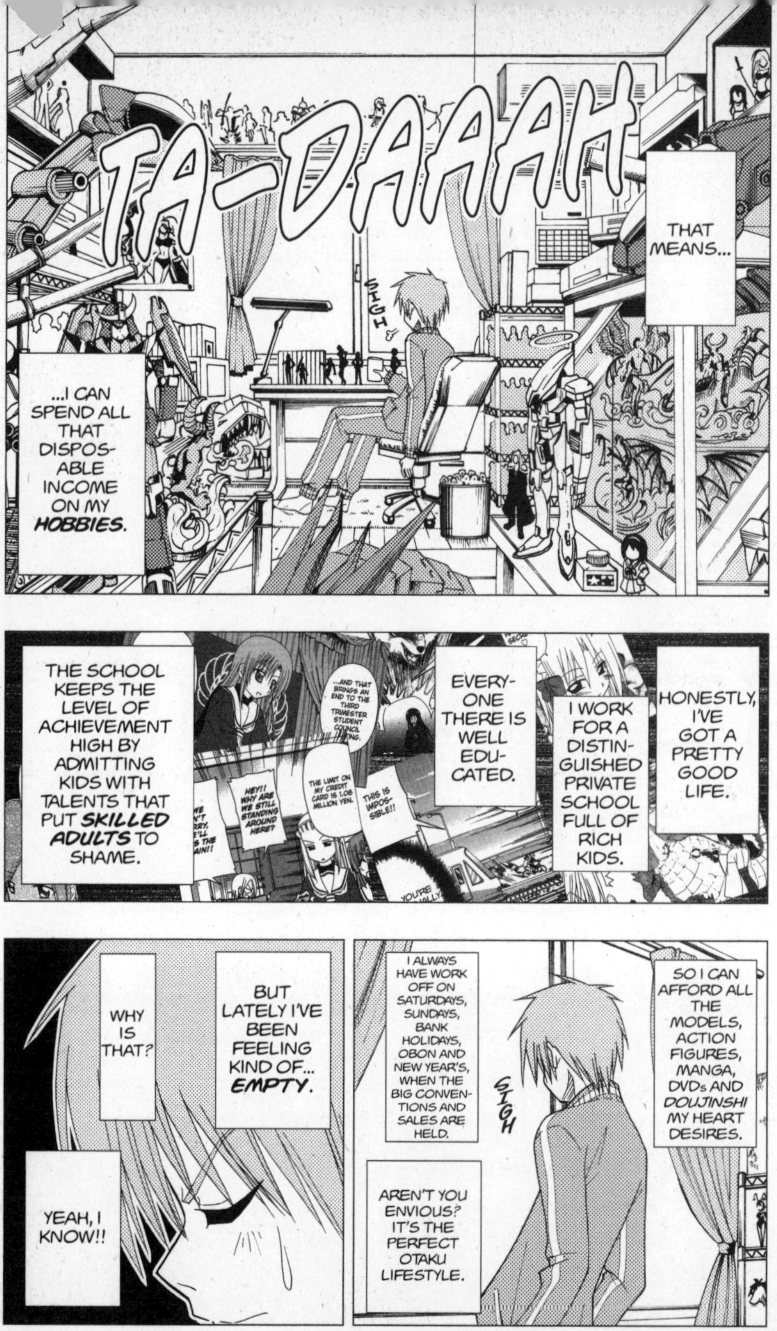
TA-DAAAH
THAT MEANS...
SIGH
...I CAN SPEND ALL THAT DISPOSABLE INCOME ON MY HOBBIES.
HONESTLY, I'VE GOT A PRETTY GOOD LIFE.
I WORK FOR A DISTINGUISHED PRIVATE SCHOOL FULL OF RICH KIDS.
EVERYONE THERE IS WELL EDUCATED.
...AND THAT BRINGS AN END TO THE THIRD TRIMESTER STUDENT COUNCIL
THIS IS IMPOSSIBLE!!
THE LIMIT ON MY CREDIT CARD IS 1.08 MILLION YEN.
HEY!! WHY ARE WE STILL STANDING AROUND HERE?
THE SCHOOL KEEPS THE LEVEL OF ACHIEVEMENT HIGH BY ADMITTING KIDS WITH TALENTS THAT PUT SKILLED ADULTS TO SHAME.
SO I CAN AFFORD ALL THE MODELS, ACTION FIGURES, MANGA, DVDs AND DOUJINSHI MY HEART DESIRES.
I ALWAYS HAVE WORK OFF ON SATURDAYS, SUNDAYS, BANK HOLIDAYS, OBON AND NEW YEAR'S, WHEN THE BIG CONVENTIONS AND SALES ARE HELD.
SIGH
AREN'T YOU ENVIOUS? IT'S THE PERFECT OTAKU LIFESTYLE.
BUT LATELY I'VE BEEN FEELING KIND OF... EMPTY.
WHY IS THAT?
YEAH, I KNOW!!

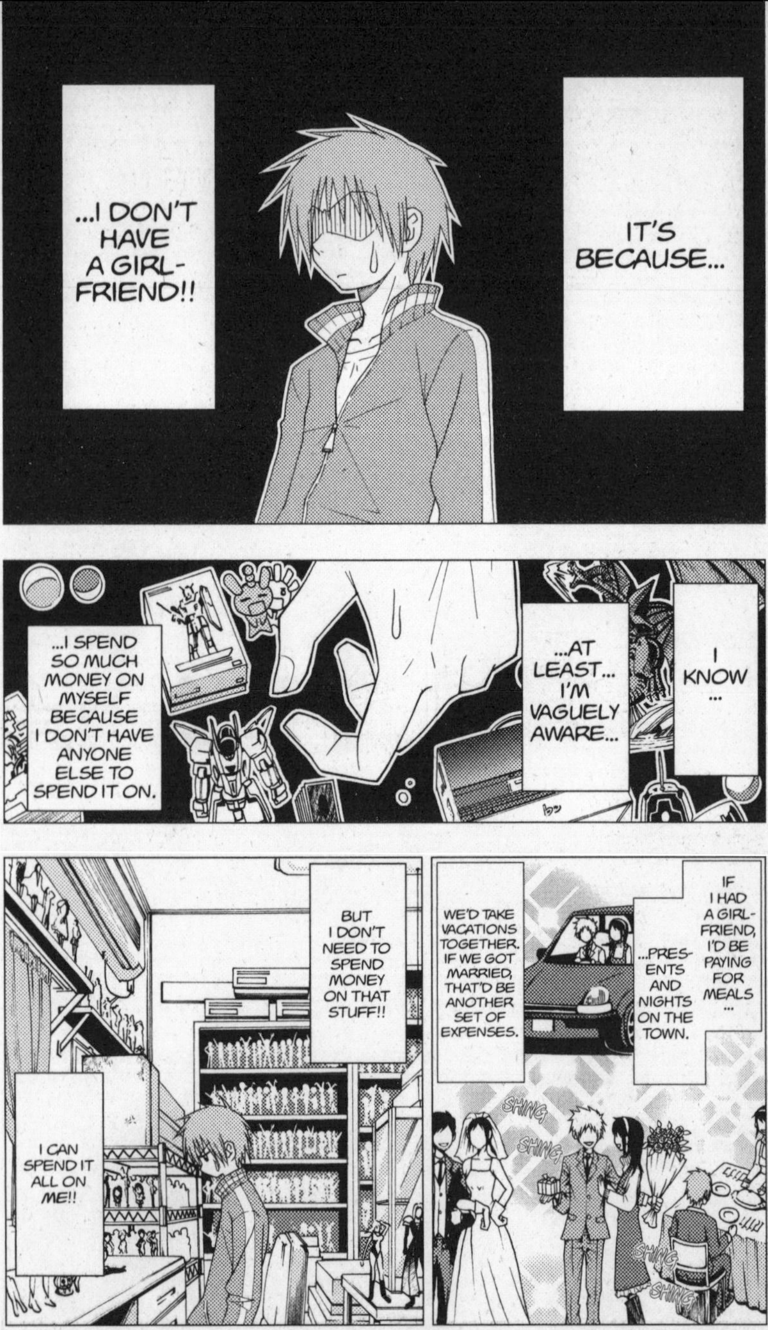
IT'S BECAUSE...
...I DON'T HAVE A GIRL-FRIEND!!
I KNOW...
...AT LEAST... I'M VAGUELY AWARE...
...I SPEND SO MUCH MONEY ON MYSELF BECAUSE I DON'T HAVE ANYONE ELSE TO SPEND IT ON.
IF I HAD A GIRL-FRIEND, I'D BE PAYING FOR MEALS...
...PRES-ENTS AND NIGHTS ON THE TOWN.
WE'D TAKE VACATIONS TOGETHER. IF WE GOT MARRIED, THAT'D BE ANOTHER SET OF EXPENSES.
SHING
SHING
SHING
SHING
BUT I DON'T NEED TO SPEND MONEY ON THAT STUFF!!
I CAN SPEND IT ALL ON ME!!

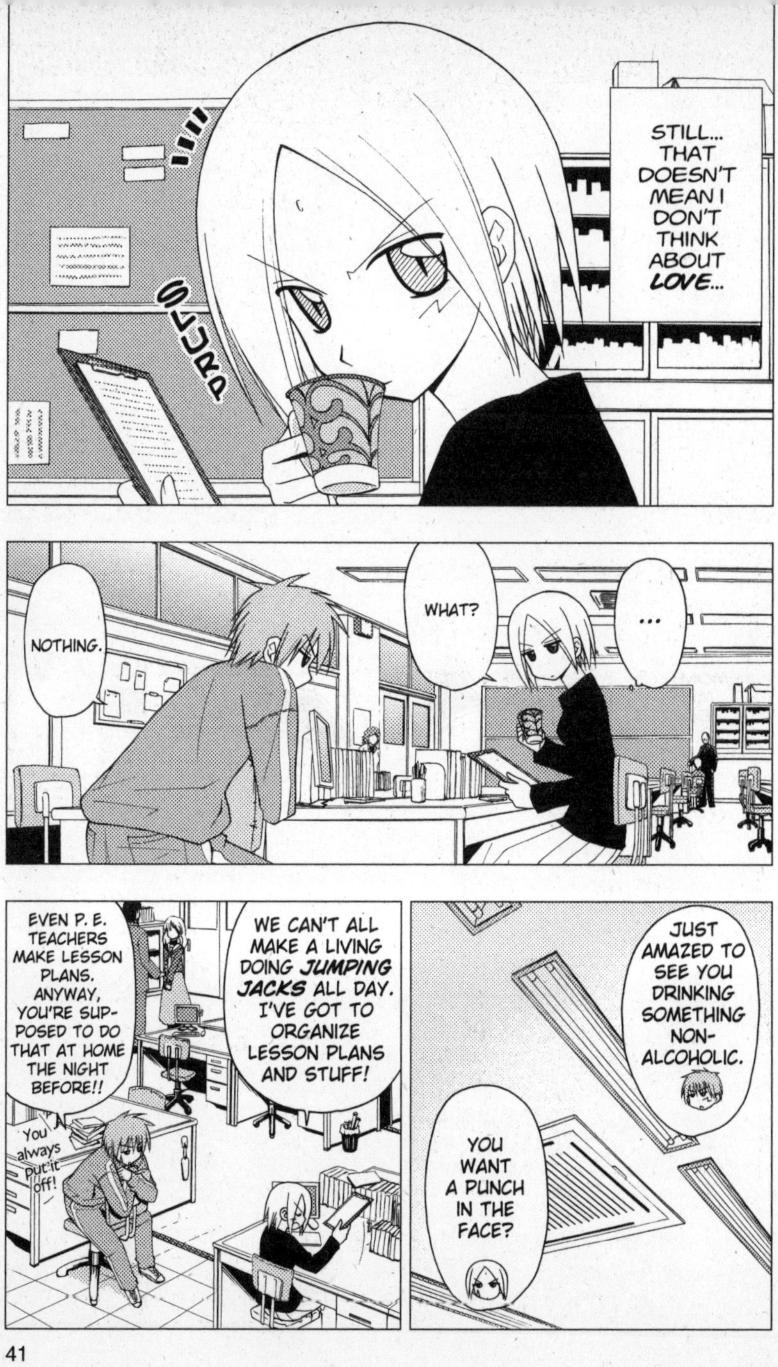
STILL... THAT DOESN'T MEAN I DON'T THINK ABOUT LOVE...
!!!!
SLURP
...
WHAT?
NOTHING.
JUST AMAZED TO SEE YOU DRINKING SOMETHING NON-ALCOHOLIC.
YOU WANT A PUNCH IN THE FACE?
WE CAN'T ALL MAKE A LIVING DOING JUMPING JACKS ALL DAY. I'VE GOT TO ORGANIZE LESSON PLANS AND STUFF!
EVEN P. E. TEACHERS MAKE LESSON PLANS. ANYWAY, YOU'RE SUPPOSED TO DO THAT AT HOME THE NIGHT BEFORE!!
You always put it off!

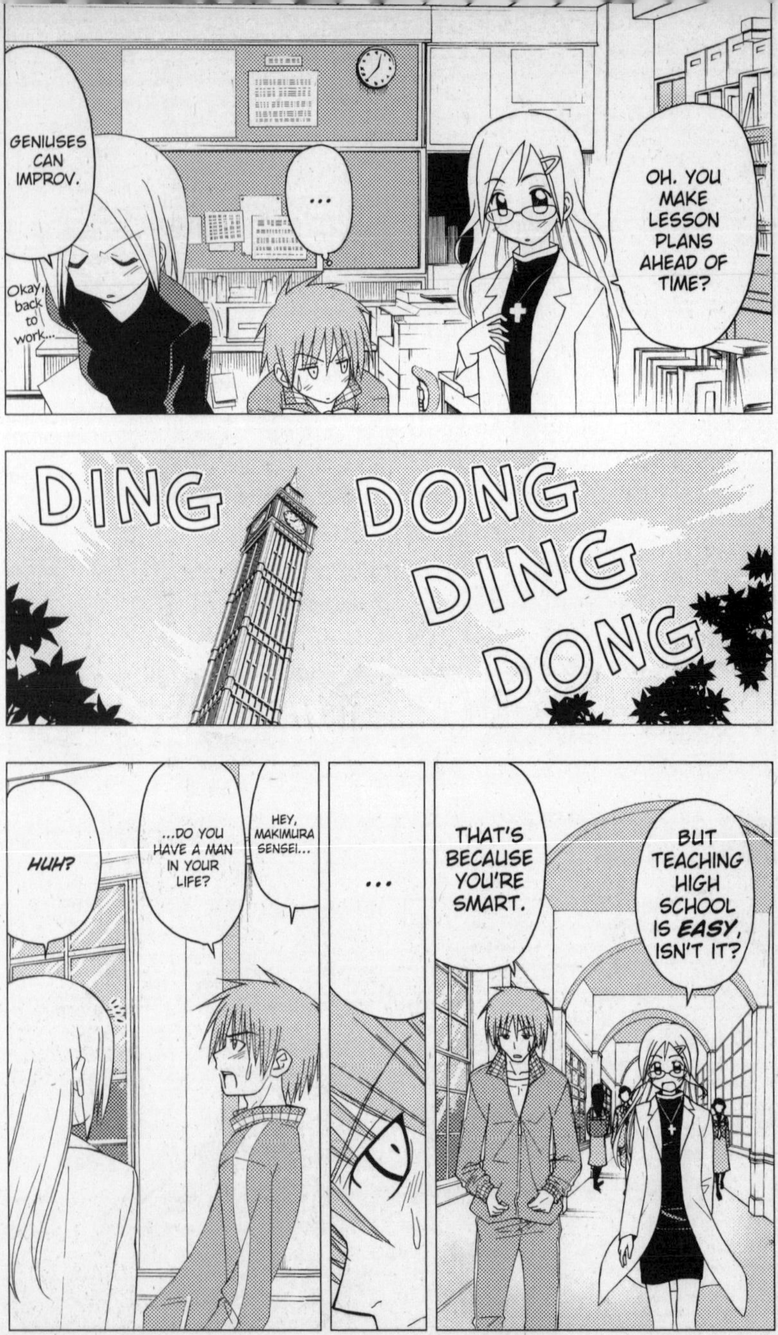
OH. YOU MAKE LESSON PLANS AHEAD OF TIME?
...
GENIUSES CAN IMPROV.
Okay, back to work...
DING DONG DING DONG
BUT TEACHING HIGH SCHOOL IS *EASY*, ISN'T IT?
THAT'S BECAUSE YOU'RE SMART.
...
HEY, MAKIMURA SENSEI...
...DO YOU HAVE A MAN IN YOUR LIFE?
HUH?

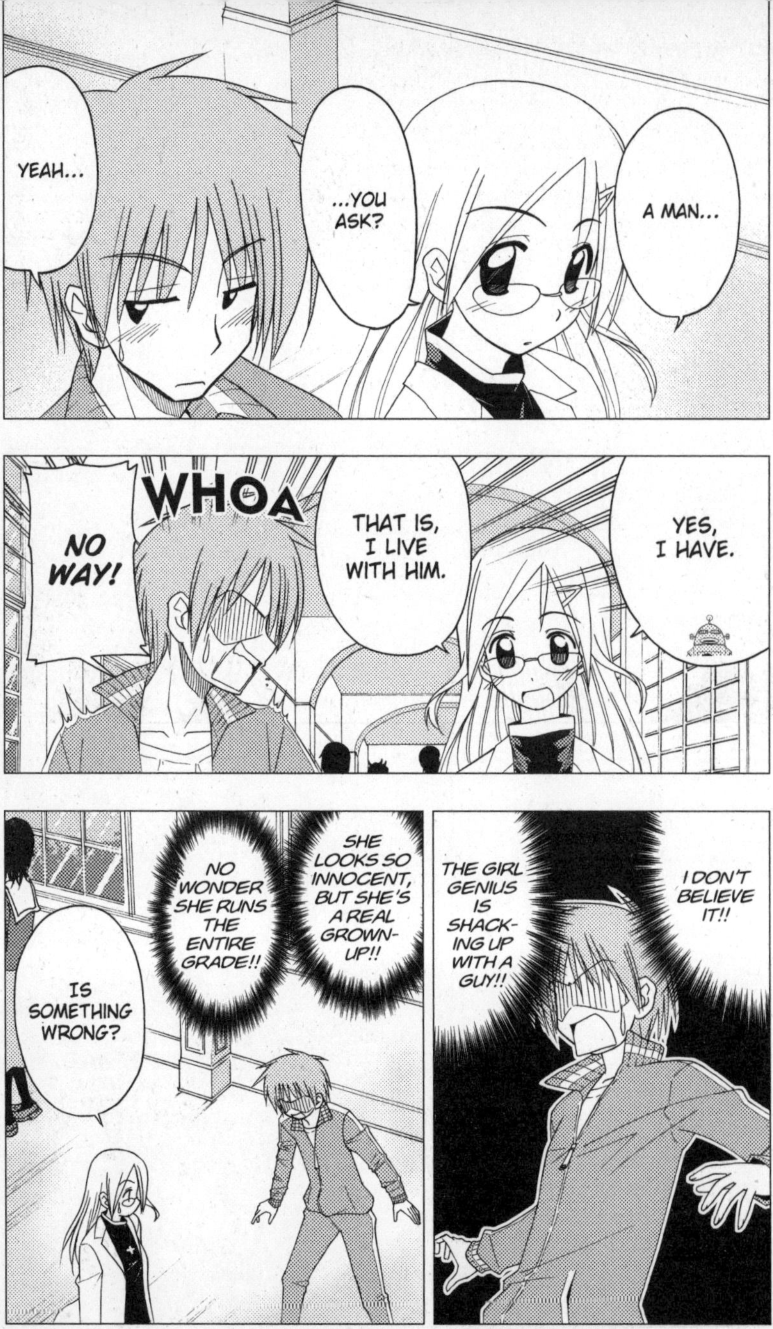
A MAN...
...YOU ASK?
YEAH...
YES, I HAVE.
THAT IS, I LIVE WITH HIM.
WHOA
NO WAY!
I DON'T BELIEVE IT!!
THE GIRL GENIUS IS SHACKING UP WITH A GUY!!
SHE LOOKS SO INNOCENT, BUT SHE'S A REAL GROWN-UP!!
NO WONDER SHE RUNS THE ENTIRE GRADE!!
IS SOMETHING WRONG?

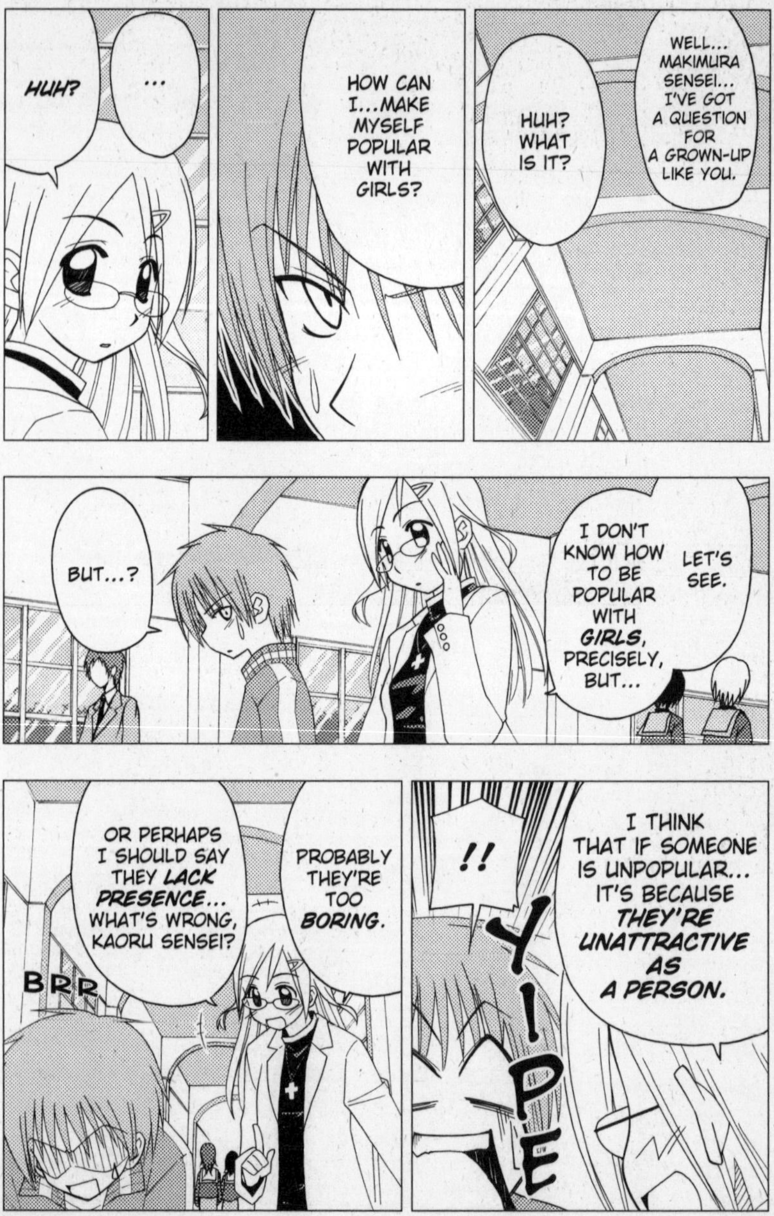
WELL... MAKIMURA SENSEI... I'VE GOT A QUESTION FOR A GROWN-UP LIKE YOU.
HUH? WHAT IS IT?
HOW CAN I...MAKE MYSELF POPULAR WITH GIRLS?
...
HUH?
LET'S SEE.
I DON'T KNOW HOW TO BE POPULAR WITH GIRLS, PRECISELY, BUT...
BUT...?
I THINK THAT IF SOMEONE IS UNPOPULAR... IT'S BECAUSE THEY'RE UNATTRACTIVE AS A PERSON.
!!
YIPE
PROBABLY THEY'RE TOO BORING.
OR PERHAPS I SHOULD SAY THEY LACK PRESENCE... WHAT'S WRONG, KAORU SENSEI?
BRR

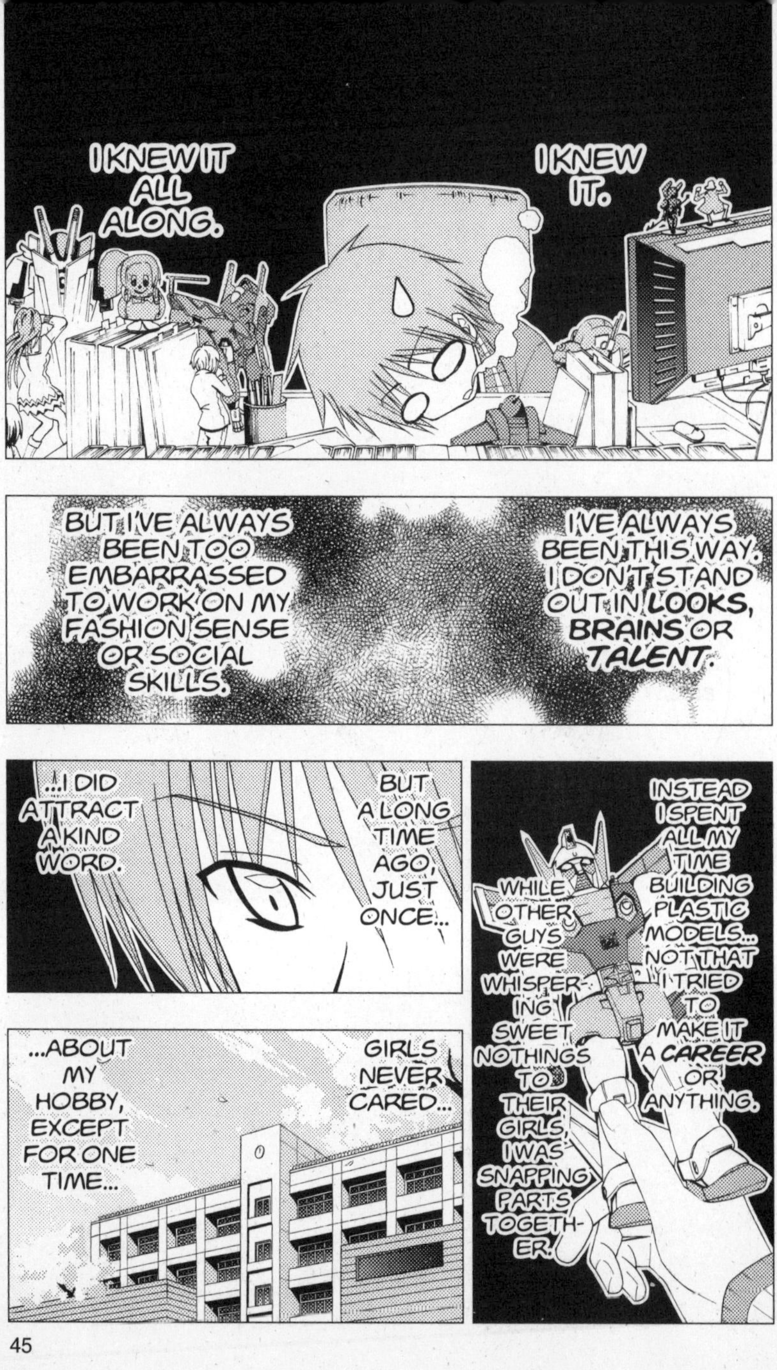
I KNEW IT.
I KNEW IT ALL ALONG.
I'VE ALWAYS BEEN THIS WAY. I DON'T STAND OUT IN **LOOKS, BRAINS** OR ***TALENT***.
BUT I'VE ALWAYS BEEN TOO EMBARRASSED TO WORK ON MY FASHION SENSE OR SOCIAL SKILLS.
INSTEAD I SPENT ALL MY TIME BUILDING PLASTIC MODELS... NOT THAT I TRIED TO MAKE IT A ***CAREER*** OR ANYTHING.
WHILE OTHER GUYS WERE WHISPER-ING SWEET NOTHINGS TO THEIR GIRLS, I WAS SNAPPING PARTS TOGETH-ER.
BUT A LONG TIME AGO, JUST ONCE...
...I DID ATTRACT A KIND WORD.
GIRLS NEVER CARED...
...ABOUT MY HOBBY, EXCEPT FOR ONE TIME...

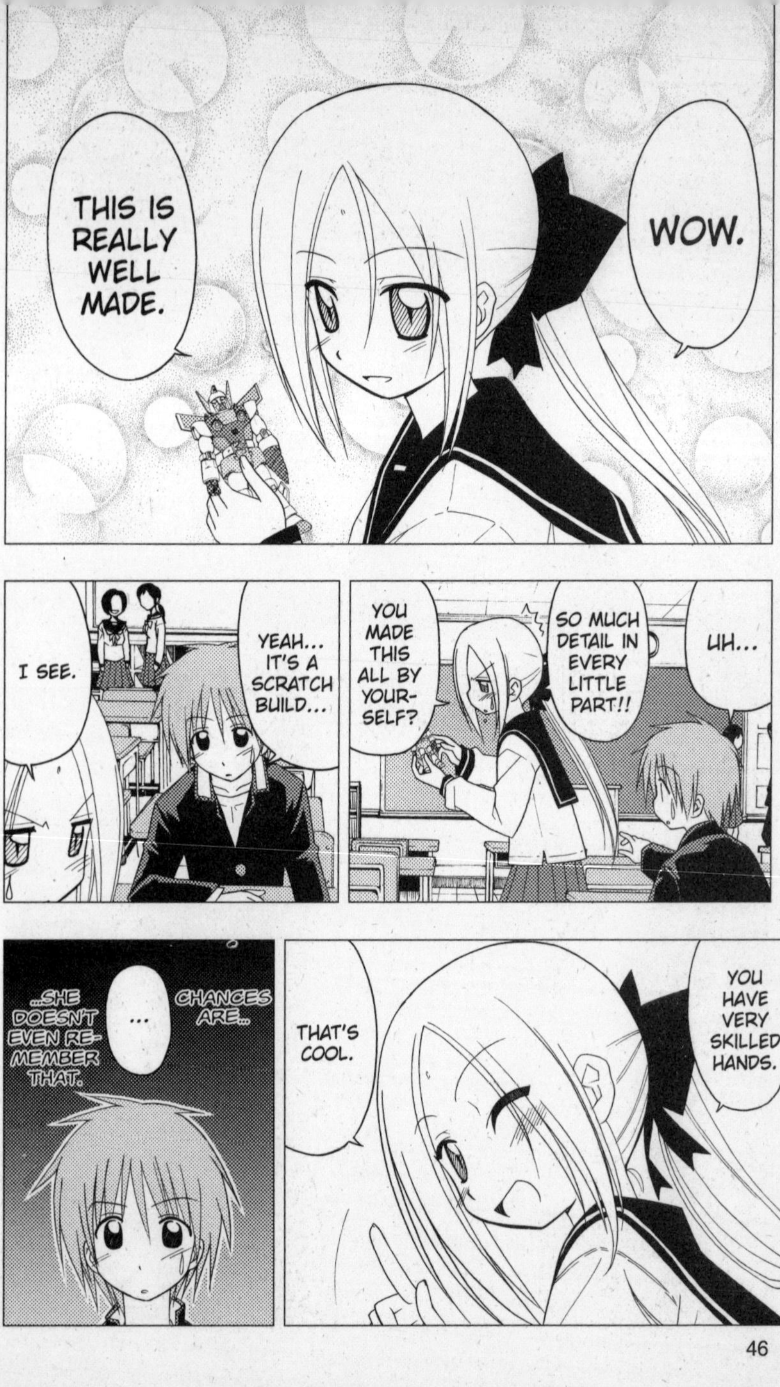
WOW.
THIS IS REALLY WELL MADE.
UH...
SO MUCH DETAIL IN EVERY LITTLE PART!!
YOU MADE THIS ALL BY YOURSELF?
YEAH... IT'S A SCRATCH BUILD...
I SEE.
YOU HAVE VERY SKILLED HANDS.
THAT'S COOL.
CHANCES ARE...
...
...SHE DOESN'T EVEN REMEMBER THAT.

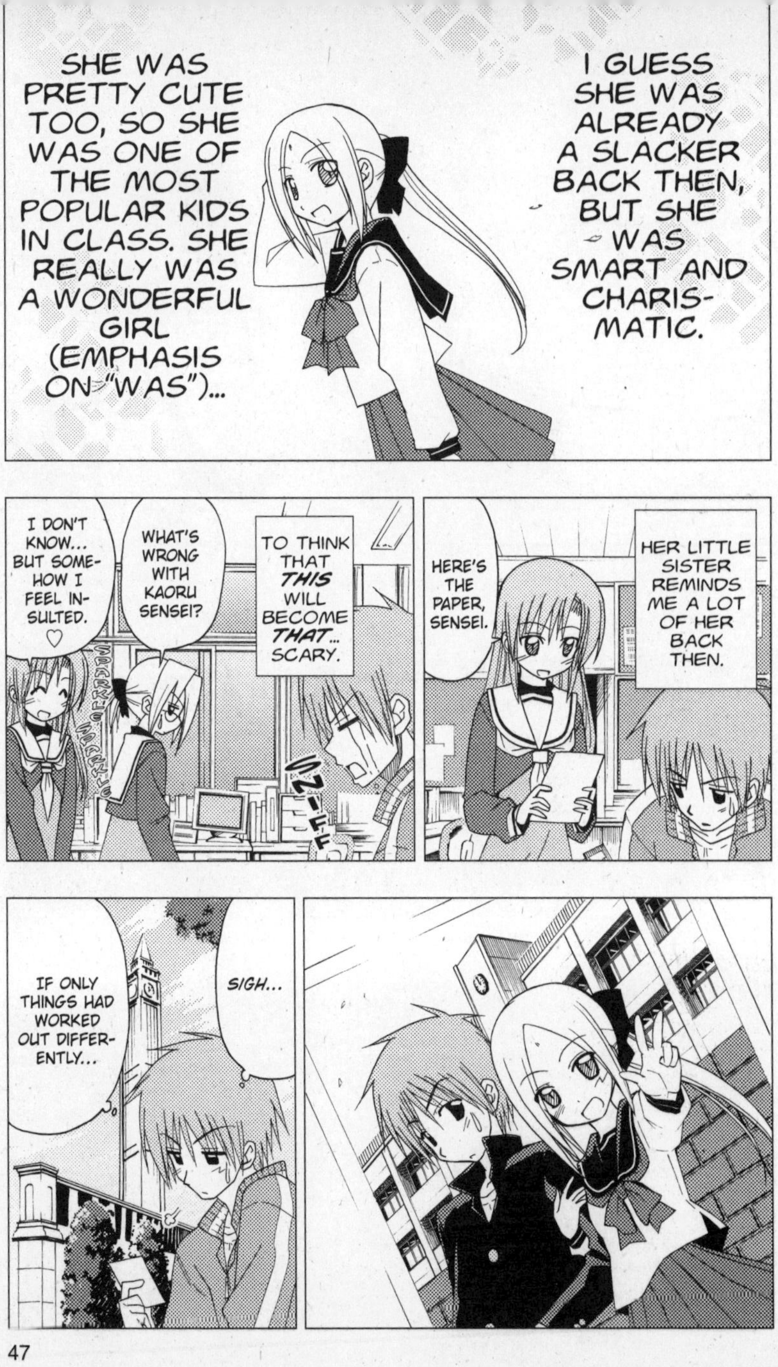
I GUESS SHE WAS ALREADY A SLACKER BACK THEN, BUT SHE WAS SMART AND CHARIS-MATIC.
SHE WAS PRETTY CUTE TOO, SO SHE WAS ONE OF THE MOST POPULAR KIDS IN CLASS. SHE REALLY WAS A WONDERFUL GIRL (EMPHASIS ON "WAS")...
HER LITTLE SISTER REMINDS ME A LOT OF HER BACK THEN.
HERE'S THE PAPER, SENSEI.
TO THINK THAT *THIS* WILL BECOME *THAT*... SCARY.
SNIFF
WHAT'S WRONG WITH KAORU SENSEI?
SPARKLE SPARKLE
I DON'T KNOW... BUT SOME-HOW I FEEL IN-SULTED. ♡
SIGH...
IF ONLY THINGS HAD WORKED OUT DIFFER-ENTLY...

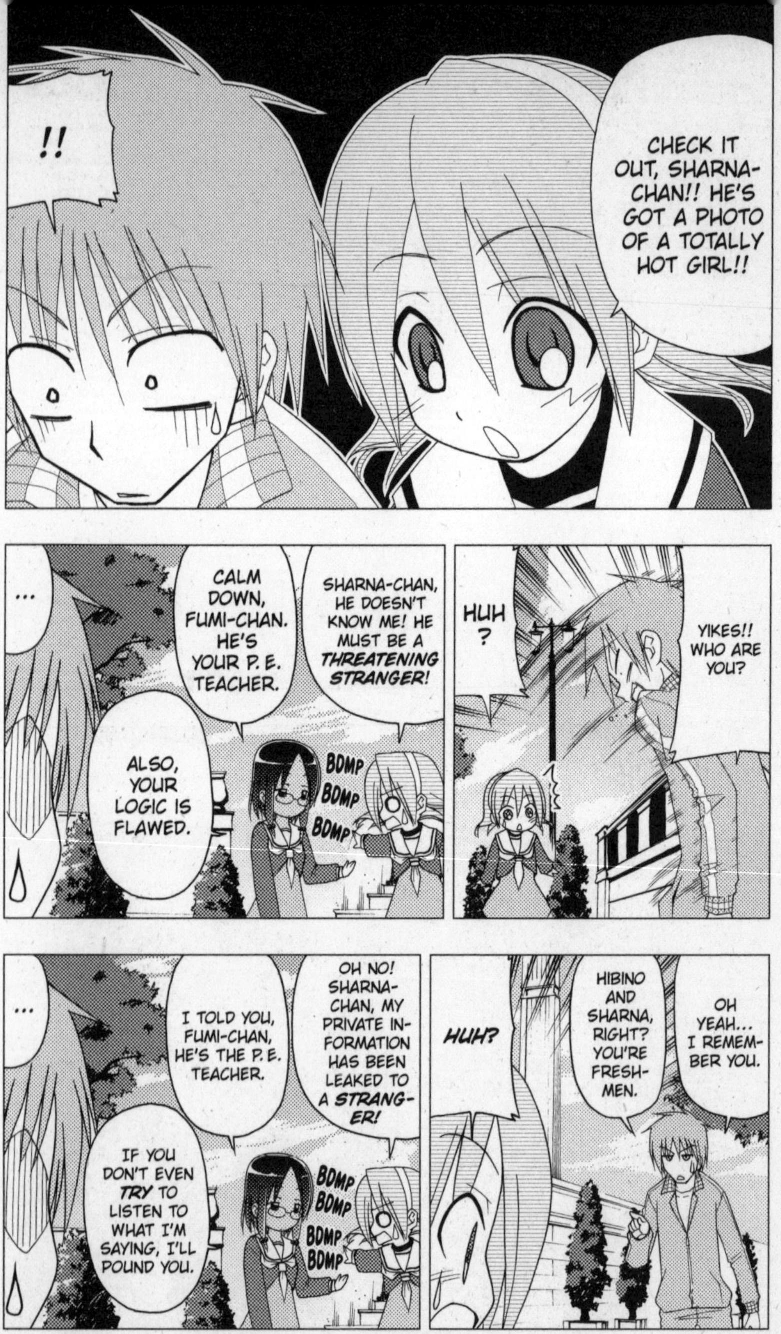
CHECK IT OUT, SHARNA-CHAN!! HE'S GOT A PHOTO OF A TOTALLY HOT GIRL!!
!!
YIKES!! WHO ARE YOU?
HUH ?
SHARNA-CHAN, HE DOESN'T KNOW ME! HE MUST BE A *THREATENING STRANGER*!
CALM DOWN, FUMI-CHAN. HE'S YOUR P. E. TEACHER.
...
ALSO, YOUR LOGIC IS FLAWED.
BDMP
BDMP
BDMP
OH YEAH... I REMEMBER YOU.
HIBINO AND SHARNA, RIGHT? YOU'RE FRESHMEN.
HUH?
OH NO! SHARNA-CHAN, MY PRIVATE INFORMATION HAS BEEN LEAKED TO A *STRANGER!*
I TOLD YOU, FUMI-CHAN, HE'S THE P.E. TEACHER.
...
IF YOU DON'T EVEN *TRY* TO LISTEN TO WHAT I'M SAYING, I'LL POUND YOU.
BDMP
BDMP
BDMP
BDMP

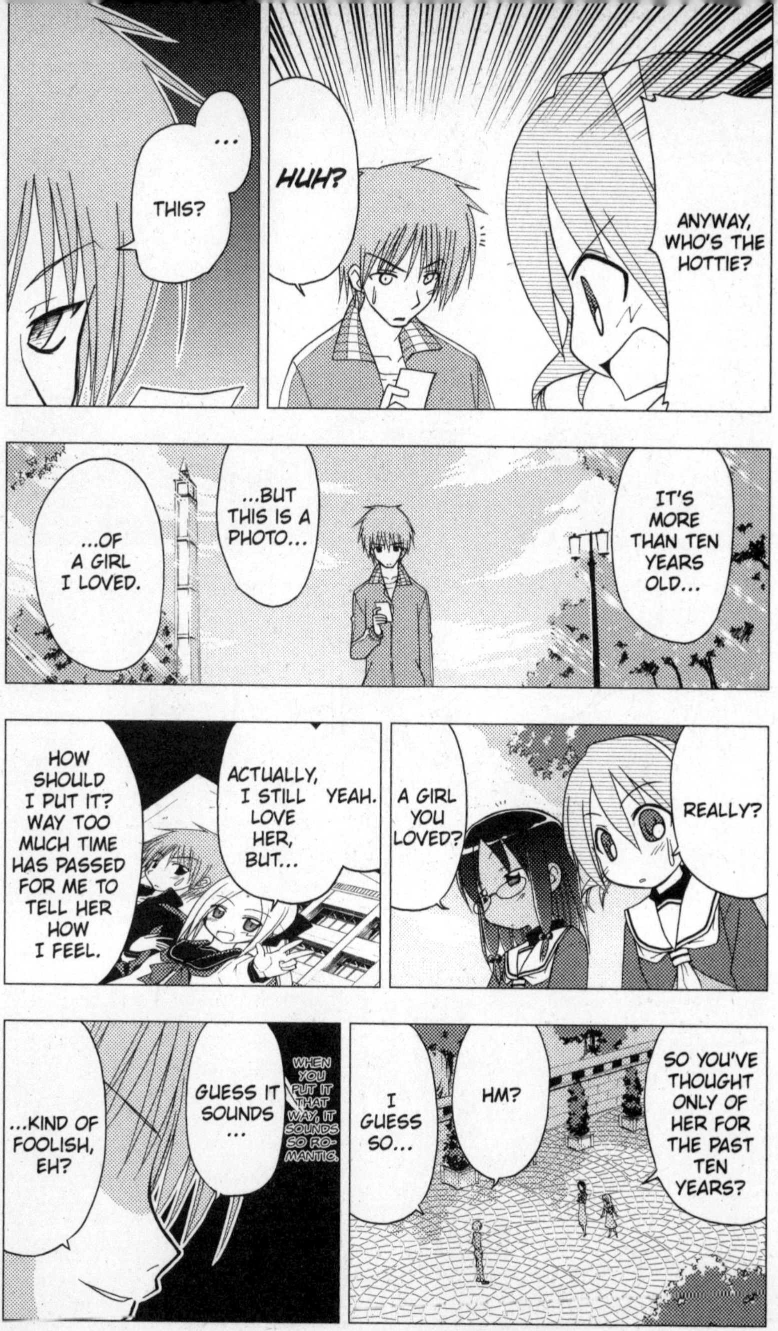
ANYWAY, WHO'S THE HOTTIE?
HUH?
... THIS?
IT'S MORE THAN TEN YEARS OLD...
...BUT THIS IS A PHOTO...
...OF A GIRL I LOVED.
REALLY?
A GIRL YOU LOVED?
YEAH.
ACTUALLY, I STILL LOVE HER, BUT...
HOW SHOULD I PUT IT? WAY TOO MUCH TIME HAS PASSED FOR ME TO TELL HER HOW I FEEL.
SO YOU'VE THOUGHT ONLY OF HER FOR THE PAST TEN YEARS?
HM?
I GUESS SO...
WHEN YOU PUT IT THAT WAY, IT SOUNDS SO RO-MANTIC.
GUESS IT SOUNDS...
...KIND OF FOOLISH, EH?

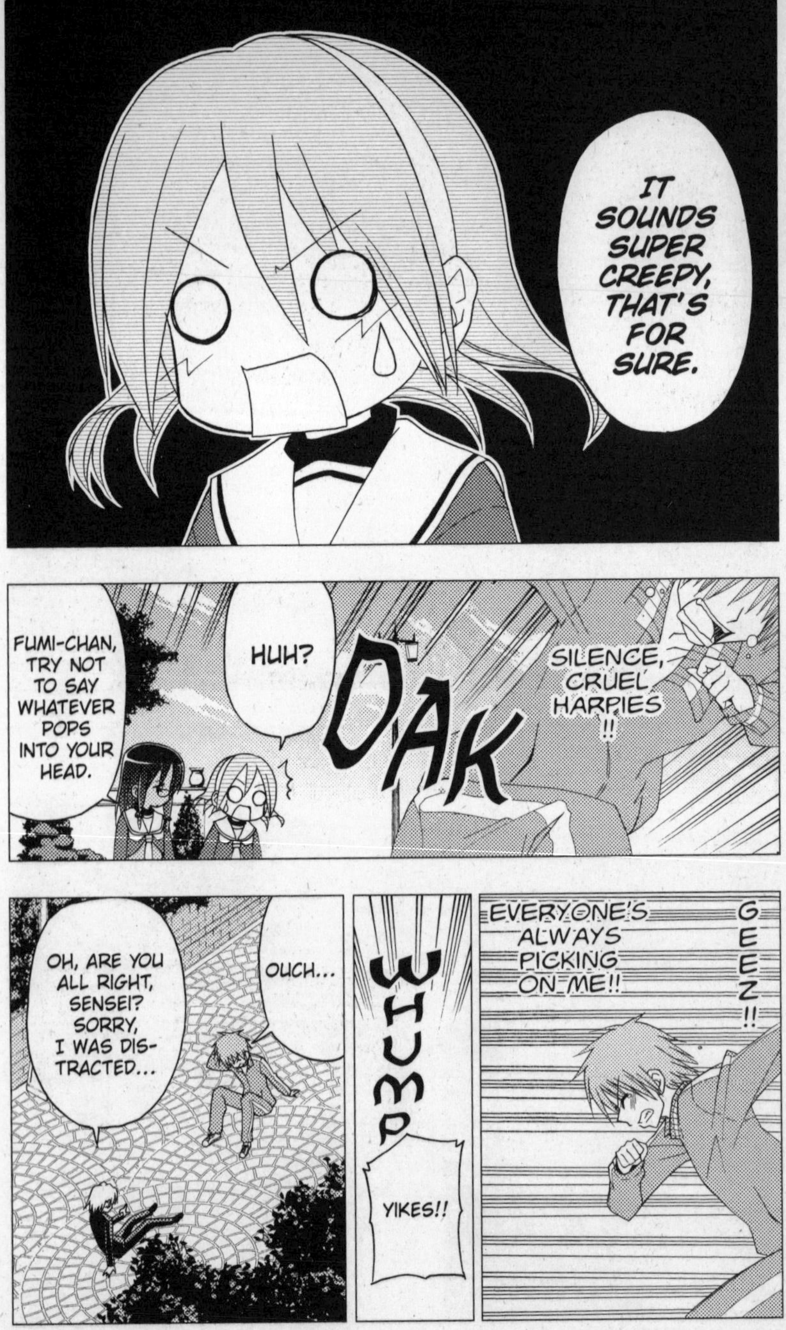
IT SOUNDS SUPER CREEPY, THAT'S FOR SURE.
SILENCE, CRUEL HARPIES!!
DAK
HUH?
FUMI-CHAN, TRY NOT TO SAY WHATEVER POPS INTO YOUR HEAD.
GEEZ!!
EVERYONE'S ALWAYS PICKING ON ME!!
WHUMP
YIKES!!
OUCH...
OH, ARE YOU ALL RIGHT, SENSEI? SORRY, I WAS DISTRACTED...

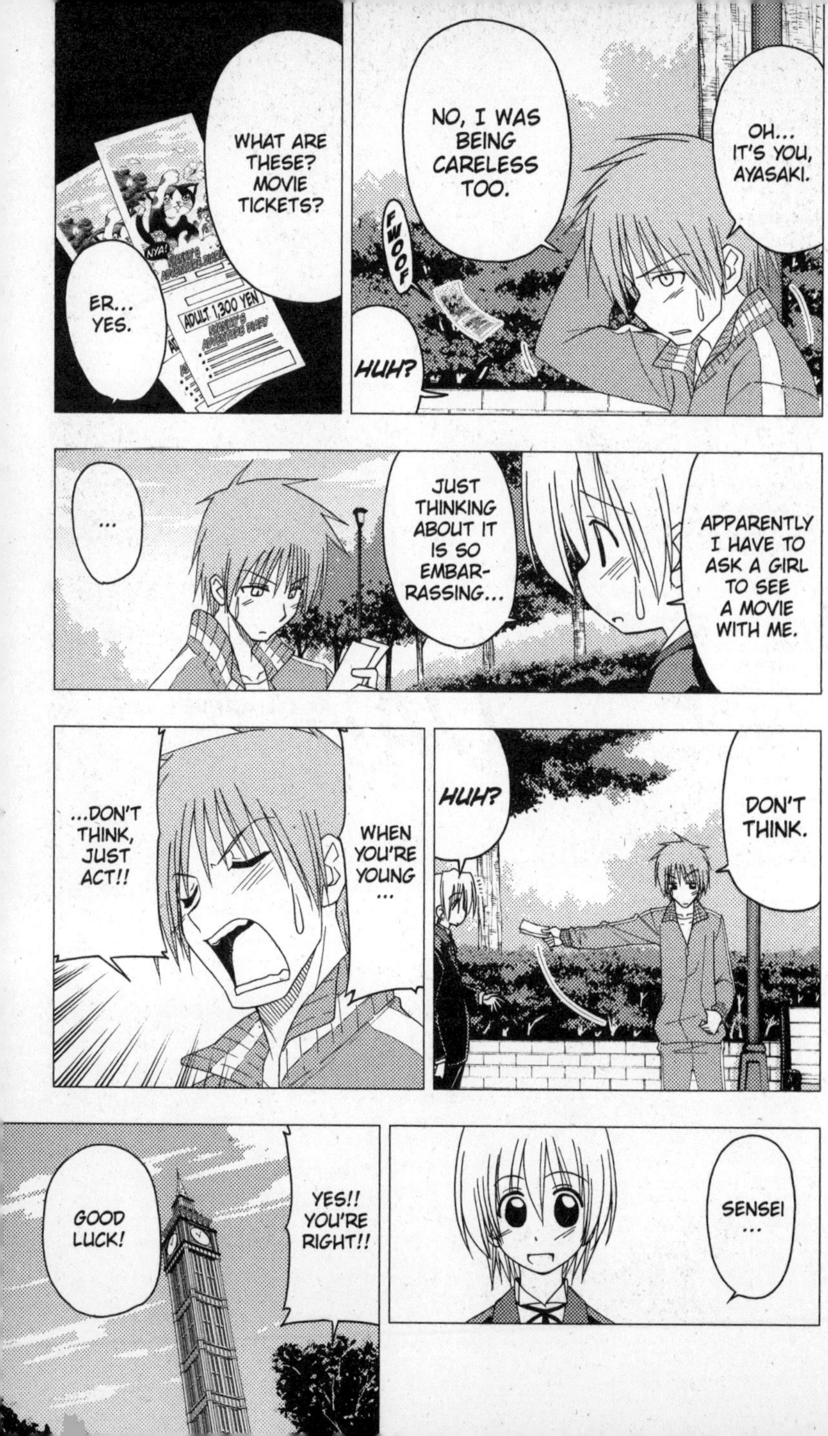
OH... IT'S YOU, AYASAKI.
NO, I WAS BEING CARELESS TOO.
FWOOF
HUH?
WHAT ARE THESE? MOVIE TICKETS?
NYA!
ADULT 1,300 YEN
NYAKO'S ADVENTURE DIARY
ER... YES.
APPARENTLY I HAVE TO ASK A GIRL TO SEE A MOVIE WITH ME.
JUST THINKING ABOUT IT IS SO EMBARRASSING...
...
DON'T THINK.
HUH?
WHEN YOU'RE YOUNG...
...DON'T THINK, JUST ACT!!
SENSEI...
YES!! YOU'RE RIGHT!!
GOOD LUCK!

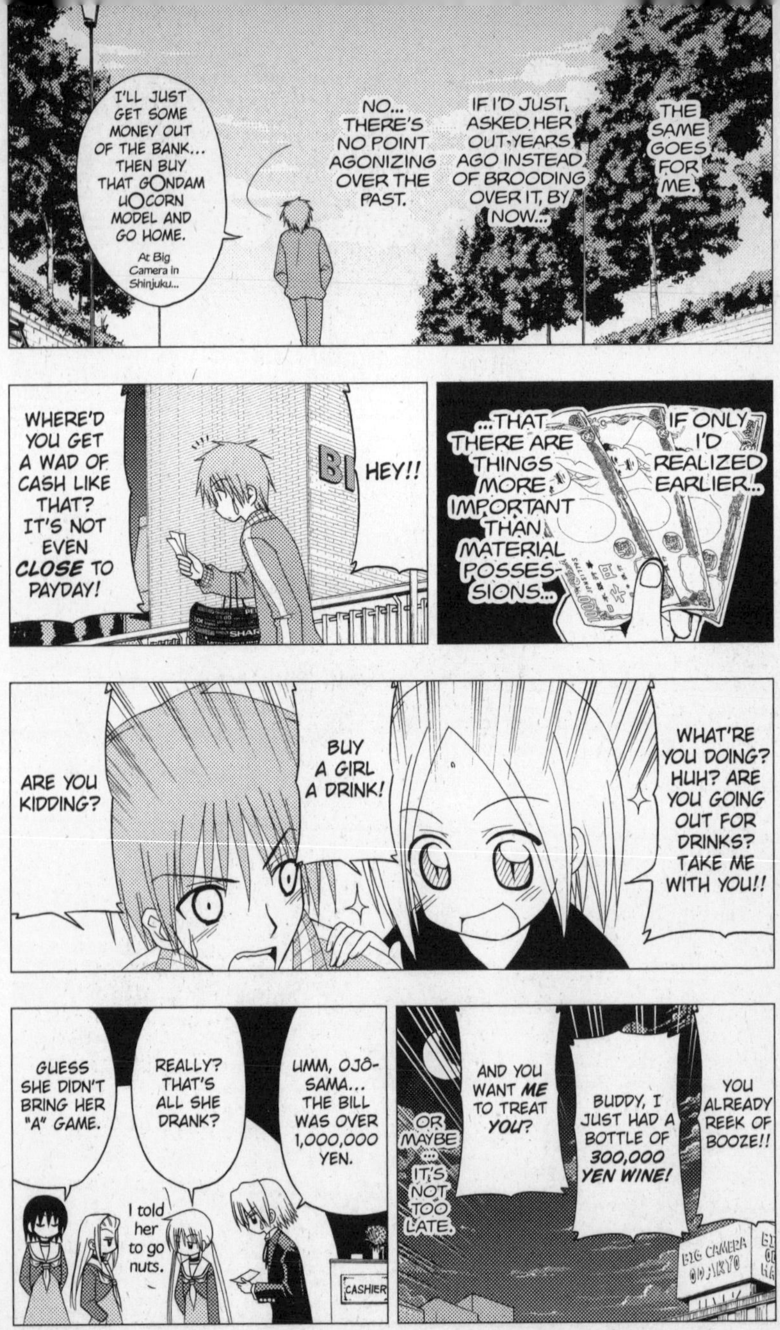
THE SAME GOES FOR ME.
IF I'D JUST ASKED HER OUT YEARS AGO INSTEAD OF BROODING OVER IT, BY NOW...
NO... THERE'S NO POINT AGONIZING OVER THE PAST.
I'LL JUST GET SOME MONEY OUT OF THE BANK... THEN BUY THAT GONDAM UNICORN MODEL AND GO HOME.
At Big Camera in Shinjuku...
IF ONLY I'D REALIZED EARLIER...
...THAT THERE ARE THINGS MORE IMPORTANT THAN MATERIAL POSSESSIONS...
HEY!!
WHERE'D YOU GET A WAD OF CASH LIKE THAT? IT'S NOT EVEN CLOSE TO PAYDAY!
WHAT'RE YOU DOING? HUH? ARE YOU GOING OUT FOR DRINKS? TAKE ME WITH YOU!!
BUY A GIRL A DRINK!
ARE YOU KIDDING?
YOU ALREADY REEK OF BOOZE!!
BUDDY, I JUST HAD A BOTTLE OF 300,000 YEN WINE!
AND YOU WANT ME TO TREAT YOU?
OR MAYBE... IT'S NOT TOO LATE.
BIG CAMERA ODAKYO
UMM, OJÔ-SAMA... THE BILL WAS OVER 1,000,000 YEN.
CASHIER
REALLY? THAT'S ALL SHE DRANK?
I told her to go nuts.
GUESS SHE DIDN'T BRING HER "A" GAME.

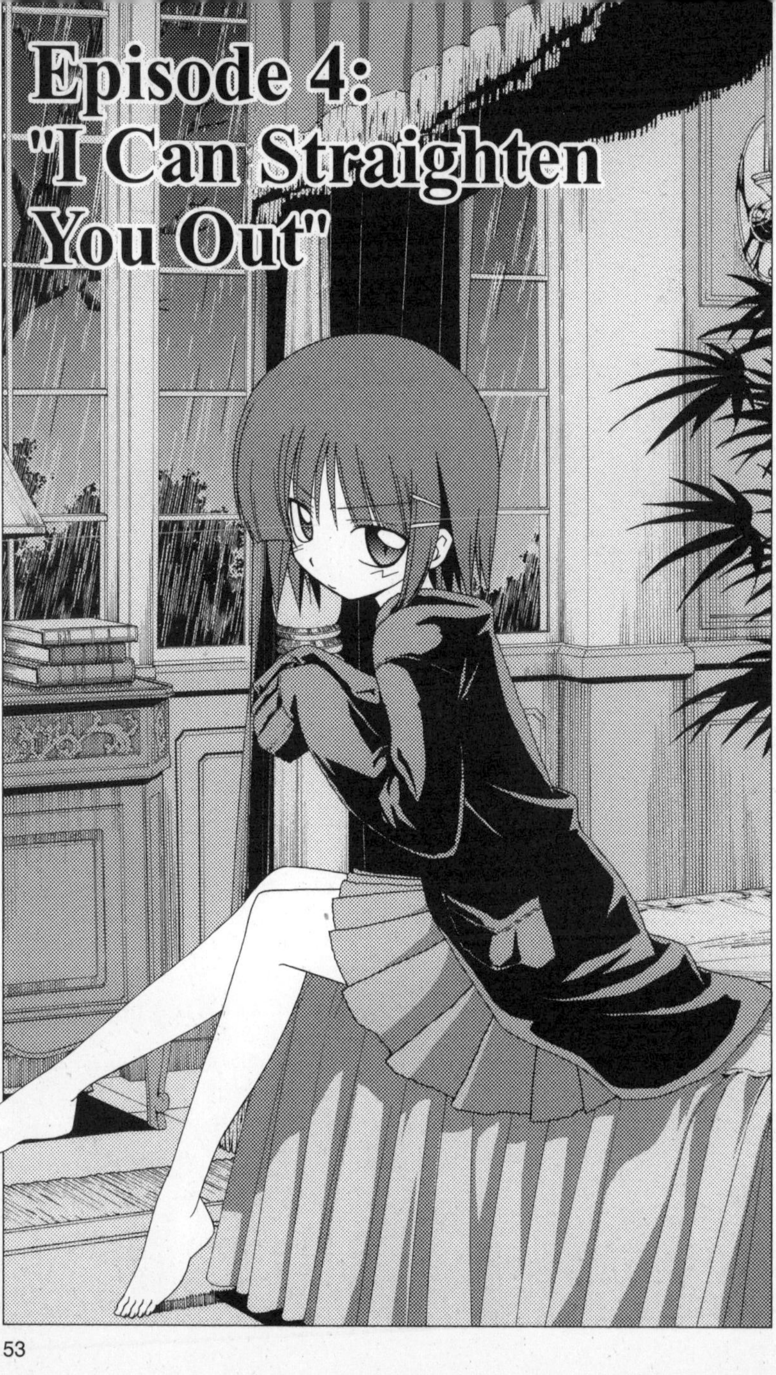
Episode 4:
"I Can Straighten You Out"

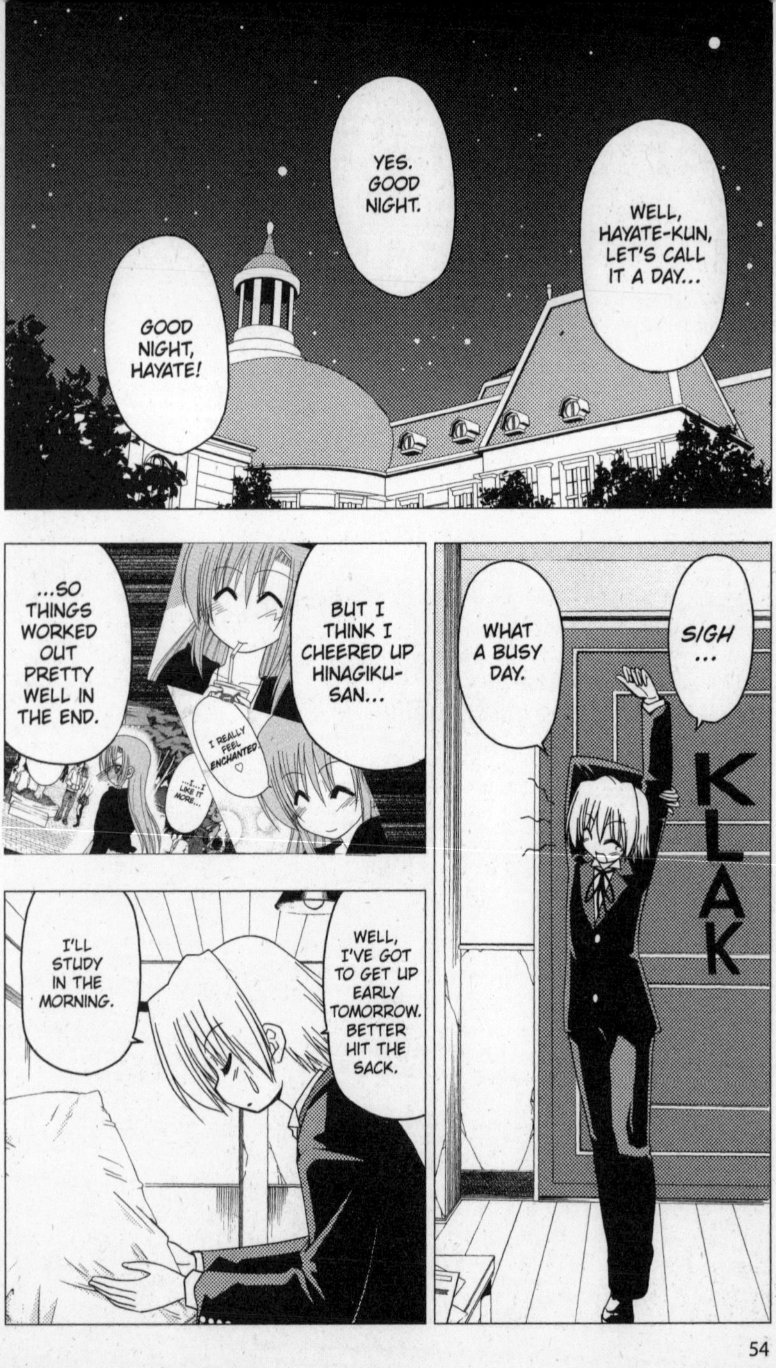
WELL, HAYATE-KUN, LET'S CALL IT A DAY...
YES. GOOD NIGHT.
GOOD NIGHT, HAYATE!
SIGH...
KLAK
WHAT A BUSY DAY.
BUT I THINK I CHEERED UP HINAGIKU-SAN...
I REALLY FEEL ENCHANTED ♡
...I...I LIKE IT MORE...
...SO THINGS WORKED OUT PRETTY WELL IN THE END.
WELL, I'VE GOT TO GET UP EARLY TOMORROW. BETTER HIT THE SACK.
I'LL STUDY IN THE MORNING.

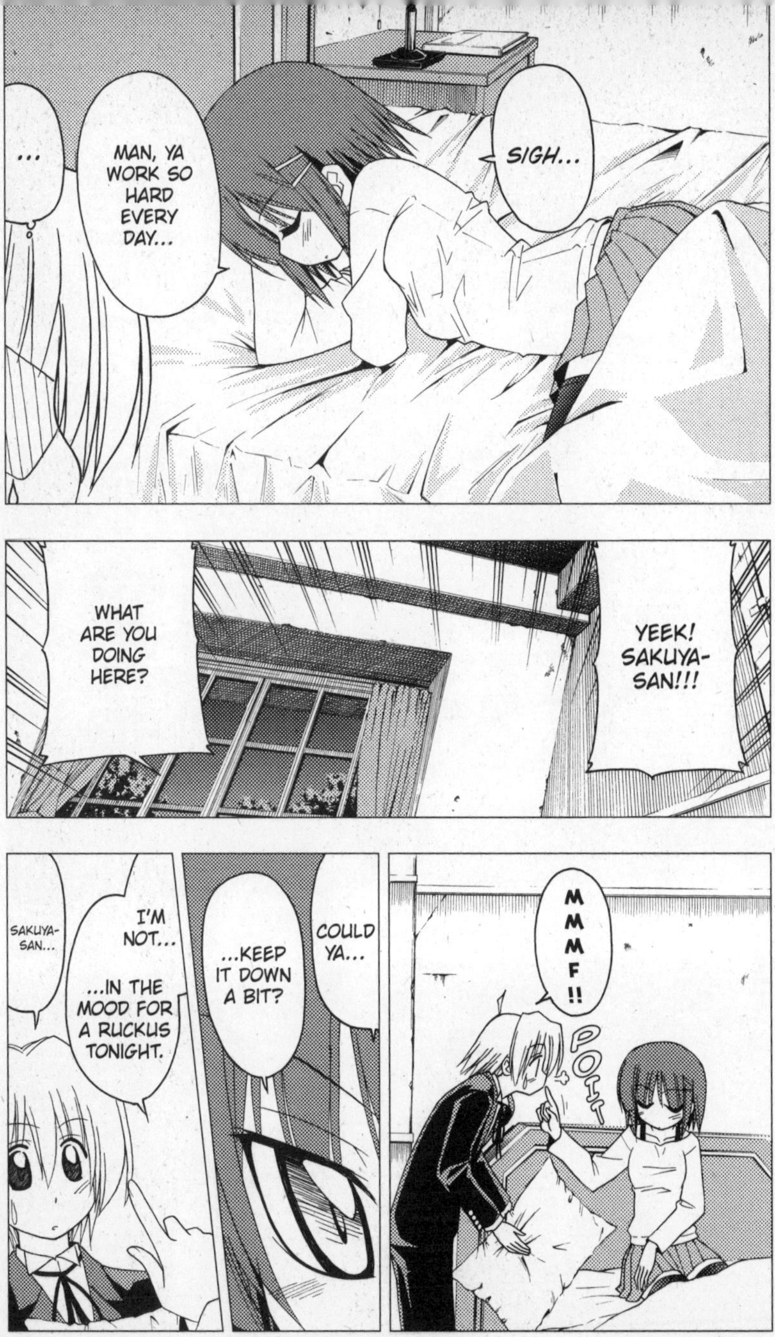
SIGH...
MAN, YA WORK SO HARD EVERY DAY...
...
YEEK! SAKUYA-SAN!!!
WHAT ARE YOU DOING HERE?
MMMF!!
POIT
COULD YA...
...KEEP IT DOWN A BIT?
I'M NOT...
...IN THE MOOD FOR A RUCKUS TONIGHT.
SAKUYA-SAN...

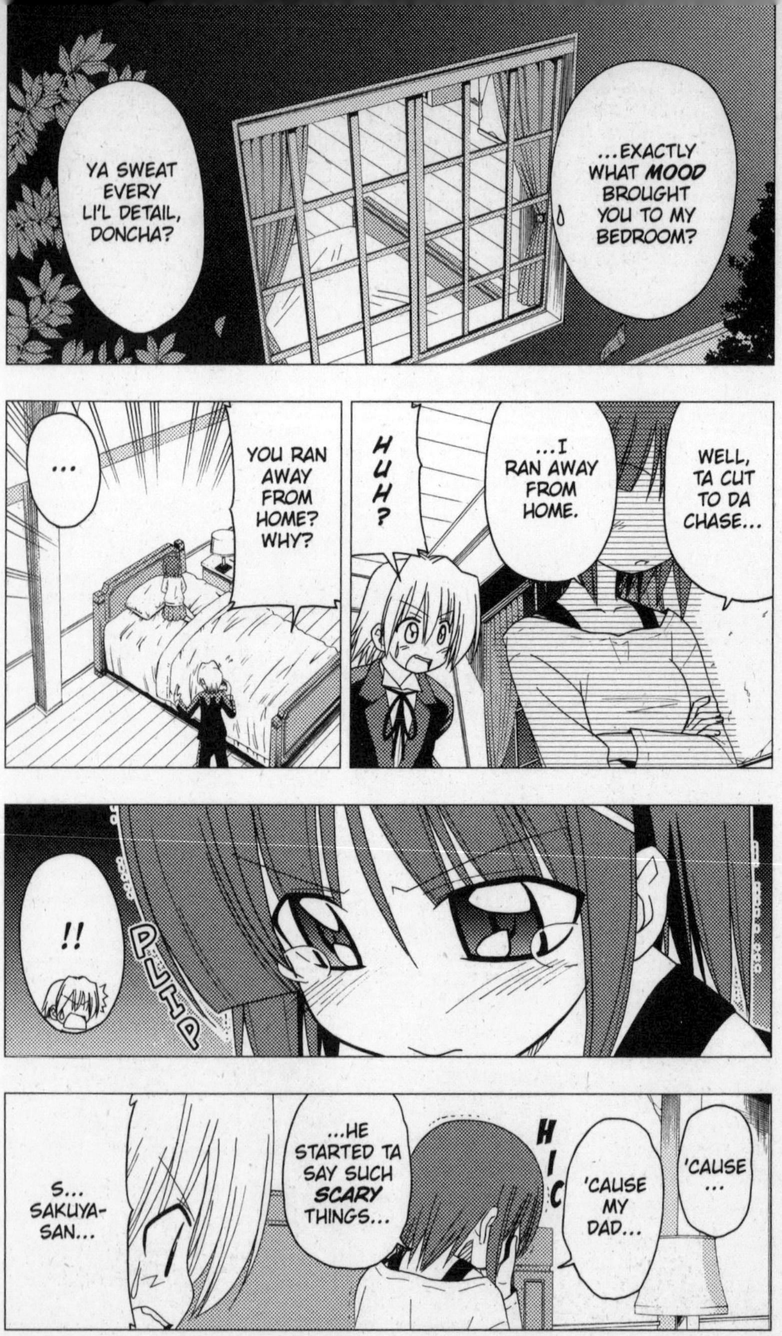
...EXACTLY WHAT MOOD BROUGHT YOU TO MY BEDROOM?
YA SWEAT EVERY LI'L DETAIL, DONCHA?
WELL, TA CUT TO DA CHASE...
...I RAN AWAY FROM HOME.
HUH?
YOU RAN AWAY FROM HOME? WHY?
...
PLIP
!!
'CAUSE...
'CAUSE MY DAD...
HIC
...HE STARTED TA SAY SUCH SCARY THINGS...
S... SAKUYA-SAN...

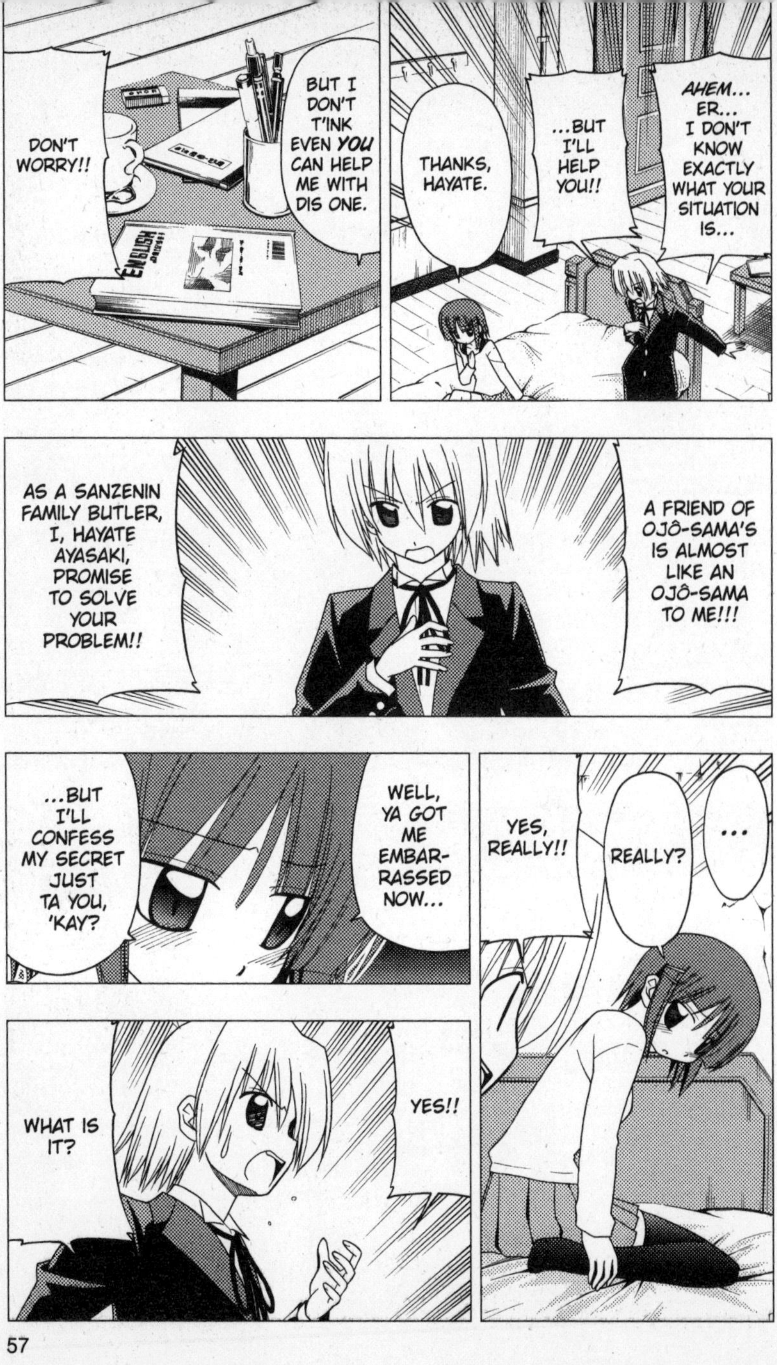
AHEM... ER... I DON'T KNOW EXACTLY WHAT YOUR SITUATION IS...
...BUT I'LL HELP YOU!!
THANKS, HAYATE.
BUT I DON'T T'INK EVEN *YOU* CAN HELP ME WITH DIS ONE.
DON'T WORRY!!
A FRIEND OF OJÔ-SAMA'S IS ALMOST LIKE AN OJÔ-SAMA TO ME!!!
AS A SANZENIN FAMILY BUTLER, I, HAYATE AYASAKI, PROMISE TO SOLVE YOUR PROBLEM!!
...
REALLY?
YES, REALLY!!
WELL, YA GOT ME EMBARRASSED NOW...
...BUT I'LL CONFESS MY SECRET JUST TA YOU, 'KAY?
YES!!
WHAT IS IT?

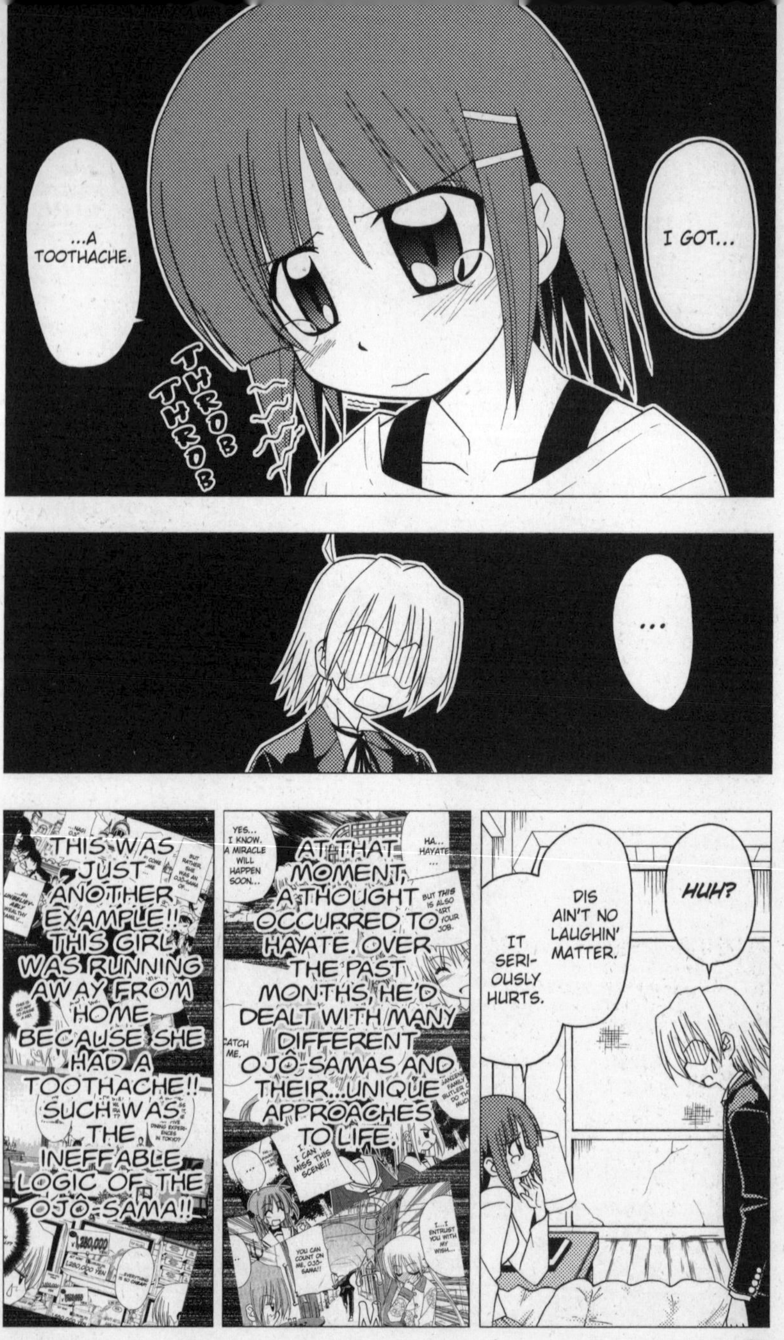
I GOT...
...A TOOTHACHE.
THROB THROB
...
HUH?
DIS AIN'T NO LAUGHIN' MATTER.
IT SERI-OUSLY HURTS.
HA... HAYATE...
YES... I KNOW. A MIRACLE WILL HAPPEN SOON...
AT THAT MOMENT, A THOUGHT OCCURRED TO HAYATE. OVER THE PAST MONTHS, HE'D DEALT WITH MANY DIFFERENT OJÔ-SAMAS AND THEIR...UNIQUE APPROACHES TO LIFE.
CATCH ME.
I...I ENTRUST YOU WITH MY WISH...
YOU CAN COUNT ON ME, OJÔ-SAMA!!
THIS WAS JUST ANOTHER EXAMPLE!! THIS GIRL WAS RUNNING AWAY FROM HOME BECAUSE SHE HAD A TOOTHACHE!! SUCH WAS THE INEFFABLE LOGIC OF THE OJÔ-SAMA!!
1,280,000 YEN

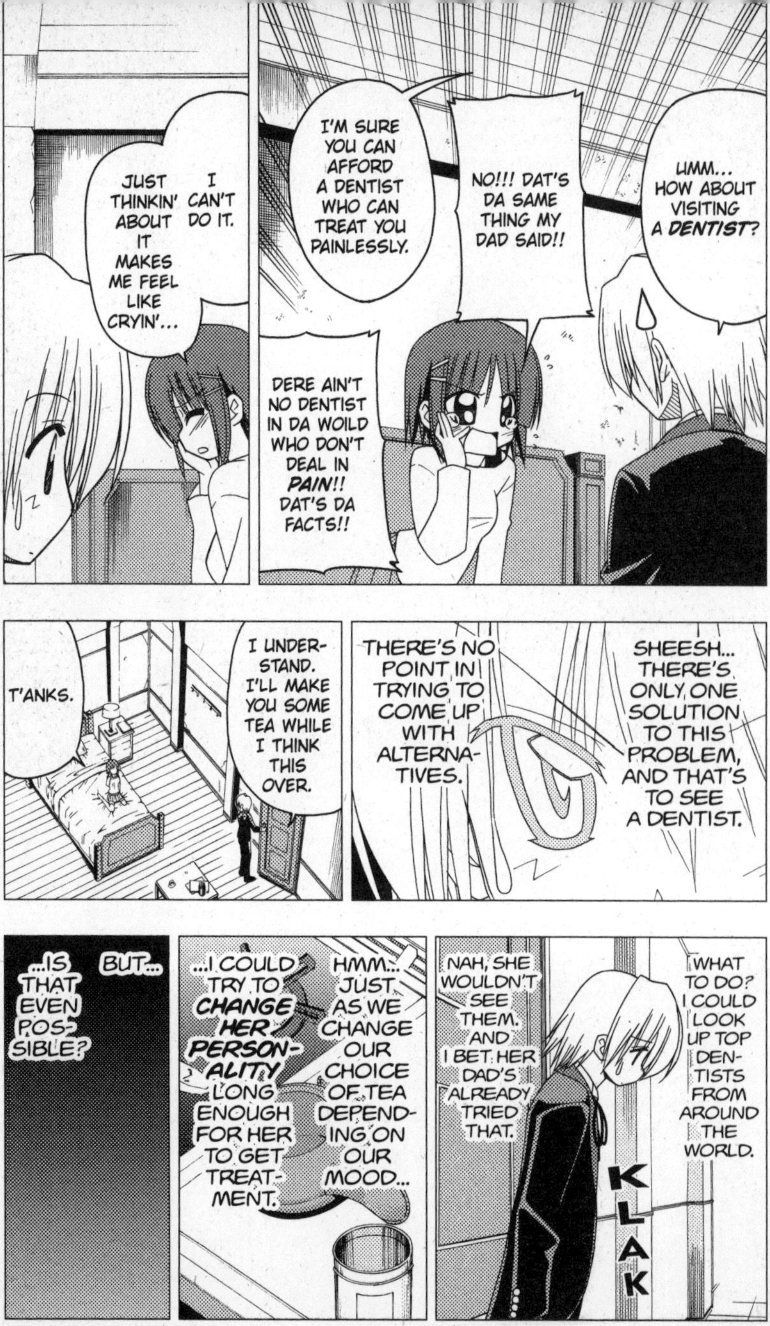
UMM... HOW ABOUT VISITING A DENTIST?
NO!!! DAT'S DA SAME THING MY DAD SAID!!
I'M SURE YOU CAN AFFORD A DENTIST WHO CAN TREAT YOU PAINLESSLY.
DERE AIN'T NO DENTIST IN DA WOILD WHO DON'T DEAL IN PAIN!! DAT'S DA FACTS!!
I CAN'T DO IT.
JUST THINKIN' ABOUT IT MAKES ME FEEL LIKE CRYIN'...
SHEESH... THERE'S ONLY ONE SOLUTION TO THIS PROBLEM, AND THAT'S TO SEE A DENTIST.
THERE'S NO POINT IN TRYING TO COME UP WITH ALTERNATIVES.
I UNDERSTAND. I'LL MAKE YOU SOME TEA WHILE I THINK THIS OVER.
T'ANKS.
WHAT TO DO? I COULD LOOK UP TOP DENTISTS FROM AROUND THE WORLD.
NAH, SHE WOULDN'T SEE THEM. AND I BET HER DAD'S ALREADY TRIED THAT.
KLAK
HMM... JUST AS WE CHANGE OUR CHOICE OF TEA DEPENDING ON OUR MOOD...
...I COULD TRY TO CHANGE HER PERSONALITY LONG ENOUGH FOR HER TO GET TREATMENT.
BUT...
...IS THAT EVEN POSSIBLE?

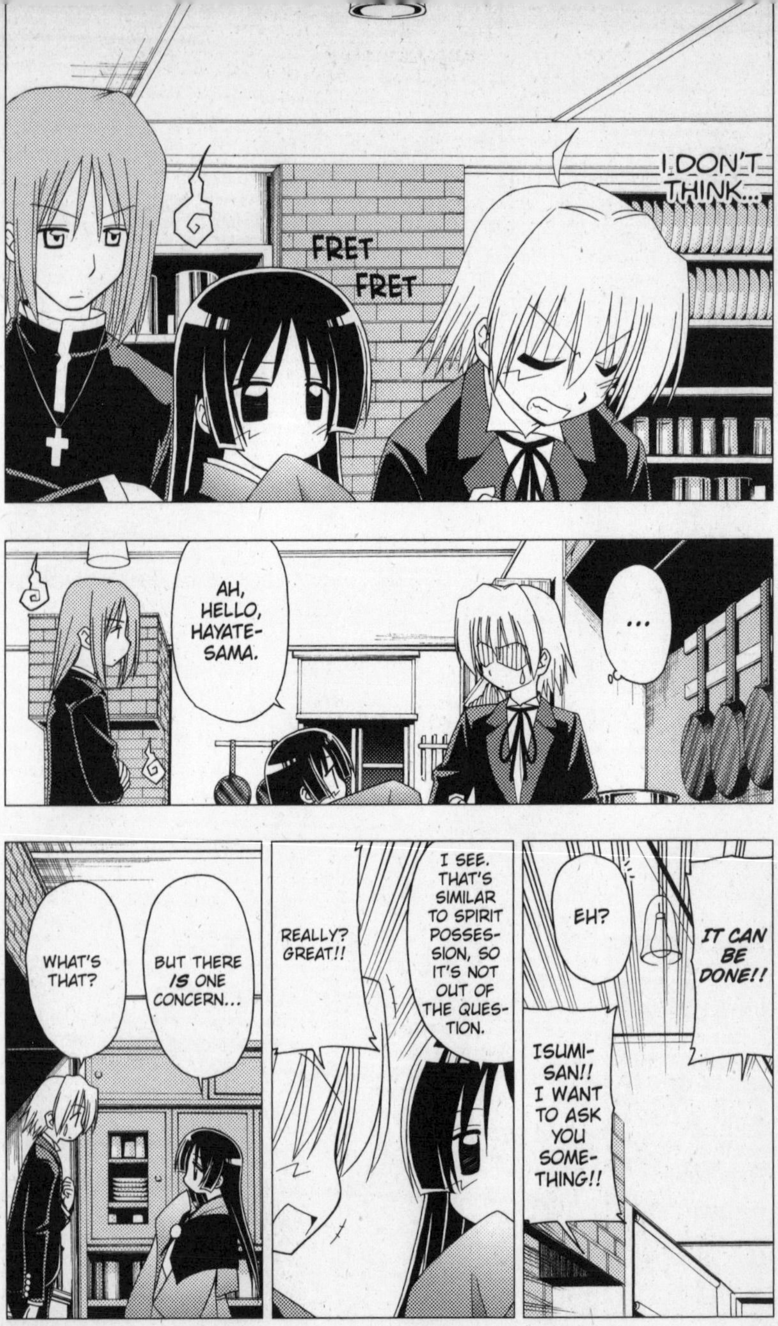
I DON'T THINK...
FRET FRET
...
AH, HELLO, HAYATE-SAMA.
IT CAN BE DONE!!
EH?
ISUMI-SAN!! I WANT TO ASK YOU SOMETHING!!
I SEE. THAT'S SIMILAR TO SPIRIT POSSESSION, SO IT'S NOT OUT OF THE QUESTION.
REALLY? GREAT!!
BUT THERE IS ONE CONCERN...
WHAT'S THAT?

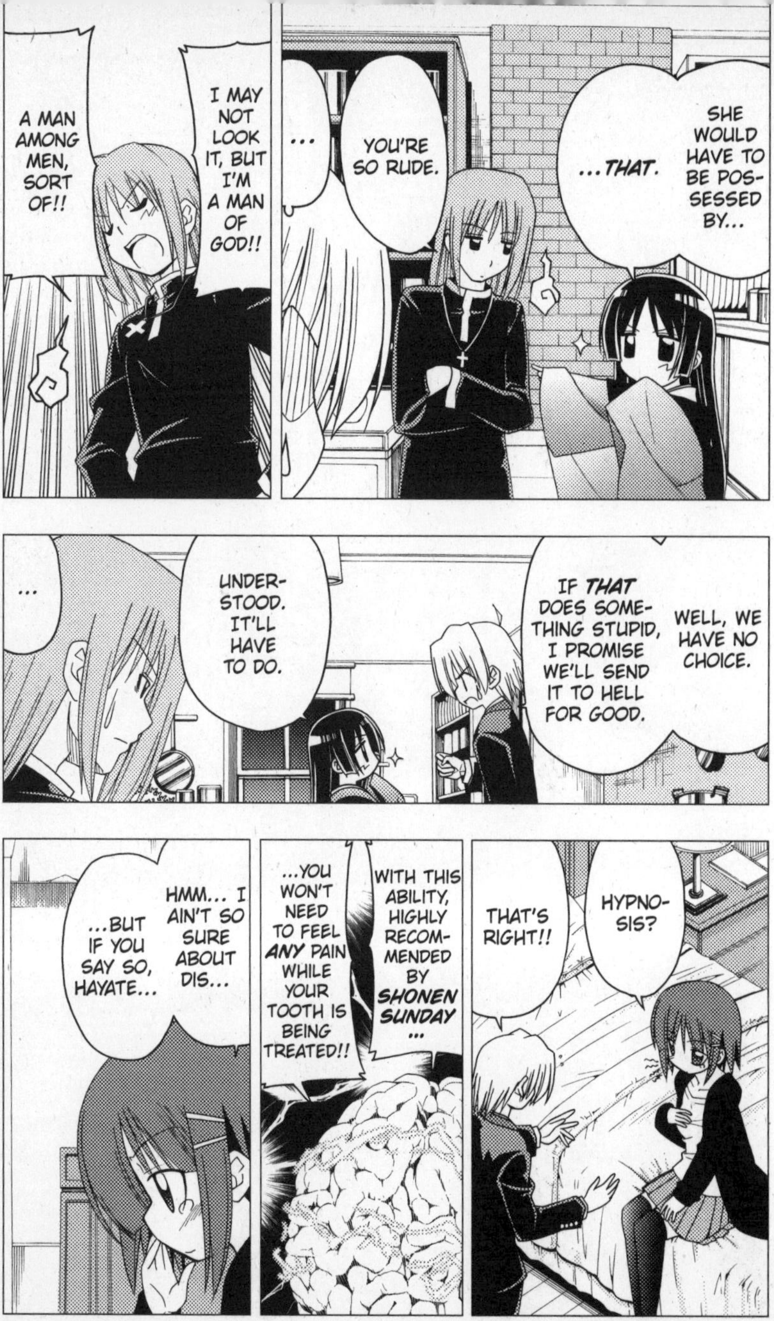
SHE WOULD HAVE TO BE POSSESSED BY...
...*THAT*.
YOU'RE SO RUDE.
...
I MAY NOT LOOK IT, BUT I'M A MAN OF GOD!!
A MAN AMONG MEN, SORT OF!!
WELL, WE HAVE NO CHOICE.
IF *THAT* DOES SOMETHING STUPID, I PROMISE WE'LL SEND IT TO HELL FOR GOOD.
UNDERSTOOD. IT'LL HAVE TO DO.
...
HYPNOSIS?
THAT'S RIGHT!!
WITH THIS ABILITY, HIGHLY RECOMMENDED BY *SHONEN SUNDAY*...
...YOU WON'T NEED TO FEEL *ANY* PAIN WHILE YOUR TOOTH IS BEING TREATED!!
HMM... I AIN'T SO SURE ABOUT DIS...
...BUT IF YOU SAY SO, HAYATE...

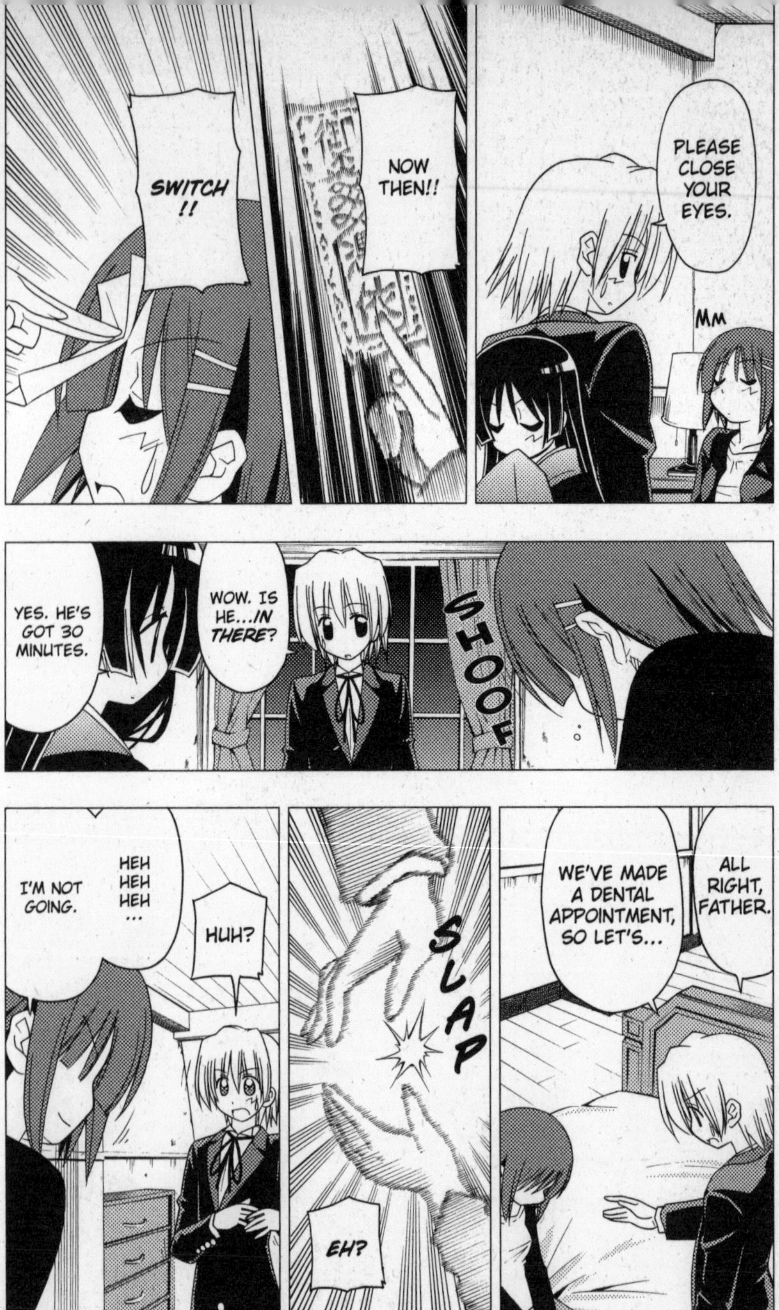
PLEASE CLOSE YOUR EYES.
MM
NOW THEN!!
SWITCH !!
SHOOF
WOW. IS HE...*IN THERE*?
YES. HE'S GOT 30 MINUTES.
ALL RIGHT, FATHER.
WE'VE MADE A DENTAL APPOINTMENT, SO LET'S...
SLAP
EH?
HUH?
HEH HEH HEH ...
I'M NOT GOING.

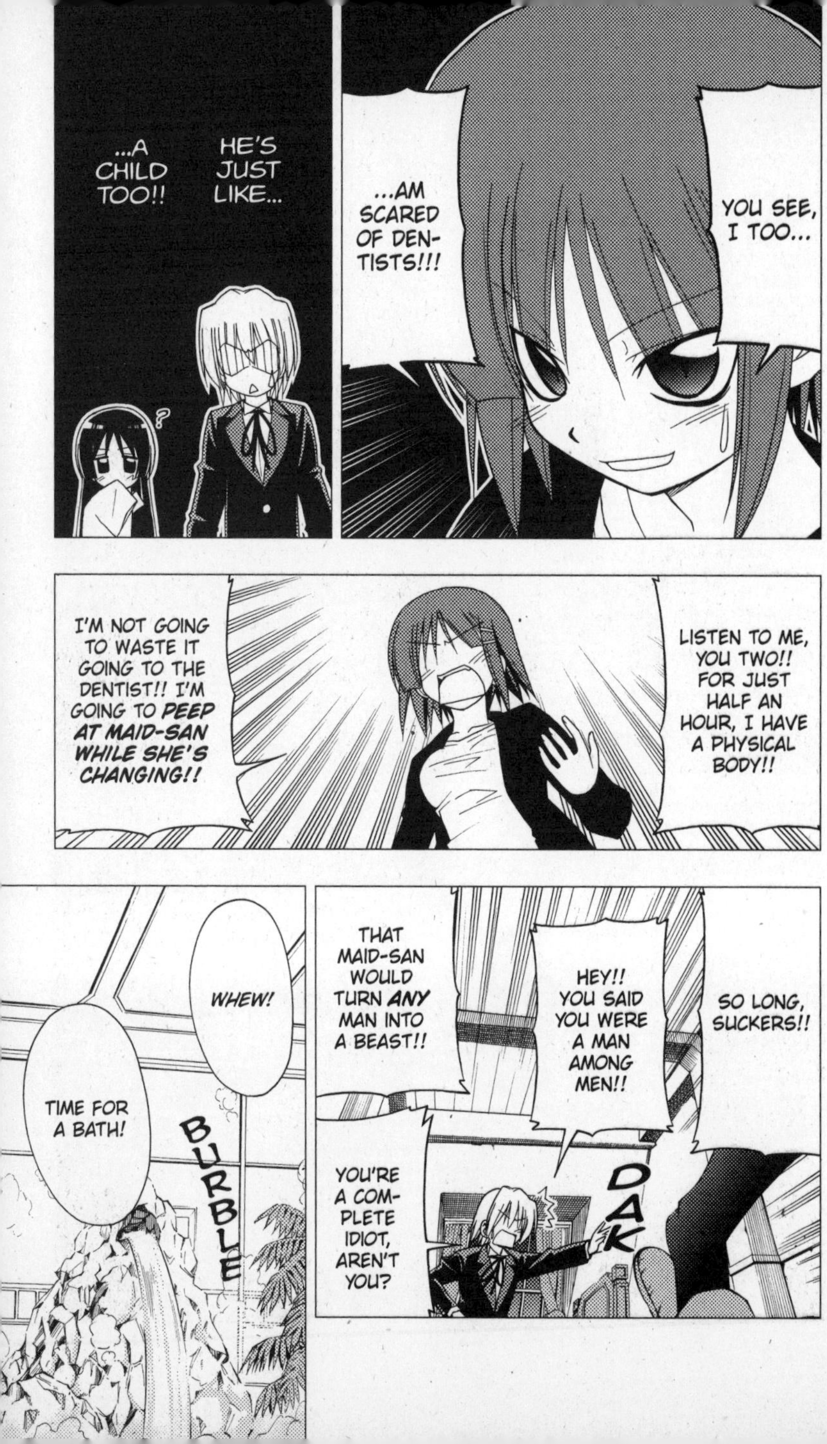
YOU SEE, I TOO...
...AM SCARED OF DEN-TISTS!!!
HE'S JUST LIKE...
...A CHILD TOO!!
?
LISTEN TO ME, YOU TWO!! FOR JUST HALF AN HOUR, I HAVE A PHYSICAL BODY!!
I'M NOT GOING TO WASTE IT GOING TO THE DENTIST!! I'M GOING TO *PEEP AT MAID-SAN WHILE SHE'S CHANGING!!*
SO LONG, SUCKERS!!
HEY!! YOU SAID YOU WERE A MAN AMONG MEN!!
THAT MAID-SAN WOULD TURN *ANY* MAN INTO A BEAST!!
DAK
YOU'RE A COM-PLETE IDIOT, AREN'T YOU?
WHEW!
TIME FOR A BATH!
BURBLE

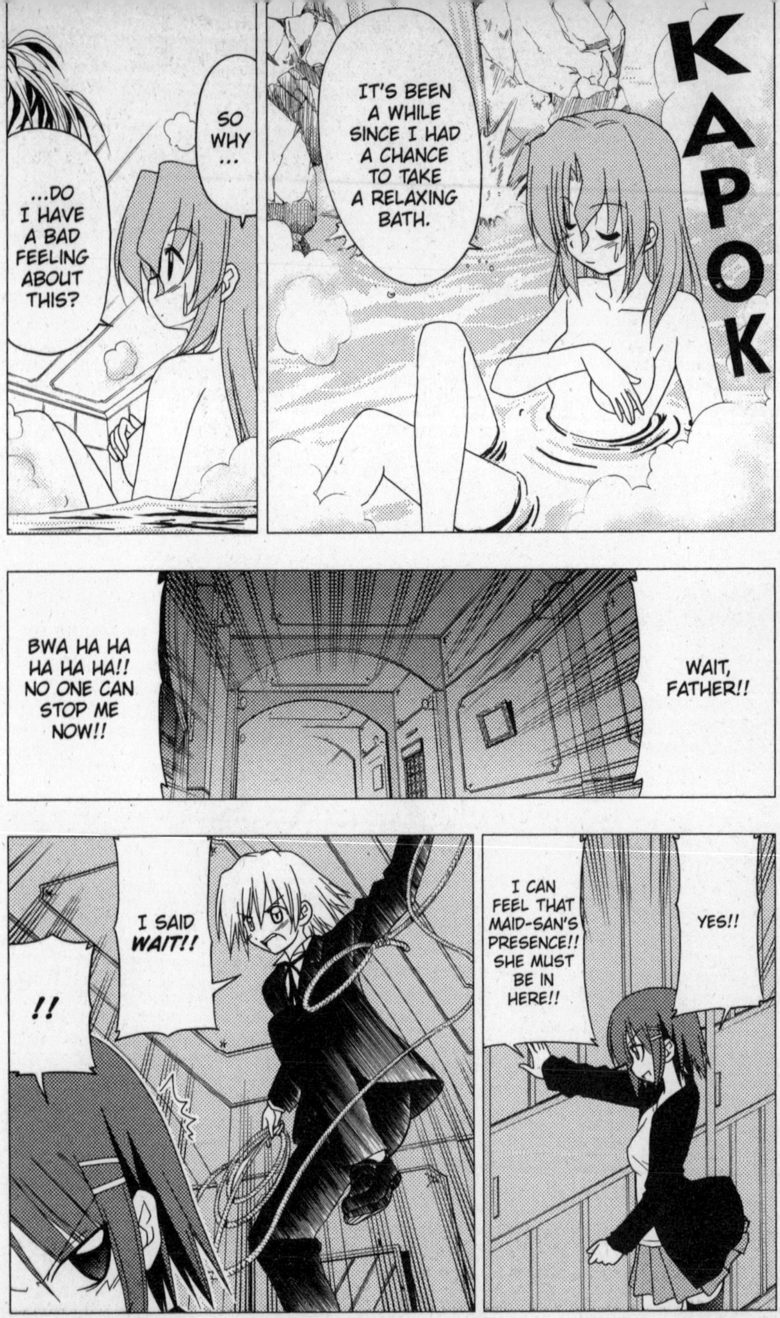
KAPOK
IT'S BEEN A WHILE SINCE I HAD A CHANCE TO TAKE A RELAXING BATH.
SO WHY...
...DO I HAVE A BAD FEELING ABOUT THIS?
WAIT, FATHER!!
BWA HA HA HA HA HA!! NO ONE CAN STOP ME NOW!!
YES!!
I CAN FEEL THAT MAID-SAN'S PRESENCE!! SHE MUST BE IN HERE!!
I SAID *WAIT!!*
!!

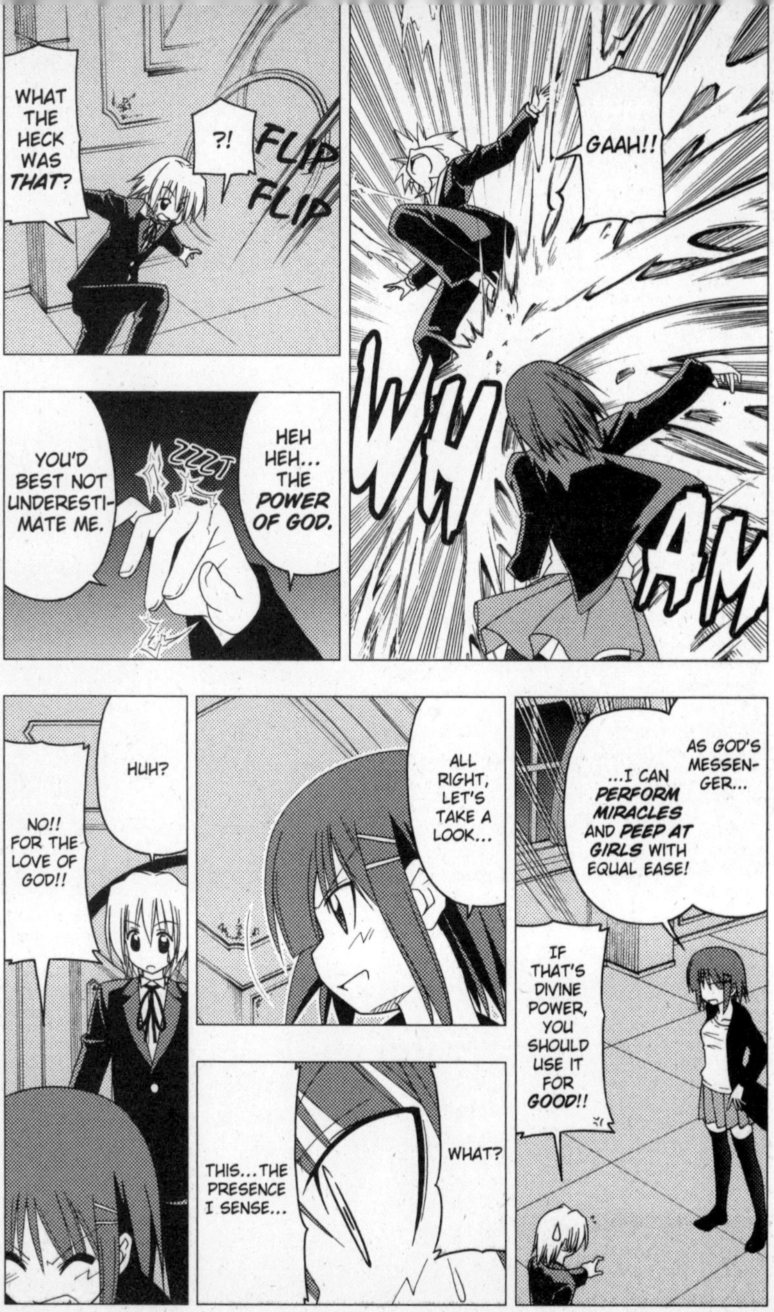
GAAH!!
WHAM
?!
FLIP FLIP
WHAT THE HECK WAS *THAT*?
HEH HEH... THE ***POWER OF GOD.***
YOU'D BEST NOT UNDERESTIMATE ME.
AS GOD'S MESSENGER...
...I CAN ***PERFORM MIRACLES*** AND ***PEEP AT GIRLS*** WITH EQUAL EASE!
IF THAT'S DIVINE POWER, YOU SHOULD USE IT FOR ***GOOD!!***
ALL RIGHT, LET'S TAKE A LOOK...
WHAT?
THIS...THE PRESENCE I SENSE...
HUH?
NO!! FOR THE LOVE OF GOD!!

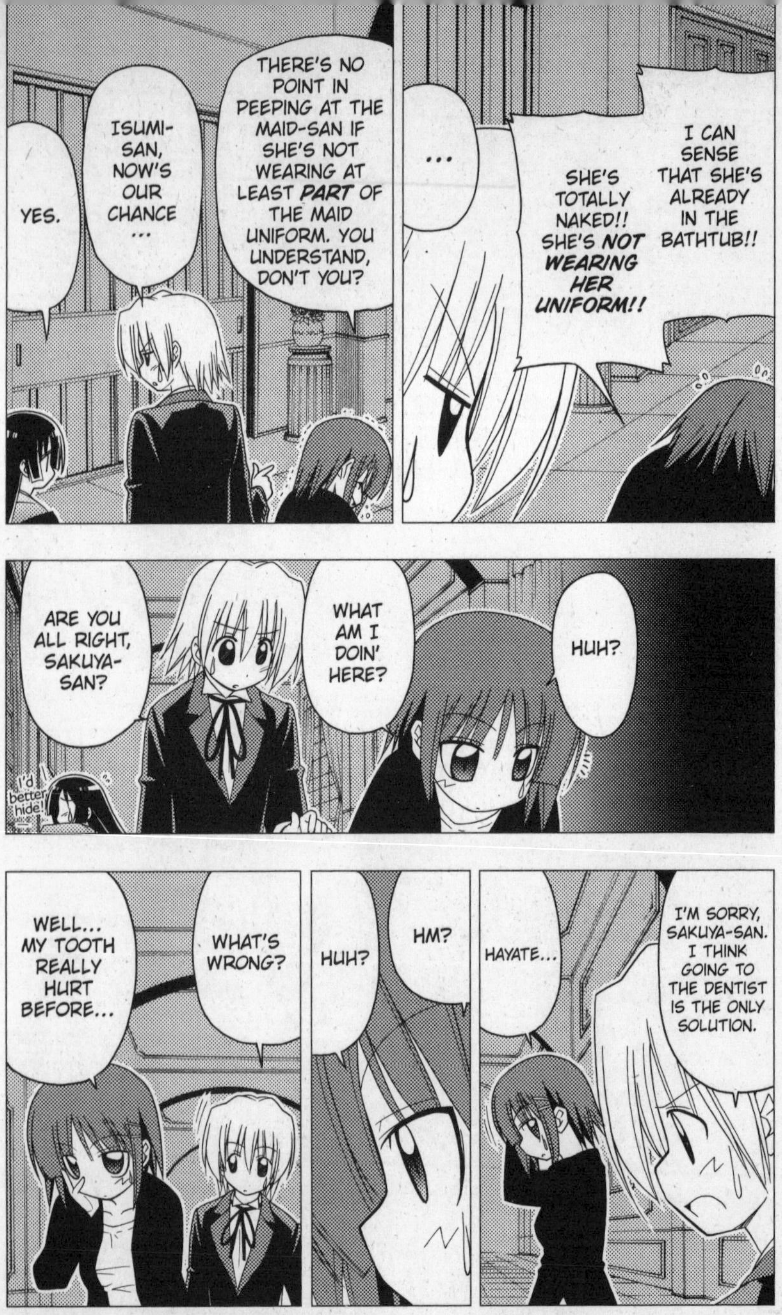
I CAN SENSE THAT SHE'S ALREADY IN THE BATHTUB!!
SHE'S TOTALLY NAKED!! SHE'S NOT WEARING HER UNIFORM!!
...
THERE'S NO POINT IN PEEPING AT THE MAID-SAN IF SHE'S NOT WEARING AT LEAST PART OF THE MAID UNIFORM. YOU UNDERSTAND, DON'T YOU?
ISUMI-SAN, NOW'S OUR CHANCE...
YES.
HUH?
WHAT AM I DOIN' HERE?
ARE YOU ALL RIGHT, SAKUYA-SAN?
I'd better hide!
I'M SORRY, SAKUYA-SAN. I THINK GOING TO THE DENTIST IS THE ONLY SOLUTION.
HAYATE...
HM?
HUH?
WHAT'S WRONG?
WELL... MY TOOTH REALLY HURT BEFORE...

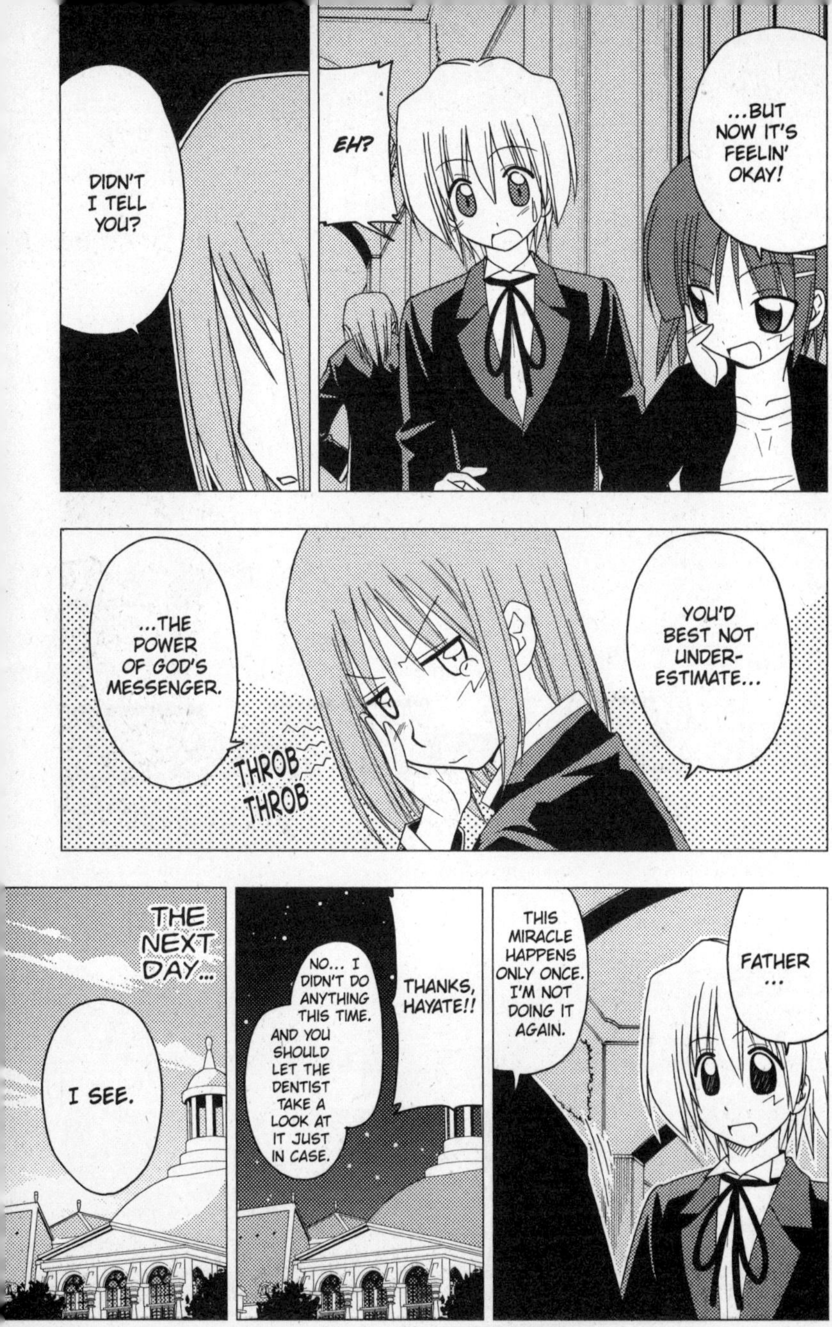
...BUT NOW IT'S FEELIN' OKAY!
EH?
DIDN'T I TELL YOU?
YOU'D BEST NOT UNDER-ESTIMATE...
...THE POWER OF GOD'S MESSENGER.
THROB THROB
FATHER ...
THIS MIRACLE HAPPENS ONLY ONCE. I'M NOT DOING IT AGAIN.
THANKS, HAYATE!!
NO... I DIDN'T DO ANYTHING THIS TIME.
AND YOU SHOULD LET THE DENTIST TAKE A LOOK AT IT JUST IN CASE.
THE NEXT DAY...
I SEE.

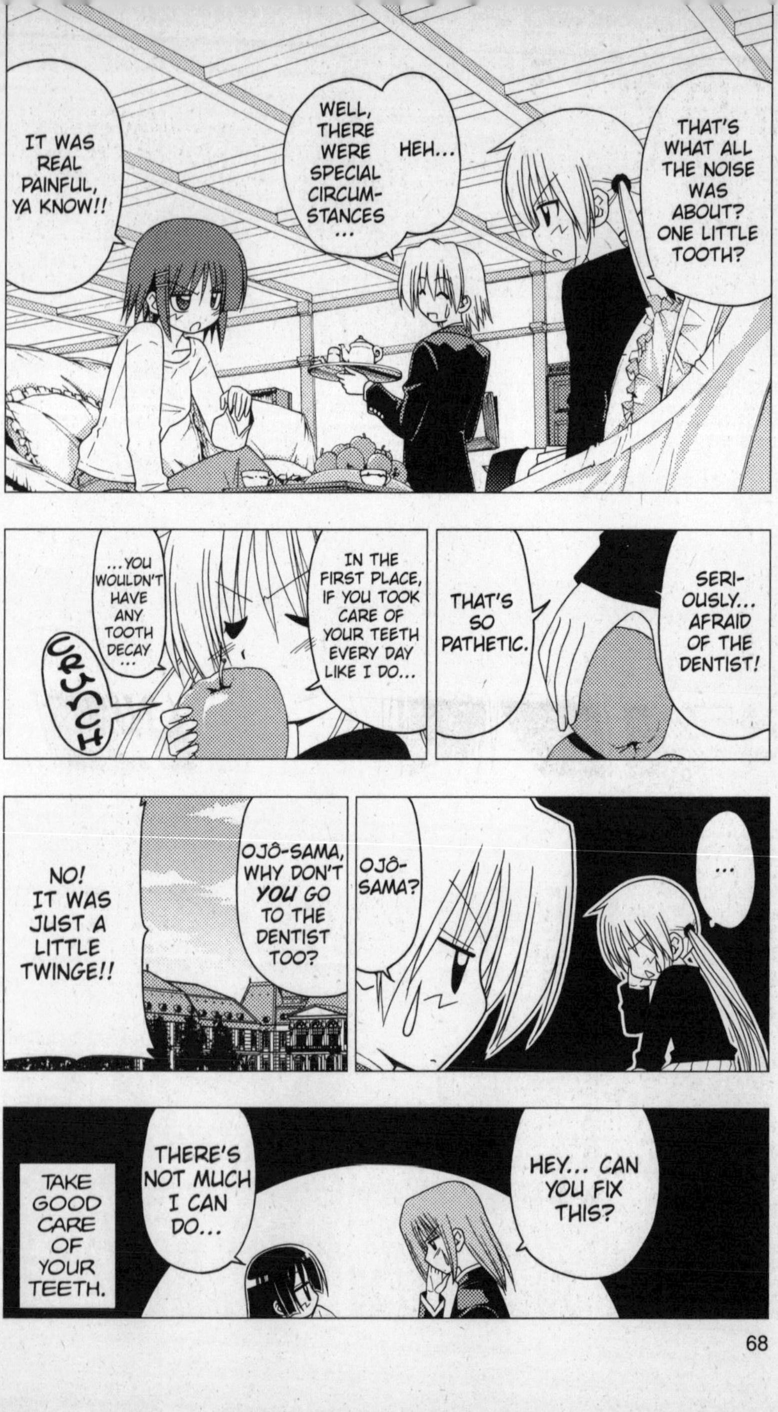
THAT'S WHAT ALL THE NOISE WAS ABOUT? ONE LITTLE TOOTH?
HEH...
WELL, THERE WERE SPECIAL CIRCUM-STANCES...
IT WAS REAL PAINFUL, YA KNOW!!
SERI-OUSLY... AFRAID OF THE DENTIST!
THAT'S SO PATHETIC.
IN THE FIRST PLACE, IF YOU TOOK CARE OF YOUR TEETH EVERY DAY LIKE I DO...
...YOU WOULDN'T HAVE ANY TOOTH DECAY...
CRUNCH
...
OJÔ-SAMA?
OJÔ-SAMA, WHY DON'T *YOU* GO TO THE DENTIST TOO?
NO! IT WAS JUST A LITTLE TWINGE!!
HEY... CAN YOU FIX THIS?
THERE'S NOT MUCH I CAN DO...
TAKE GOOD CARE OF YOUR TEETH.

Episode 5:
"Enough Is Enough for an Unforgettable Memory"

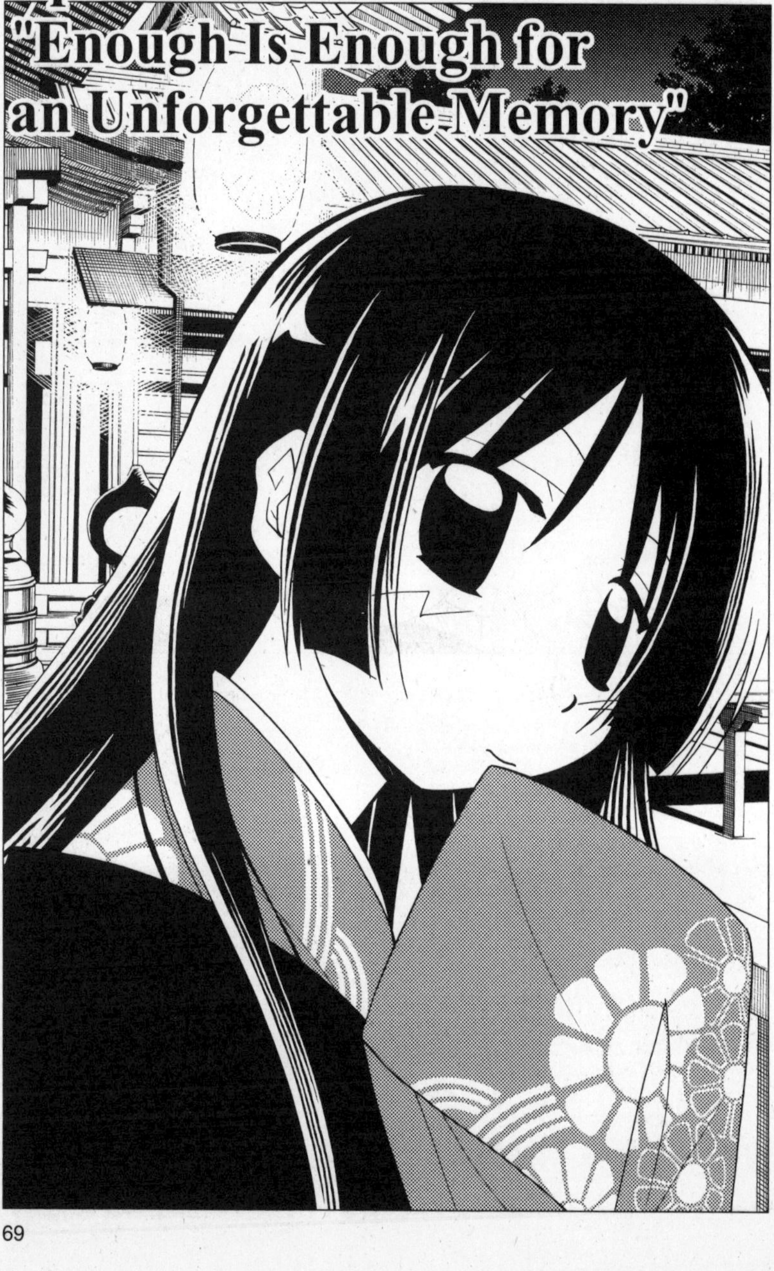

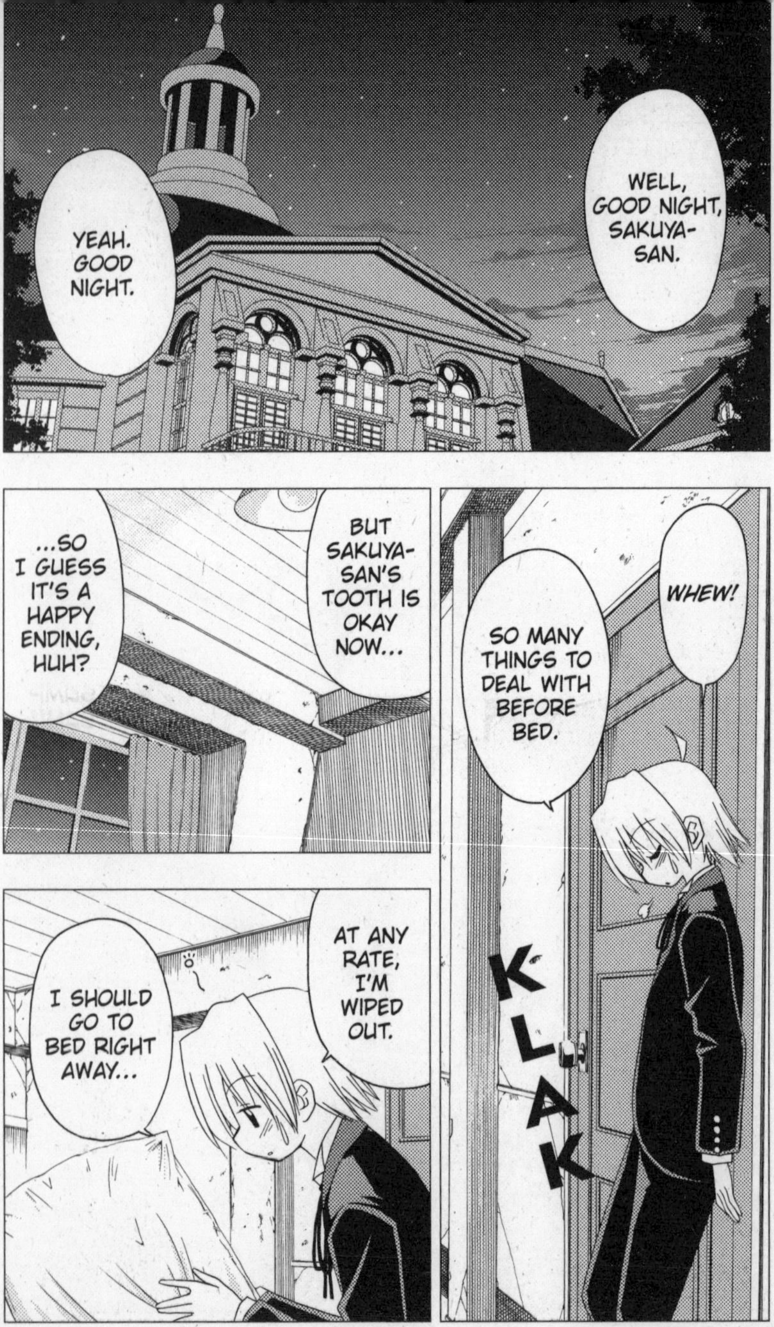
WELL, GOOD NIGHT, SAKUYA-SAN.
YEAH. GOOD NIGHT.
WHEW!
SO MANY THINGS TO DEAL WITH BEFORE BED.
KLAK
BUT SAKUYA-SAN'S TOOTH IS OKAY NOW...
...SO I GUESS IT'S A HAPPY ENDING, HUH?
AT ANY RATE, I'M WIPED OUT.
I SHOULD GO TO BED RIGHT AWAY...

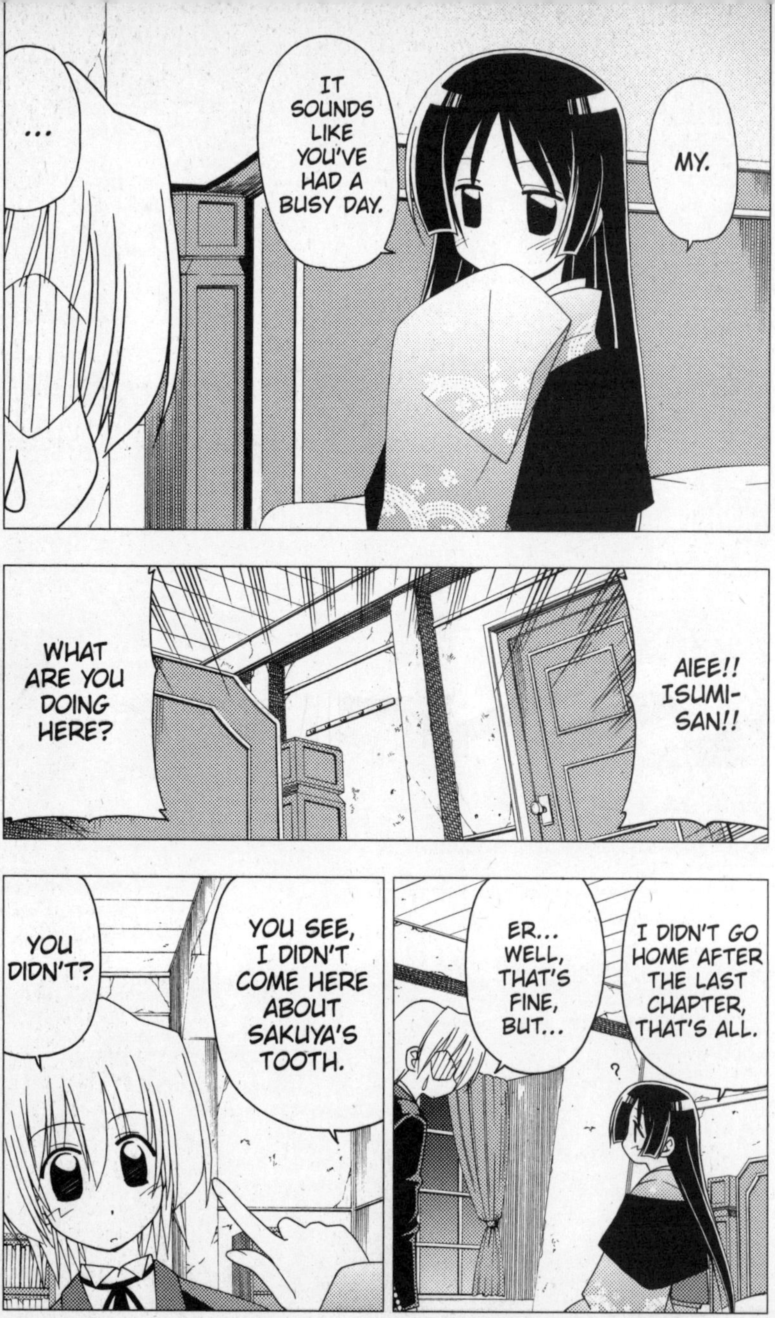
MY.
IT SOUNDS LIKE YOU'VE HAD A BUSY DAY.
...
AIEE!! ISUMI-SAN!!
WHAT ARE YOU DOING HERE?
I DIDN'T GO HOME AFTER THE LAST CHAPTER, THAT'S ALL.
ER... WELL, THAT'S FINE, BUT...
?
YOU SEE, I DIDN'T COME HERE ABOUT SAKUYA'S TOOTH.
YOU DIDN'T?

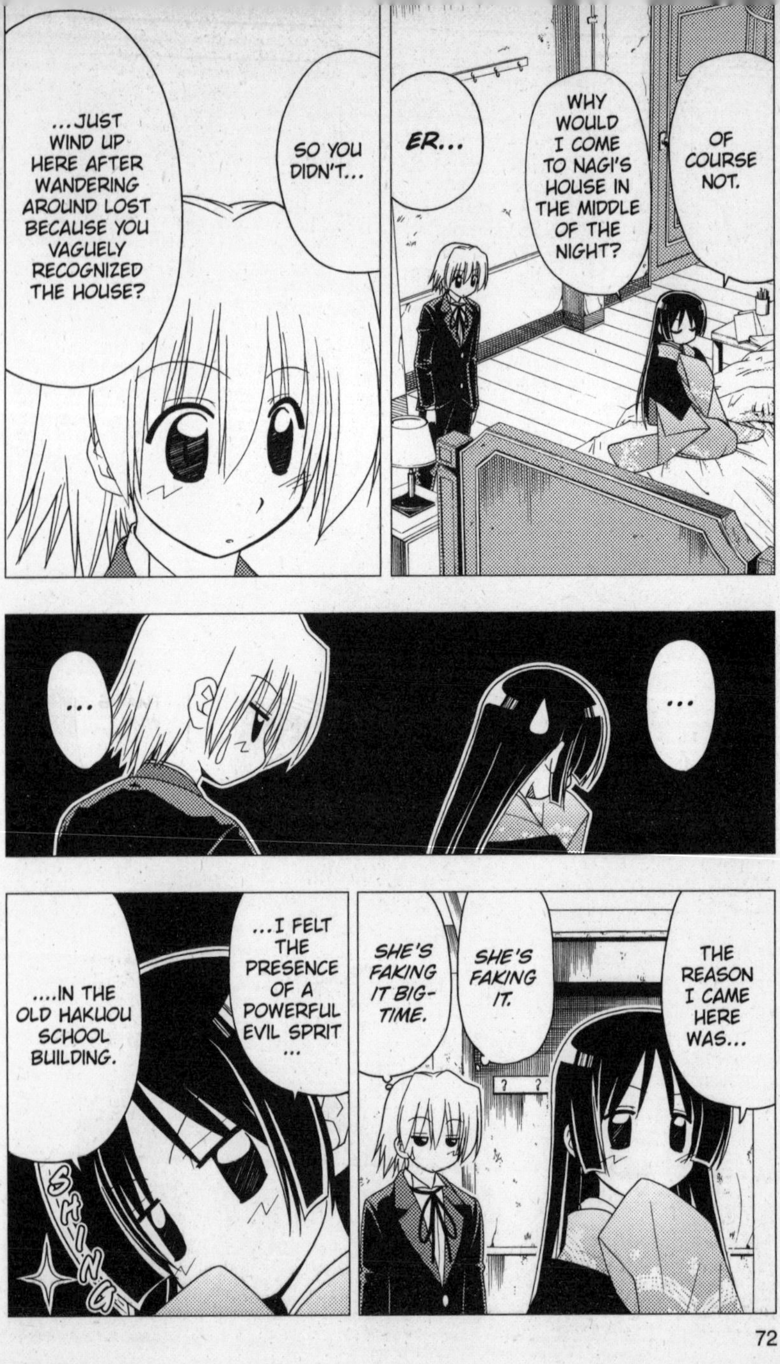
OF COURSE NOT.
WHY WOULD I COME TO NAGI'S HOUSE IN THE MIDDLE OF THE NIGHT?
ER...
SO YOU DIDN'T...
...JUST WIND UP HERE AFTER WANDERING AROUND LOST BECAUSE YOU VAGUELY RECOGNIZED THE HOUSE?
...
...
THE REASON I CAME HERE WAS...
SHE'S FAKING IT.
SHE'S FAKING IT BIG-TIME.
...I FELT THE PRESENCE OF A POWERFUL EVIL SPRIT ...
....IN THE OLD HAKUOU SCHOOL BUILDING.
SHING

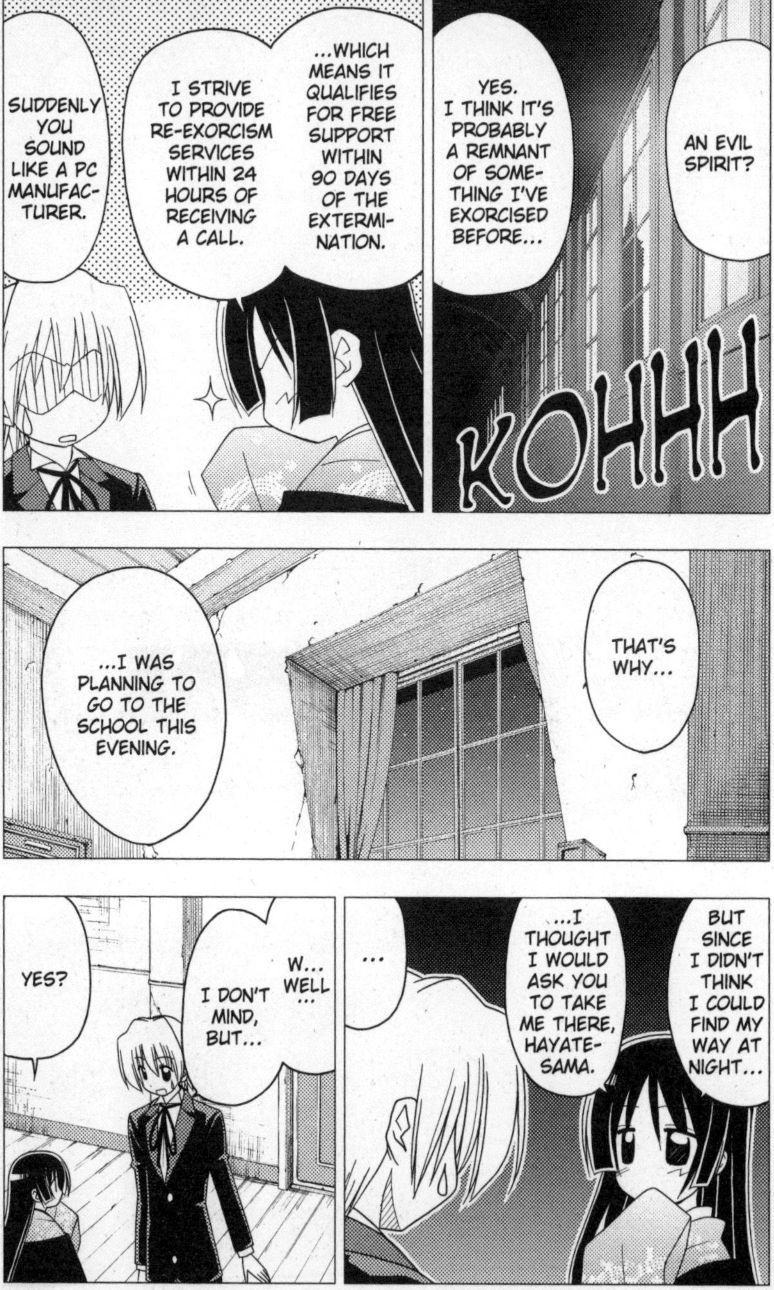
AN EVIL SPIRIT?
YES. I THINK IT'S PROBABLY A REMNANT OF SOME-THING I'VE EXORCISED BEFORE...
KOHHH
...WHICH MEANS IT QUALIFIES FOR FREE SUPPORT WITHIN 90 DAYS OF THE EXTERMI-NATION.
I STRIVE TO PROVIDE RE-EXORCISM SERVICES WITHIN 24 HOURS OF RECEIVING A CALL.
SUDDENLY YOU SOUND LIKE A PC MANUFAC-TURER.
THAT'S WHY...
...I WAS PLANNING TO GO TO THE SCHOOL THIS EVENING.
BUT SINCE I DIDN'T THINK I COULD FIND MY WAY AT NIGHT...
...I THOUGHT I WOULD ASK YOU TO TAKE ME THERE, HAYATE-SAMA.
...
W... WELL...
I DON'T MIND, BUT...
YES?

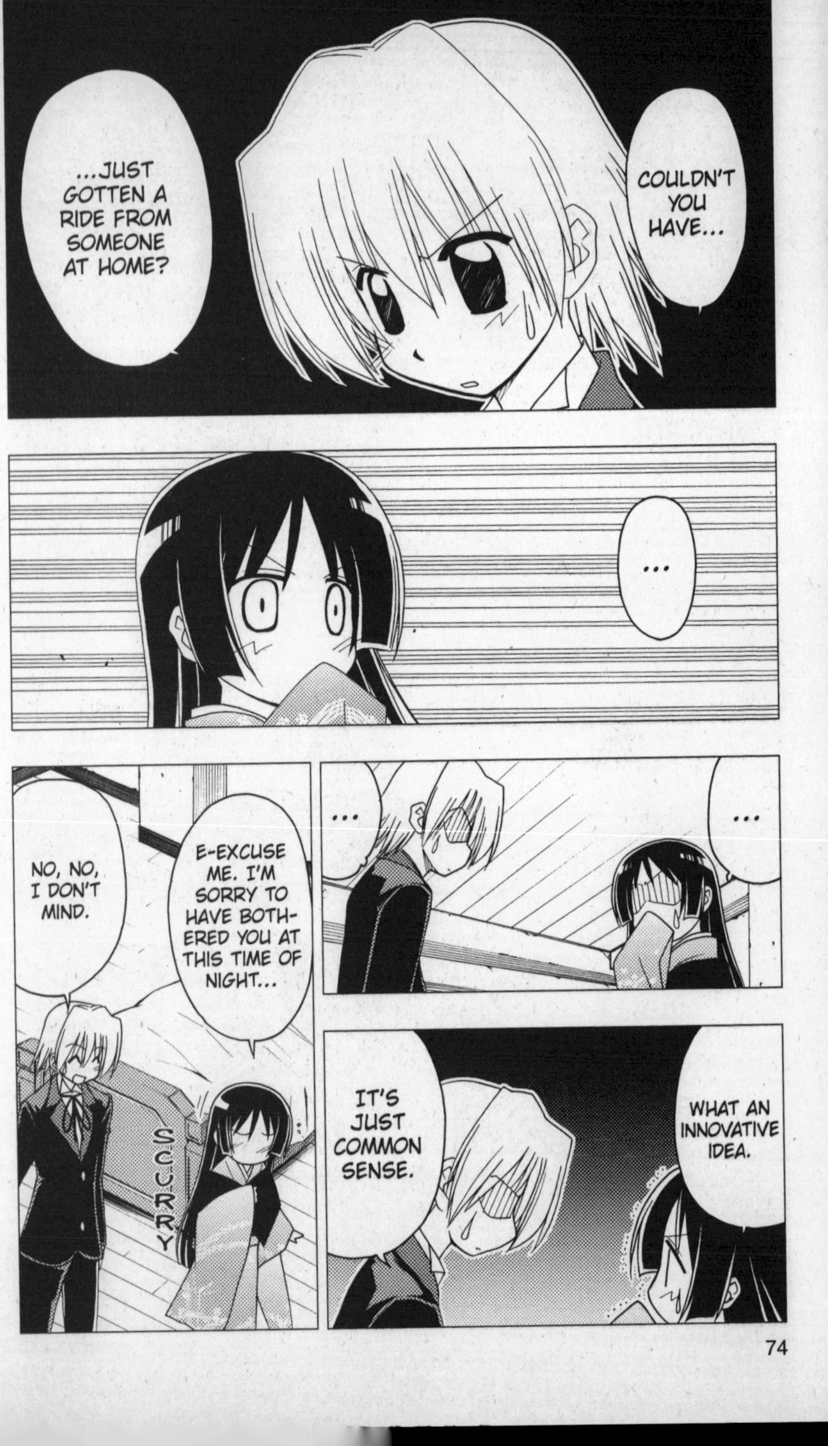
COULDN'T YOU HAVE...
...JUST GOTTEN A RIDE FROM SOMEONE AT HOME?
...
...
...
WHAT AN INNOVATIVE IDEA.
IT'S JUST COMMON SENSE.
E-EXCUSE ME. I'M SORRY TO HAVE BOTH-ERED YOU AT THIS TIME OF NIGHT...
SCURRY
NO, NO, I DON'T MIND.

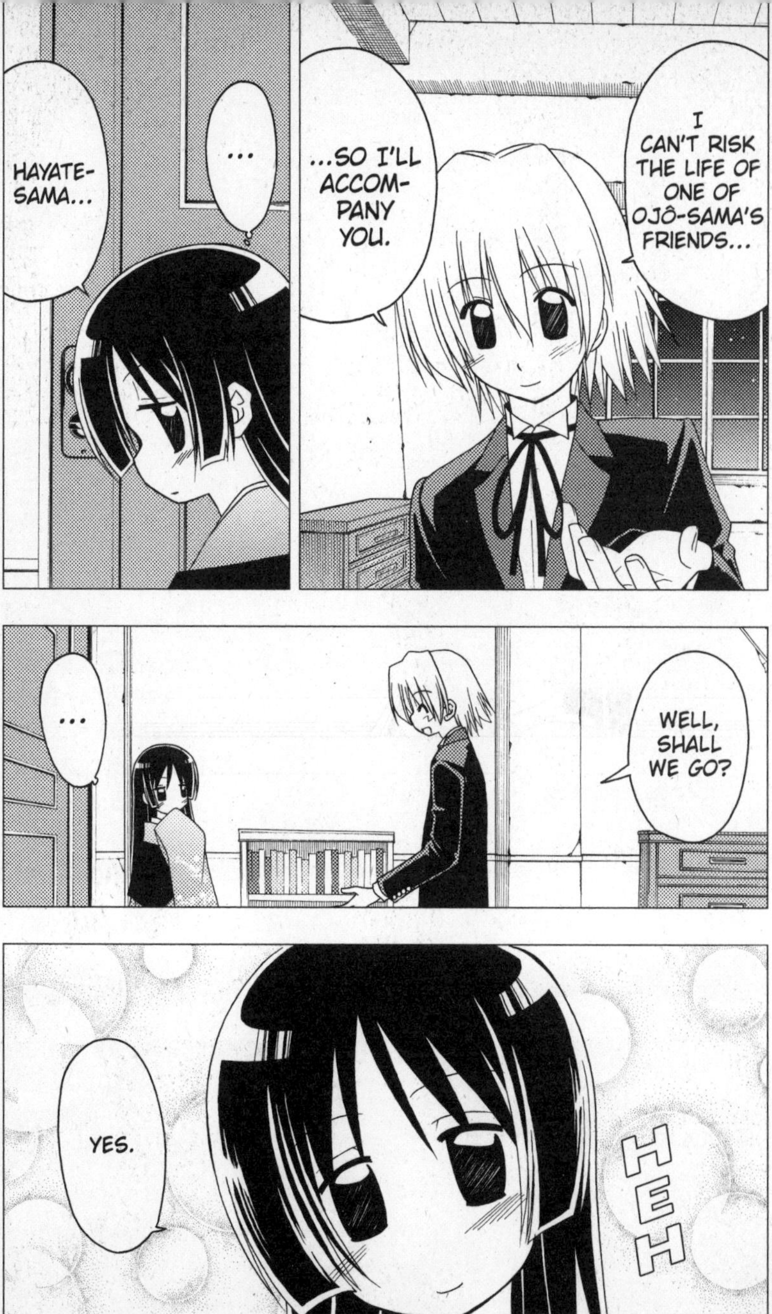
I CAN'T RISK THE LIFE OF ONE OF OJÔ-SAMA'S FRIENDS...
...SO I'LL ACCOMPANY YOU.
...
HAYATE-SAMA...
WELL, SHALL WE GO?
...
HEH
YES.

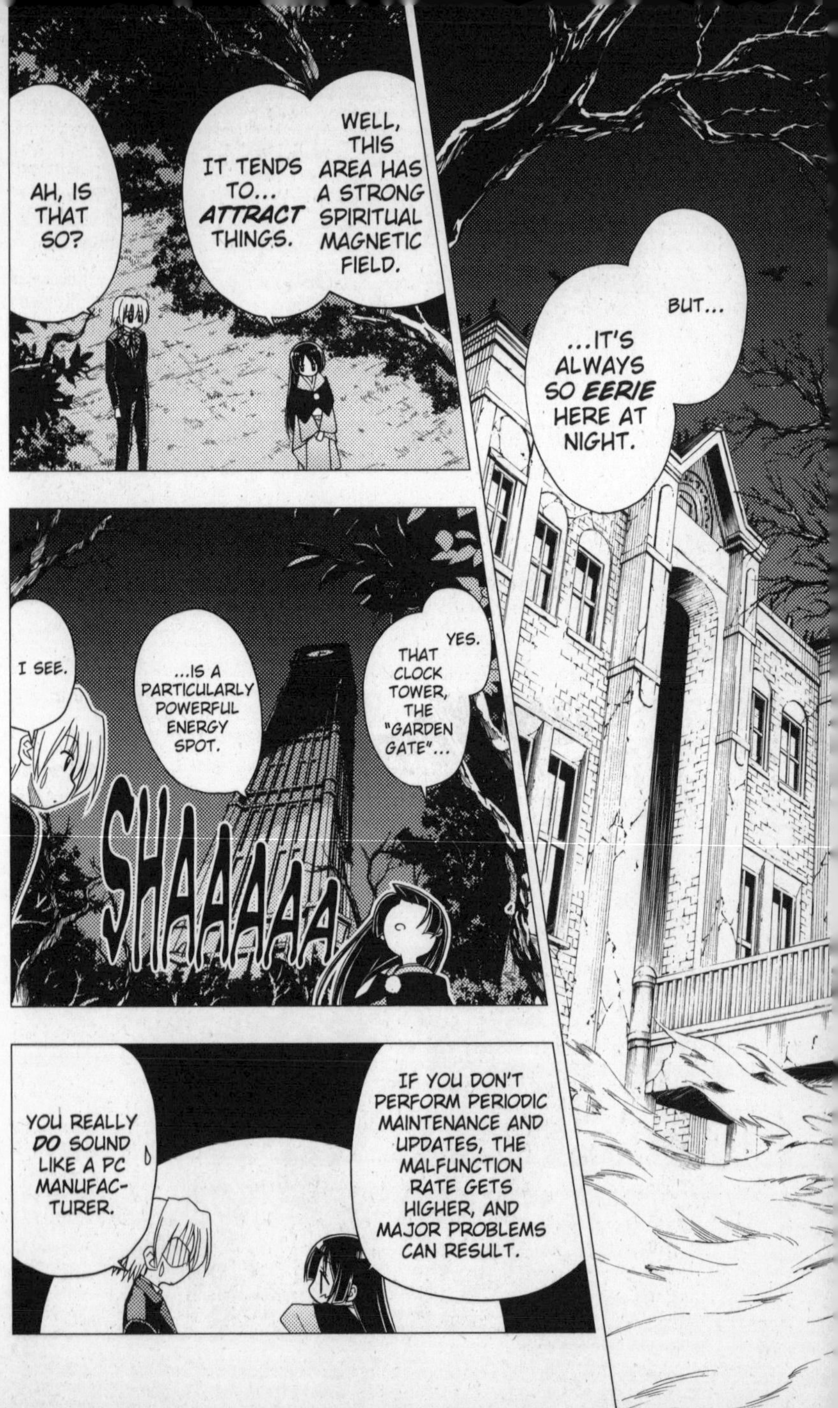
BUT... ...IT'S ALWAYS SO EERIE HERE AT NIGHT.
WELL, THIS AREA HAS A STRONG SPIRITUAL MAGNETIC FIELD.
IT TENDS TO... ATTRACT THINGS.
AH, IS THAT SO?
YES. THAT CLOCK TOWER, THE "GARDEN GATE"...
...IS A PARTICULARLY POWERFUL ENERGY SPOT.
I SEE.
SHAAAAAA
IF YOU DON'T PERFORM PERIODIC MAINTENANCE AND UPDATES, THE MALFUNCTION RATE GETS HIGHER, AND MAJOR PROBLEMS CAN RESULT.
YOU REALLY DO SOUND LIKE A PC MANUFAC-TURER.

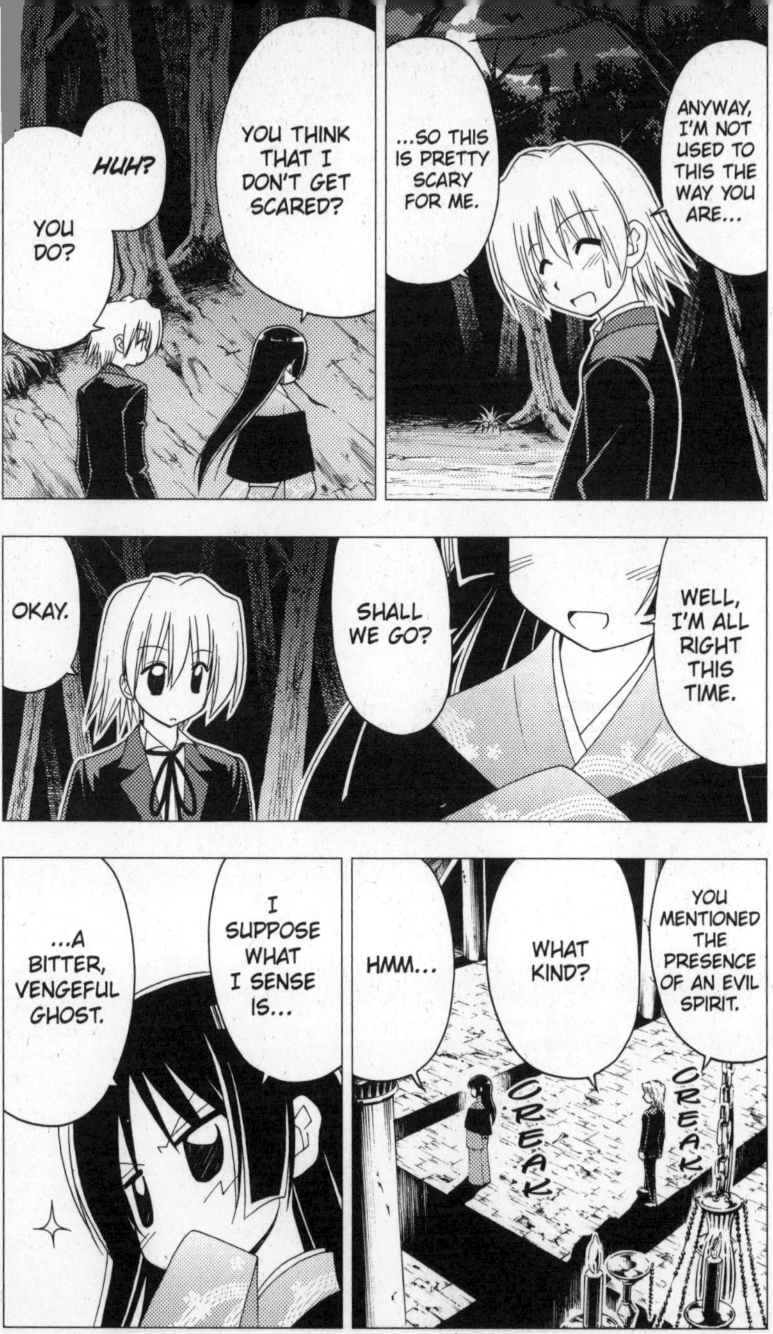
ANYWAY, I'M NOT USED TO THIS THE WAY YOU ARE...
...SO THIS IS PRETTY SCARY FOR ME.
YOU THINK THAT I DON'T GET SCARED?
HUH?
YOU DO?
WELL, I'M ALL RIGHT THIS TIME.
SHALL WE GO?
OKAY.
YOU MENTIONED THE PRESENCE OF AN EVIL SPIRIT.
WHAT KIND?
CREAK
CREAK
HMM...
I SUPPOSE WHAT I SENSE IS...
...A BITTER, VENGEFUL GHOST.

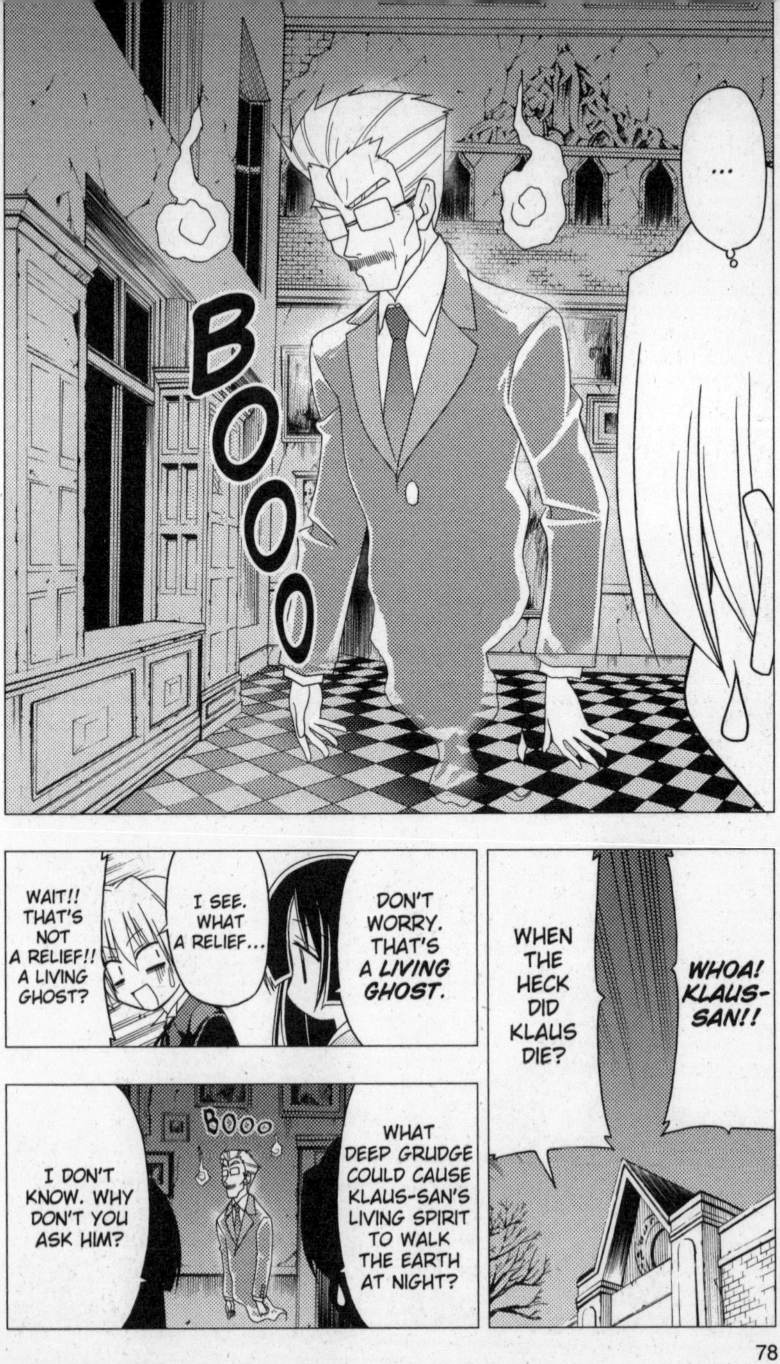
...
BOOOOO
WHOA! KLAUS-SAN!!
WHEN THE HECK DID KLAUS DIE?
DON'T WORRY. THAT'S A *LIVING GHOST*.
I SEE. WHAT A RELIEF...
WAIT!! THAT'S NOT A RELIEF!! A LIVING GHOST?
WHAT DEEP GRUDGE COULD CAUSE KLAUS-SAN'S LIVING SPIRIT TO WALK THE EARTH AT NIGHT?
BOOO
I DON'T KNOW. WHY DON'T YOU ASK HIM?

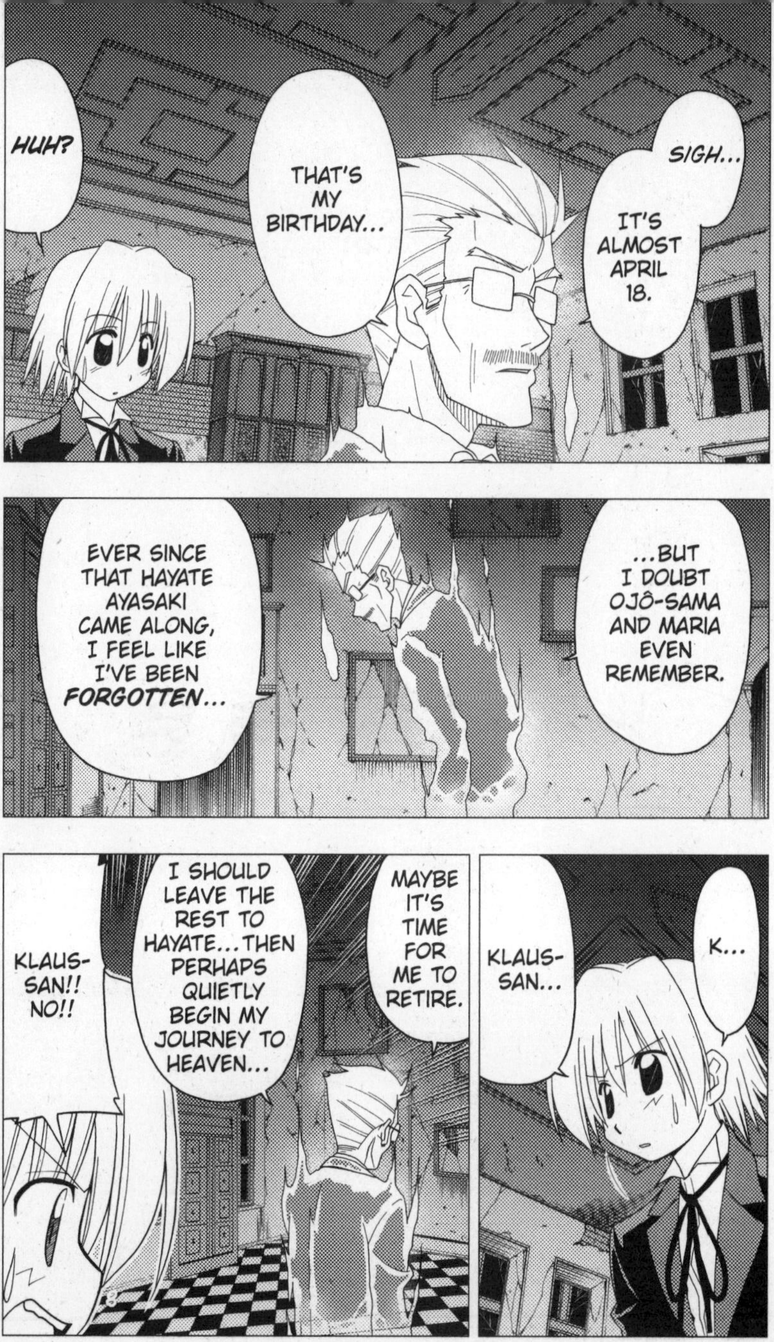
SIGH...
IT'S ALMOST APRIL 18.
THAT'S MY BIRTHDAY...
HUH?
...BUT I DOUBT OJÔ-SAMA AND MARIA EVEN REMEMBER.
EVER SINCE THAT HAYATE AYASAKI CAME ALONG, I FEEL LIKE I'VE BEEN FORGOTTEN...
K...
KLAUS-SAN...
MAYBE IT'S TIME FOR ME TO RETIRE.
I SHOULD LEAVE THE REST TO HAYATE... THEN PERHAPS QUIETLY BEGIN MY JOURNEY TO HEAVEN...
KLAUS-SAN!! NO!!

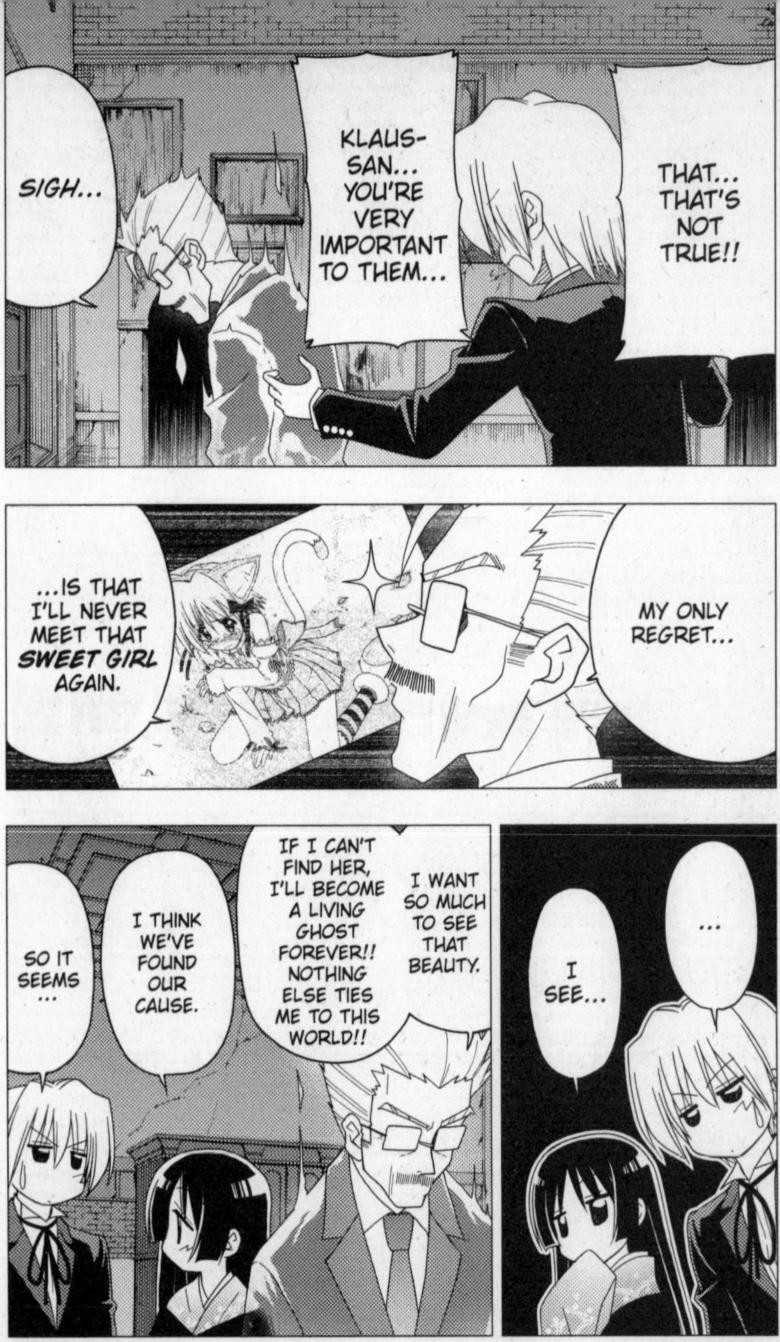
THAT... THAT'S NOT TRUE!!
KLAUS-SAN... YOU'RE VERY IMPORTANT TO THEM...
SIGH...
MY ONLY REGRET...
...IS THAT I'LL NEVER MEET THAT **SWEET GIRL** AGAIN.
...
I SEE...
I WANT SO MUCH TO SEE THAT BEAUTY.
IF I CAN'T FIND HER, I'LL BECOME A LIVING GHOST FOREVER!! NOTHING ELSE TIES ME TO THIS WORLD!!
I THINK WE'VE FOUND OUR CAUSE.
SO IT SEEMS...

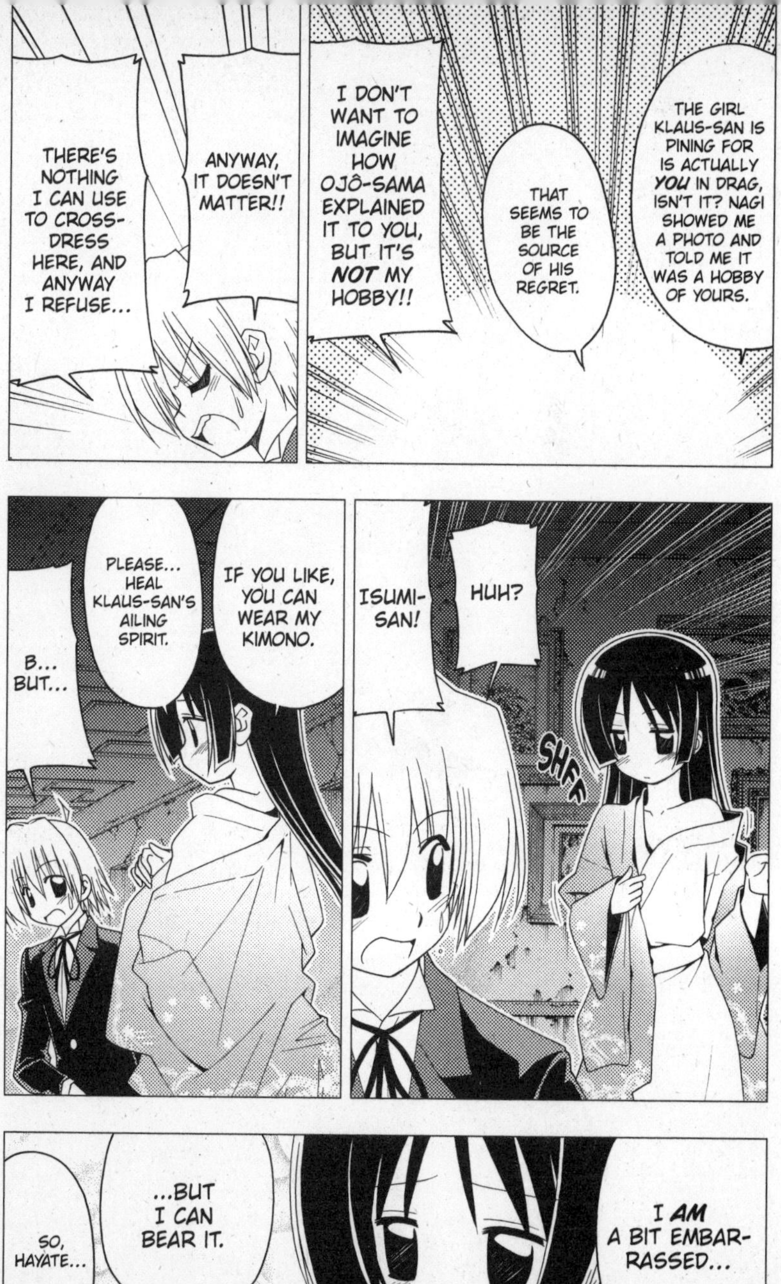
THE GIRL KLAUS-SAN IS PINING FOR IS ACTUALLY *YOU* IN DRAG, ISN'T IT? NAGI SHOWED ME A PHOTO AND TOLD ME IT WAS A HOBBY OF YOURS.
THAT SEEMS TO BE THE SOURCE OF HIS REGRET.
I DON'T WANT TO IMAGINE HOW OJÔ-SAMA EXPLAINED IT TO YOU, BUT IT'S *NOT* MY HOBBY!!
ANYWAY, IT DOESN'T MATTER!!
THERE'S NOTHING I CAN USE TO CROSS-DRESS HERE, AND ANYWAY I REFUSE...
HUH?
SHFF
ISUMI-SAN!
IF YOU LIKE, YOU CAN WEAR MY KIMONO.
PLEASE... HEAL KLAUS-SAN'S AILING SPIRIT.
B... BUT...
I *AM* A BIT EMBARRASSED...
...BUT I CAN BEAR IT.
SO, HAYATE...

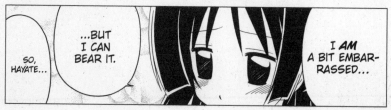

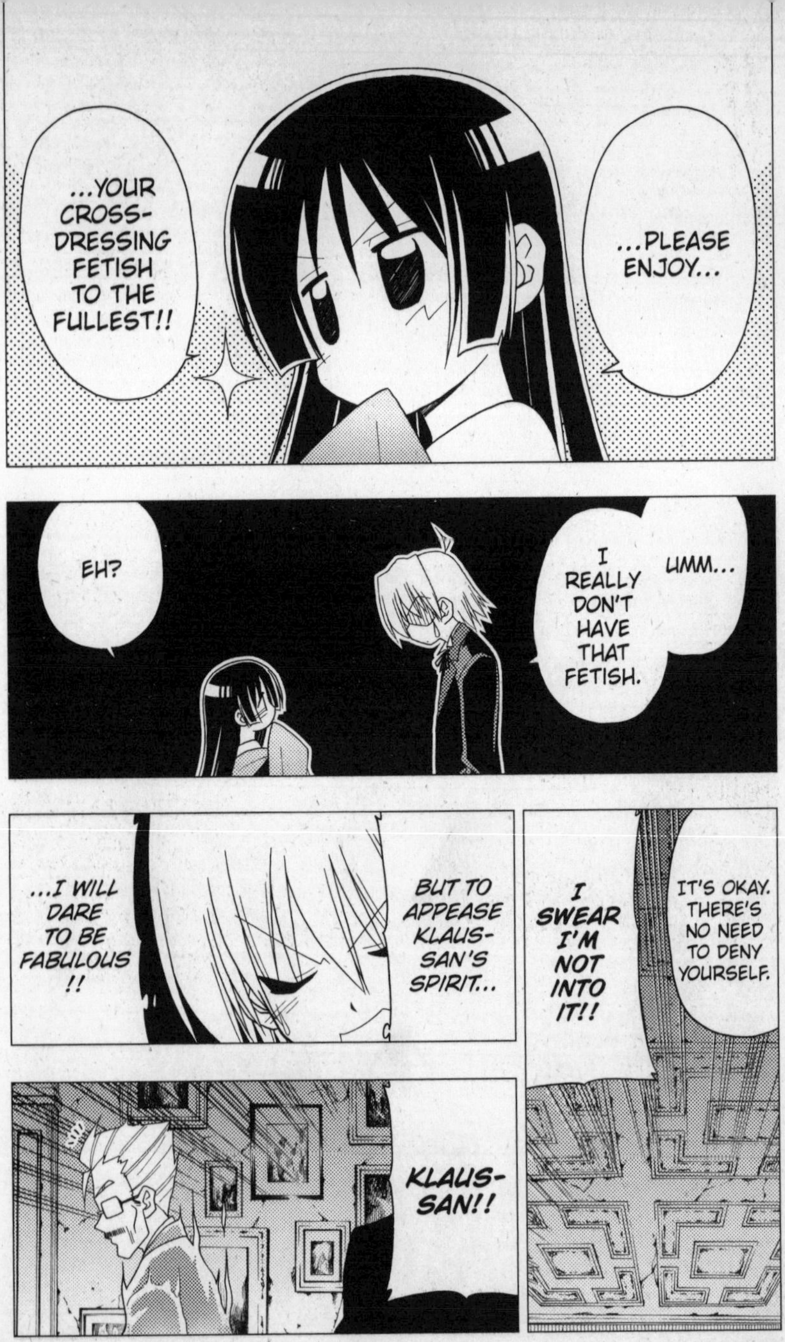
...PLEASE ENJOY...
...YOUR CROSS-DRESSING FETISH TO THE FULLEST!!
UMM...
I REALLY DON'T HAVE THAT FETISH.
EH?
IT'S OKAY. THERE'S NO NEED TO DENY YOURSELF.
I SWEAR I'M NOT INTO IT!!
BUT TO APPEASE KLAUS-SAN'S SPIRIT...
...I WILL DARE TO BE FABULOUS!!
KLAUS-SAN!!

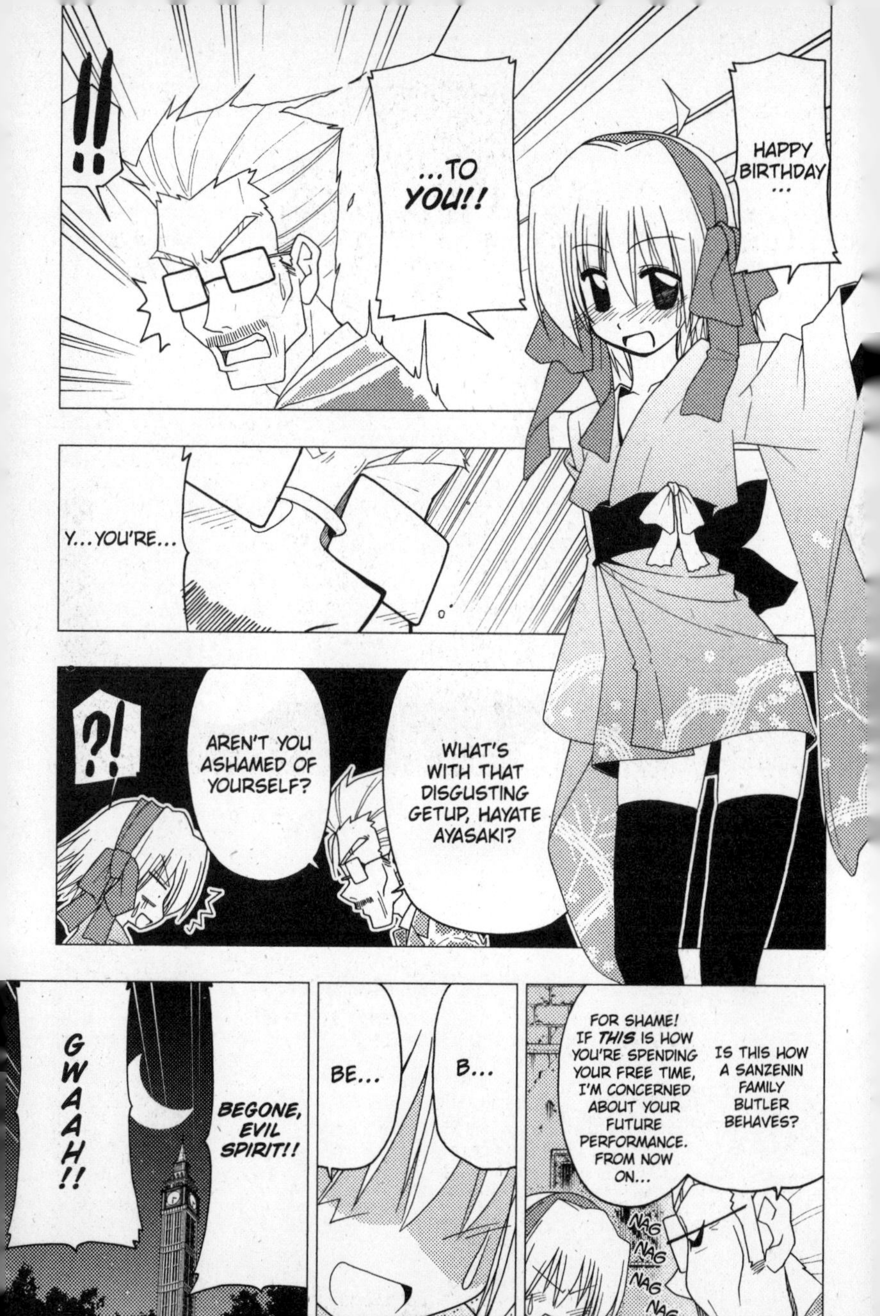
HAPPY BIRTHDAY...
...TO *YOU!!*
!!
Y...YOU'RE...
WHAT'S WITH THAT DISGUSTING GETUP, HAYATE AYASAKI?
AREN'T YOU ASHAMED OF YOURSELF?
?!
IS THIS HOW A SANZENIN FAMILY BUTLER BEHAVES?
FOR SHAME! IF *THIS* IS HOW YOU'RE SPENDING YOUR FREE TIME, I'M CONCERNED ABOUT YOUR FUTURE PERFORMANCE. FROM NOW ON...
NAG NAG NAG NAG
B...
BE...
BEGONE, EVIL SPIRIT!!
GWAAAH!!

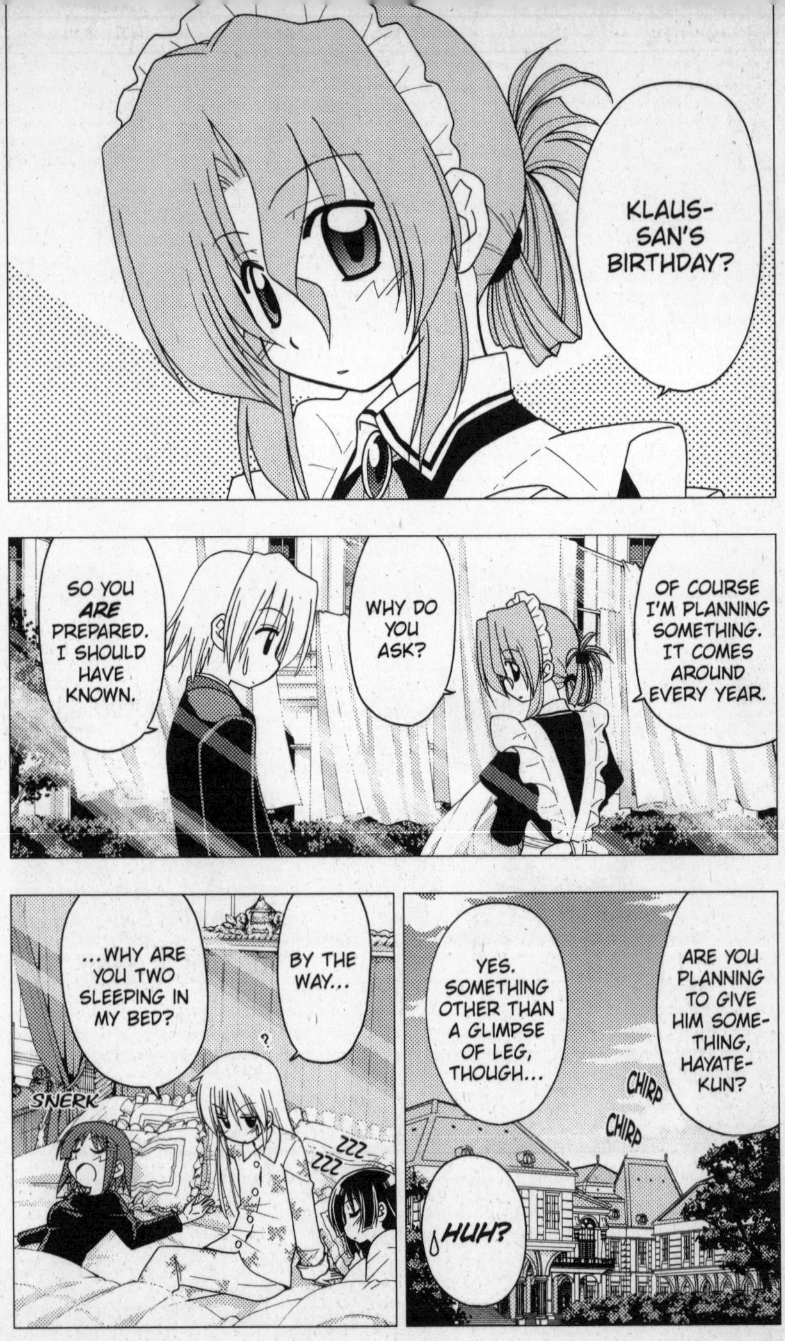
KLAUS-SAN'S BIRTHDAY?
OF COURSE I'M PLANNING SOMETHING. IT COMES AROUND EVERY YEAR.
WHY DO YOU ASK?
SO YOU *ARE* PREPARED. I SHOULD HAVE KNOWN.
ARE YOU PLANNING TO GIVE HIM SOMETHING, HAYATE-KUN?
CHIRP
CHIRP
YES. SOMETHING OTHER THAN A GLIMPSE OF LEG, THOUGH...
HUH?
BY THE WAY...
...WHY ARE YOU TWO SLEEPING IN MY BED?
?
SNERK
ZZZ
ZZZ

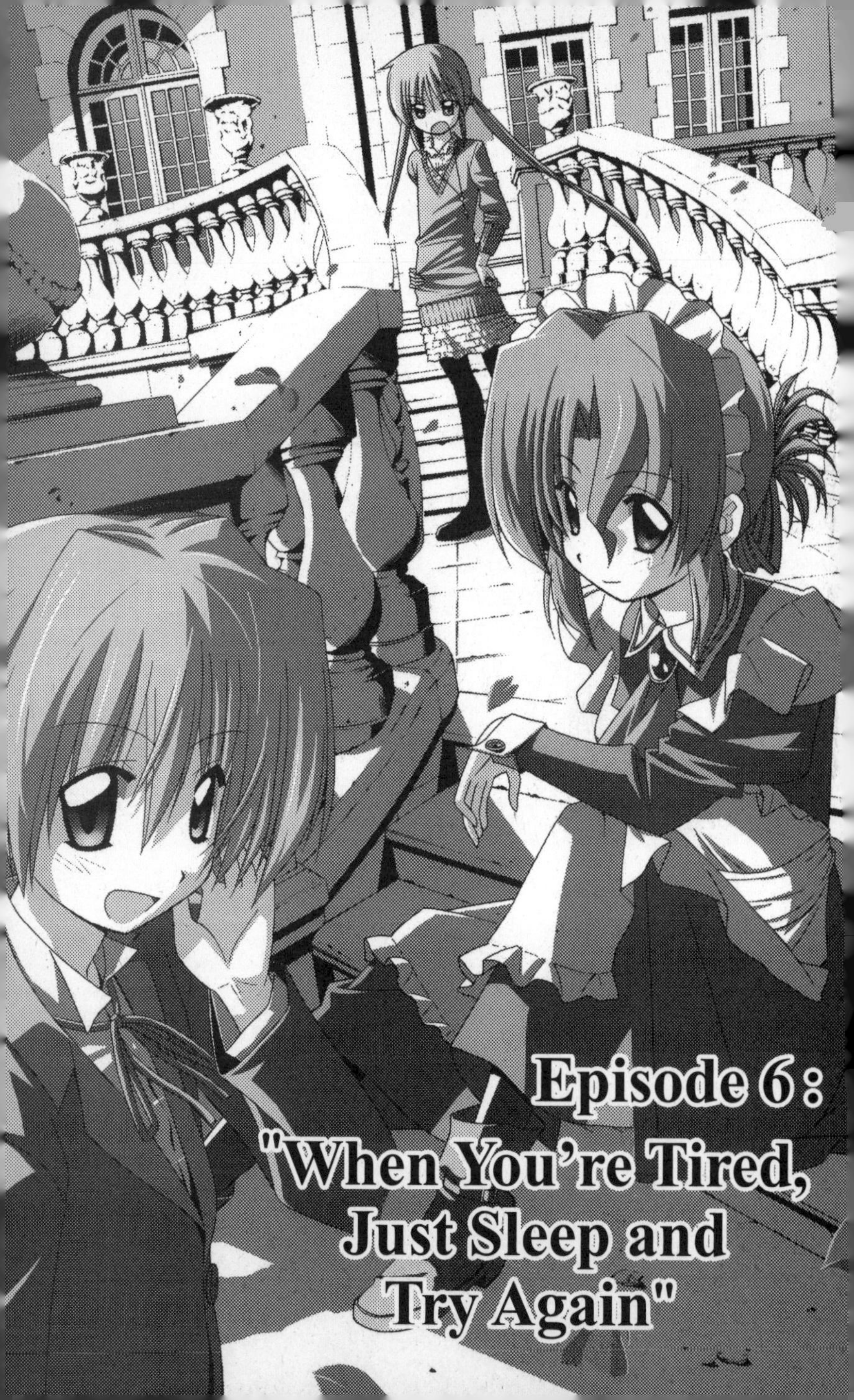
Episode 6 :
"When You're Tired, Just Sleep and Try Again"

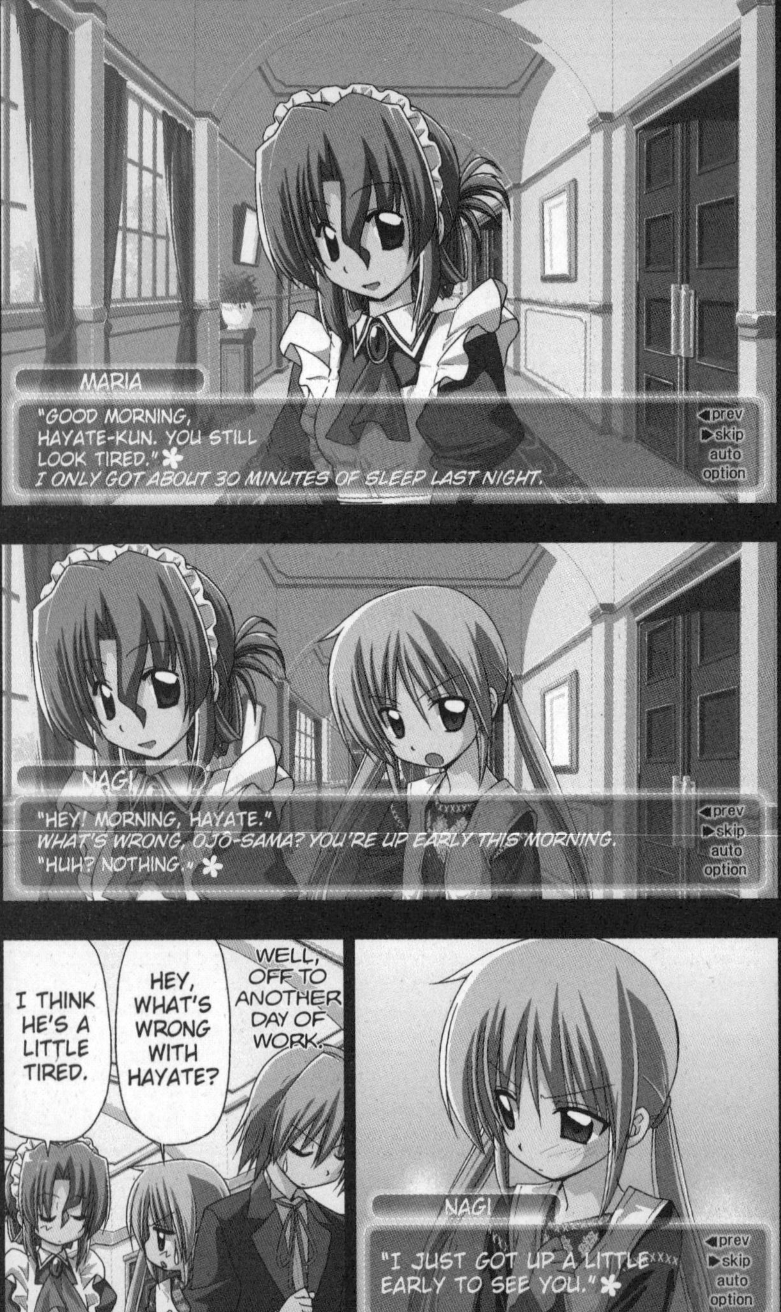
MARIA
"GOOD MORNING, HAYATE-KUN. YOU STILL LOOK TIRED."
I ONLY GOT ABOUT 30 MINUTES OF SLEEP LAST NIGHT.
prev
skip
auto
option
NAGI
"HEY! MORNING, HAYATE."
WHAT'S WRONG, OJŌ-SAMA? YOU'RE UP EARLY THIS MORNING.
"HUH? NOTHING."
prev
skip
auto
option
NAGI
"I JUST GOT UP A LITTLE EARLY TO SEE YOU."
prev
skip
auto
option
WELL, OFF TO ANOTHER DAY OF WORK.
HEY, WHAT'S WRONG WITH HAYATE?
I THINK HE'S A LITTLE TIRED.

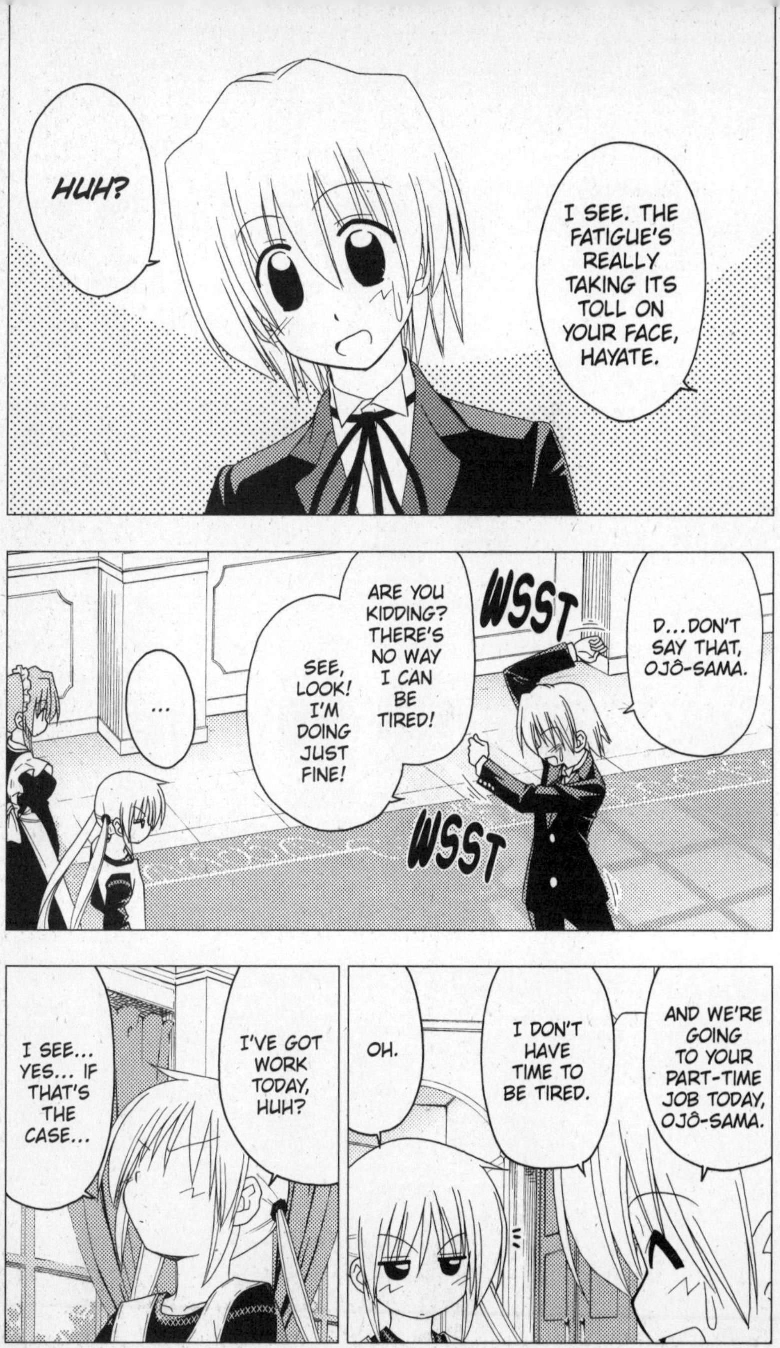
I SEE. THE FATIGUE'S REALLY TAKING ITS TOLL ON YOUR FACE, HAYATE.
HUH?
D...DON'T SAY THAT, OJÔ-SAMA.
WSST
ARE YOU KIDDING? THERE'S NO WAY I CAN BE TIRED!
SEE, LOOK! I'M DOING JUST FINE!
WSST
...
AND WE'RE GOING TO YOUR PART-TIME JOB TODAY, OJÔ-SAMA.
I DON'T HAVE TIME TO BE TIRED.
OH.
I'VE GOT WORK TODAY, HUH?
I SEE... YES... IF THAT'S THE CASE...

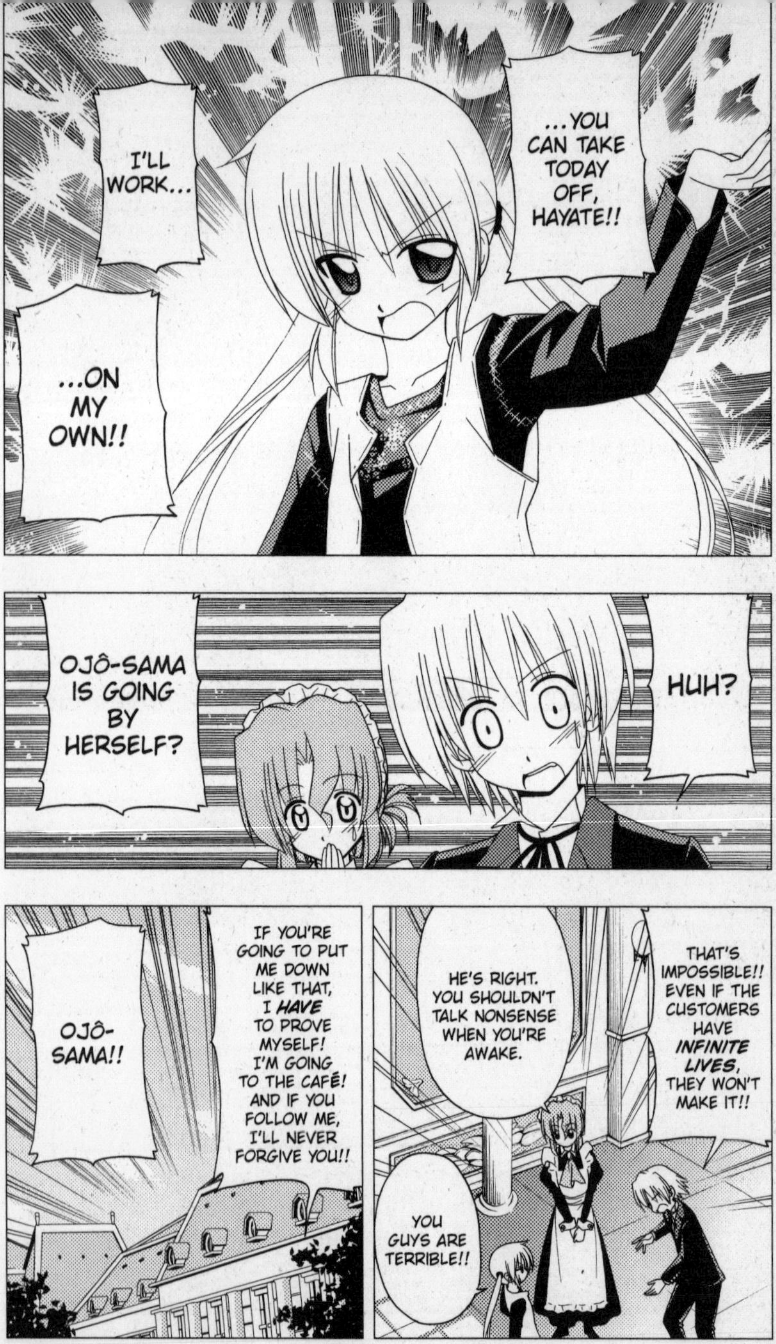
...YOU CAN TAKE TODAY OFF, HAYATE!!
I'LL WORK...
...ON MY OWN!!
HUH?
OJÔ-SAMA IS GOING BY HERSELF?
THAT'S IMPOSSIBLE!! EVEN IF THE CUSTOMERS HAVE *INFINITE LIVES*, THEY WON'T MAKE IT!!
HE'S RIGHT. YOU SHOULDN'T TALK NONSENSE WHEN YOU'RE AWAKE.
YOU GUYS ARE TERRIBLE!!
IF YOU'RE GOING TO PUT ME DOWN LIKE THAT, I *HAVE* TO PROVE MYSELF! I'M GOING TO THE CAFÉ! AND IF YOU FOLLOW ME, I'LL NEVER FORGIVE YOU!!
OJÔ-SAMA!!

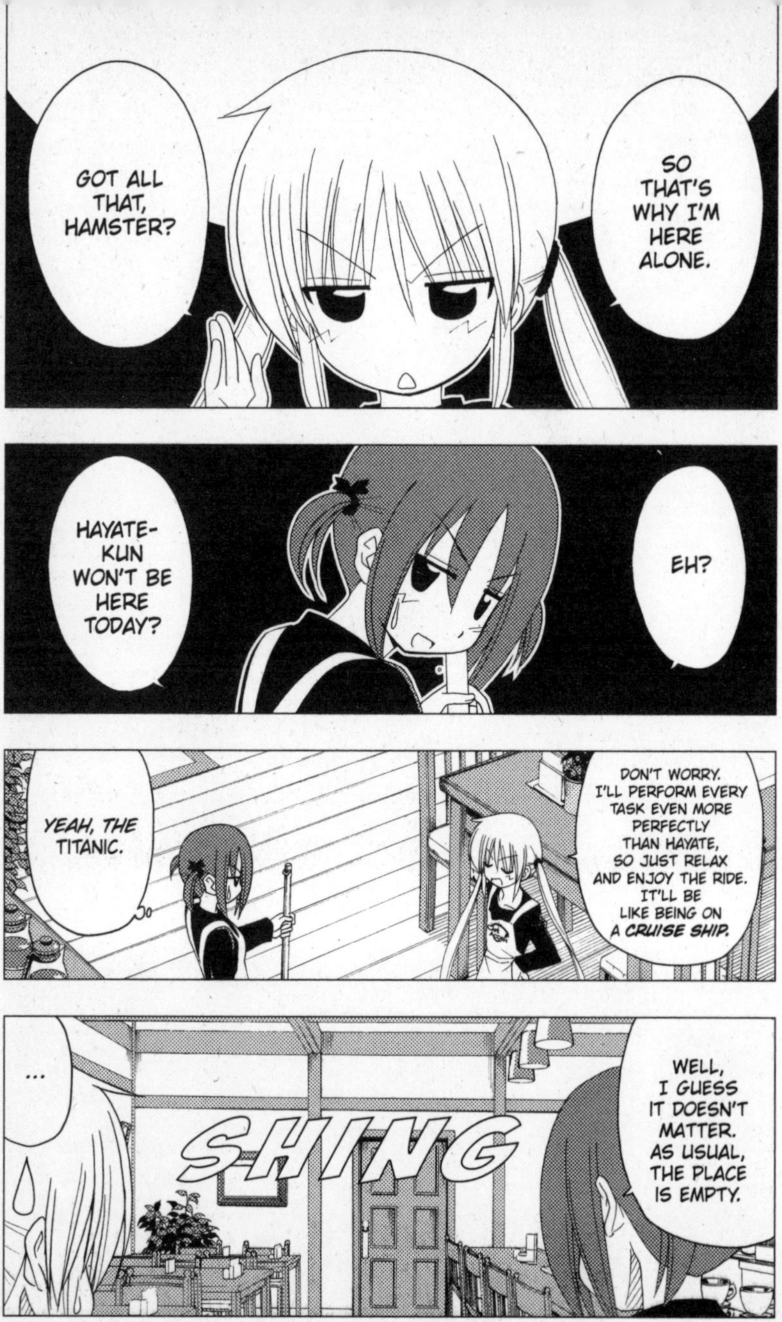
SO THAT'S WHY I'M HERE ALONE.
GOT ALL THAT, HAMSTER?
EH?
HAYATE-KUN WON'T BE HERE TODAY?
DON'T WORRY. I'LL PERFORM EVERY TASK EVEN MORE PERFECTLY THAN HAYATE, SO JUST RELAX AND ENJOY THE RIDE. IT'LL BE LIKE BEING ON A *CRUISE SHIP.*
YEAH, THE TITANIC.
WELL, I GUESS IT DOESN'T MATTER. AS USUAL, THE PLACE IS EMPTY.
SHING
...

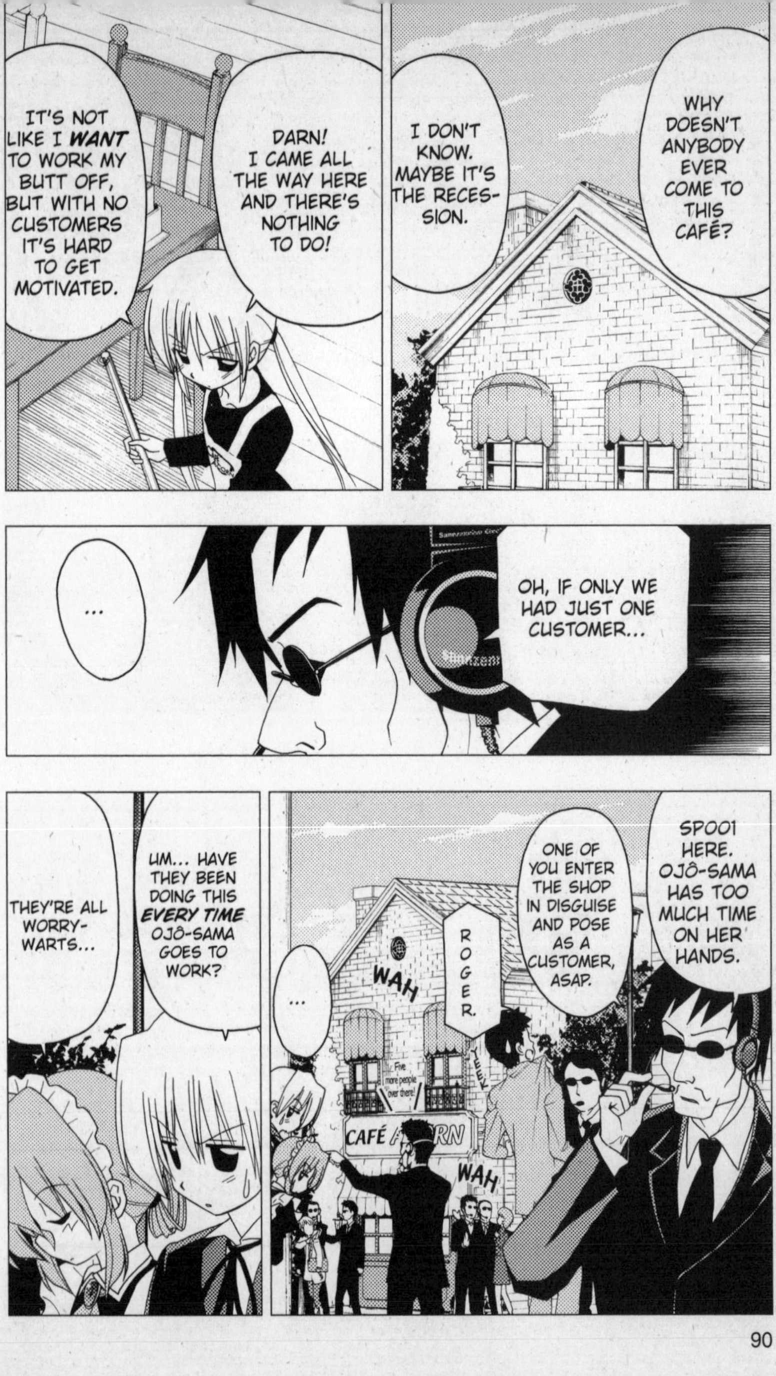
WHY DOESN'T ANYBODY EVER COME TO THIS CAFÉ?
I DON'T KNOW. MAYBE IT'S THE RECES-SION.
DARN! I CAME ALL THE WAY HERE AND THERE'S NOTHING TO DO!
IT'S NOT LIKE I ***WANT*** TO WORK MY BUTT OFF, BUT WITH NO CUSTOMERS IT'S HARD TO GET MOTIVATED.
OH, IF ONLY WE HAD JUST ONE CUSTOMER...
...
SP001 HERE. OJÔ-SAMA HAS TOO MUCH TIME ON HER HANDS.
ONE OF YOU ENTER THE SHOP IN DISGUISE AND POSE AS A CUSTOMER, ASAP.
ROGER.
...
WAH
Five more people over there!
CAFÉ
WAH
UM... HAVE THEY BEEN DOING THIS ***EVERY TIME*** OJÔ-SAMA GOES TO WORK?
THEY'RE ALL WORRY-WARTS...

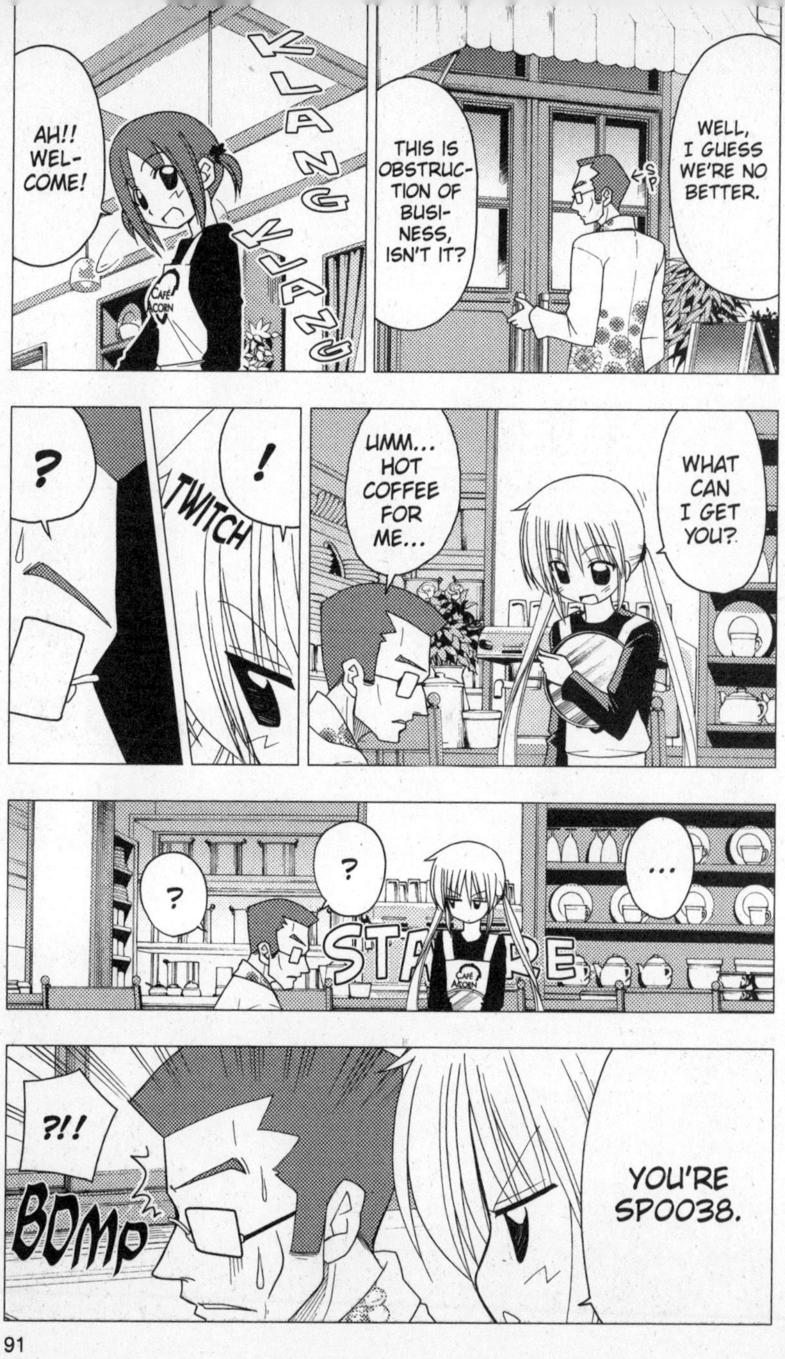

WELL, I GUESS WE'RE NO BETTER.
SP
THIS IS OBSTRUCTION OF BUSINESS, ISN'T IT?
KLANG KLANG
AH!! WELCOME!
CAFÉ ACORN
WHAT CAN I GET YOU?
UMM... HOT COFFEE FOR ME...
!
TWITCH
?
...
?
?
STARE
CAFÉ ACORN
YOU'RE SP0038.
?!!
BOMP

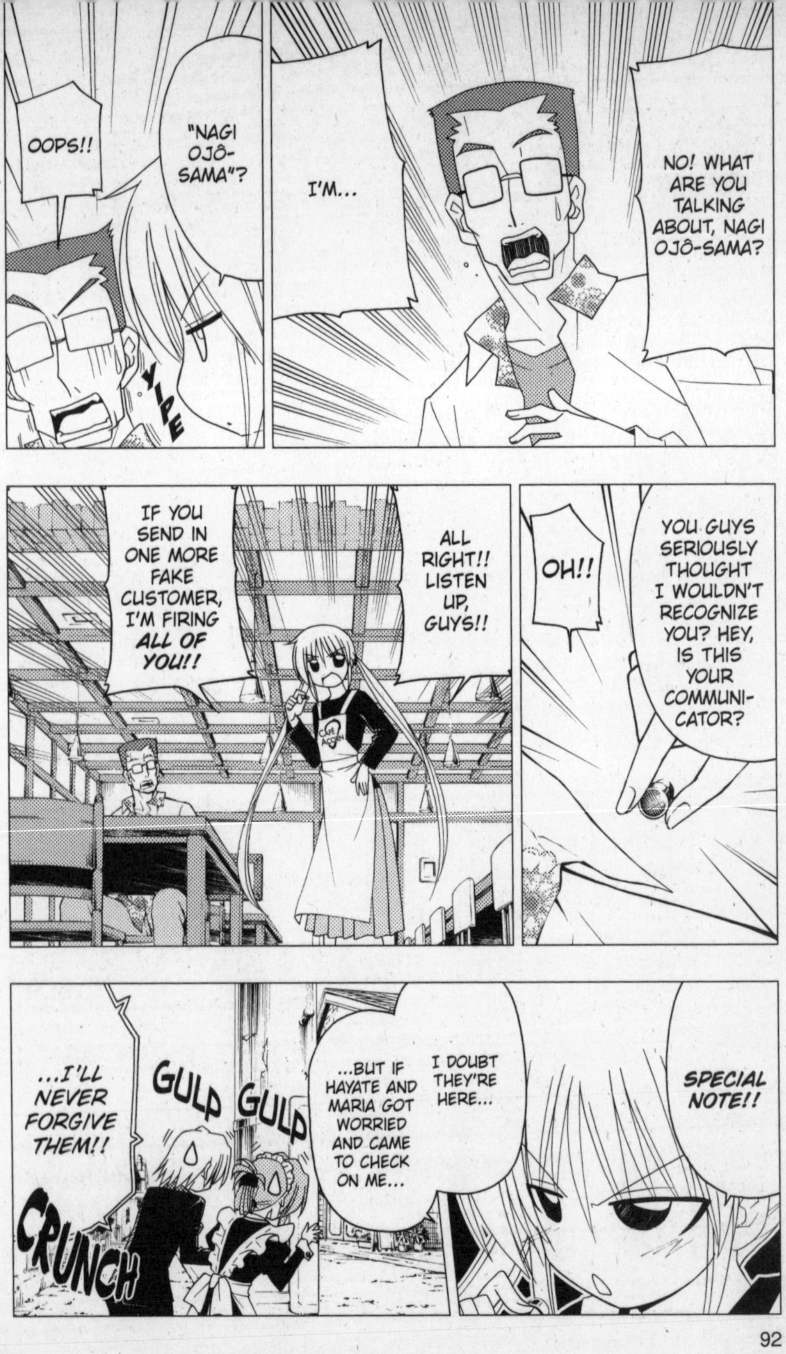
NO! WHAT ARE YOU TALKING ABOUT, NAGI OJÔ-SAMA?
I'M...
"NAGI OJÔ-SAMA"?
OOPS!!
YIPE
YOU GUYS SERIOUSLY THOUGHT I WOULDN'T RECOGNIZE YOU? HEY, IS THIS YOUR COMMUNI-CATOR?
OH!!
ALL RIGHT!! LISTEN UP, GUYS!!
IF YOU SEND IN ONE MORE FAKE CUSTOMER, I'M FIRING ALL OF YOU!!
CAFÉ ACORN
SPECIAL NOTE!!
I DOUBT THEY'RE HERE...
...BUT IF HAYATE AND MARIA GOT WORRIED AND CAME TO CHECK ON ME...
GULP GULP
...I'LL NEVER FORGIVE THEM!!
CRUNCH

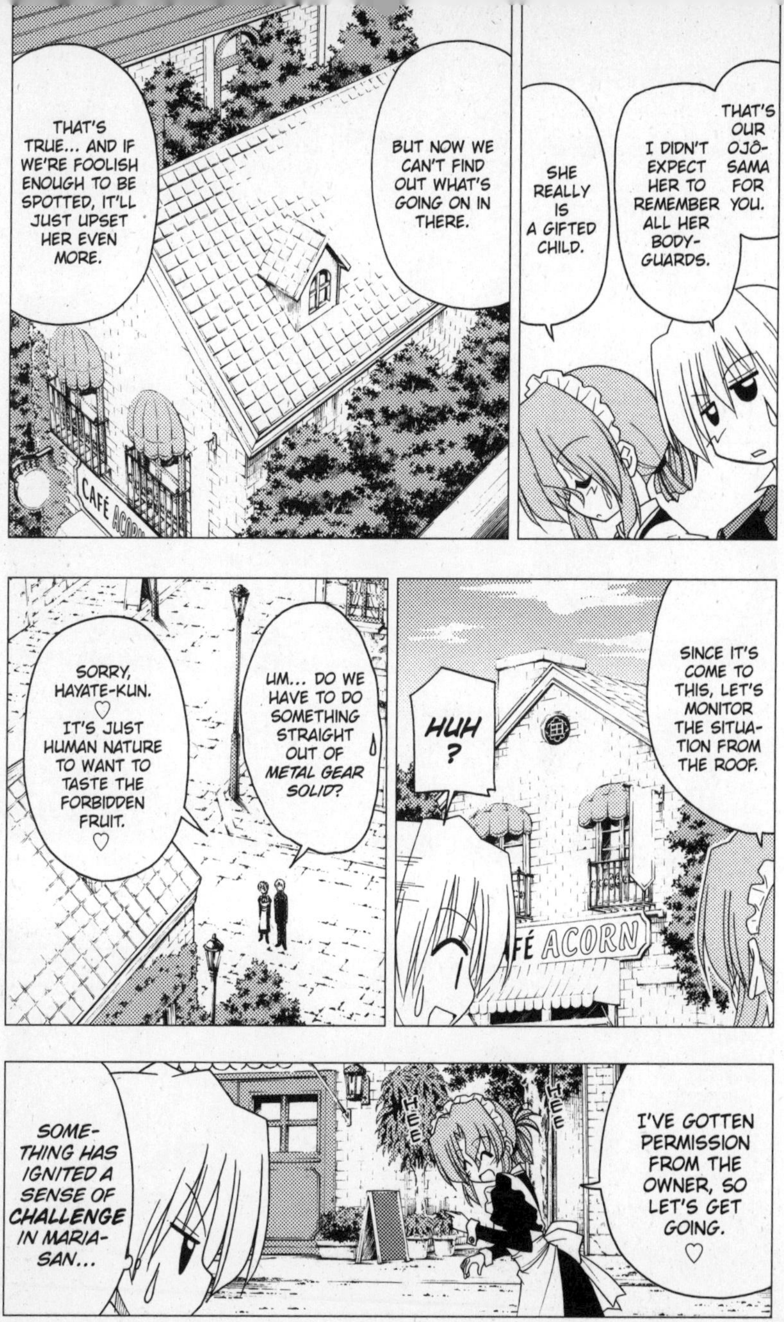
THAT'S OUR OJÔ-SAMA FOR YOU.
I DIDN'T EXPECT HER TO REMEMBER ALL HER BODY-GUARDS.
SHE REALLY IS A GIFTED CHILD.
BUT NOW WE CAN'T FIND OUT WHAT'S GOING ON IN THERE.
THAT'S TRUE... AND IF WE'RE FOOLISH ENOUGH TO BE SPOTTED, IT'LL JUST UPSET HER EVEN MORE.
CAFÉ ACORN
SINCE IT'S COME TO THIS, LET'S MONITOR THE SITUATION FROM THE ROOF.
HUH?
FÉ ACORN
UM... DO WE HAVE TO DO SOMETHING STRAIGHT OUT OF *METAL GEAR SOLID*?
SORRY, HAYATE-KUN. ♡ IT'S JUST HUMAN NATURE TO WANT TO TASTE THE FORBIDDEN FRUIT. ♡
I'VE GOTTEN PERMISSION FROM THE OWNER, SO LET'S GET GOING. ♡
HEE
HEE
SOME-THING HAS IGNITED A SENSE OF **CHALLENGE** IN MARIA-SAN...

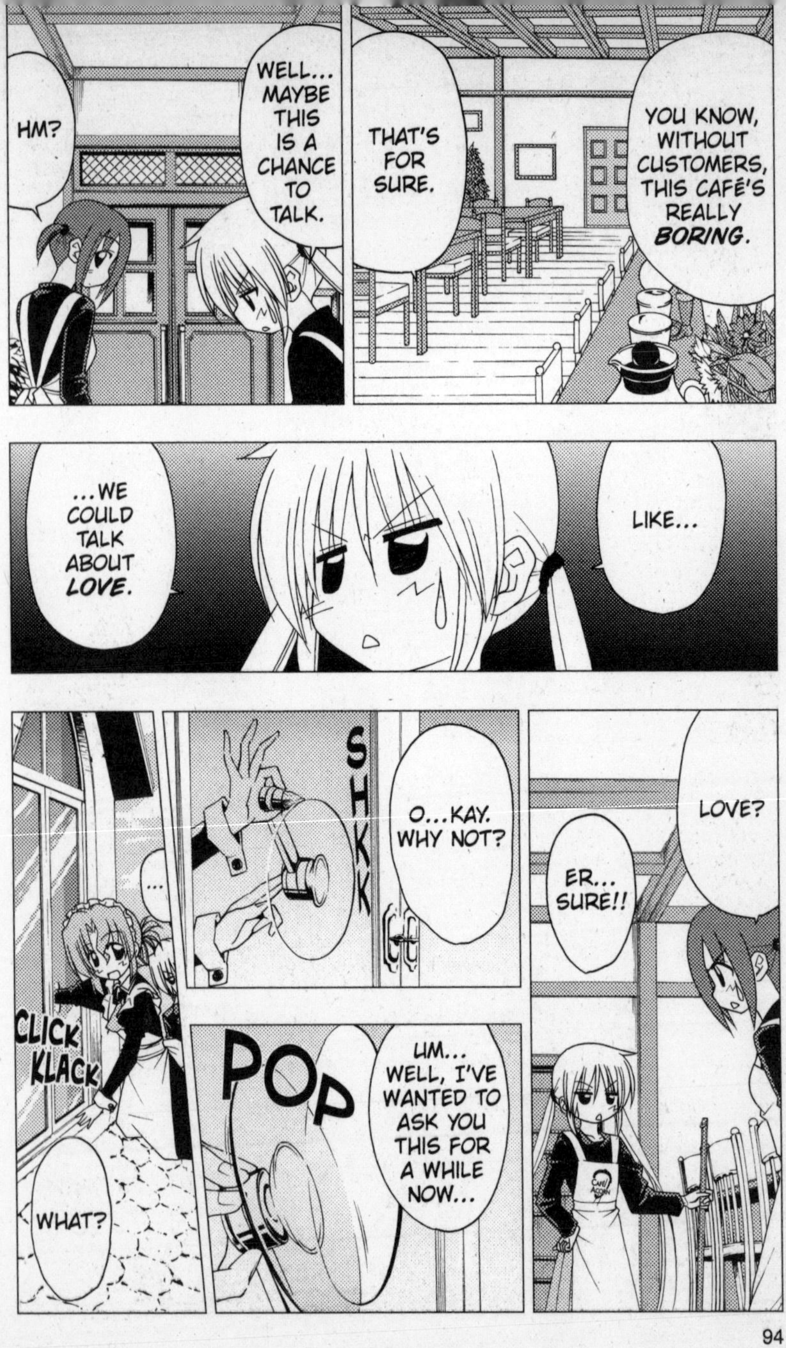
YOU KNOW, WITHOUT CUSTOMERS, THIS CAFÉ'S REALLY BORING.
THAT'S FOR SURE.
WELL... MAYBE THIS IS A CHANCE TO TALK.
HM?
LIKE...
...WE COULD TALK ABOUT LOVE.
LOVE?
ER... SURE!!
SHKK
O...KAY. WHY NOT?
POP
UM... WELL, I'VE WANTED TO ASK YOU THIS FOR A WHILE NOW...
...
CLICK KLACK
WHAT?

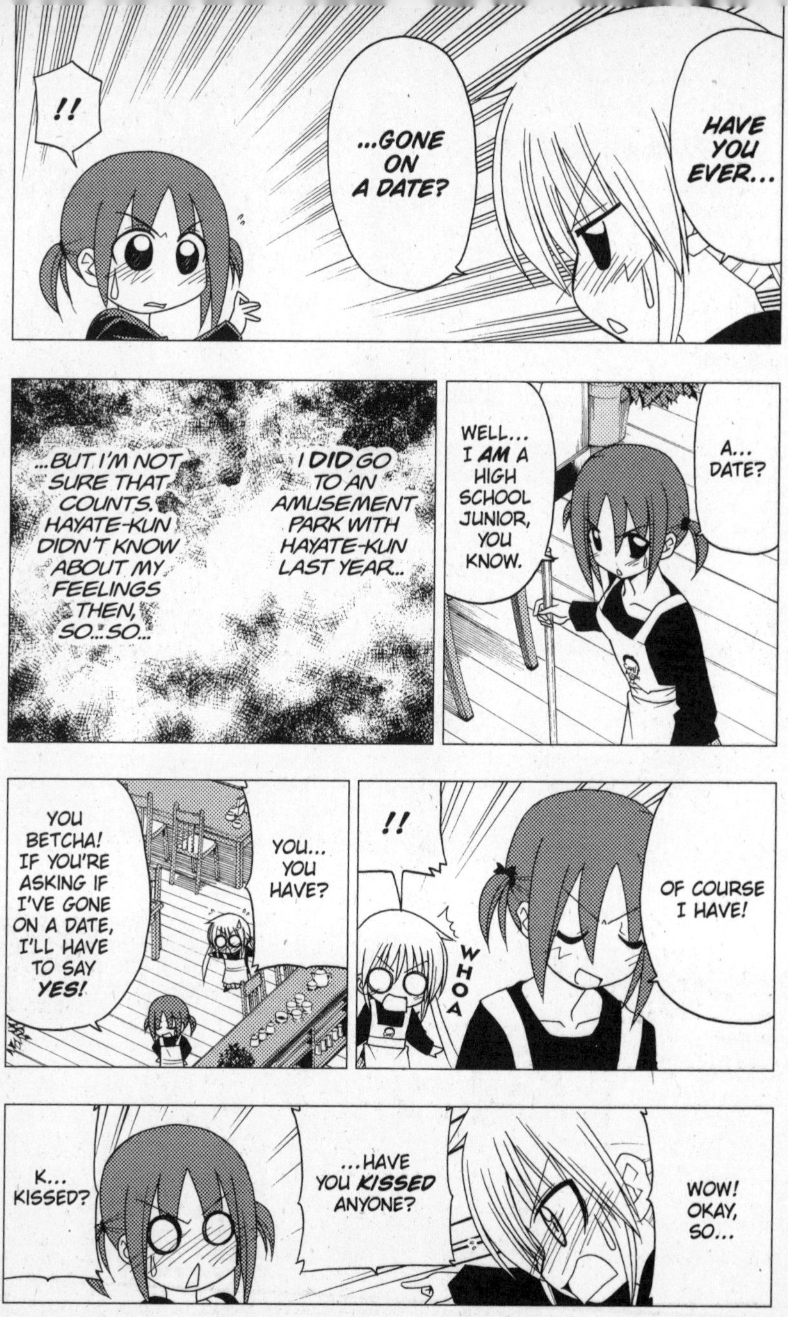
HAVE YOU EVER...
...GONE ON A DATE?
!!
A... DATE?
WELL... I AM A HIGH SCHOOL JUNIOR, YOU KNOW.
I DID GO TO AN AMUSEMENT PARK WITH HAYATE-KUN LAST YEAR...
...BUT I'M NOT SURE THAT COUNTS. HAYATE-KUN DIDN'T KNOW ABOUT MY FEELINGS THEN, SO...SO...
OF COURSE I HAVE!
!!
WHOA
YOU... YOU HAVE?
YOU BETCHA! IF YOU'RE ASKING IF I'VE GONE ON A DATE, I'LL HAVE TO SAY YES!
WOW! OKAY, SO...
...HAVE YOU KISSED ANYONE?
K... KISSED?

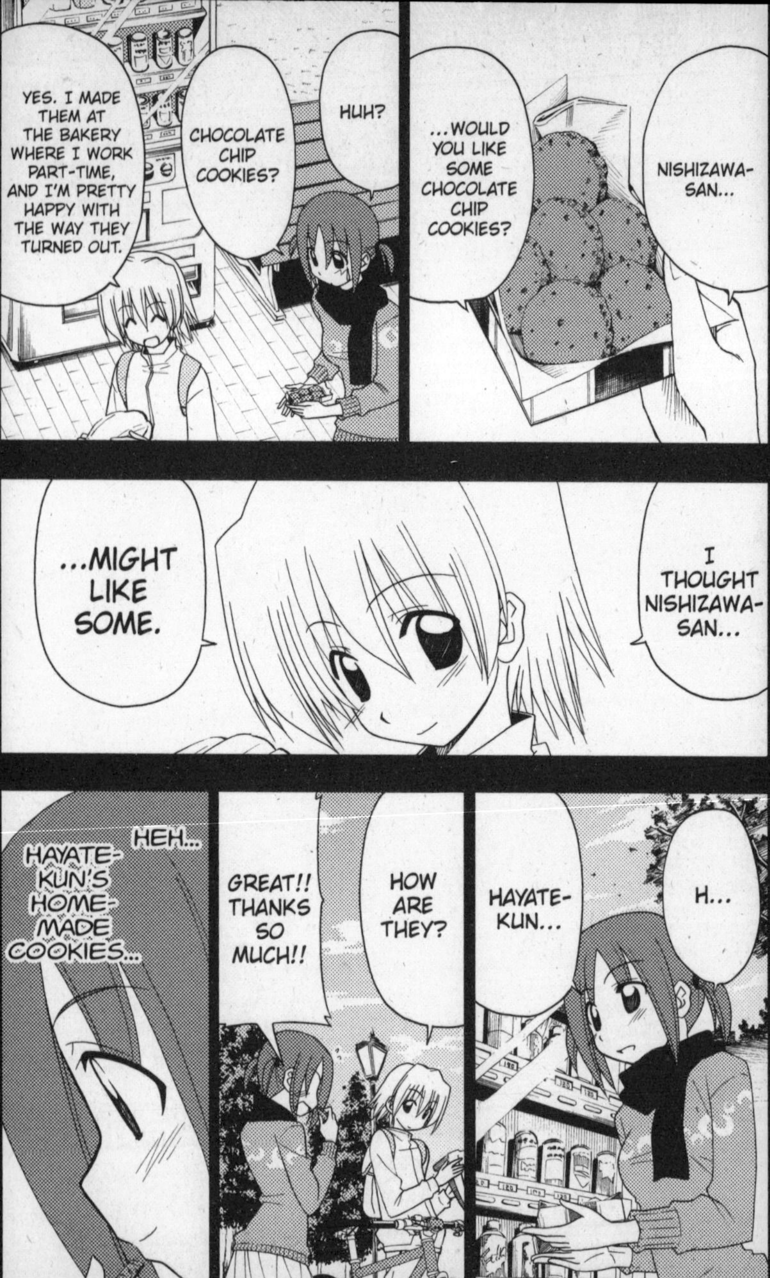
NISHIZAWA-SAN...
...WOULD YOU LIKE SOME CHOCOLATE CHIP COOKIES?
HUH?
CHOCOLATE CHIP COOKIES?
YES. I MADE THEM AT THE BAKERY WHERE I WORK PART-TIME, AND I'M PRETTY HAPPY WITH THE WAY THEY TURNED OUT.
I THOUGHT NISHIZAWA-SAN...
...MIGHT LIKE SOME.
H...
HAYATE-KUN...
HOW ARE THEY?
GREAT!! THANKS SO MUCH!!
HEH... HAYATE-KUN'S HOME-MADE COOKIES...

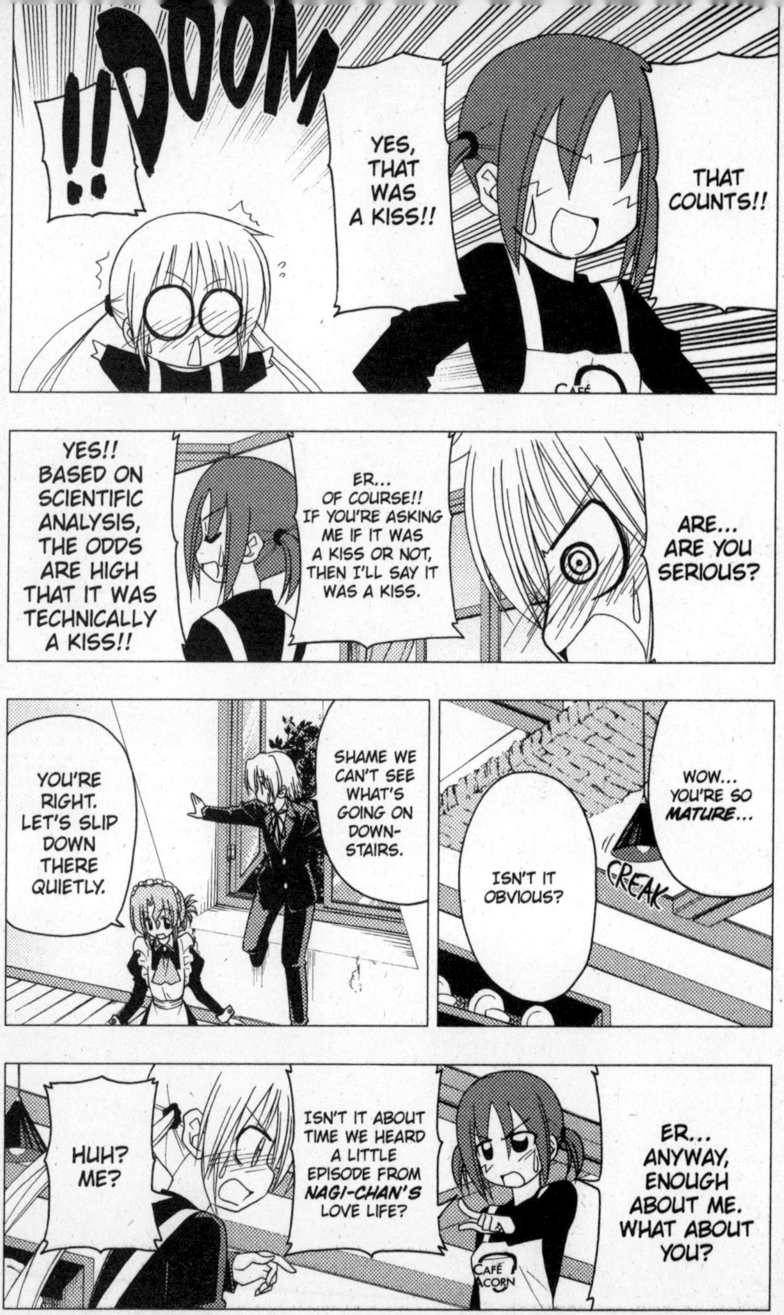
THAT COUNTS!!
YES, THAT WAS A KISS!!
DOOM
!!
CAFÉ
ARE... ARE YOU SERIOUS?
ER... OF COURSE!! IF YOU'RE ASKING ME IF IT WAS A KISS OR NOT, THEN I'LL SAY IT WAS A KISS.
YES!! BASED ON SCIENTIFIC ANALYSIS, THE ODDS ARE HIGH THAT IT WAS TECHNICALLY A KISS!!
WOW... YOU'RE SO MATURE...
CREAK
ISN'T IT OBVIOUS?
SHAME WE CAN'T SEE WHAT'S GOING ON DOWN-STAIRS.
YOU'RE RIGHT. LET'S SLIP DOWN THERE QUIETLY.
ER... ANYWAY, ENOUGH ABOUT ME. WHAT ABOUT YOU?
CAFÉ ACORN
ISN'T IT ABOUT TIME WE HEARD A LITTLE EPISODE FROM NAGI-CHAN'S LOVE LIFE?
HUH? ME?

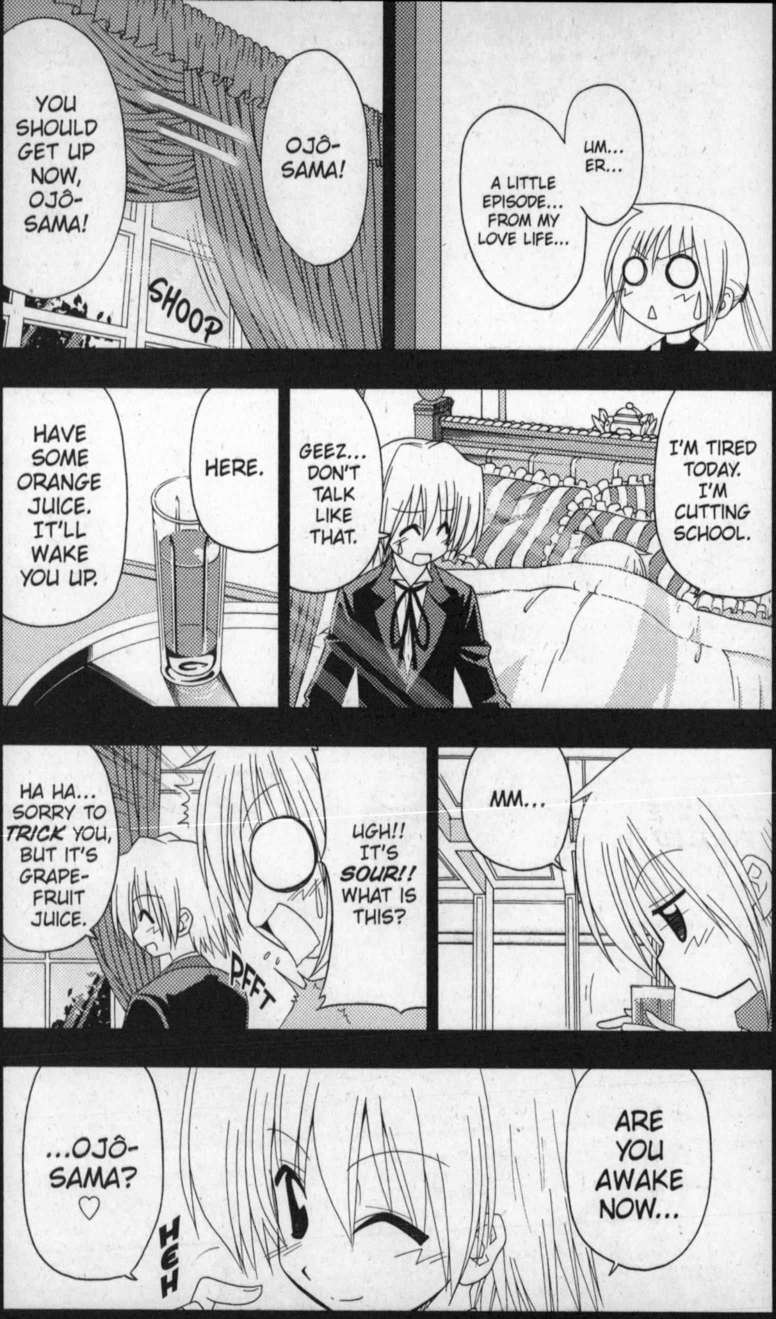
UM... ER... A LITTLE EPISODE... FROM MY LOVE LIFE...
OJÔ-SAMA!
YOU SHOULD GET UP NOW, OJÔ-SAMA!
SHOOP
I'M TIRED TODAY. I'M CUTTING SCHOOL.
GEEZ... DON'T TALK LIKE THAT.
HERE.
HAVE SOME ORANGE JUICE. IT'LL WAKE YOU UP.
MM...
UGH!! IT'S SOUR!! WHAT IS THIS?
PFFT
HA HA... SORRY TO TRICK YOU, BUT IT'S GRAPE-FRUIT JUICE.
ARE YOU AWAKE NOW...
HEH
...OJÔ-SAMA? ♡

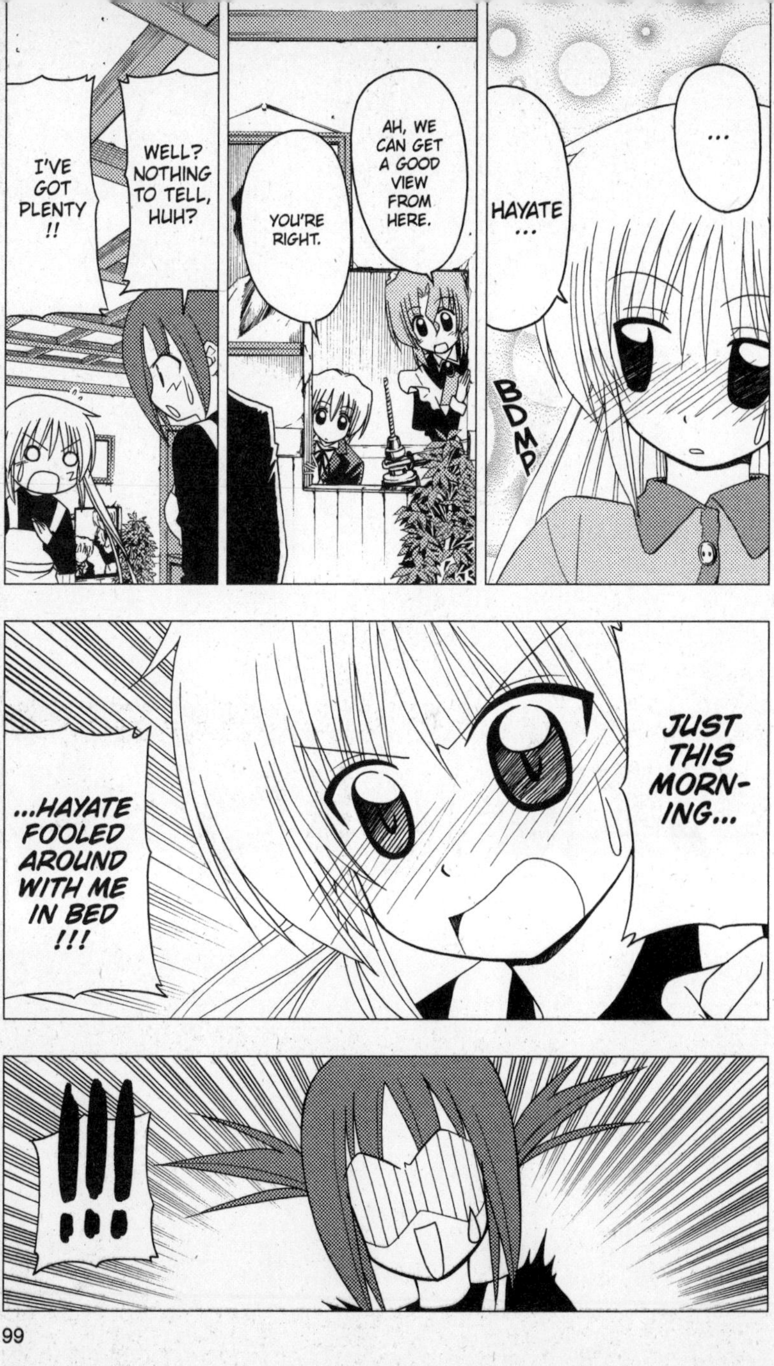
...
HAYATE ...
BDMP
AH, WE CAN GET A GOOD VIEW FROM HERE.
YOU'RE RIGHT.
WELL? NOTHING TO TELL, HUH?
I'VE GOT PLENTY !!
JUST THIS MORN-ING...
...HAYATE FOOLED AROUND WITH ME IN BED !!!
!!!

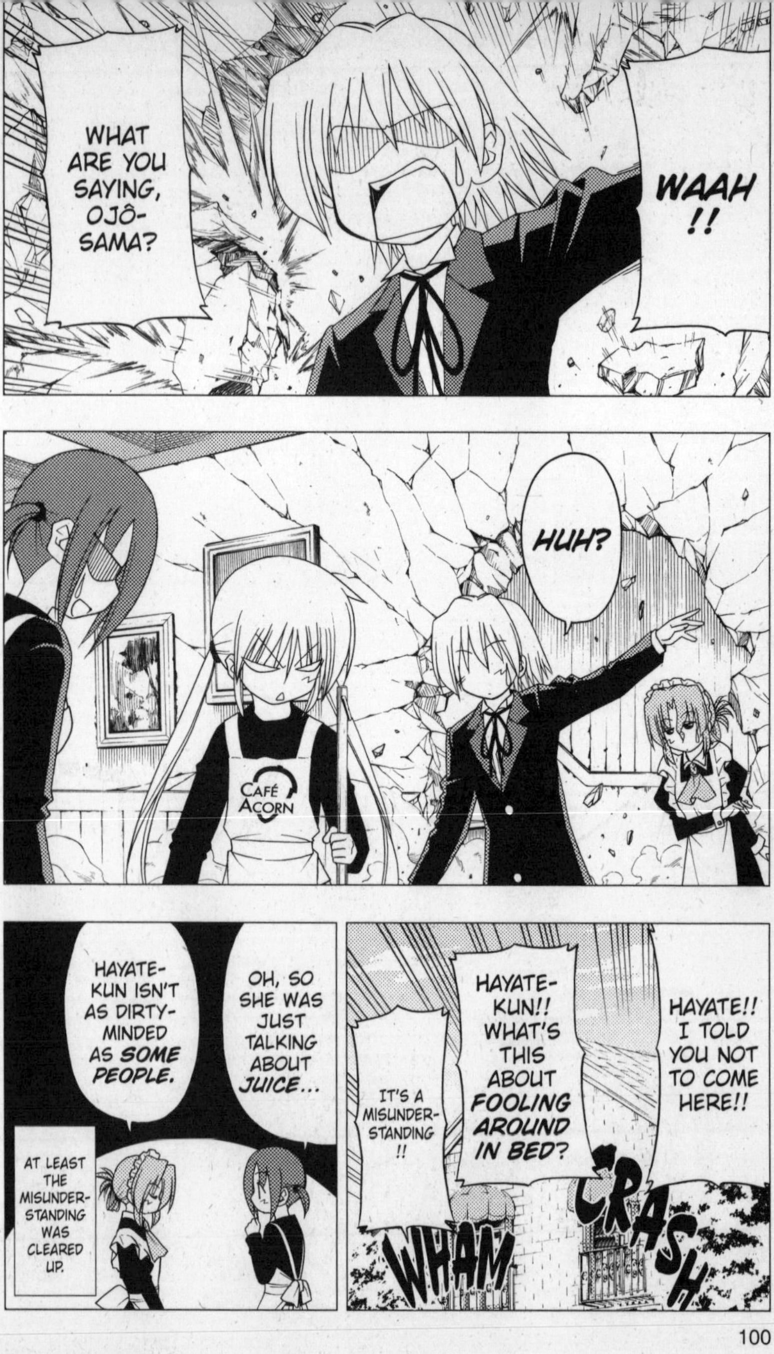
WAAH!!
WHAT ARE YOU SAYING, OJÔ-SAMA?
HUH?
CAFÉ ACORN
HAYATE!! I TOLD YOU NOT TO COME HERE!!
HAYATE-KUN!! WHAT'S THIS ABOUT FOOLING AROUND IN BED?
IT'S A MISUNDER-STANDING!!
CRASH
WHAM
OH, SO SHE WAS JUST TALKING ABOUT JUICE...
HAYATE-KUN ISN'T AS DIRTY-MINDED AS SOME PEOPLE.
AT LEAST THE MISUNDER-STANDING WAS CLEARED UP.

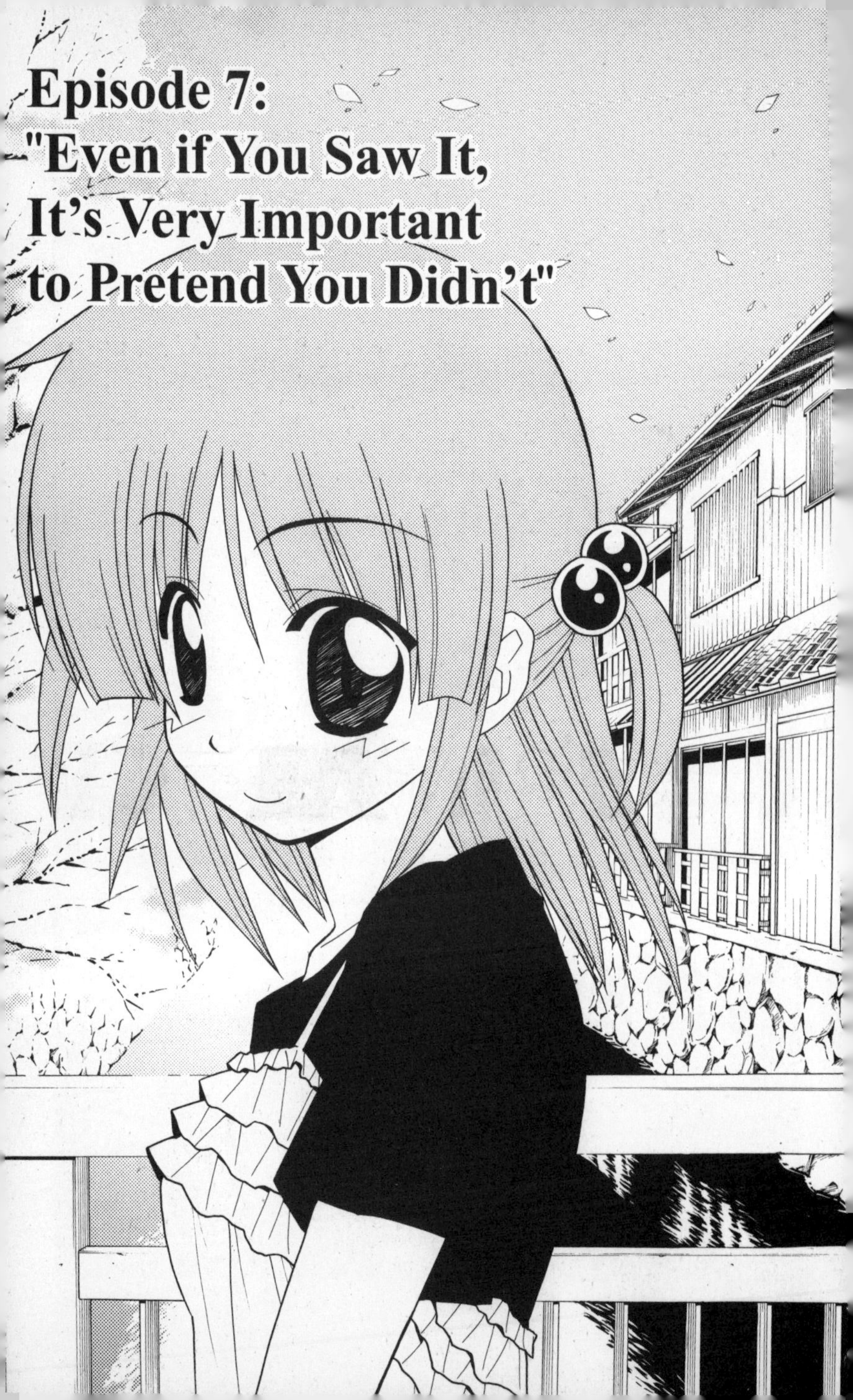
Episode 7:
"Even if You Saw It,
It's Very Important
to Pretend You Didn't"

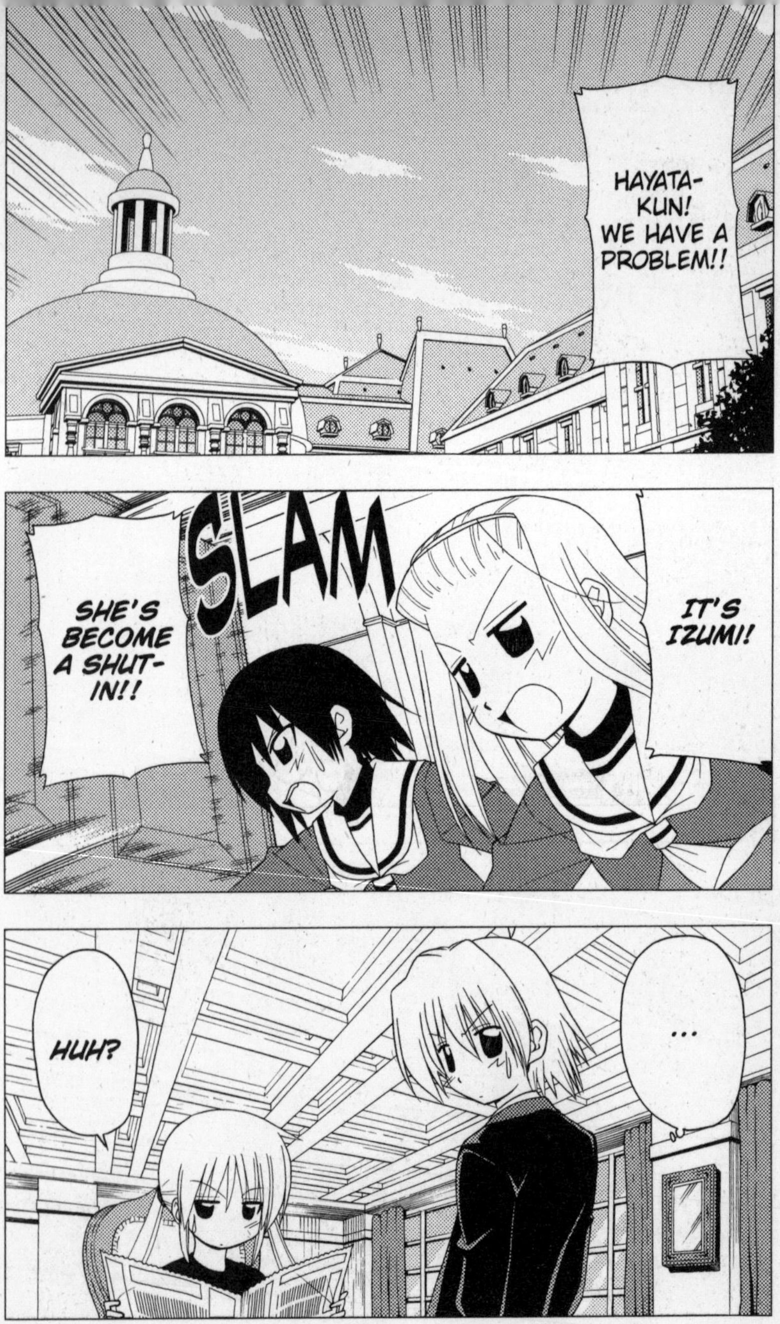
HAYATA-KUN! WE HAVE A PROBLEM!!
SLAM
IT'S IZUMI!
SHE'S BECOME A SHUT-IN!!
...
HUH?

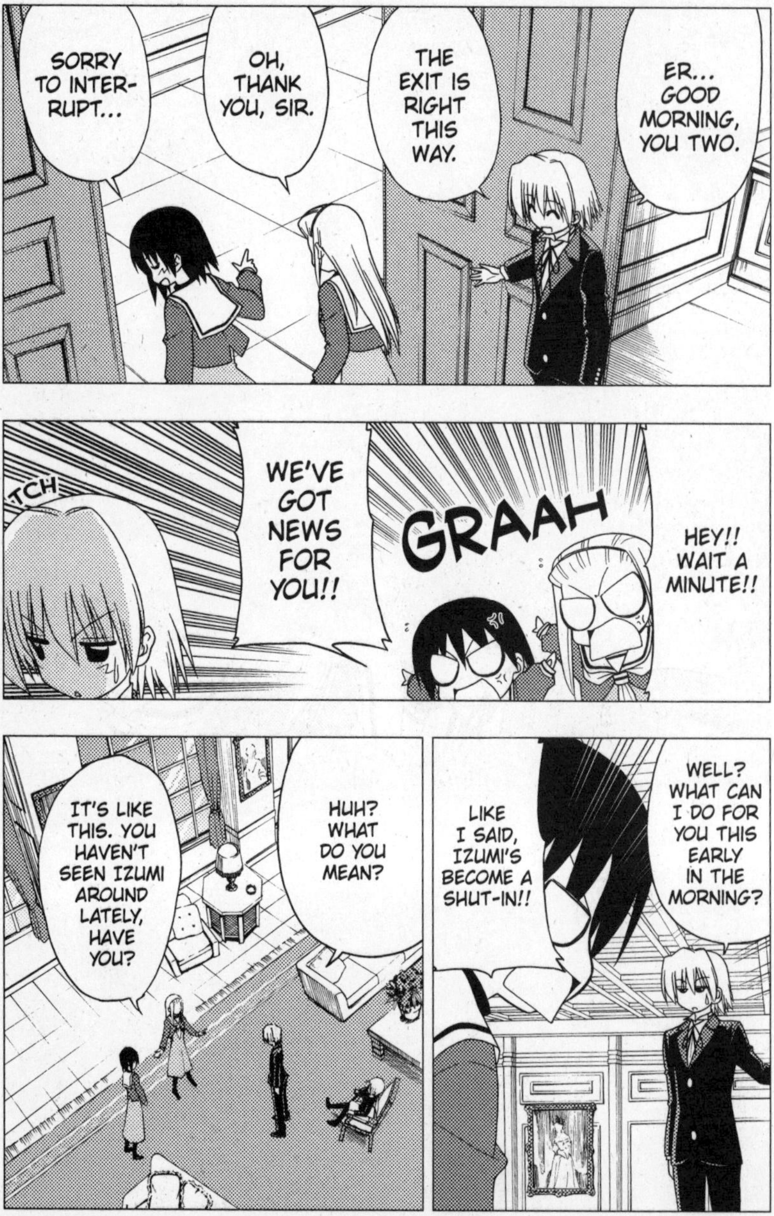
ER... GOOD MORNING, YOU TWO.
THE EXIT IS RIGHT THIS WAY.
OH, THANK YOU, SIR.
SORRY TO INTER-RUPT...
HEY!! WAIT A MINUTE!!
GRAAH
WE'VE GOT NEWS FOR YOU!!
TCH
WELL? WHAT CAN I DO FOR YOU THIS EARLY IN THE MORNING?
LIKE I SAID, IZUMI'S BECOME A SHUT-IN!!
HUH? WHAT DO YOU MEAN?
IT'S LIKE THIS. YOU HAVEN'T SEEN IZUMI AROUND LATELY, HAVE YOU?

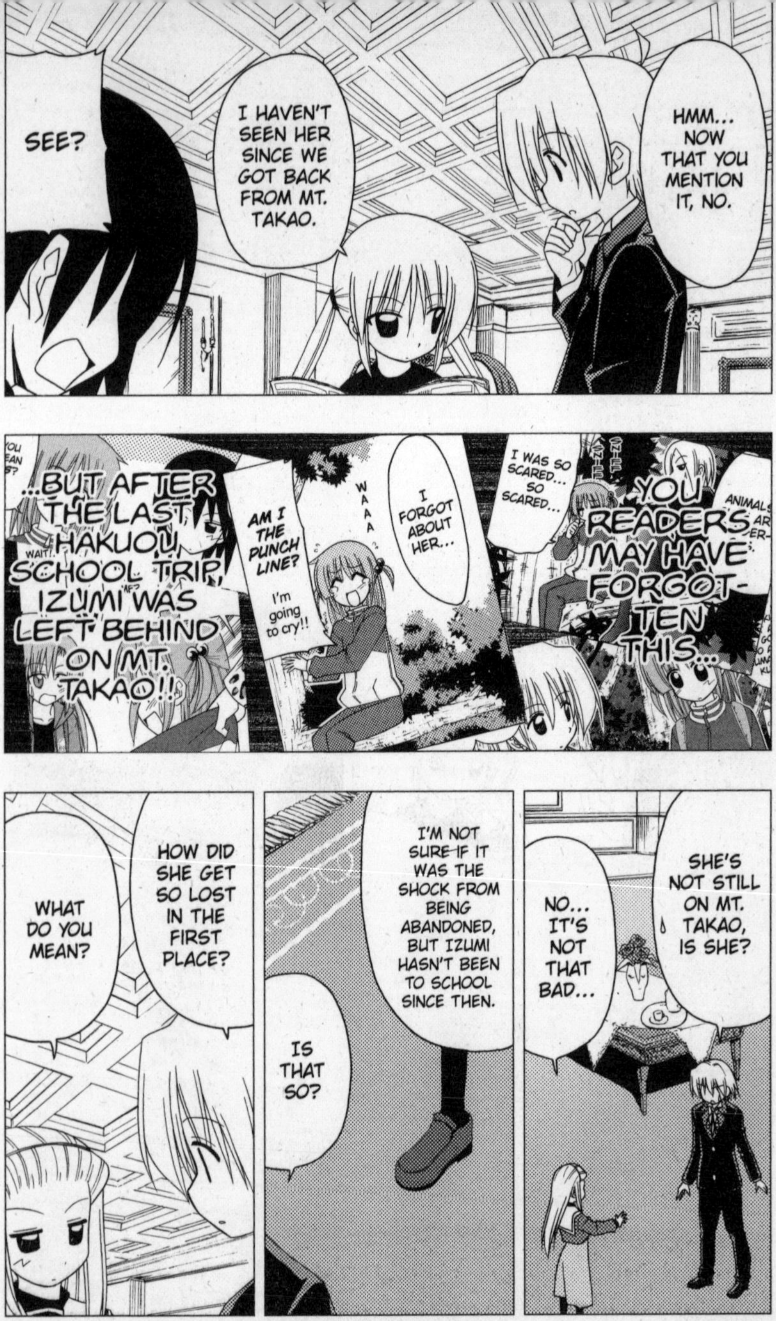
HMM... NOW THAT YOU MENTION IT, NO.
I HAVEN'T SEEN HER SINCE WE GOT BACK FROM MT. TAKAO.
SEE?
YOU READERS MAY HAVE FORGOTTEN THIS...
SNIFF SNIFF
I WAS SO SCARED... SO SCARED...
I FORGOT ABOUT HER...
WAAA
AM I THE PUNCH LINE?
I'm going to cry!!
...BUT AFTER THE LAST HAKUOU SCHOOL TRIP, IZUMI WAS LEFT BEHIND ON MT. TAKAO!!
WAIT!!
SHE'S NOT STILL ON MT. TAKAO, IS SHE?
NO... IT'S NOT THAT BAD...
I'M NOT SURE IF IT WAS THE SHOCK FROM BEING ABANDONED, BUT IZUMI HASN'T BEEN TO SCHOOL SINCE THEN.
IS THAT SO?
HOW DID SHE GET SO LOST IN THE FIRST PLACE?
WHAT DO YOU MEAN?

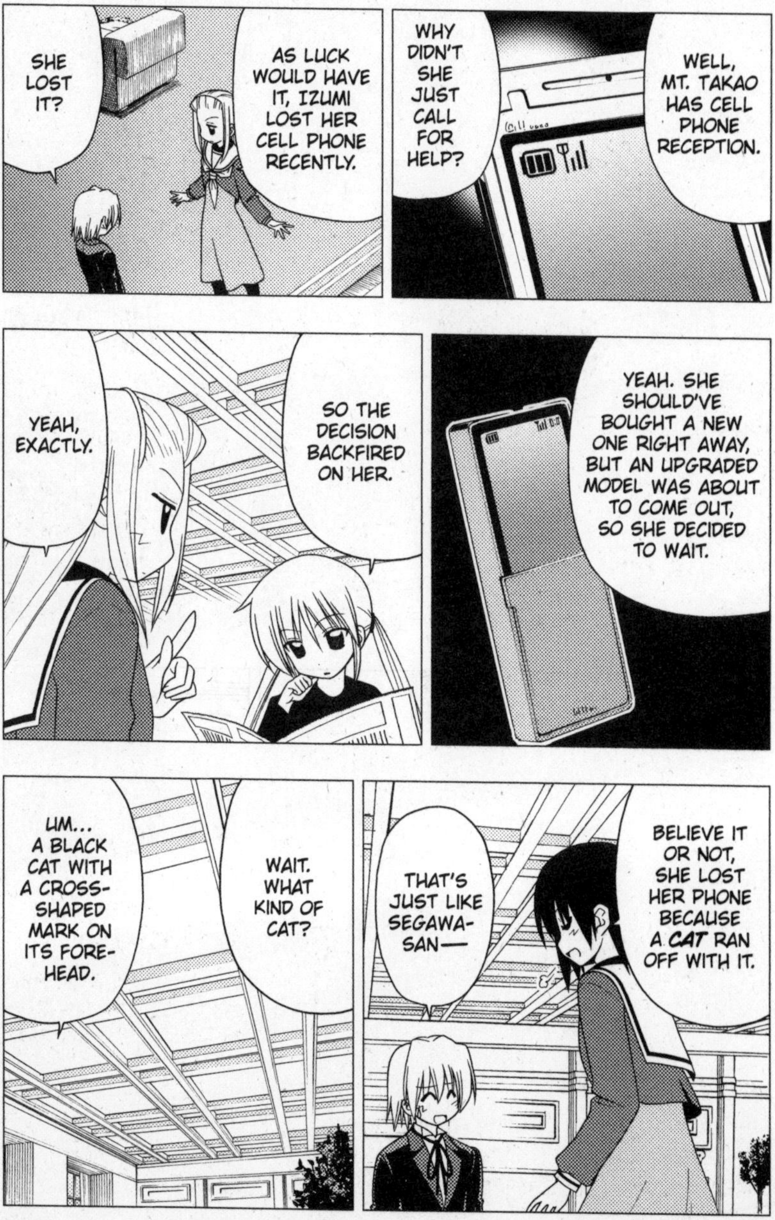
WELL, MT. TAKAO HAS CELL PHONE RECEPTION.
WHY DIDN'T SHE JUST CALL FOR HELP?
AS LUCK WOULD HAVE IT, IZUMI LOST HER CELL PHONE RECENTLY.
SHE LOST IT?
YEAH. SHE SHOULD'VE BOUGHT A NEW ONE RIGHT AWAY, BUT AN UPGRADED MODEL WAS ABOUT TO COME OUT, SO SHE DECIDED TO WAIT.
SO THE DECISION BACKFIRED ON HER.
YEAH, EXACTLY.
BELIEVE IT OR NOT, SHE LOST HER PHONE BECAUSE A *CAT* RAN OFF WITH IT.
THAT'S JUST LIKE SEGAWA-SAN—
WAIT. WHAT KIND OF CAT?
UM... A BLACK CAT WITH A CROSS-SHAPED MARK ON ITS FORE-HEAD.

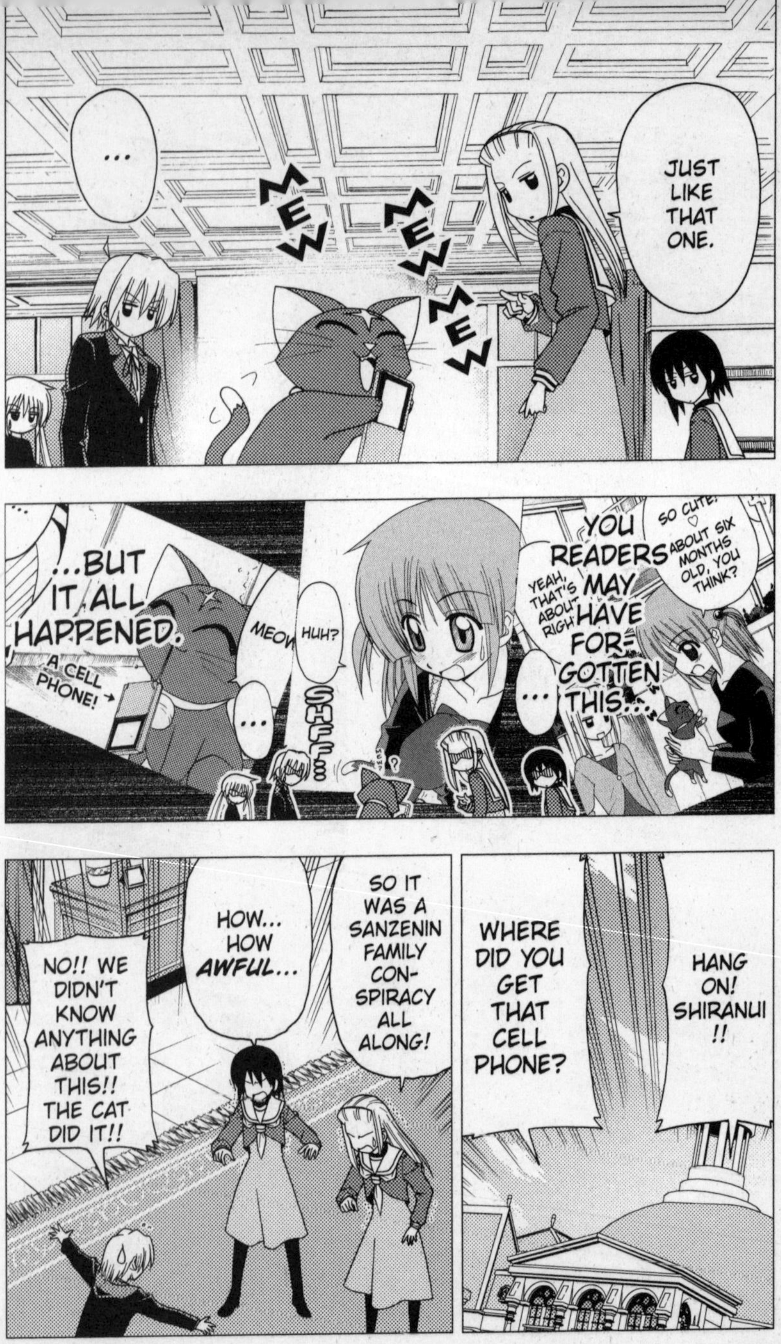
JUST LIKE THAT ONE.
MEW MEW MEW MEW
...
SO CUTE! ♡ ABOUT SIX MONTHS OLD, YOU THINK?
YEAH, THAT'S ABOUT RIGHT
YOU READERS MAY HAVE FOR-GOTTEN THIS...
...
HUH?
SHFF...
MEOW
...
...BUT IT ALL HAPPENED.
A CELL PHONE!
HANG ON! SHIRANUI !!
WHERE DID YOU GET THAT CELL PHONE?
SO IT WAS A SANZENIN FAMILY CON-SPIRACY ALL ALONG!
HOW... HOW AWFUL...
NO!! WE DIDN'T KNOW ANYTHING ABOUT THIS!! THE CAT DID IT!!

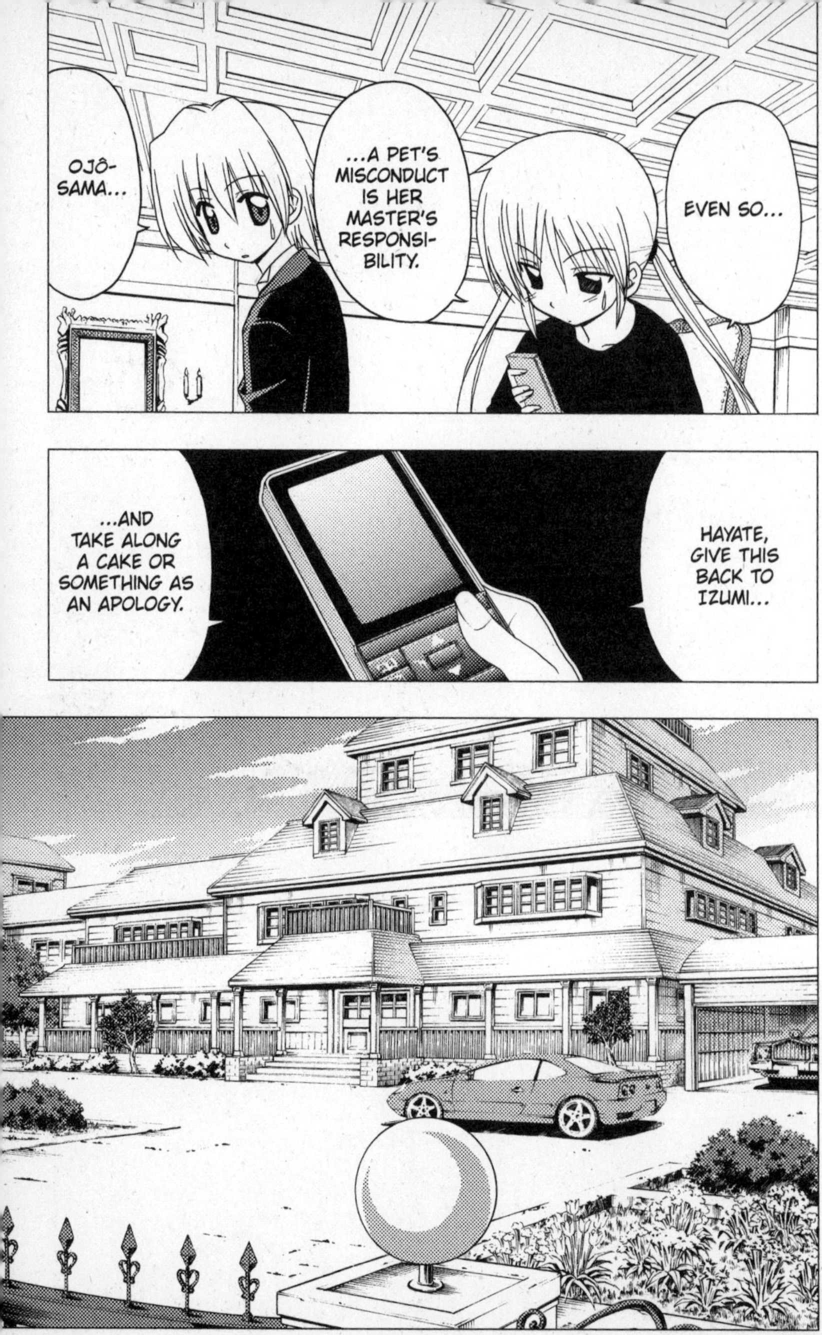
EVEN SO...
...A PET'S MISCONDUCT IS HER MASTER'S RESPONSIBILITY.
OJÔ-SAMA...
HAYATE, GIVE THIS BACK TO IZUMI...
...AND TAKE ALONG A CAKE OR SOMETHING AS AN APOLOGY.

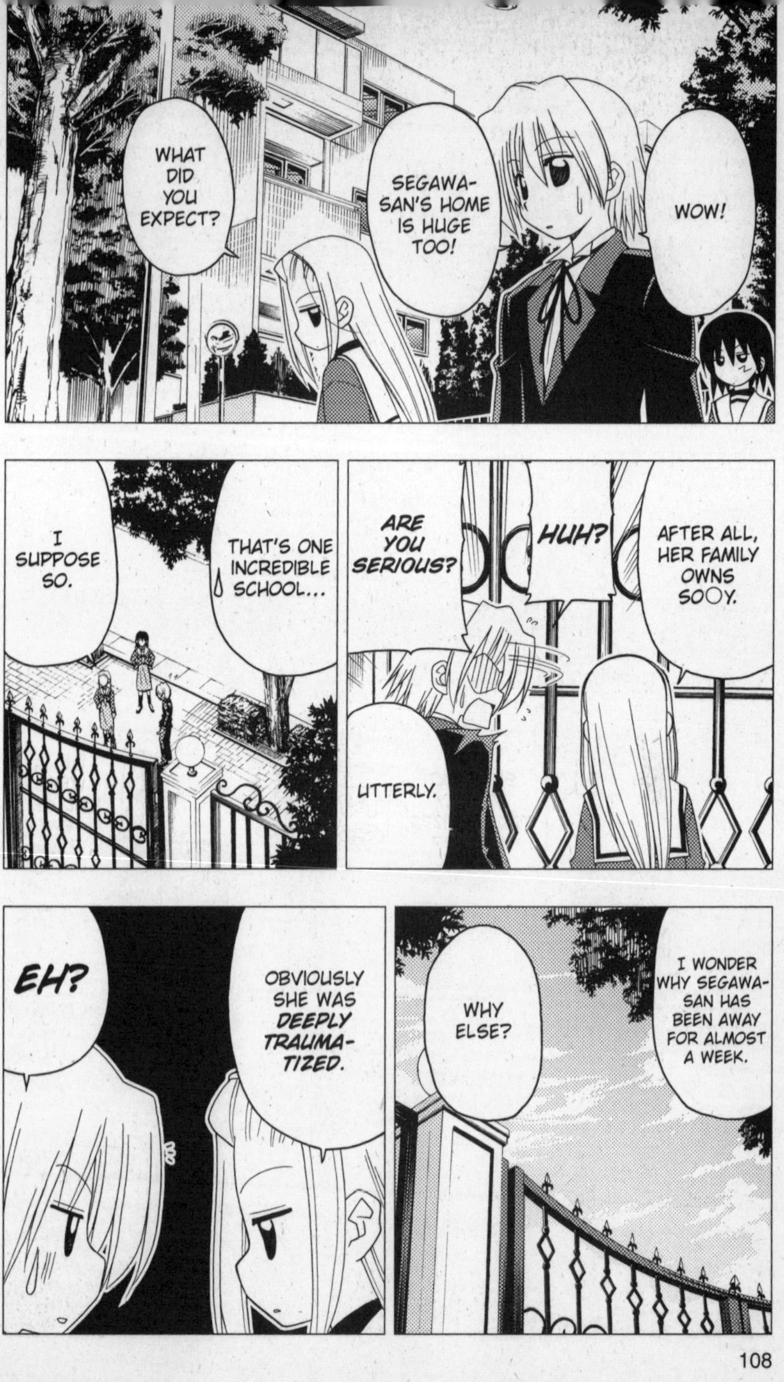
WOW!
SEGAWA-SAN'S HOME IS HUGE TOO!
WHAT DID YOU EXPECT?
AFTER ALL, HER FAMILY OWNS SO○Y.
HUH?
ARE YOU SERIOUS?
UTTERLY.
THAT'S ONE INCREDIBLE SCHOOL...
I SUPPOSE SO.
I WONDER WHY SEGAWA-SAN HAS BEEN AWAY FOR ALMOST A WEEK.
WHY ELSE?
OBVIOUSLY SHE WAS DEEPLY TRAUMATIZED.
EH?

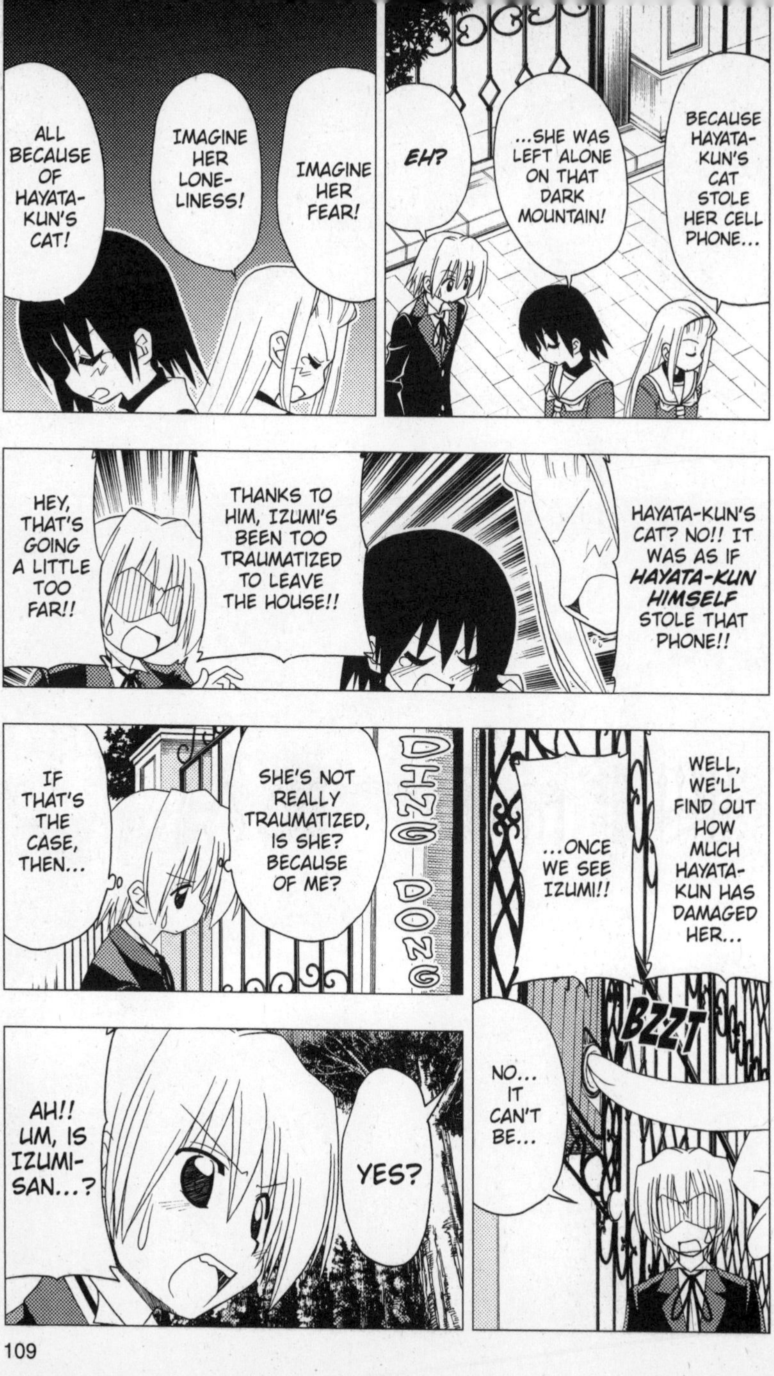
BECAUSE HAYATA-KUN'S CAT STOLE HER CELL PHONE...
...SHE WAS LEFT ALONE ON THAT DARK MOUNTAIN!
EH?
IMAGINE HER FEAR!
IMAGINE HER LONE-LINESS!
ALL BECAUSE OF HAYATA-KUN'S CAT!
HAYATA-KUN'S CAT? NO!! IT WAS AS IF *HAYATA-KUN HIMSELF* STOLE THAT PHONE!!
THANKS TO HIM, IZUMI'S BEEN TOO TRAUMATIZED TO LEAVE THE HOUSE!!
HEY, THAT'S GOING A LITTLE TOO FAR!!
WELL, WE'LL FIND OUT HOW MUCH HAYATA-KUN HAS DAMAGED HER...
...ONCE WE SEE IZUMI!!
BZZT
NO... IT CAN'T BE...
DING DONG
SHE'S NOT REALLY TRAUMATIZED, IS SHE? BECAUSE OF ME?
IF THAT'S THE CASE, THEN...
YES?
AH!! UM, IS IZUMI-SAN...?

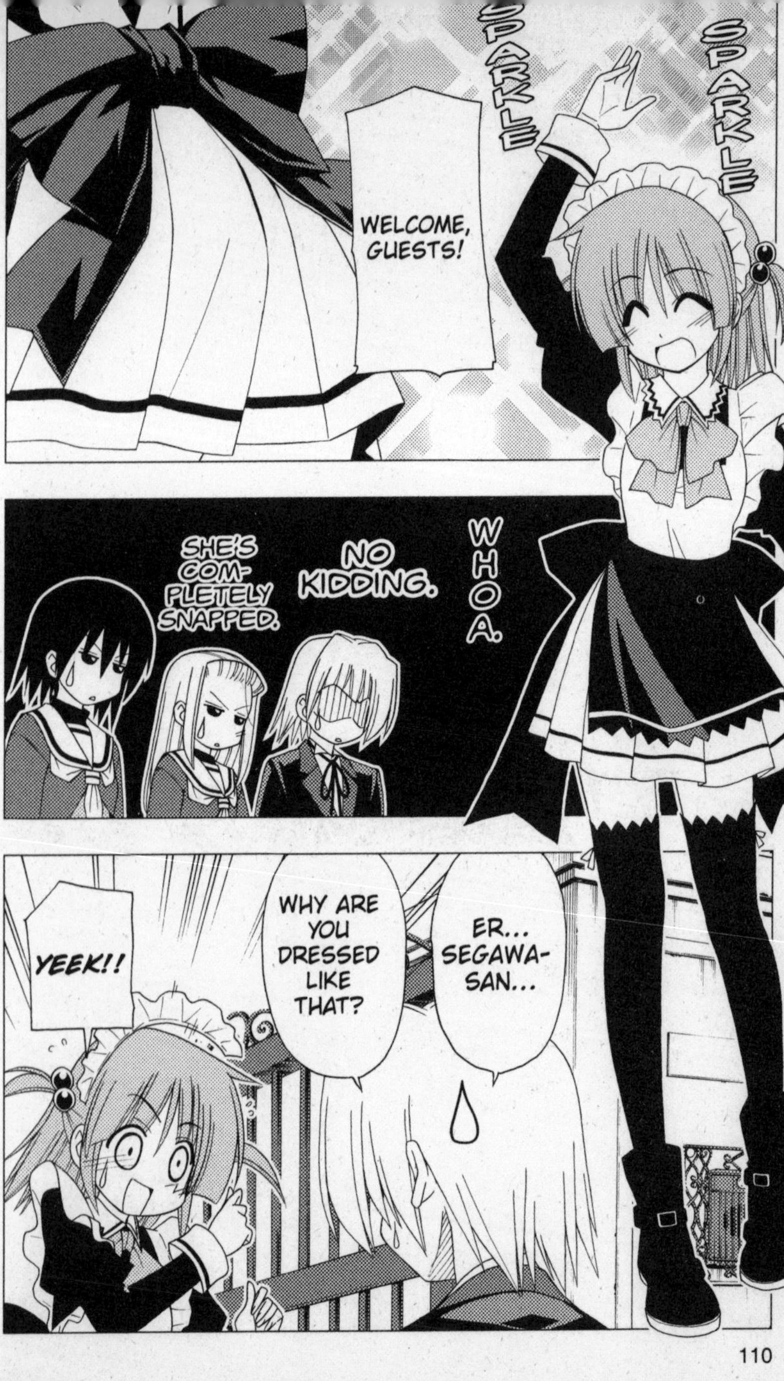
SPARKLE
SPARKLE
WELCOME, GUESTS!
WHOA.
NO KIDDING.
SHE'S COM-PLETELY SNAPPED.
ER... SEGAWA-SAN...
WHY ARE YOU DRESSED LIKE THAT?
YEEK!!

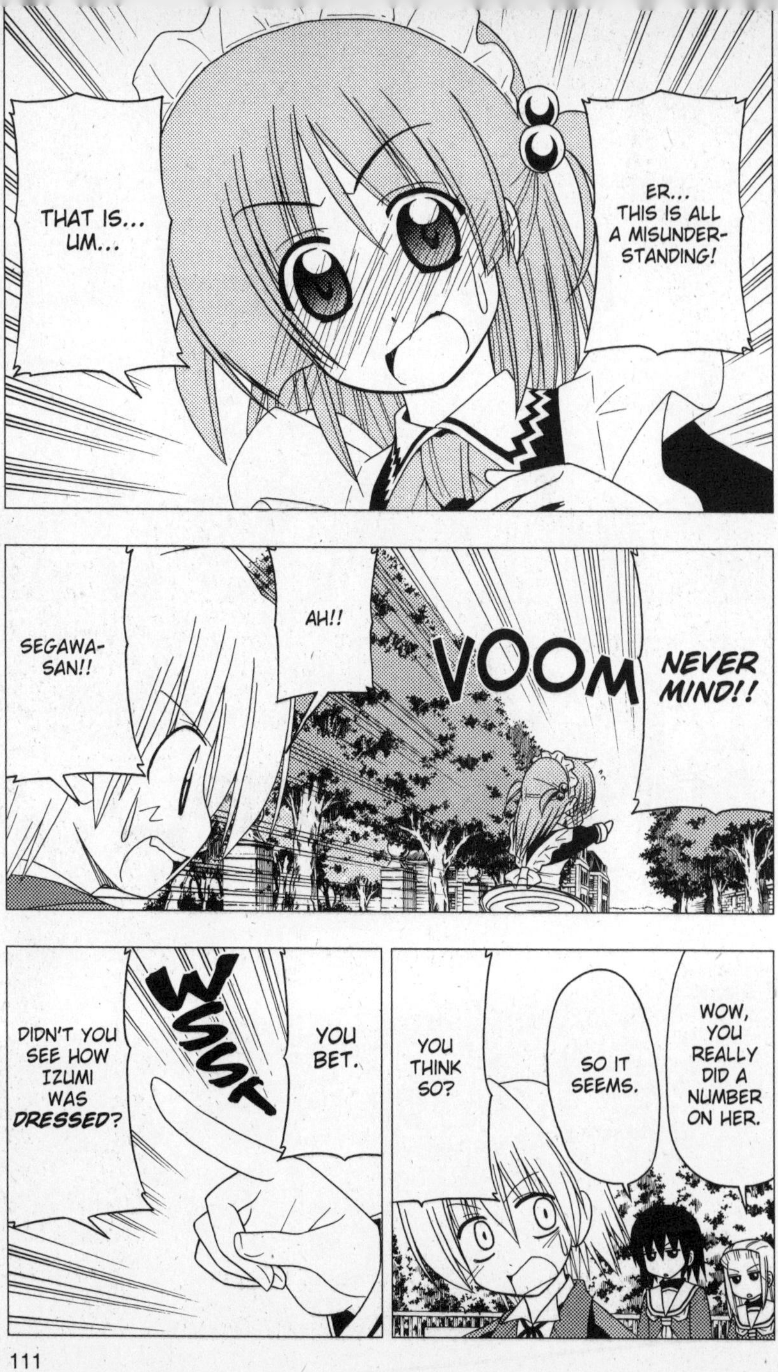
ER... THIS IS ALL A MISUNDER-STANDING!
THAT IS... UM...
NEVER MIND!!
VOOM
AH!!
SEGAWA-SAN!!
WOW, YOU REALLY DID A NUMBER ON HER.
SO IT SEEMS.
YOU THINK SO?
YOU BET.
WSST
DIDN'T YOU SEE HOW IZUMI WAS **DRESSED**?

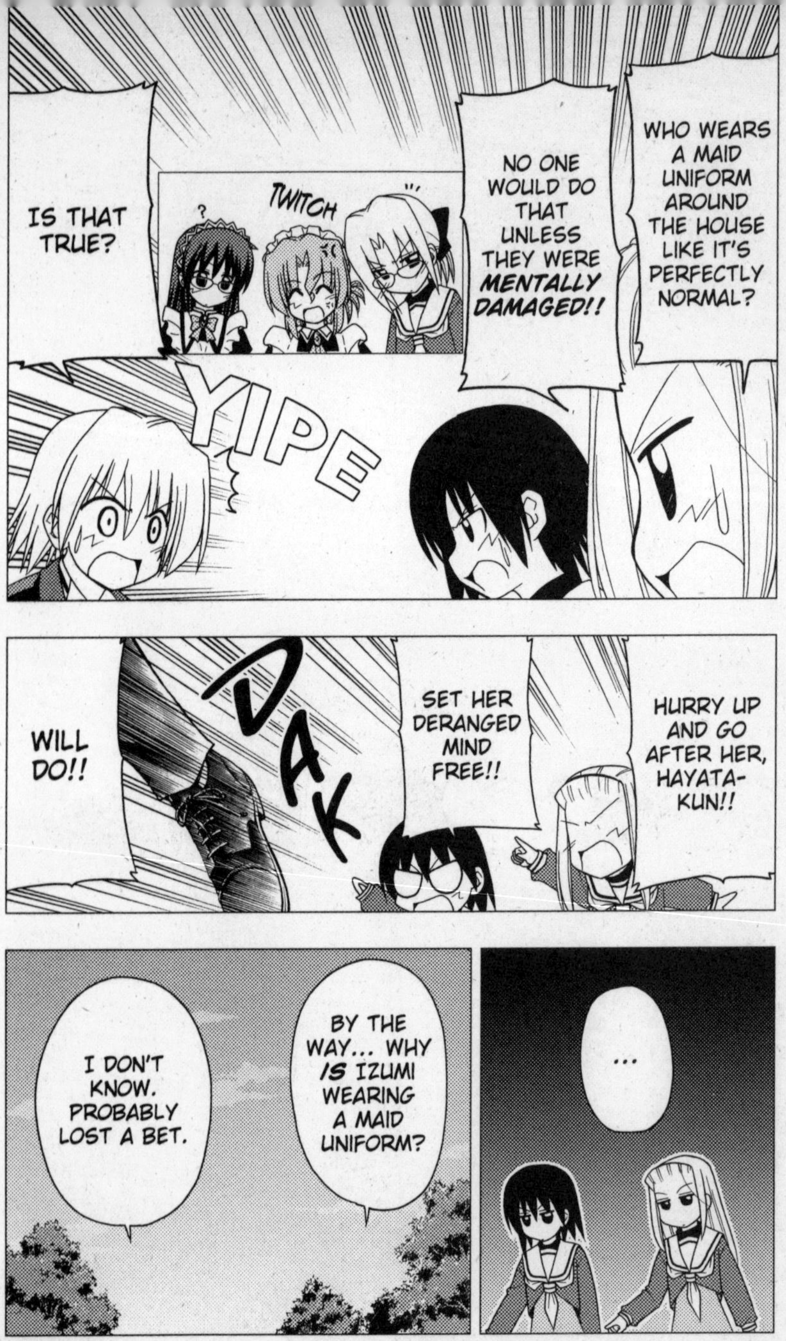
WHO WEARS A MAID UNIFORM AROUND THE HOUSE LIKE IT'S PERFECTLY NORMAL?
NO ONE WOULD DO THAT UNLESS THEY WERE *MENTALLY DAMAGED!!*
TWITCH
IS THAT TRUE?
YIPE
HURRY UP AND GO AFTER HER, HAYATA-KUN!!
SET HER DERANGED MIND FREE!!
DAK
WILL DO!!
...
BY THE WAY... WHY *IS* IZUMI WEARING A MAID UNIFORM?
I DON'T KNOW. PROBABLY LOST A BET.

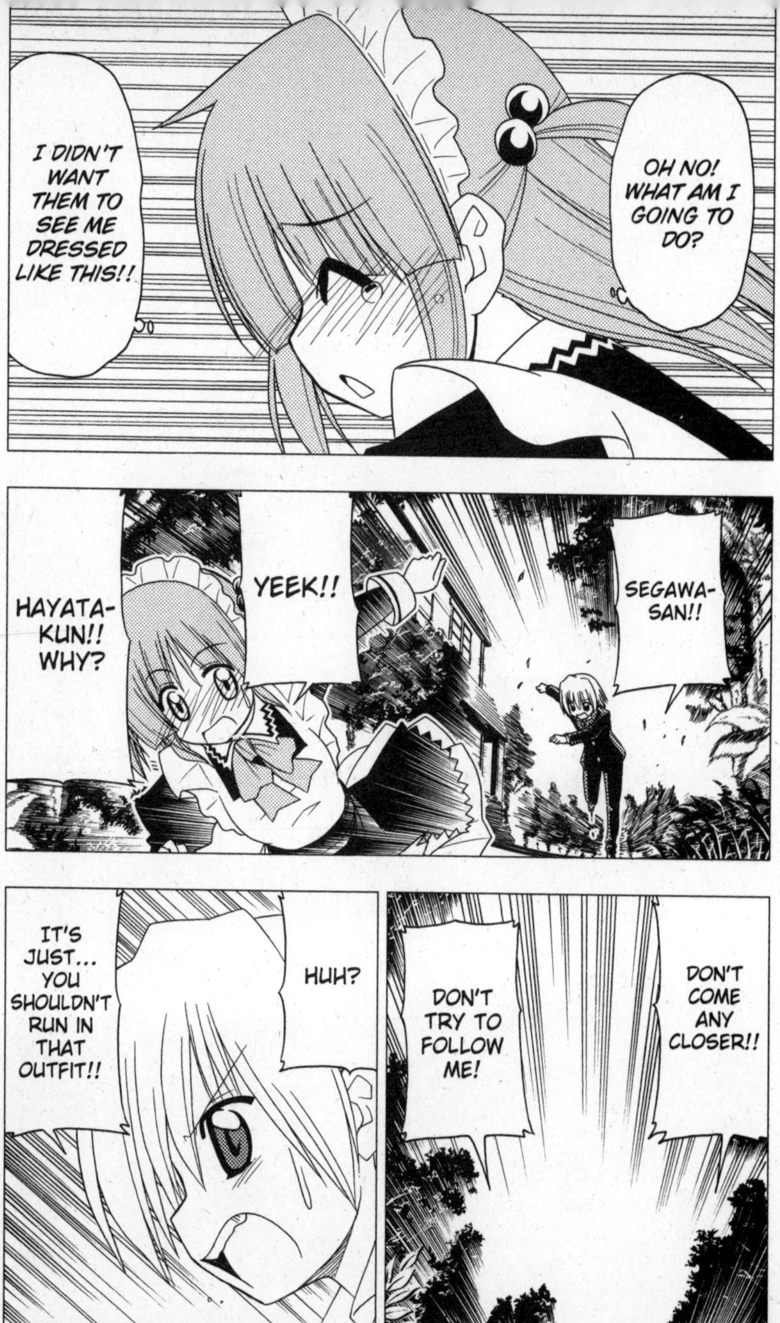
OH NO! WHAT AM I GOING TO DO?
I DIDN'T WANT THEM TO SEE ME DRESSED LIKE THIS!!
SEGAWA-SAN!!
YEEK!!
HAYATA-KUN!! WHY?
DON'T COME ANY CLOSER!!
DON'T TRY TO FOLLOW ME!
HUH?
IT'S JUST... YOU SHOULDN'T RUN IN THAT OUTFIT!!

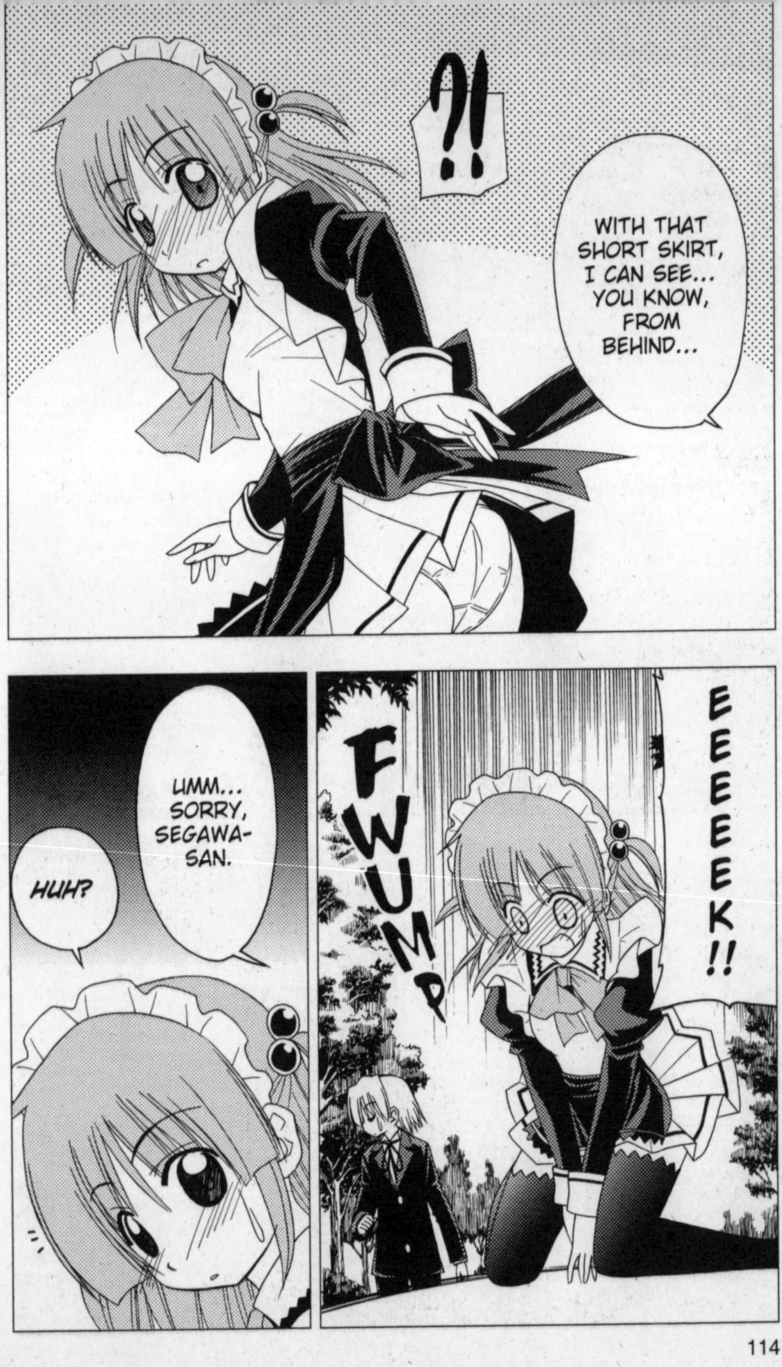
WITH THAT SHORT SKIRT, I CAN SEE... YOU KNOW, FROM BEHIND...
?!
EEEEEK!!
FWUMP
UMM... SORRY, SEGAWA-SAN.
HUH?

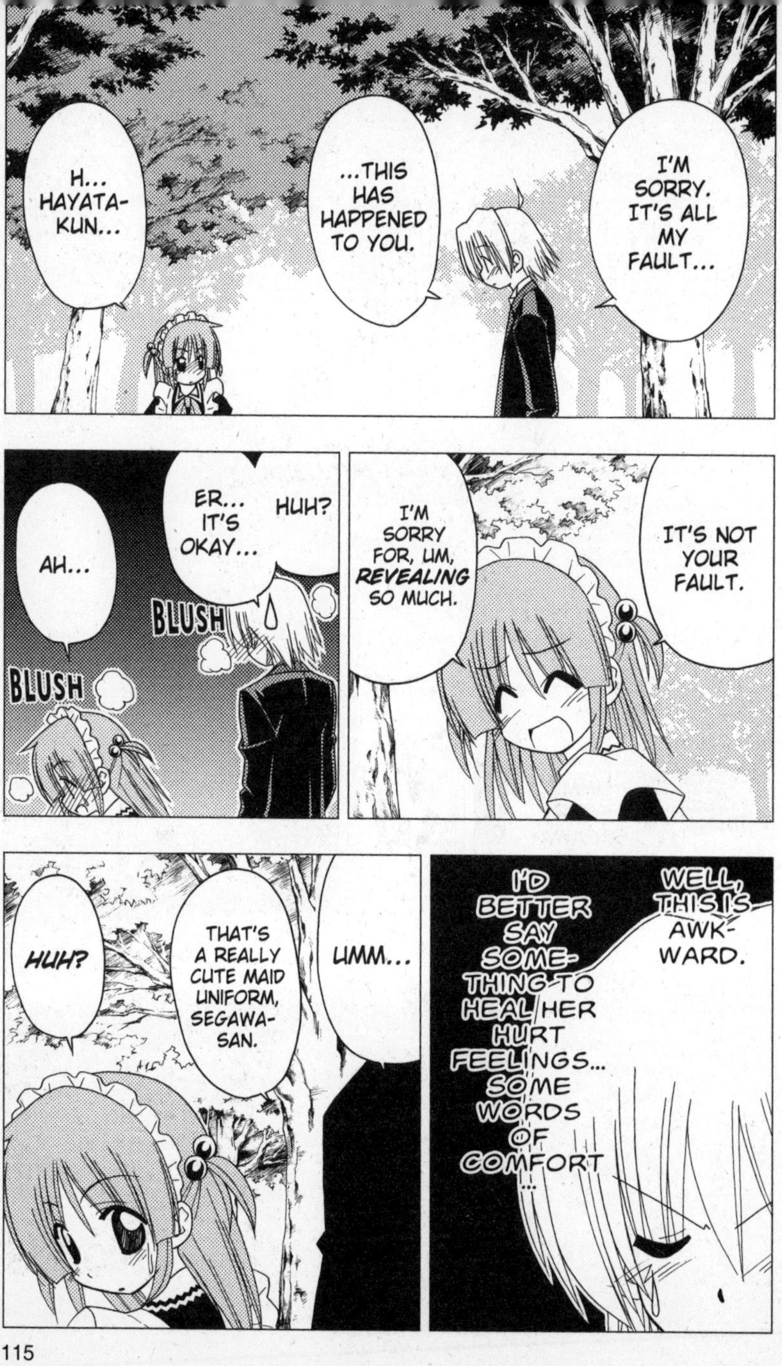
I'M SORRY. IT'S ALL MY FAULT...
...THIS HAS HAPPENED TO YOU.
H... HAYATA-KUN...
IT'S NOT YOUR FAULT.
I'M SORRY FOR, UM, *REVEALING* SO MUCH.
HUH?
ER... IT'S OKAY...
BLUSH
AH...
BLUSH
WELL, THIS IS AWK-WARD.
I'D BETTER SAY SOME-THING TO HEAL HER HURT FEELINGS... SOME WORDS OF COMFORT...
UMM...
THAT'S A REALLY CUTE MAID UNIFORM, SEGAWA-SAN.
HUH?

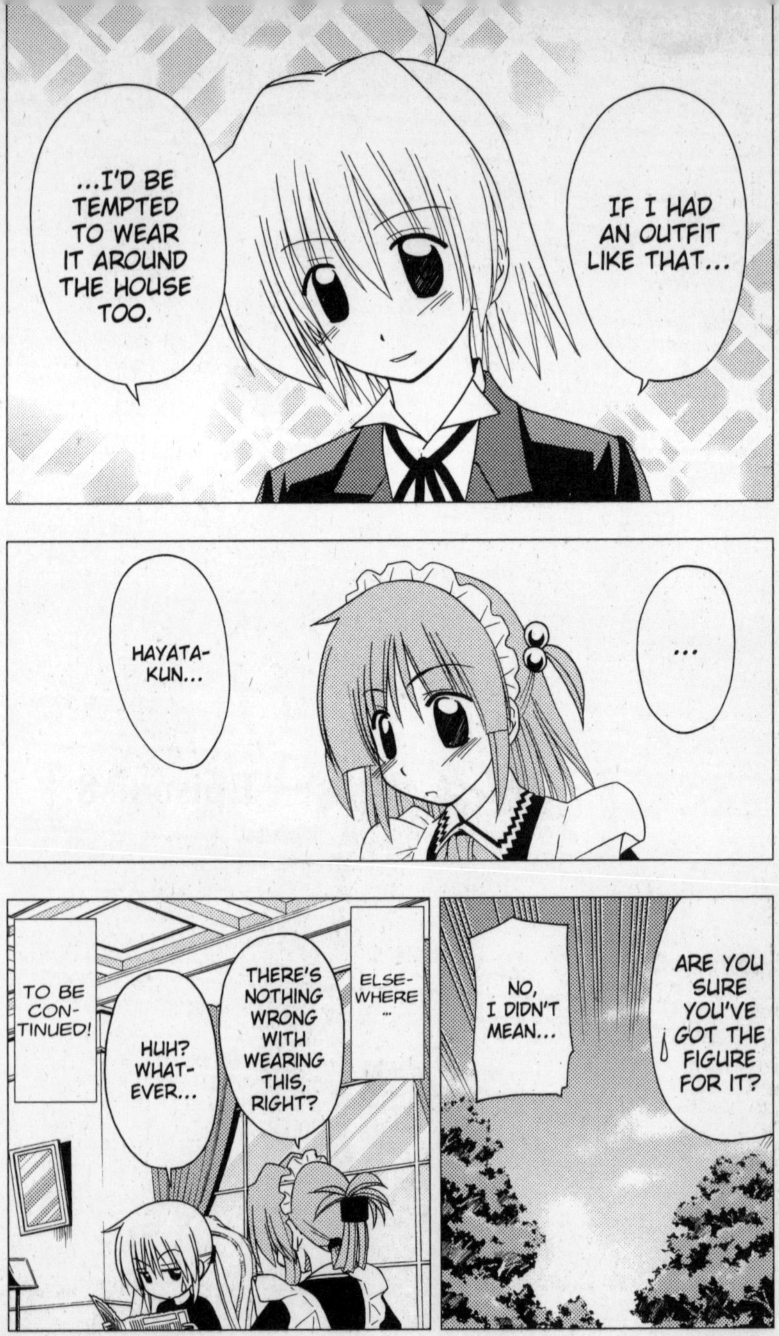
IF I HAD AN OUTFIT LIKE THAT...
...I'D BE TEMPTED TO WEAR IT AROUND THE HOUSE TOO.
...
HAYATA-KUN...
ARE YOU SURE YOU'VE GOT THE FIGURE FOR IT?
NO, I DIDN'T MEAN...
ELSE-WHERE...
THERE'S NOTHING WRONG WITH WEARING THIS, RIGHT?
HUH? WHAT-EVER...
TO BE CON-TINUED!

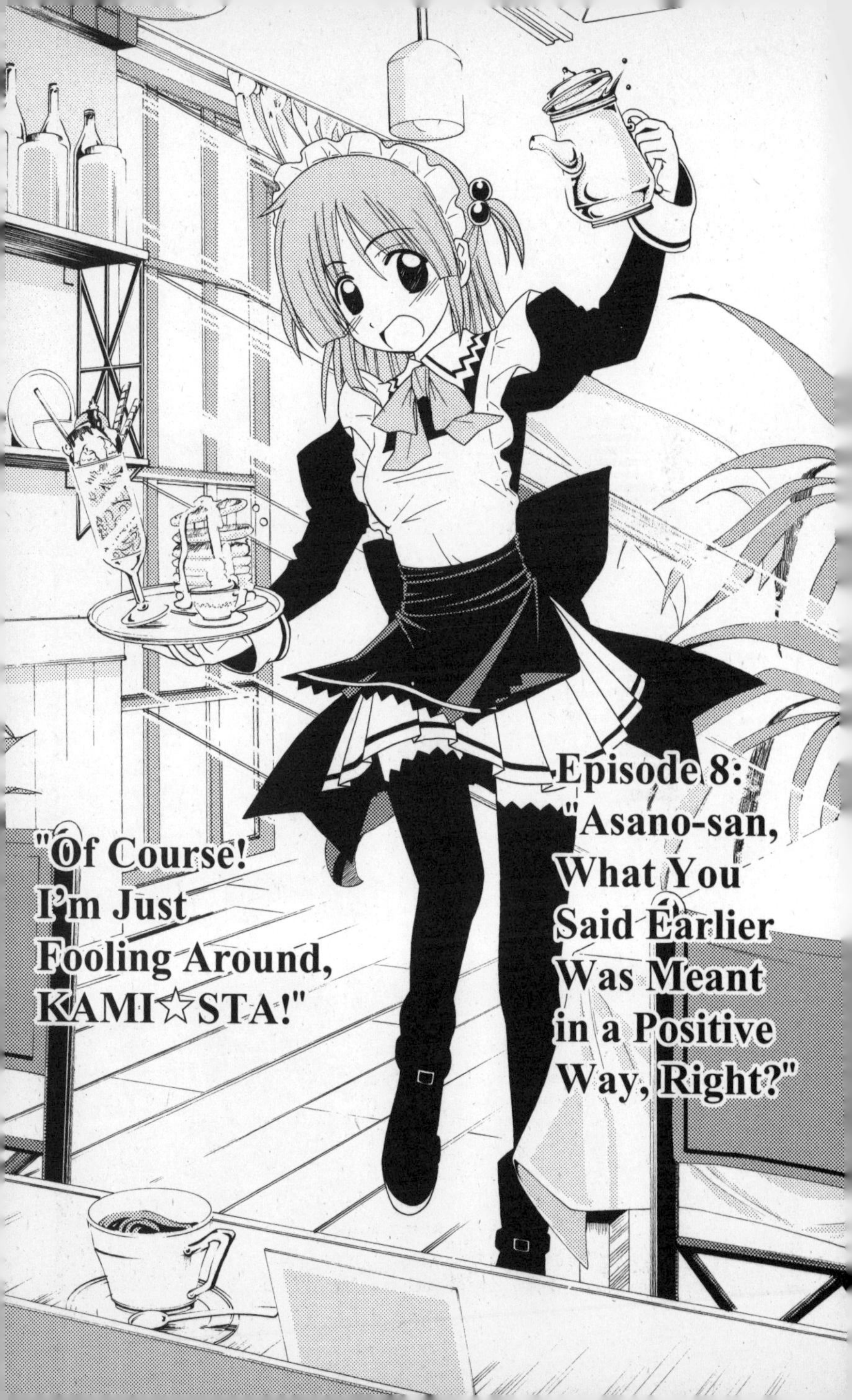
Episode 8: "Asano-san, What You Said Earlier Was Meant in a Positive Way, Right?"
"Of Course! I'm Just Fooling Around, KAMI☆STA!"

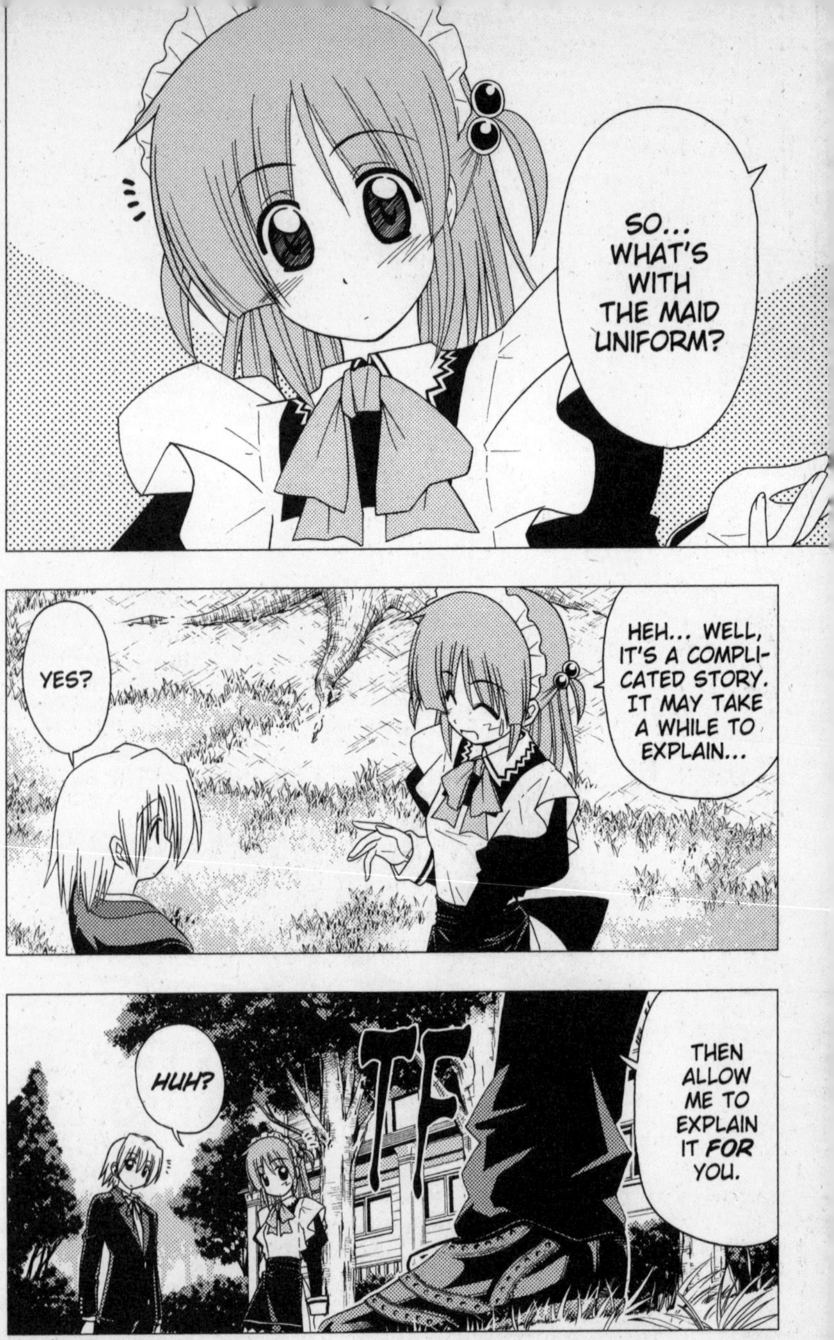
SO... WHAT'S WITH THE MAID UNIFORM?
HEH... WELL, IT'S A COMPLICATED STORY. IT MAY TAKE A WHILE TO EXPLAIN...
YES?
THEN ALLOW ME TO EXPLAIN IT *FOR* YOU.
HUH?

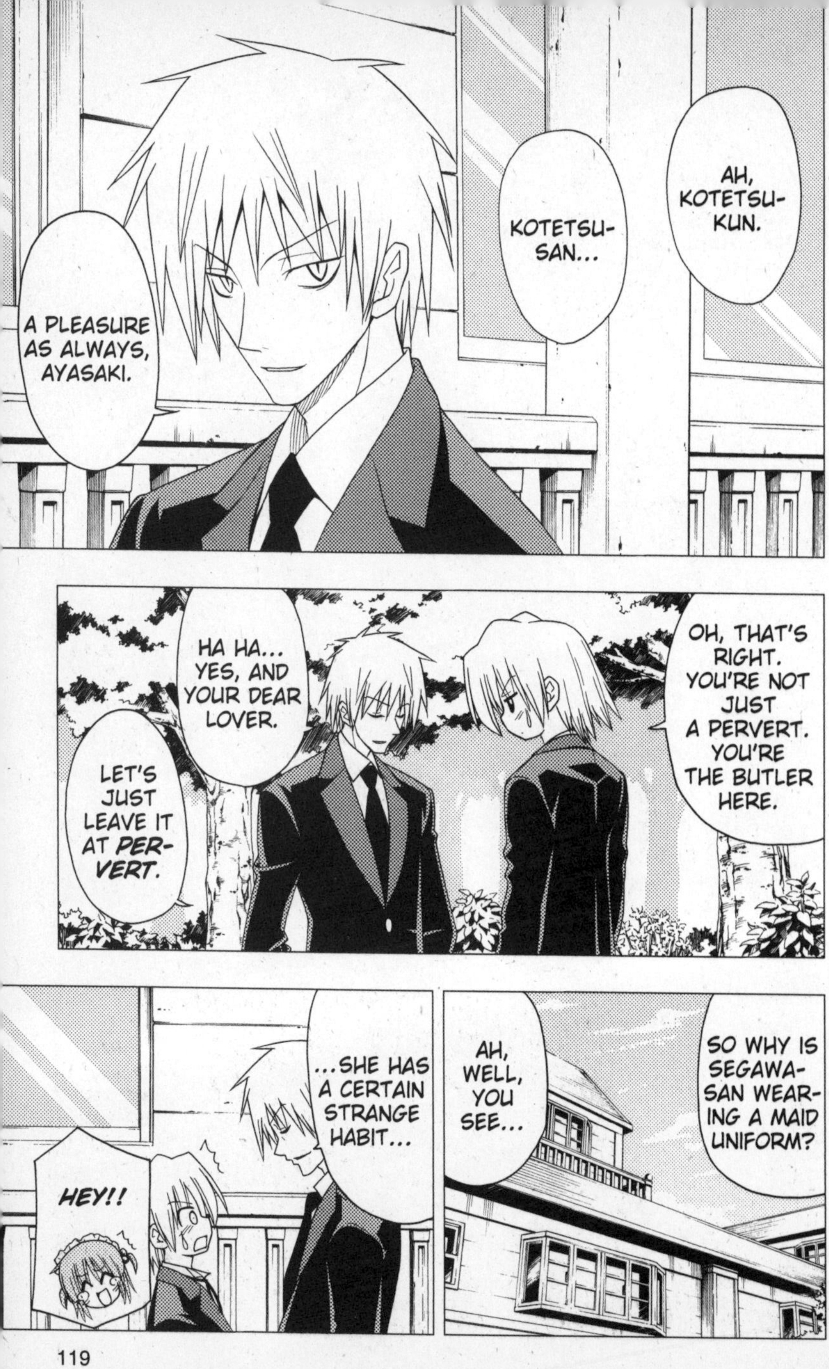
AH, KOTETSU-KUN.
KOTETSU-SAN...
A PLEASURE AS ALWAYS, AYASAKI.
OH, THAT'S RIGHT. YOU'RE NOT JUST A PERVERT. YOU'RE THE BUTLER HERE.
HA HA... YES, AND YOUR DEAR LOVER.
LET'S JUST LEAVE IT AT *PERVERT*.
SO WHY IS SEGAWA-SAN WEARING A MAID UNIFORM?
AH, WELL, YOU SEE...
...SHE HAS A CERTAIN STRANGE HABIT...
HEY!!

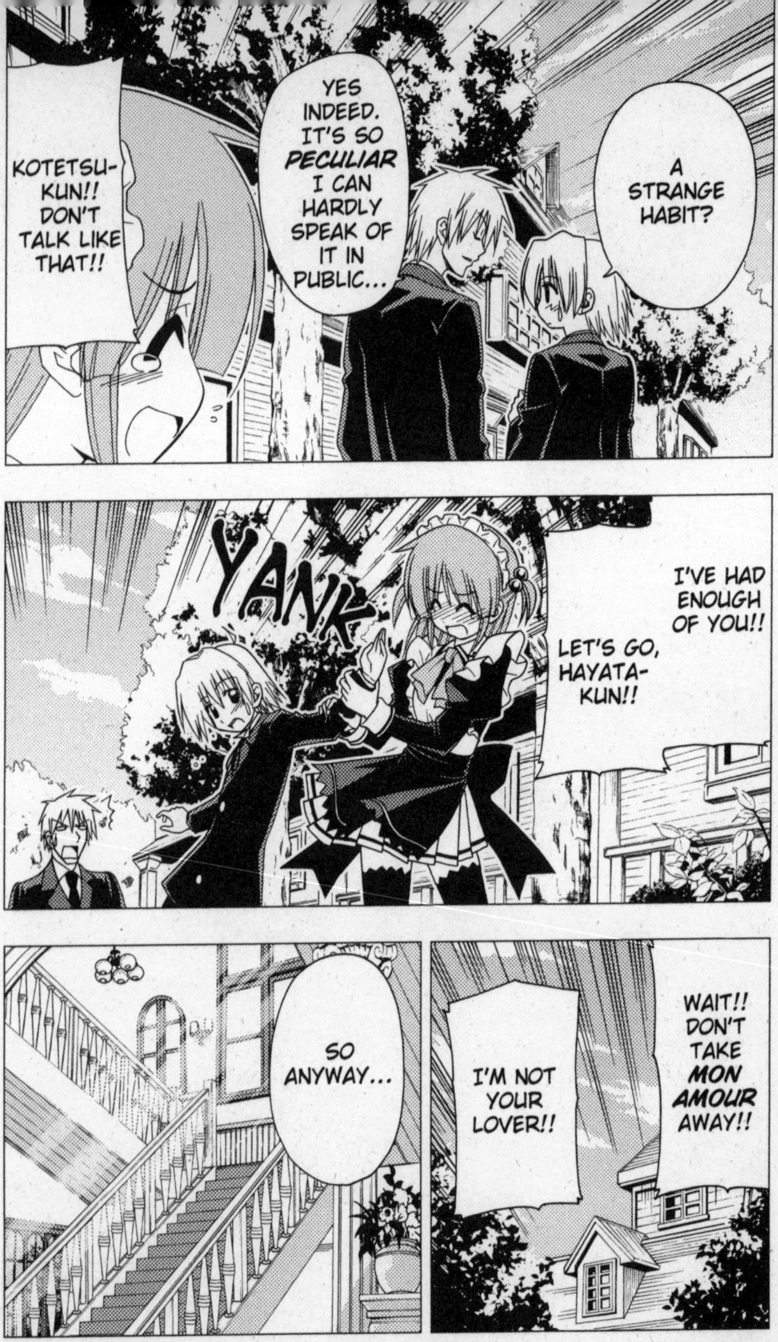
A STRANGE HABIT?
YES INDEED. IT'S SO *PECULIAR* I CAN HARDLY SPEAK OF IT IN PUBLIC...
KOTETSU-KUN!! DON'T TALK LIKE THAT!!
I'VE HAD ENOUGH OF YOU!!
LET'S GO, HAYATA-KUN!!
YANK
WAIT!! DON'T TAKE *MON AMOUR* AWAY!!
I'M NOT YOUR LOVER!!
SO ANYWAY...

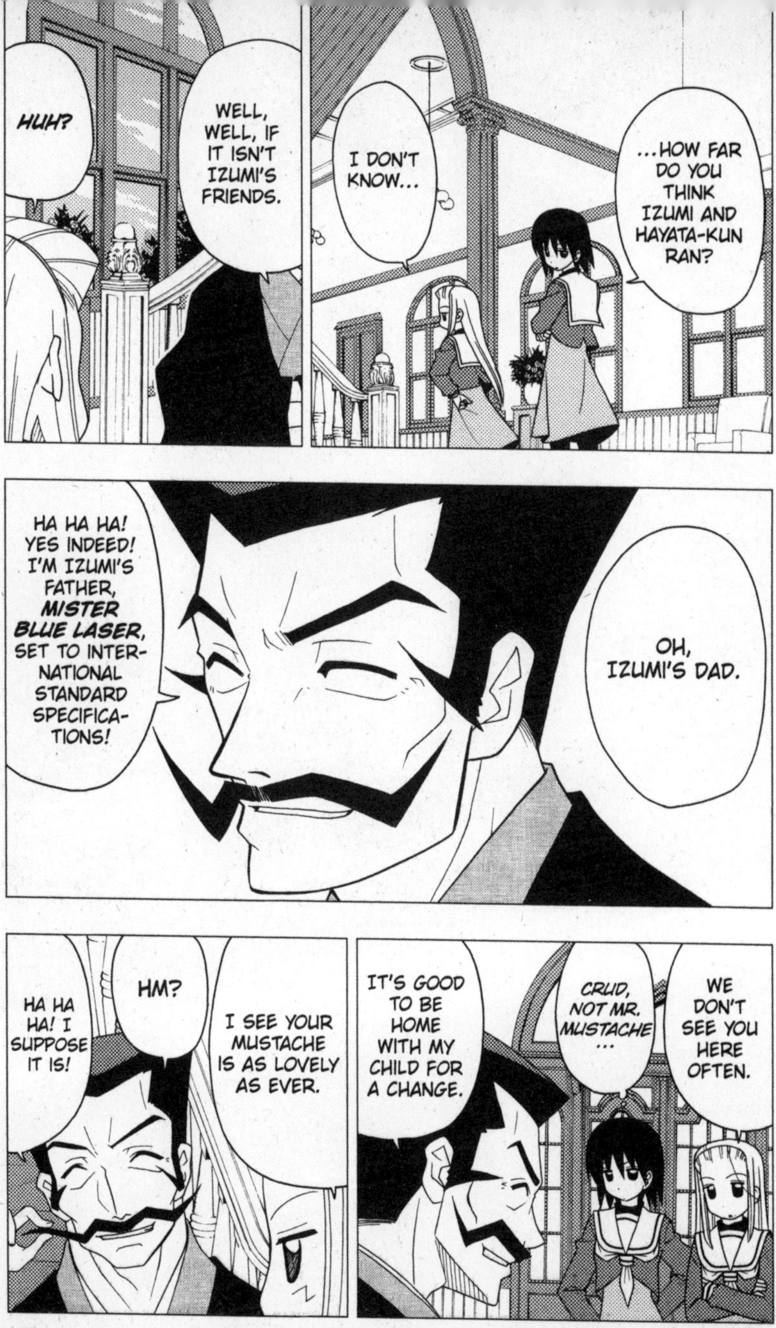
...HOW FAR DO YOU THINK IZUMI AND HAYATA-KUN RAN?
I DON'T KNOW...
WELL, WELL, IF IT ISN'T IZUMI'S FRIENDS.
HUH?
OH, IZUMI'S DAD.
HA HA HA! YES INDEED! I'M IZUMI'S FATHER, ***MISTER BLUE LASER***, SET TO INTER-NATIONAL STANDARD SPECIFICA-TIONS!
WE DON'T SEE YOU HERE OFTEN.
CRUD, NOT MR. MUSTACHE...
IT'S GOOD TO BE HOME WITH MY CHILD FOR A CHANGE.
I SEE YOUR MUSTACHE IS AS LOVELY AS EVER.
HM?
HA HA HA! I SUPPOSE IT IS!

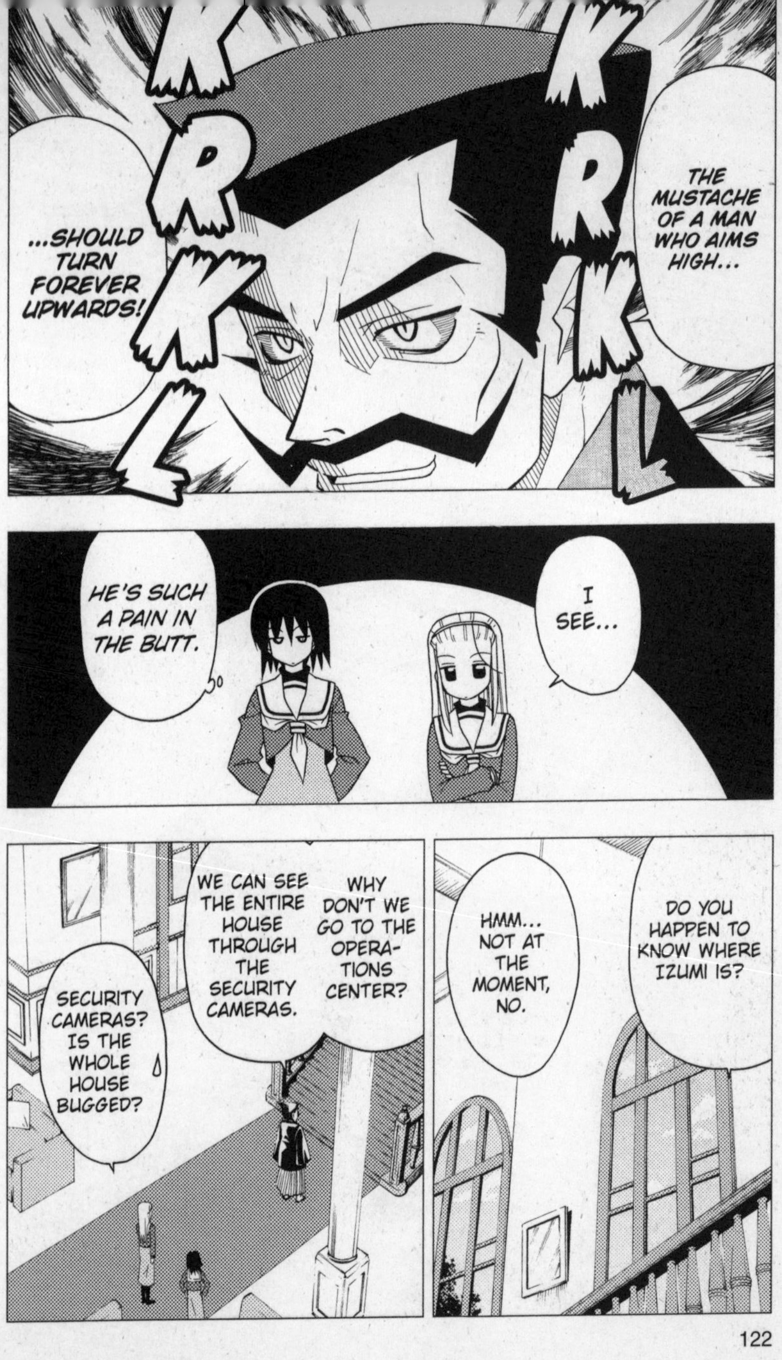
KRKL
THE MUSTACHE OF A MAN WHO AIMS HIGH...
KRKL
...SHOULD TURN FOREVER UPWARDS!
I SEE...
HE'S SUCH A PAIN IN THE BUTT.
DO YOU HAPPEN TO KNOW WHERE IZUMI IS?
HMM... NOT AT THE MOMENT, NO.
WHY DON'T WE GO TO THE OPERA-TIONS CENTER?
WE CAN SEE THE ENTIRE HOUSE THROUGH THE SECURITY CAMERAS.
SECURITY CAMERAS? IS THE WHOLE HOUSE BUGGED?

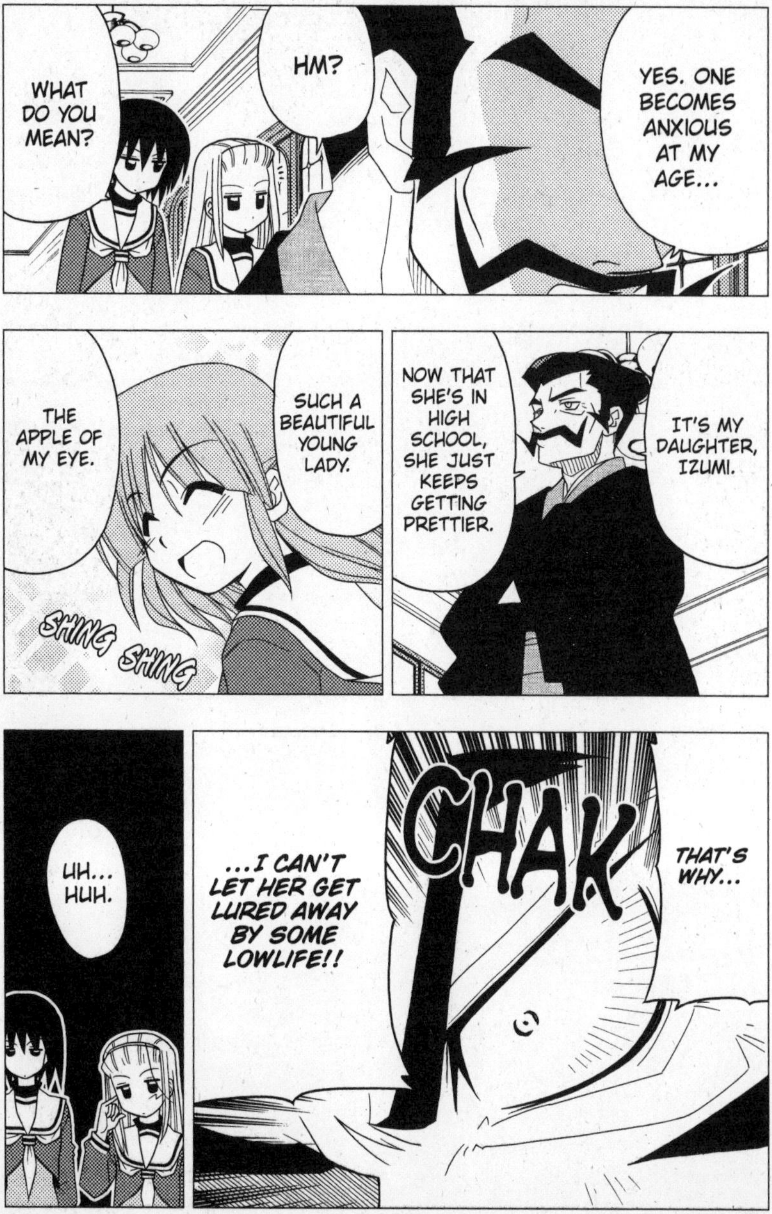
YES. ONE BECOMES ANXIOUS AT MY AGE...
HM?
WHAT DO YOU MEAN?
IT'S MY DAUGHTER, IZUMI.
NOW THAT SHE'S IN HIGH SCHOOL, SHE JUST KEEPS GETTING PRETTIER.
SUCH A BEAUTIFUL YOUNG LADY.
THE APPLE OF MY EYE.
SHING SHING
THAT'S WHY...
CHAK
...I CAN'T LET HER GET LURED AWAY BY SOME LOWLIFE!!
UH... HUH.

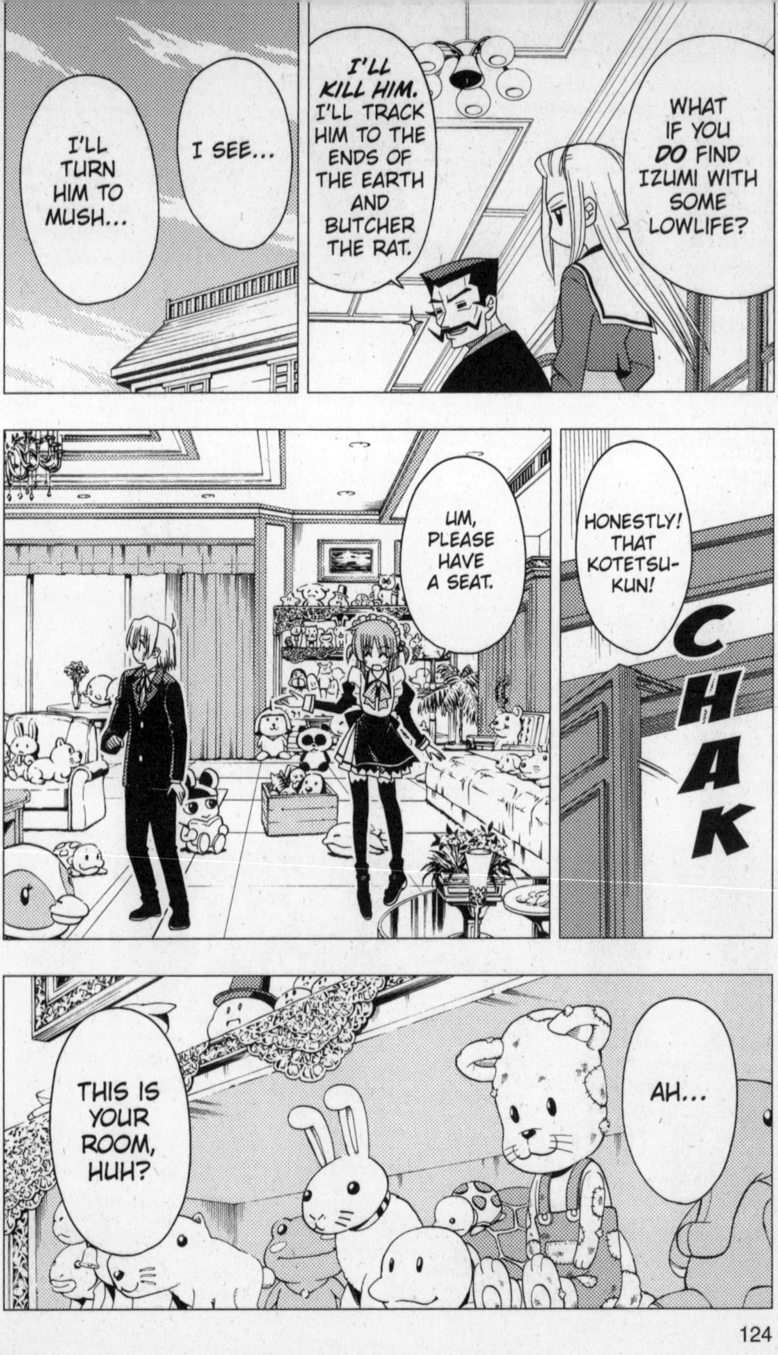
WHAT IF YOU DO FIND IZUMI WITH SOME LOWLIFE?
I'LL KILL HIM. I'LL TRACK HIM TO THE ENDS OF THE EARTH AND BUTCHER THE RAT.
I SEE...
I'LL TURN HIM TO MUSH...
HONESTLY! THAT KOTETSU-KUN!
CHAK
UM, PLEASE HAVE A SEAT.
AH...
THIS IS YOUR ROOM, HUH?

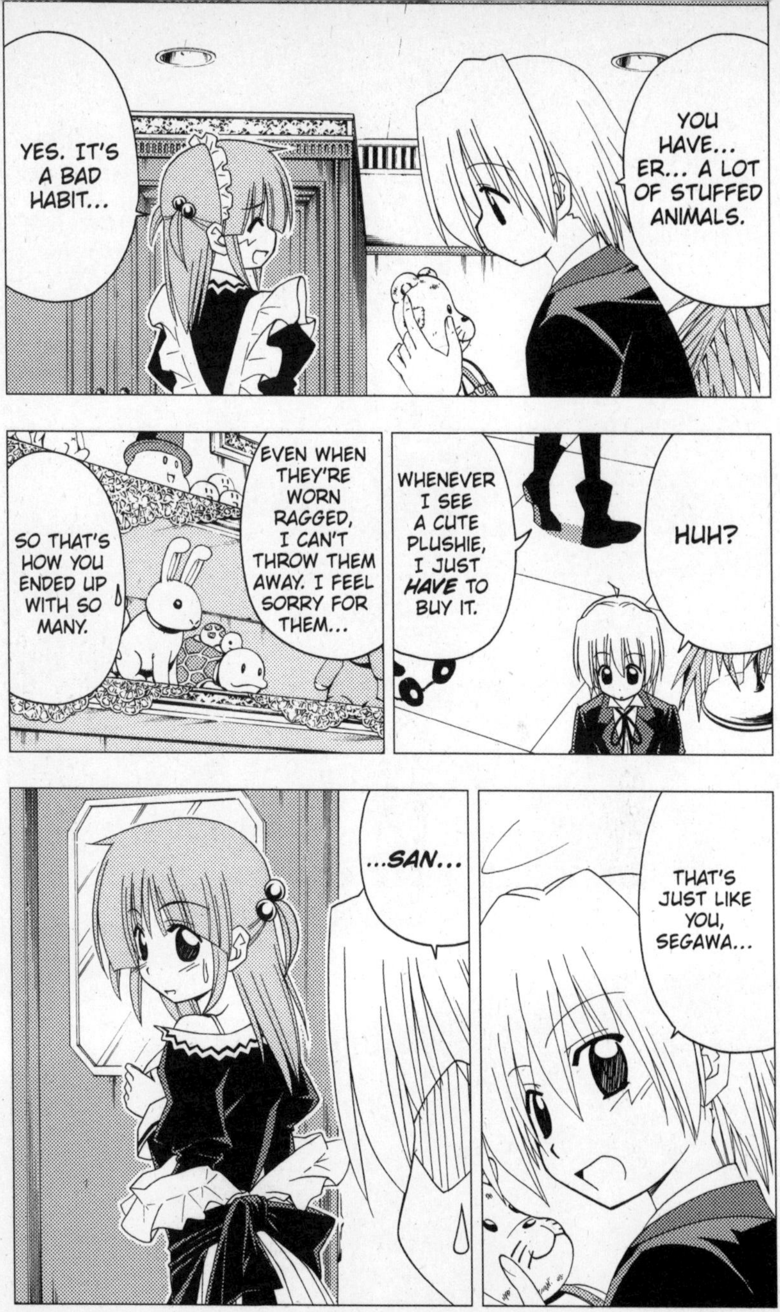
YOU HAVE... ER... A LOT OF STUFFED ANIMALS.
YES. IT'S A BAD HABIT...
HUH?
WHENEVER I SEE A CUTE PLUSHIE, I JUST *HAVE* TO BUY IT.
EVEN WHEN THEY'RE WORN RAGGED, I CAN'T THROW THEM AWAY. I FEEL SORRY FOR THEM...
SO THAT'S HOW YOU ENDED UP WITH SO MANY.
THAT'S JUST LIKE YOU, SEGAWA...
...*SAN*...

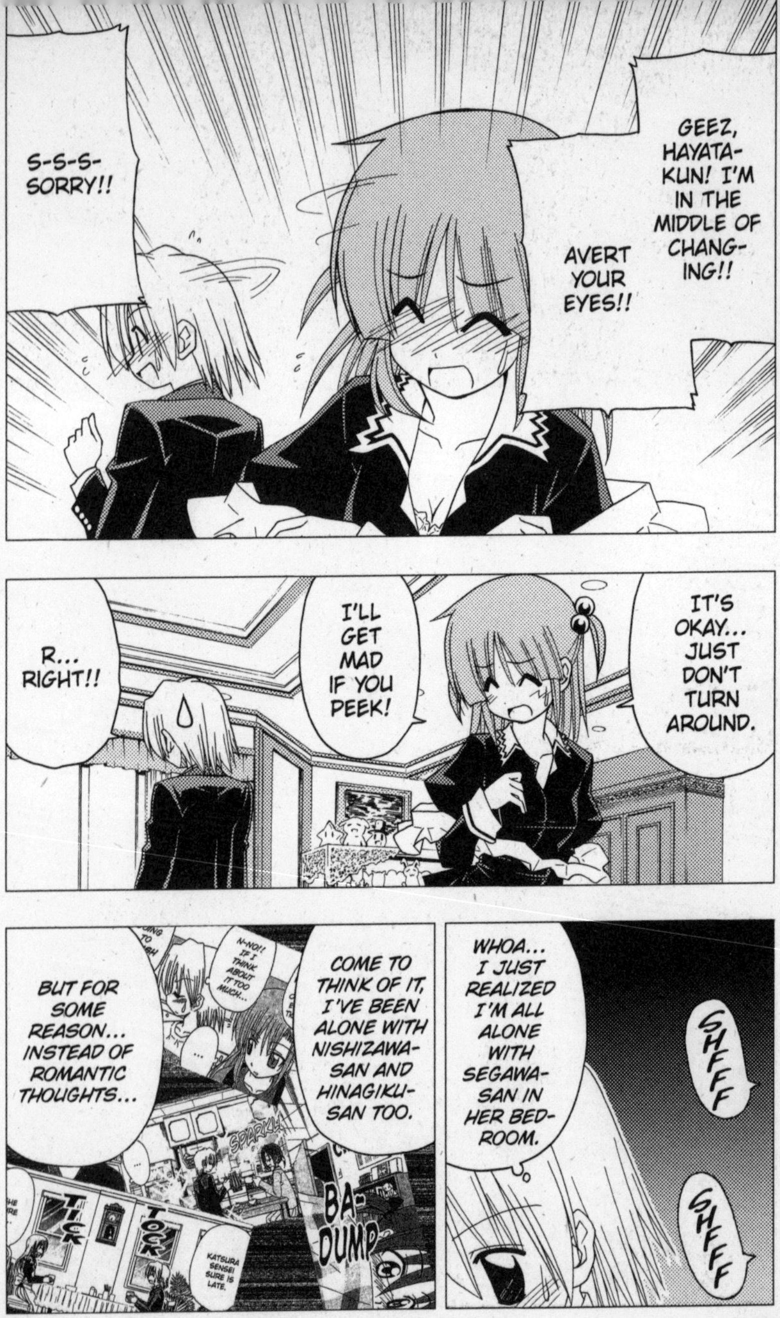
GEEZ, HAYATA-KUN! I'M IN THE MIDDLE OF CHANGING!!
AVERT YOUR EYES!!
S-S-S-SORRY!!
IT'S OKAY... JUST DON'T TURN AROUND.
I'LL GET MAD IF YOU PEEK!
R... RIGHT!!
SHFFF
SHFFF
WHOA... I JUST REALIZED I'M ALL ALONE WITH SEGAWA-SAN IN HER BEDROOM.
COME TO THINK OF IT, I'VE BEEN ALONE WITH NISHIZAWA-SAN AND HINAGIKU-SAN TOO.
N-NO!! IF I THINK ABOUT IT TOO MUCH...
...
SPARKLE
BA-DUMP
BUT FOR SOME REASON... INSTEAD OF ROMANTIC THOUGHTS...
...
TICK
TOCK
KATSURA SENSEI SURE IS LATE.

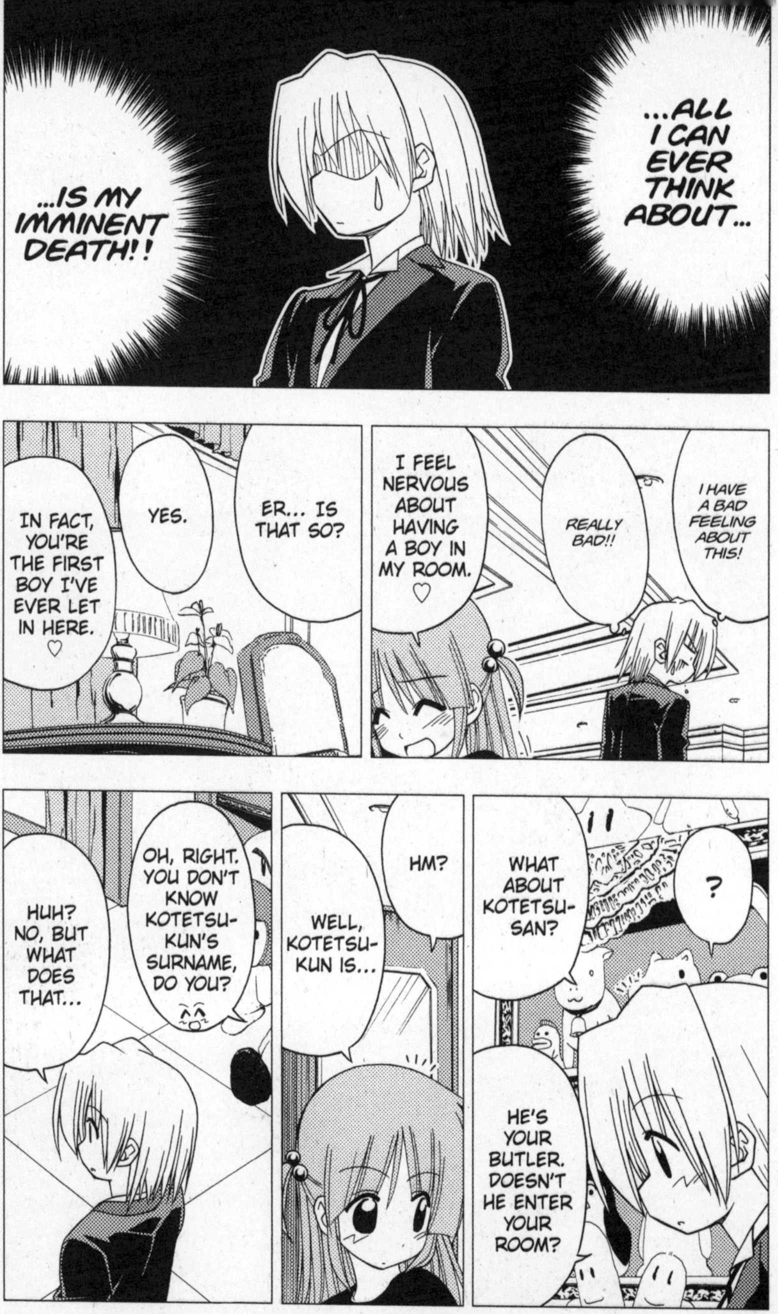
...ALL I CAN EVER THINK ABOUT...
...IS MY IMMINENT DEATH!!
I HAVE A BAD FEELING ABOUT THIS!
REALLY BAD!!
I FEEL NERVOUS ABOUT HAVING A BOY IN MY ROOM. ♡
ER... IS THAT SO?
YES.
IN FACT, YOU'RE THE FIRST BOY I'VE EVER LET IN HERE. ♡
?
WHAT ABOUT KOTETSU-SAN?
HE'S YOUR BUTLER. DOESN'T HE ENTER YOUR ROOM?
HM?
WELL, KOTETSU-KUN IS...
OH, RIGHT. YOU DON'T KNOW KOTETSU-KUN'S SURNAME, DO YOU?
HUH? NO, BUT WHAT DOES THAT...

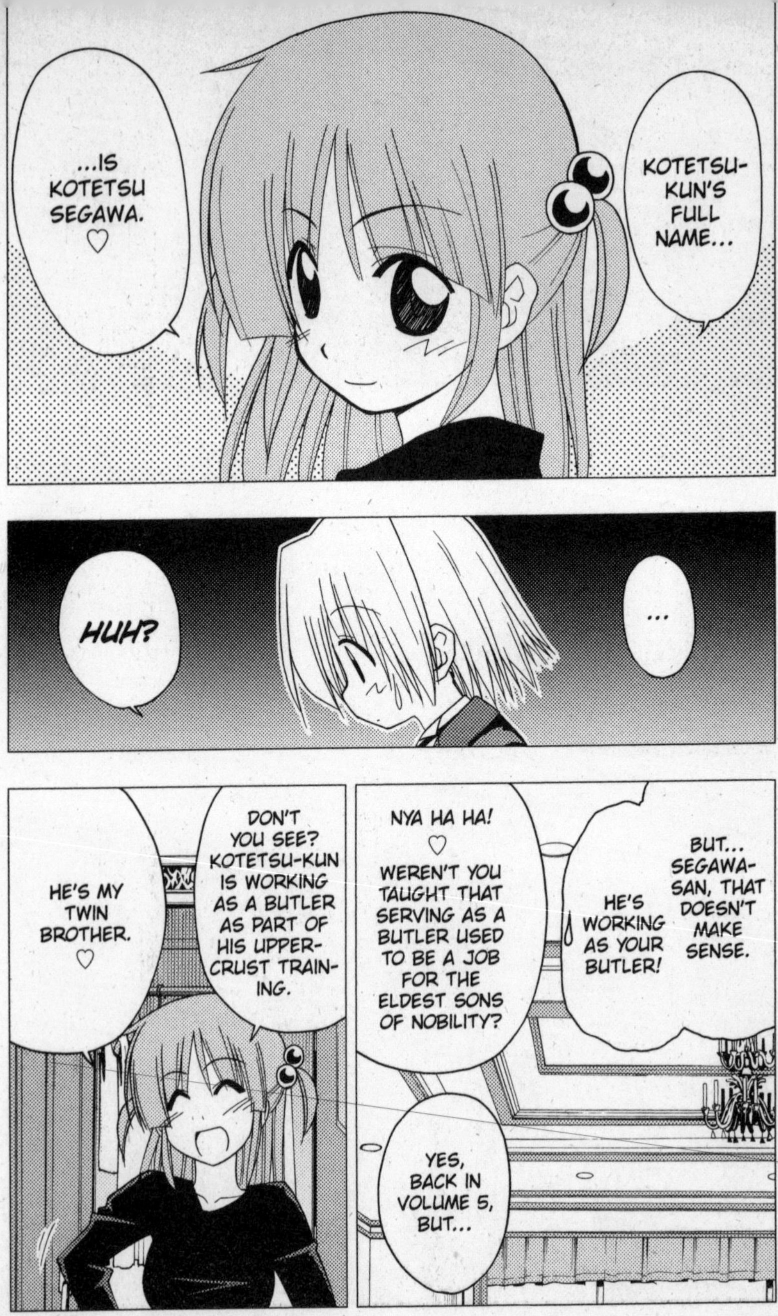
KOTETSU-KUN'S FULL NAME...
...IS KOTETSU SEGAWA. ♡
...
HUH?
BUT... SEGAWA-SAN, THAT DOESN'T MAKE SENSE.
HE'S WORKING AS YOUR BUTLER!
NYA HA HA! ♡ WEREN'T YOU TAUGHT THAT SERVING AS A BUTLER USED TO BE A JOB FOR THE ELDEST SONS OF NOBILITY?
YES, BACK IN VOLUME 5, BUT...
DON'T YOU SEE? KOTETSU-KUN IS WORKING AS A BUTLER AS PART OF HIS UPPER-CRUST TRAINING.
HE'S MY TWIN BROTHER. ♡

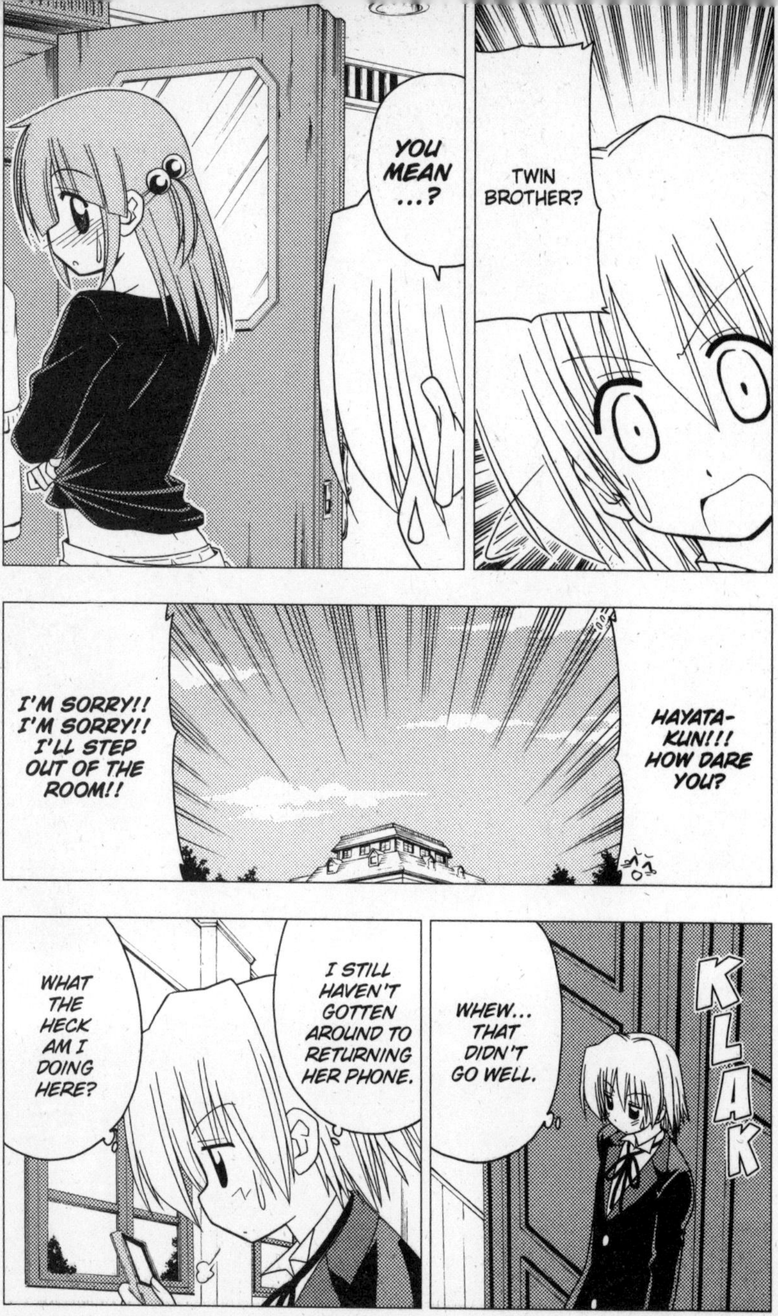
TWIN BROTHER?
YOU MEAN ...?
HAYATA-KUN!!! HOW DARE YOU?
I'M SORRY!! I'M SORRY!! I'LL STEP OUT OF THE ROOM!!
KLAK
WHEW... THAT DIDN'T GO WELL.
I STILL HAVEN'T GOTTEN AROUND TO RETURNING HER PHONE.
WHAT THE HECK AM I DOING HERE?

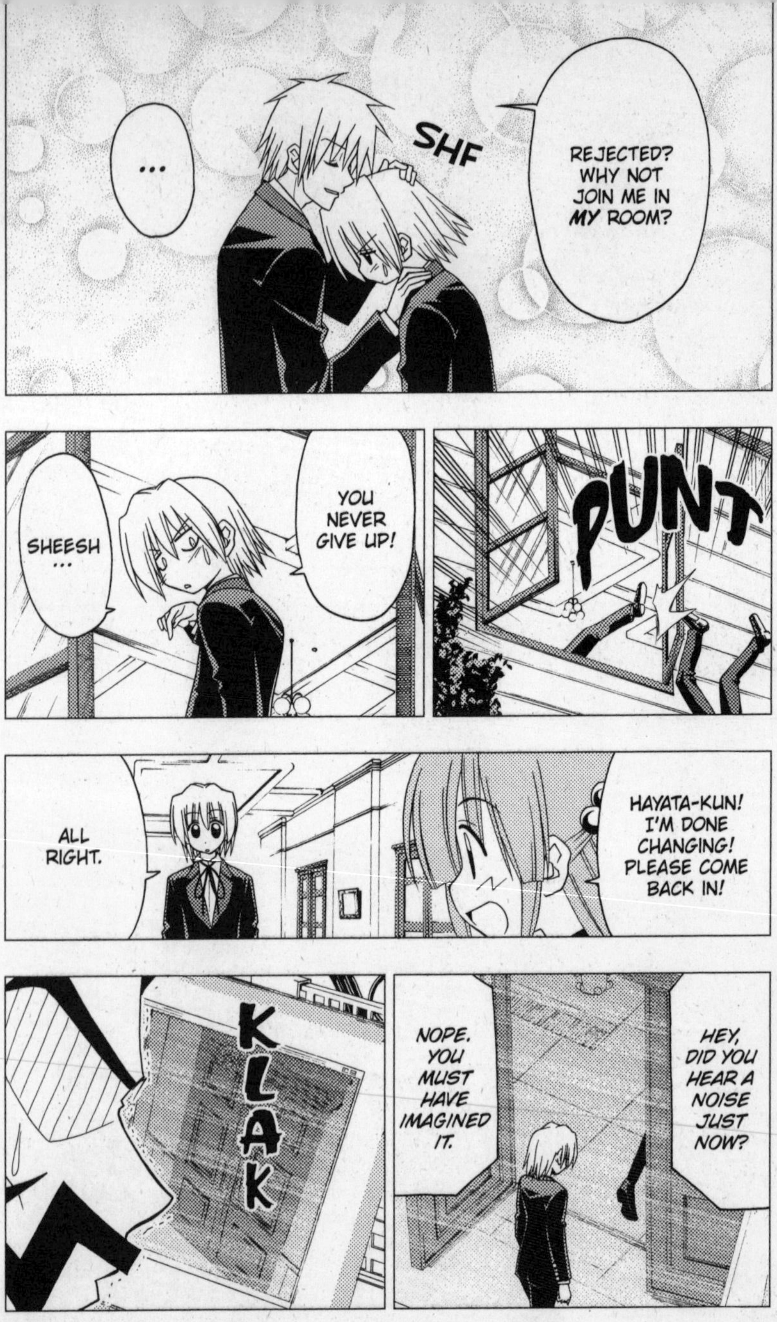
REJECTED? WHY NOT JOIN ME IN MY ROOM?
SHF
...
PUNT
YOU NEVER GIVE UP!
SHEESH ...
HAYATA-KUN! I'M DONE CHANGING! PLEASE COME BACK IN!
ALL RIGHT.
HEY, DID YOU HEAR A NOISE JUST NOW?
NOPE. YOU MUST HAVE IMAGINED IT.
KLAK

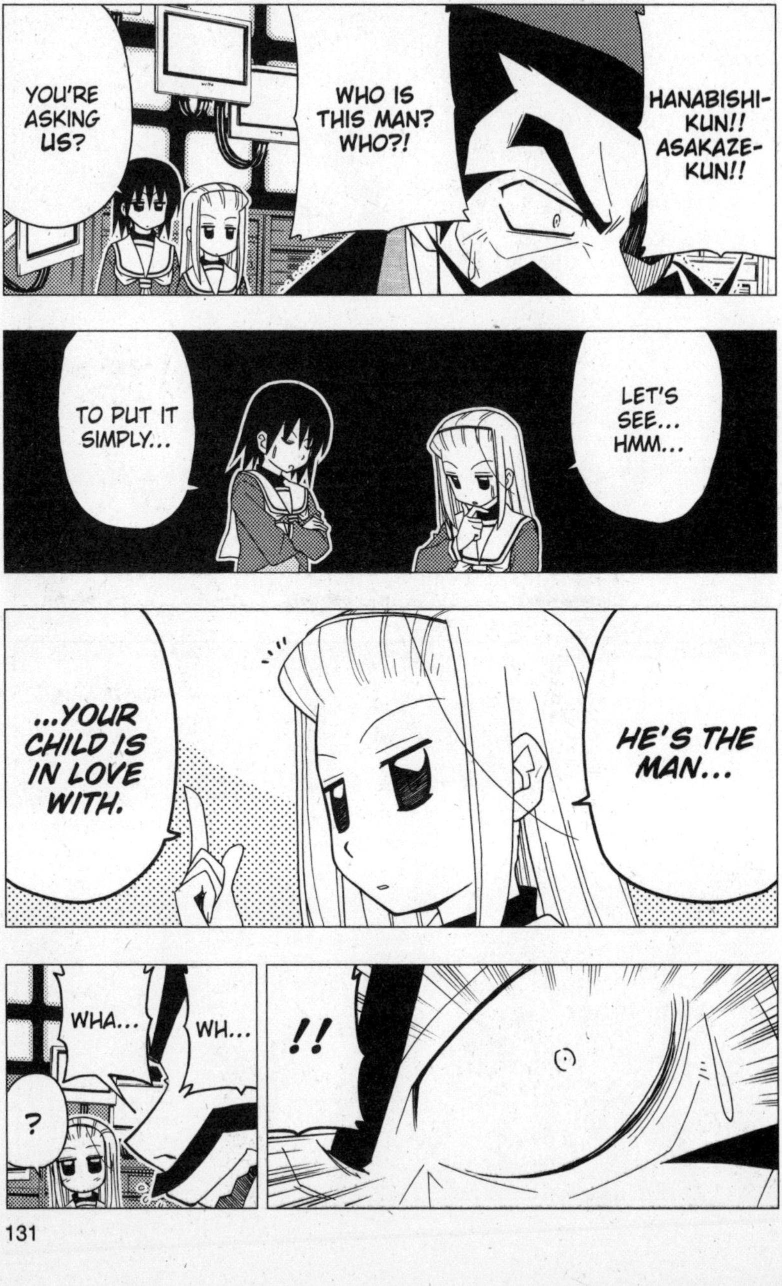
HANABISHI-KUN!! ASAKAZE-KUN!!
WHO IS THIS MAN? WHO?!
YOU'RE ASKING US?
LET'S SEE... HMM...
TO PUT IT SIMPLY...
HE'S THE MAN...
...YOUR CHILD IS IN LOVE WITH.
!!
WH...
WHA...
?

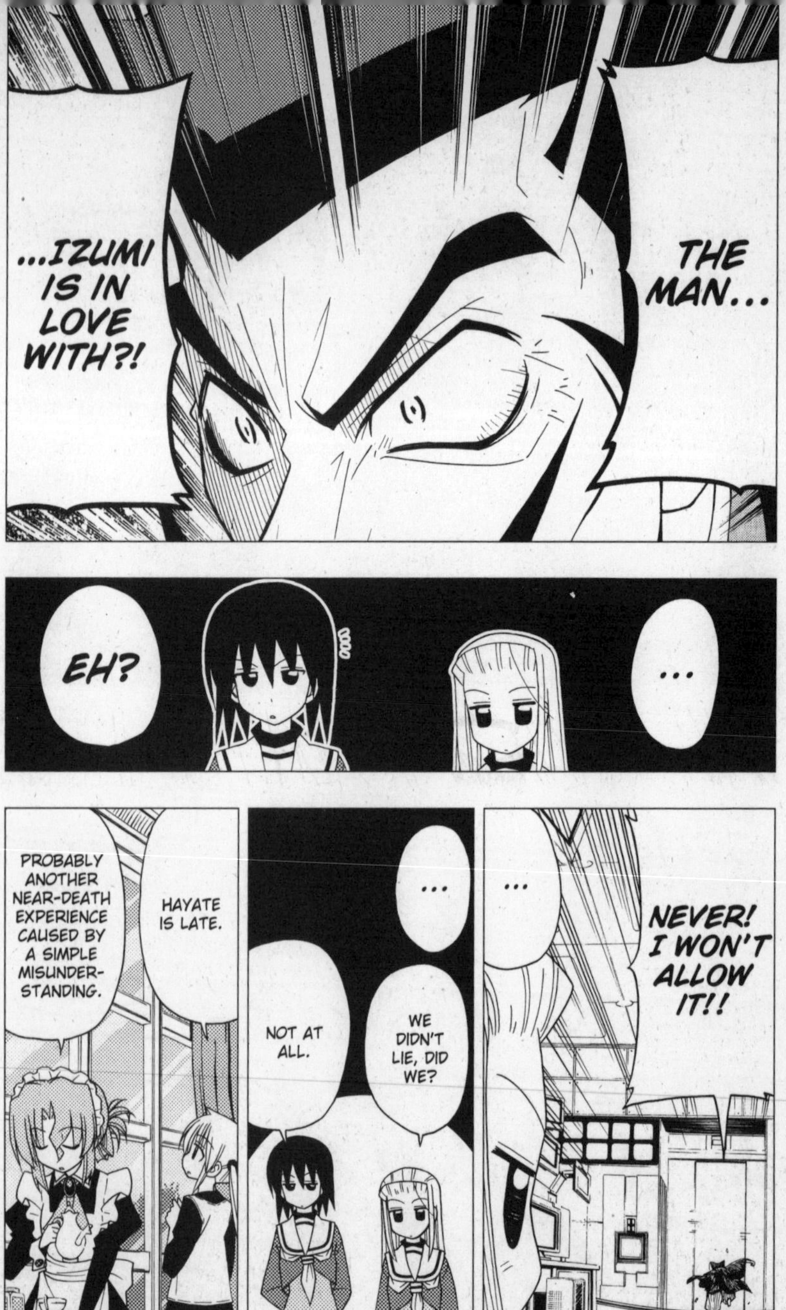
THE MAN...
...IZUMI IS IN LOVE WITH?!
...
EH?
NEVER! I WON'T ALLOW IT!!
...
...
WE DIDN'T LIE, DID WE?
NOT AT ALL.
HAYATE IS LATE.
PROBABLY ANOTHER NEAR-DEATH EXPERIENCE CAUSED BY A SIMPLE MISUNDER-STANDING.

Episode 9: "When You Beat the Bushes, Snakes Appear, Corpses Apear, Nothing Good Happens"

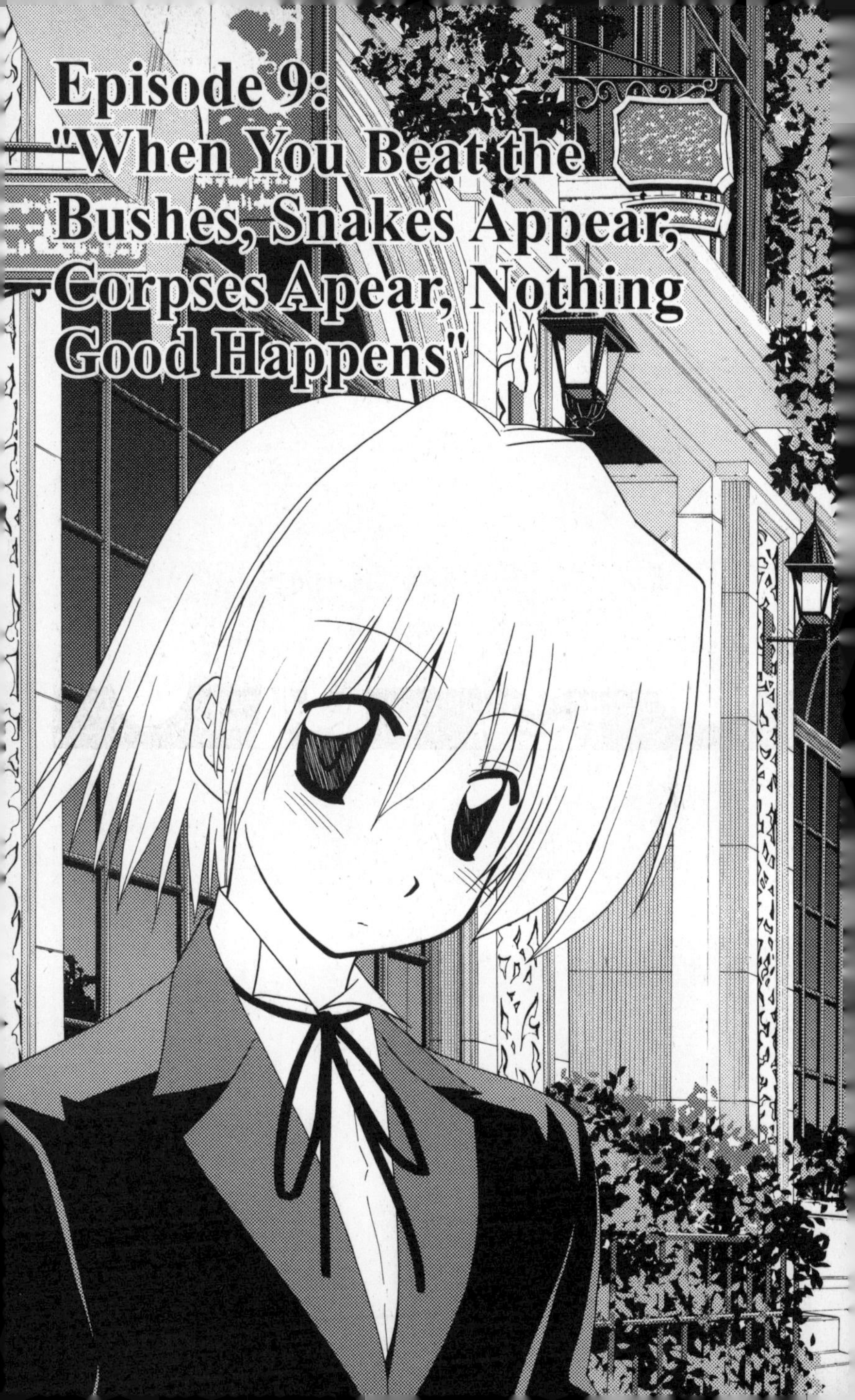

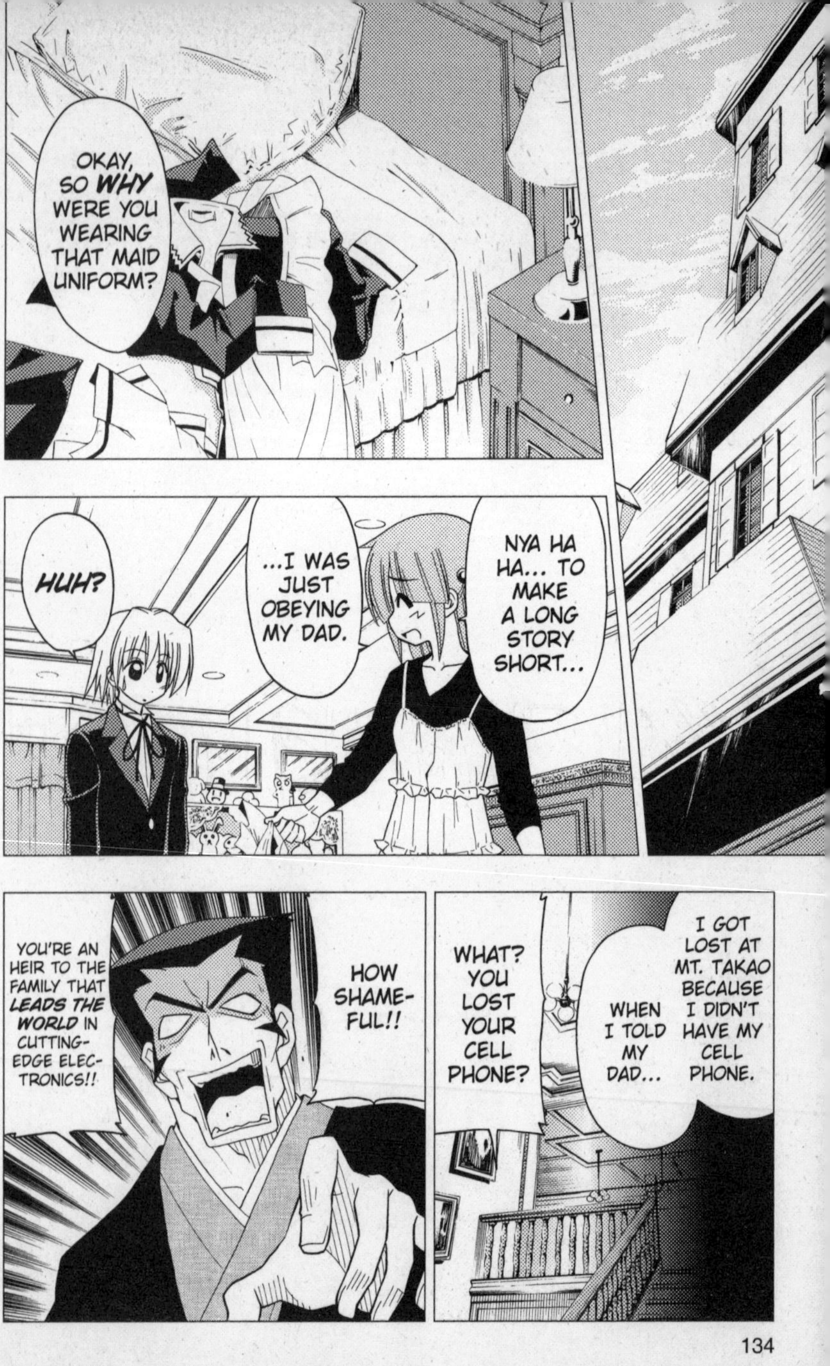
OKAY, SO WHY WERE YOU WEARING THAT MAID UNIFORM?
NYA HA HA... TO MAKE A LONG STORY SHORT...
...I WAS JUST OBEYING MY DAD.
HUH?
I GOT LOST AT MT. TAKAO BECAUSE I DIDN'T HAVE MY CELL PHONE.
WHEN I TOLD MY DAD...
WHAT? YOU LOST YOUR CELL PHONE?
HOW SHAME-FUL!!
YOU'RE AN HEIR TO THE FAMILY THAT LEADS THE WORLD IN CUTTING-EDGE ELEC-TRONICS!!

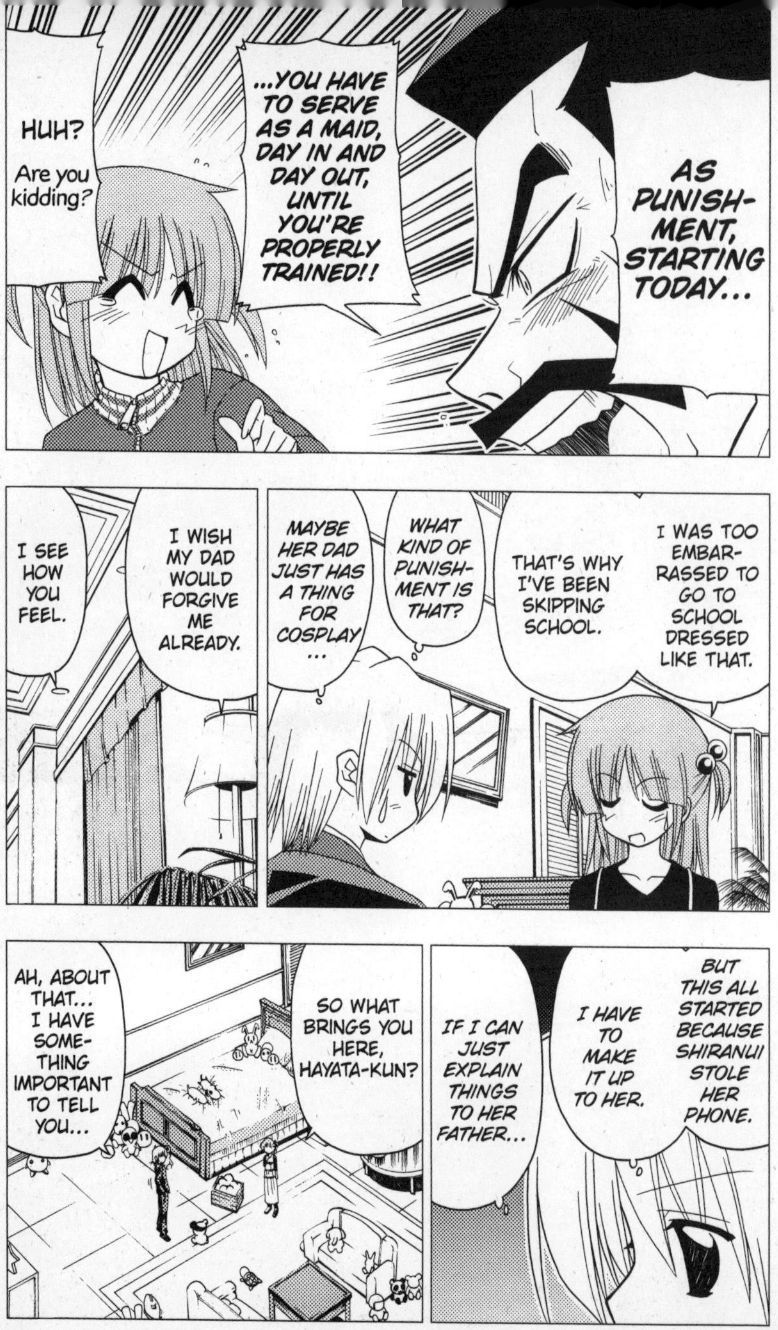
AS PUNISH-MENT, STARTING TODAY...
...YOU HAVE TO SERVE AS A MAID, DAY IN AND DAY OUT, UNTIL YOU'RE PROPERLY TRAINED!!
HUH?
Are you kidding?
I WAS TOO EMBAR-RASSED TO GO TO SCHOOL DRESSED LIKE THAT.
THAT'S WHY I'VE BEEN SKIPPING SCHOOL.
WHAT KIND OF PUNISH-MENT IS THAT?
MAYBE HER DAD JUST HAS A THING FOR COSPLAY...
I WISH MY DAD WOULD FORGIVE ME ALREADY.
I SEE HOW YOU FEEL.
BUT THIS ALL STARTED BECAUSE SHIRANUI STOLE HER PHONE.
I HAVE TO MAKE IT UP TO HER.
IF I CAN JUST EXPLAIN THINGS TO HER FATHER...
SO WHAT BRINGS YOU HERE, HAYATA-KUN?
AH, ABOUT THAT... I HAVE SOME-THING IMPORTANT TO TELL YOU...

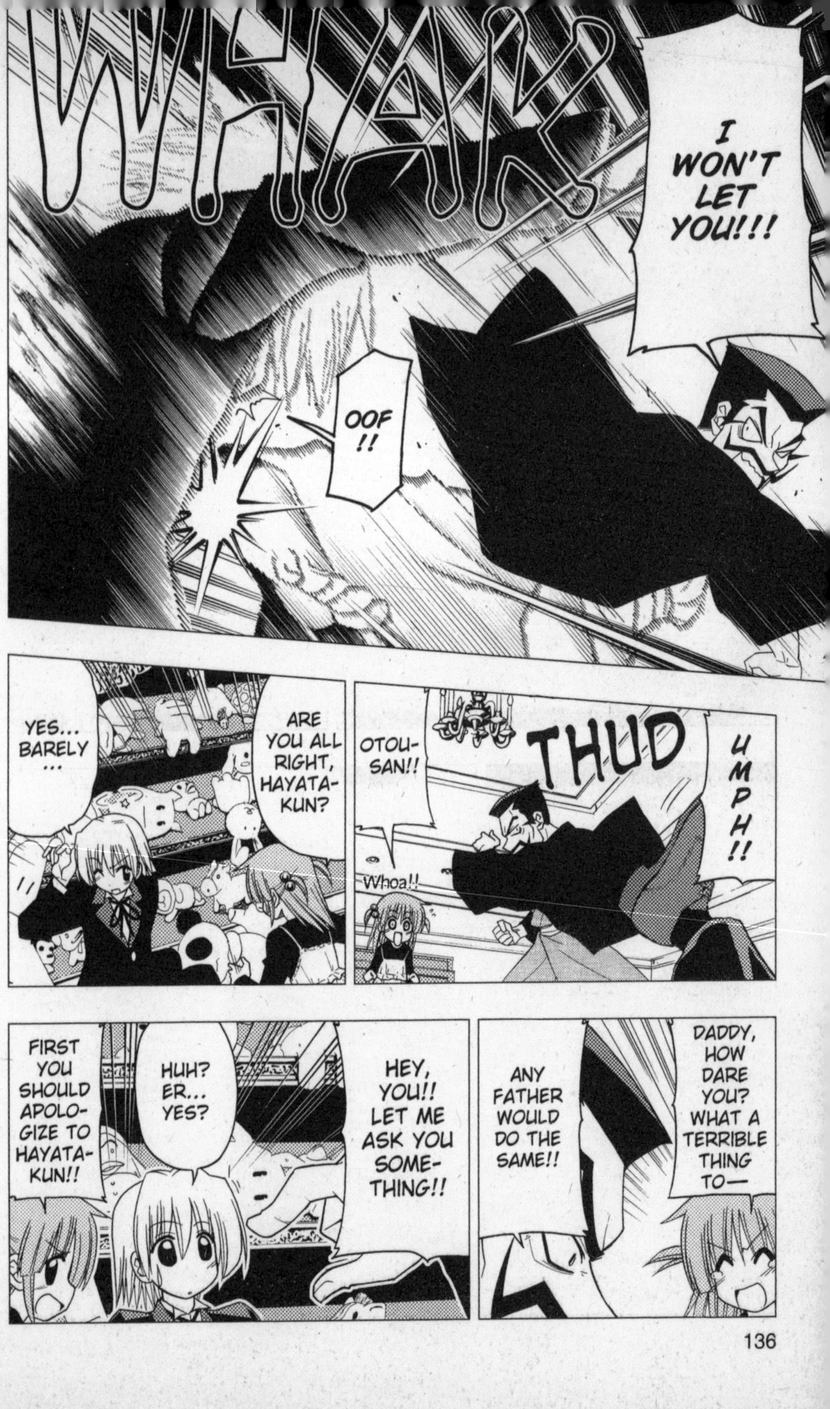
I WON'T LET YOU!!!
WHAK
OOF!!
UMPH!!
THUD
OTOU-SAN!!
Whoa!!
ARE YOU ALL RIGHT, HAYATA-KUN?
YES... BARELY...
DADDY, HOW DARE YOU? WHAT A TERRIBLE THING TO—
ANY FATHER WOULD DO THE SAME!!
HEY, YOU!! LET ME ASK YOU SOME-THING!!
HUH? ER... YES?
FIRST YOU SHOULD APOLOGIZE TO HAYATA-KUN!!

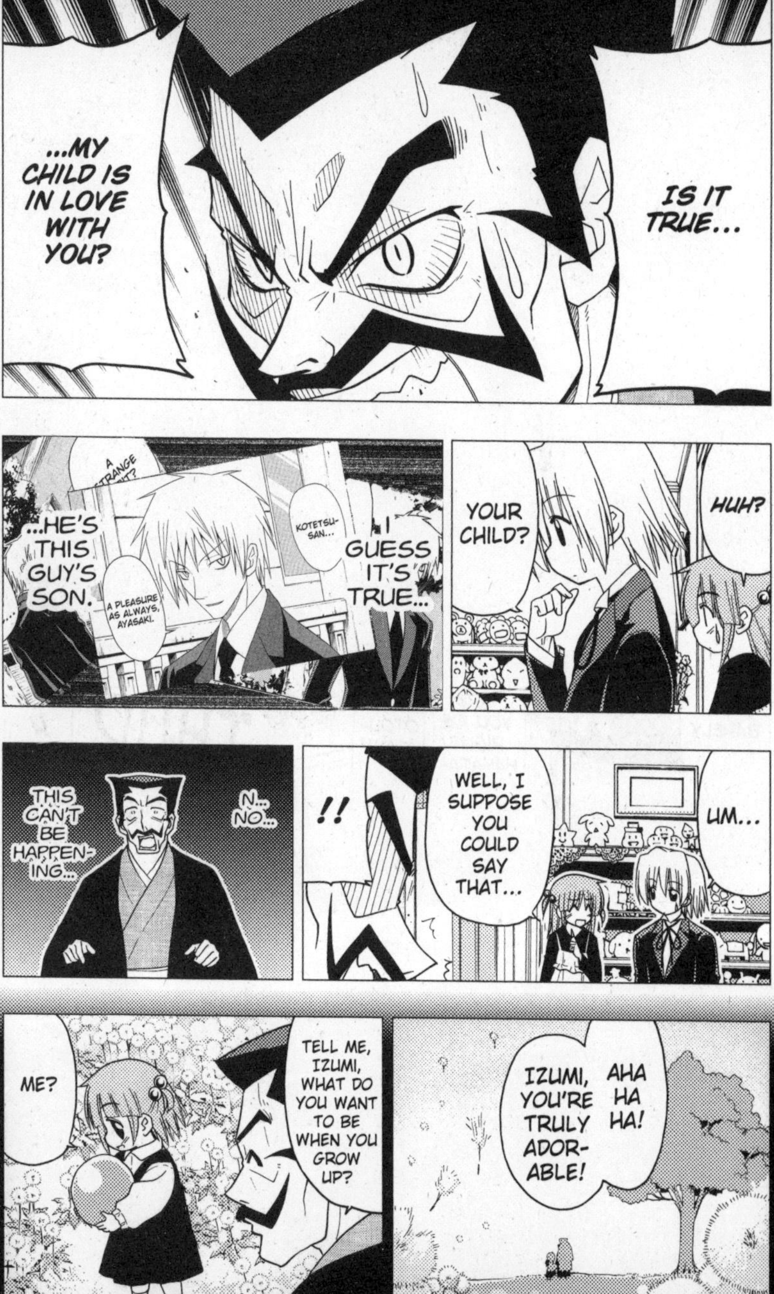
IS IT TRUE...
...MY CHILD IS IN LOVE WITH YOU?
HUH?
YOUR CHILD?
I GUESS IT'S TRUE...
KOTETSU-SAN...
A PLEASURE AS ALWAYS, AYASAKI.
...HE'S THIS GUY'S SON.
UM...
WELL, I SUPPOSE YOU COULD SAY THAT...
!!
N... NO...
THIS CAN'T BE HAPPENING...
AHA HA HA!
IZUMI, YOU'RE TRULY ADORABLE!
TELL ME, IZUMI, WHAT DO YOU WANT TO BE WHEN YOU GROW UP?
ME?

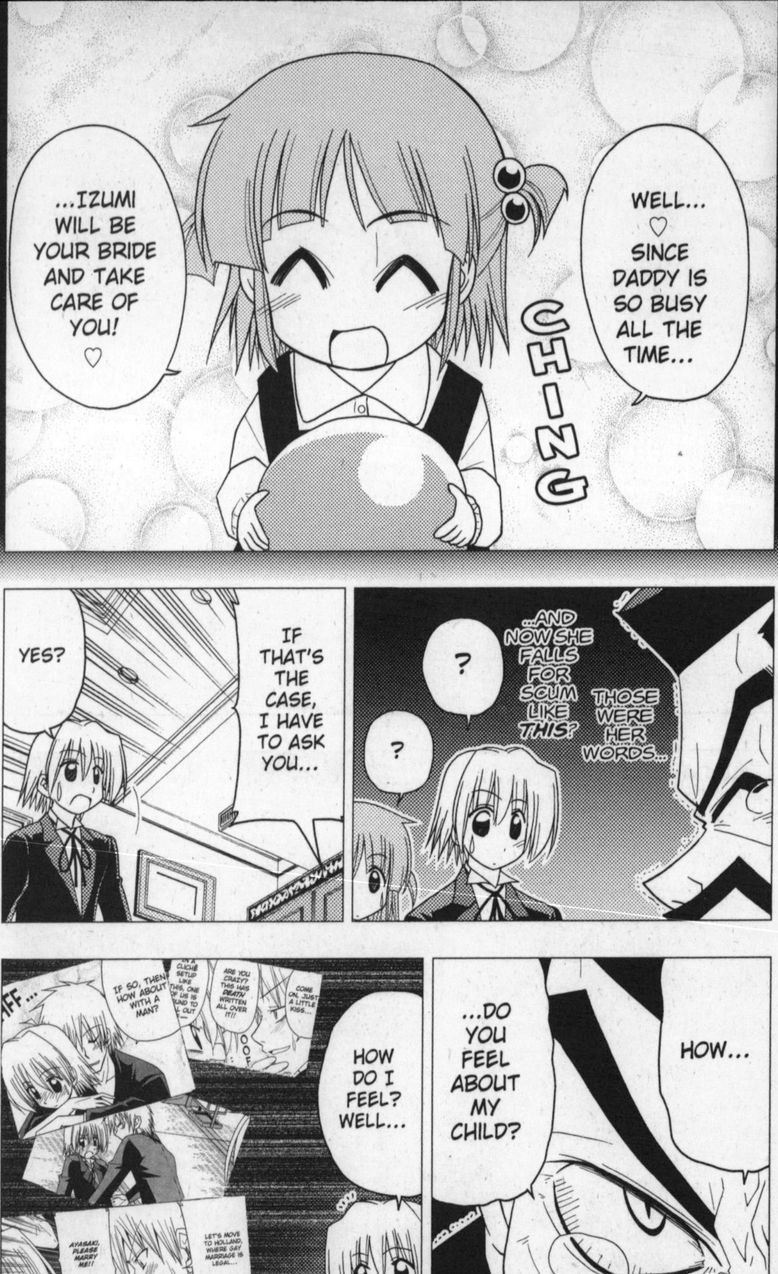
WELL... ♡ SINCE DADDY IS SO BUSY ALL THE TIME...
CHING
...IZUMI WILL BE YOUR BRIDE AND TAKE CARE OF YOU! ♡
...AND NOW SHE FALLS FOR SCUM LIKE *THIS*?
THOSE WERE HER WORDS...
?
?
IF THAT'S THE CASE, I HAVE TO ASK YOU...
YES?
HOW...
...DO YOU FEEL ABOUT MY CHILD?
HOW DO I FEEL? WELL...
COME ON, JUST A LITTLE KISS...
ARE YOU CRAZY? THIS HAS *DEATH* WRITTEN ALL OVER IT!!
OOF
CLICHÉ SETUP LIKE THIS, ONE
IF SO, THEN HOW ABOUT WITH A MAN?
LET'S MOVE TO HOLLAND, WHERE GAY MARRIAGE IS LEGAL...
AYASAKI, PLEASE MARRY ME!!

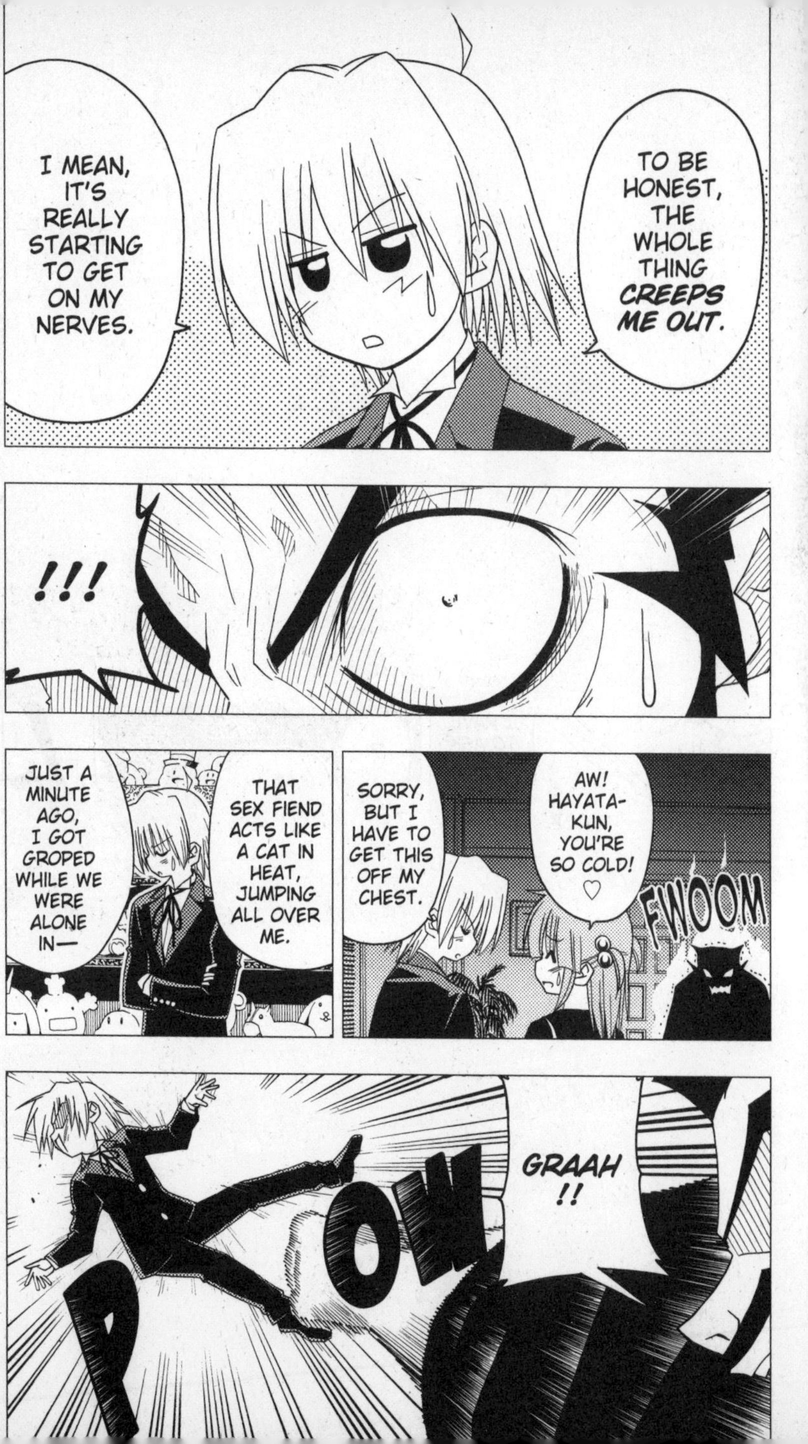
TO BE HONEST, THE WHOLE THING CREEPS ME OUT.
I MEAN, IT'S REALLY STARTING TO GET ON MY NERVES.
!!!
AW! HAYATA-KUN, YOU'RE SO COLD! ♡
FWOOM
SORRY, BUT I HAVE TO GET THIS OFF MY CHEST.
THAT SEX FIEND ACTS LIKE A CAT IN HEAT, JUMPING ALL OVER ME.
JUST A MINUTE AGO, I GOT GROPED WHILE WE WERE ALONE IN—
GRAAH !!
POW

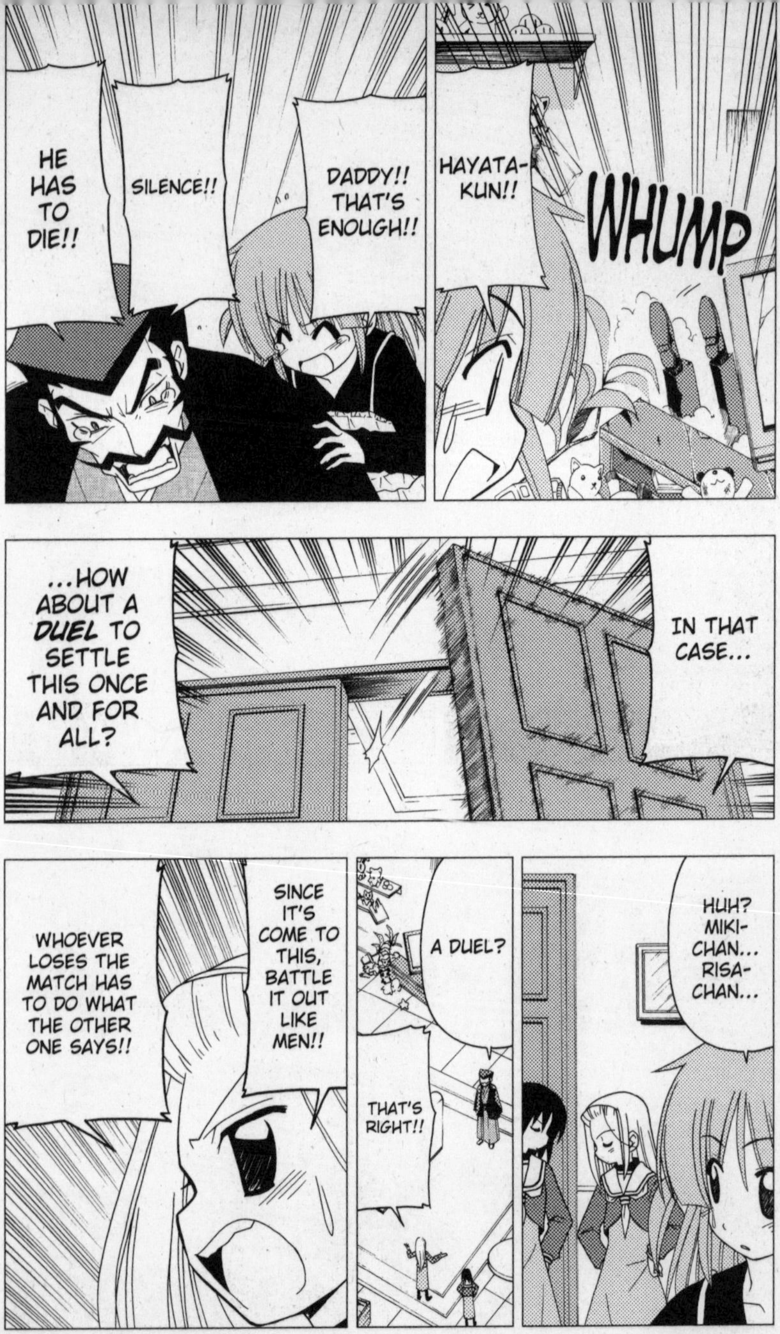
HAYATA-KUN!!
WHUMP
DADDY!! THAT'S ENOUGH!!
SILENCE!!
HE HAS TO DIE!!
IN THAT CASE...
...HOW ABOUT A DUEL TO SETTLE THIS ONCE AND FOR ALL?
HUH? MIKI-CHAN... RISA-CHAN...
A DUEL?
THAT'S RIGHT!!
SINCE IT'S COME TO THIS, BATTLE IT OUT LIKE MEN!!
WHOEVER LOSES THE MATCH HAS TO DO WHAT THE OTHER ONE SAYS!!

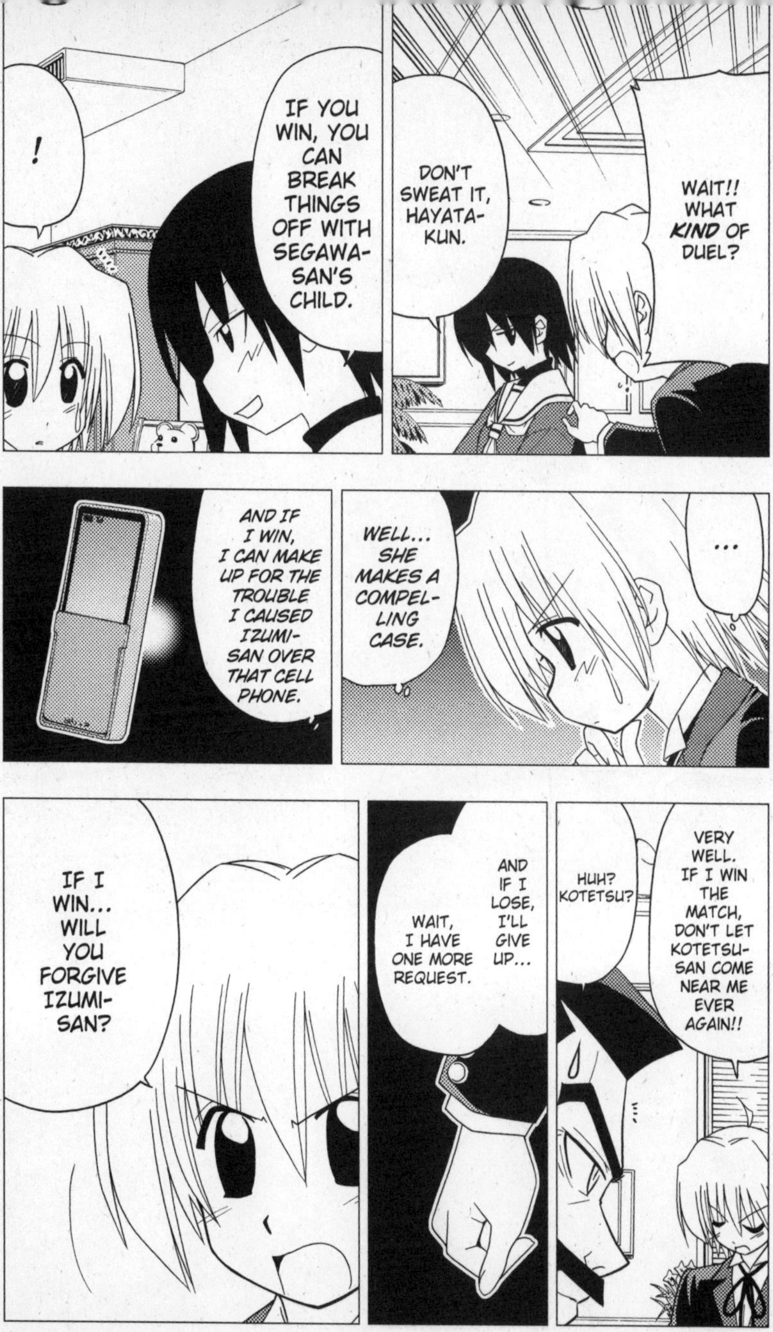
WAIT!! WHAT *KIND* OF DUEL?
DON'T SWEAT IT, HAYATA-KUN.
IF YOU WIN, YOU CAN BREAK THINGS OFF WITH SEGAWA-SAN'S CHILD.
!
...
WELL... SHE MAKES A COMPELLING CASE.
AND IF I WIN, I CAN MAKE UP FOR THE TROUBLE I CAUSED IZUMI-SAN OVER THAT CELL PHONE.
VERY WELL. IF I WIN THE MATCH, DON'T LET KOTETSU-SAN COME NEAR ME EVER AGAIN!!
HUH? KOTETSU?
AND IF I LOSE, I'LL GIVE UP...
WAIT, I HAVE ONE MORE REQUEST.
IF I WIN... WILL YOU FORGIVE IZUMI-SAN?

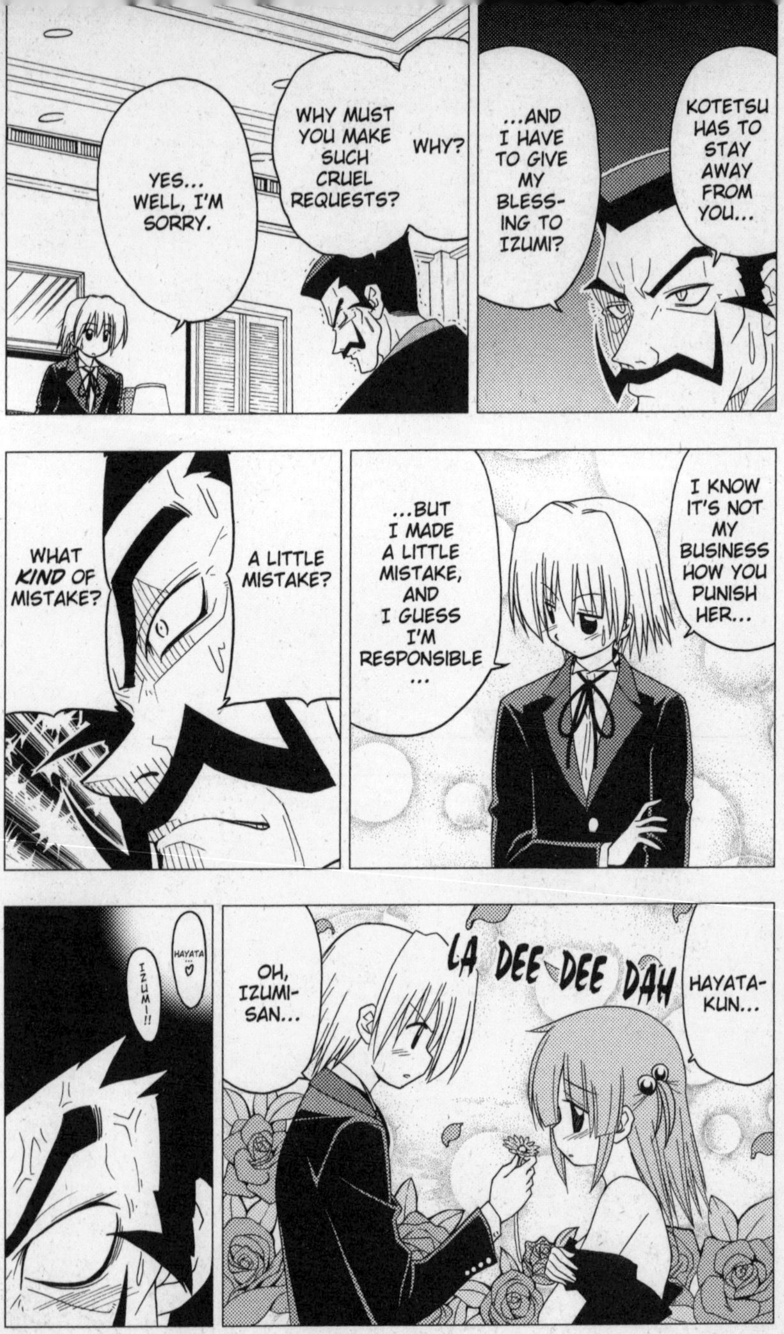
KOTETSU HAS TO STAY AWAY FROM YOU...
...AND I HAVE TO GIVE MY BLESS-ING TO IZUMI?
WHY?
WHY MUST YOU MAKE SUCH CRUEL REQUESTS?
YES... WELL, I'M SORRY.
I KNOW IT'S NOT MY BUSINESS HOW YOU PUNISH HER...
...BUT I MADE A LITTLE MISTAKE, AND I GUESS I'M RESPONSIBLE ...
A LITTLE MISTAKE?
WHAT *KIND* OF MISTAKE?
HAYATA-KUN...
LA DEE DEE DAH
OH, IZUMI-SAN...
HAYATA... ♡
IZUMI!!

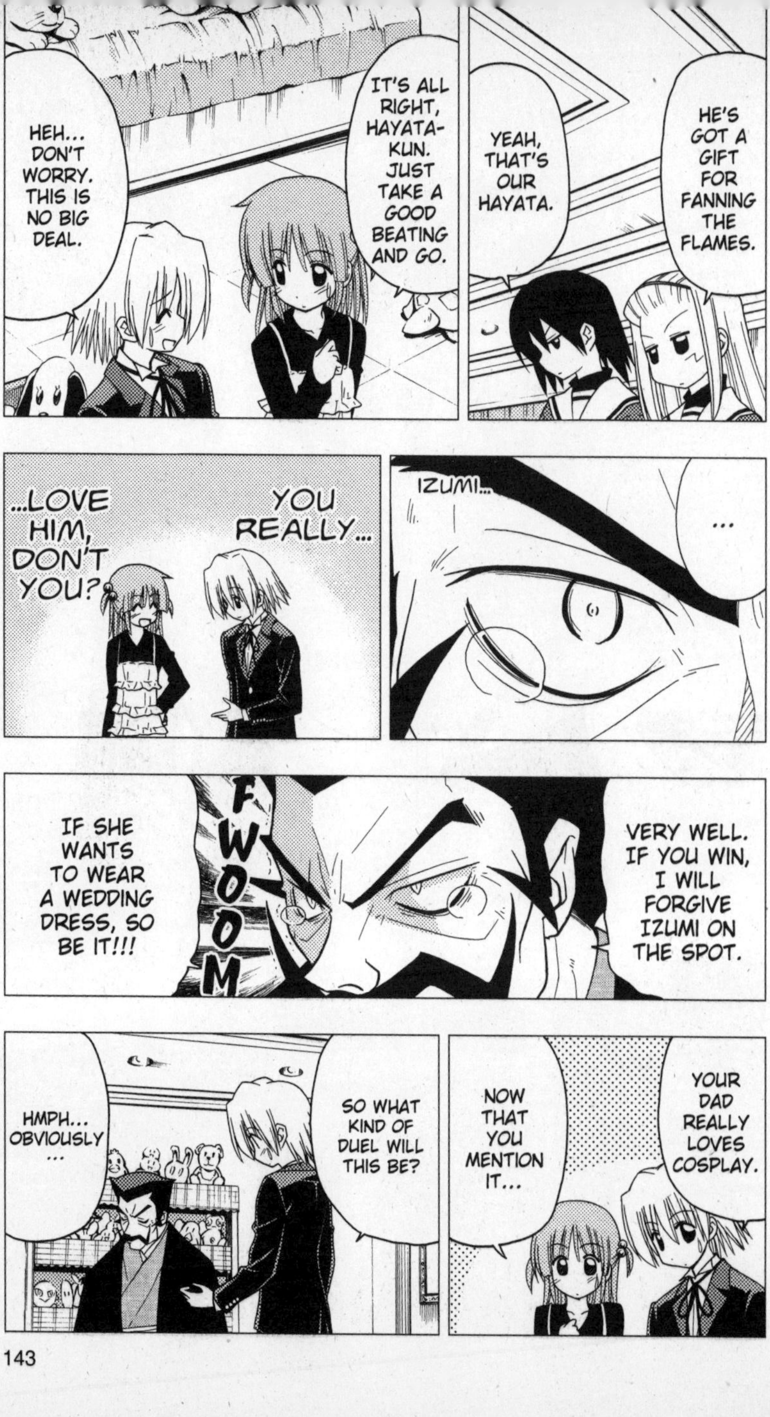
HE'S GOT A GIFT FOR FANNING THE FLAMES.
YEAH, THAT'S OUR HAYATA.
IT'S ALL RIGHT, HAYATA-KUN. JUST TAKE A GOOD BEATING AND GO.
HEH... DON'T WORRY. THIS IS NO BIG DEAL.
...
IZUMI...
YOU REALLY...
...LOVE HIM, DON'T YOU?
VERY WELL. IF YOU WIN, I WILL FORGIVE IZUMI ON THE SPOT.
FWOOM
IF SHE WANTS TO WEAR A WEDDING DRESS, SO BE IT!!!
YOUR DAD REALLY LOVES COSPLAY.
NOW THAT YOU MENTION IT...
SO WHAT KIND OF DUEL WILL THIS BE?
HMPH... OBVIOUSLY...

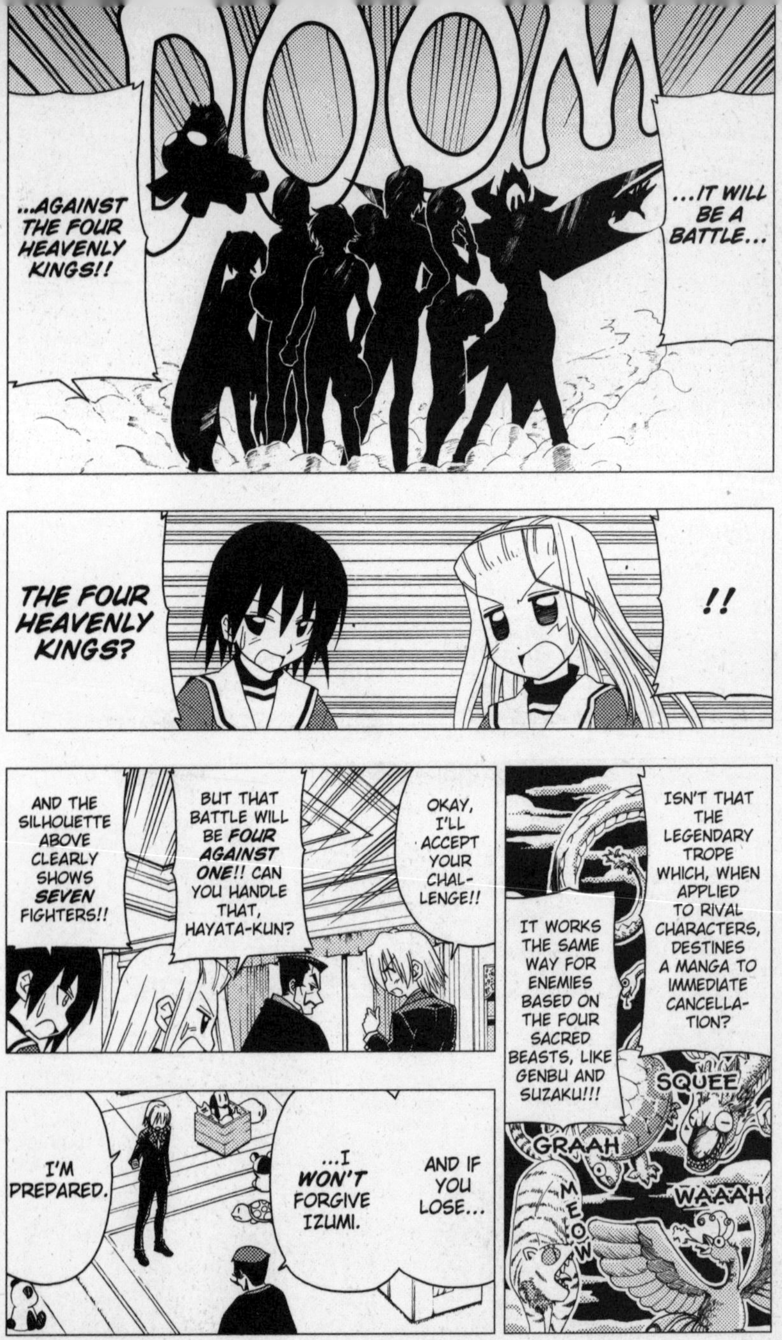
...IT WILL BE A BATTLE...
...AGAINST THE FOUR HEAVENLY KINGS!!
!!
THE FOUR HEAVENLY KINGS?
ISN'T THAT THE LEGENDARY TROPE WHICH, WHEN APPLIED TO RIVAL CHARACTERS, DESTINES A MANGA TO IMMEDIATE CANCELLA-TION?
IT WORKS THE SAME WAY FOR ENEMIES BASED ON THE FOUR SACRED BEASTS, LIKE GENBU AND SUZAKU!!!
SQUEE
GRAAH
WAAAH
MEOW
OKAY, I'LL ACCEPT YOUR CHAL-LENGE!!
BUT THAT BATTLE WILL BE FOUR AGAINST ONE!! CAN YOU HANDLE THAT, HAYATA-KUN?
AND THE SILHOUETTE ABOVE CLEARLY SHOWS SEVEN FIGHTERS!!
AND IF YOU LOSE...
...I WON'T FORGIVE IZUMI.
I'M PREPARED.

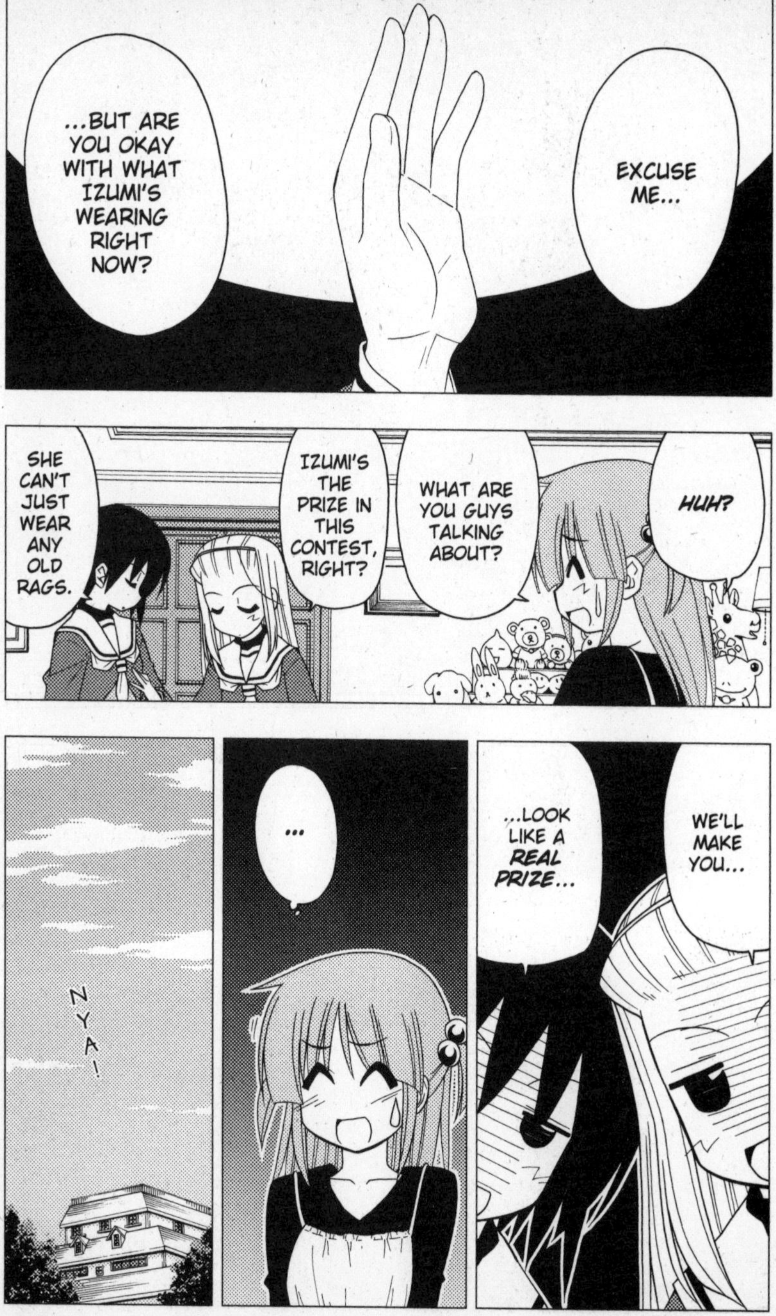
EXCUSE ME...
...BUT ARE YOU OKAY WITH WHAT IZUMI'S WEARING RIGHT NOW?
HUH?
WHAT ARE YOU GUYS TALKING ABOUT?
IZUMI'S THE PRIZE IN THIS CONTEST, RIGHT?
SHE CAN'T JUST WEAR ANY OLD RAGS.
WE'LL MAKE YOU...
...LOOK LIKE A ***REAL PRIZE***...
...
NYA!

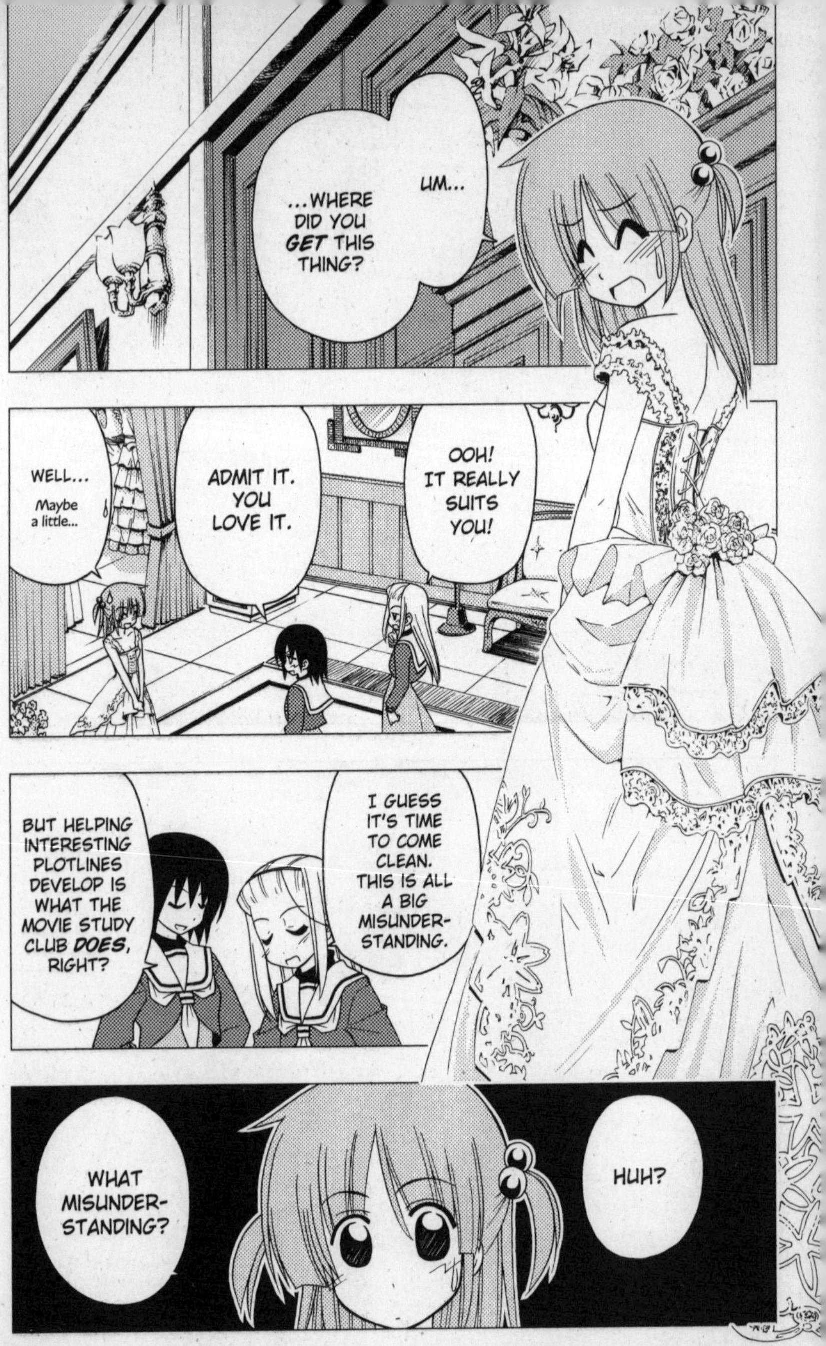
UM...
...WHERE DID YOU GET THIS THING?
OOH! IT REALLY SUITS YOU!
ADMIT IT. YOU LOVE IT.
WELL... Maybe a little...
I GUESS IT'S TIME TO COME CLEAN. THIS IS ALL A BIG MISUNDER-STANDING.
BUT HELPING INTERESTING PLOTLINES DEVELOP IS WHAT THE MOVIE STUDY CLUB DOES, RIGHT?
HUH?
WHAT MISUNDER-STANDING?

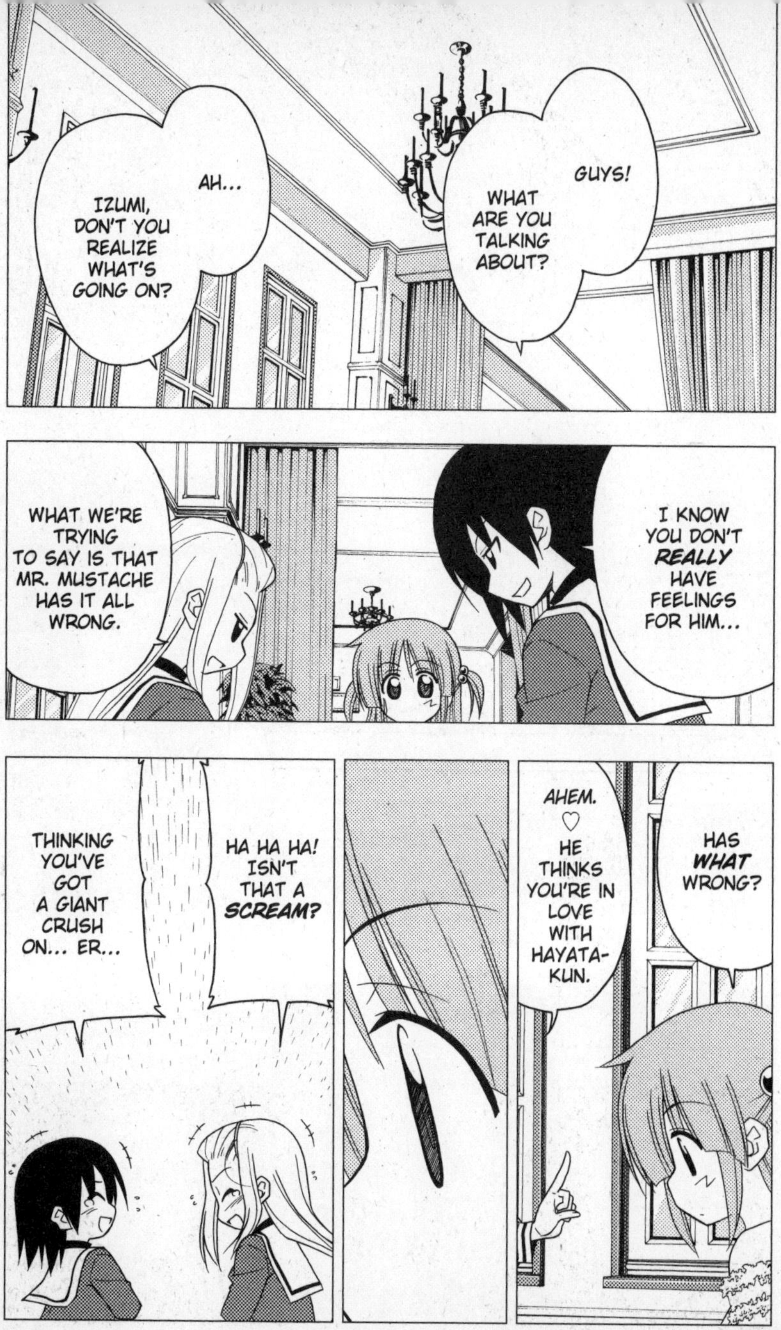
GUYS! WHAT ARE YOU TALKING ABOUT?
AH... IZUMI, DON'T YOU REALIZE WHAT'S GOING ON?
I KNOW YOU DON'T *REALLY* HAVE FEELINGS FOR HIM...
WHAT WE'RE TRYING TO SAY IS THAT MR. MUSTACHE HAS IT ALL WRONG.
HAS *WHAT* WRONG?
AHEM. ♡ HE THINKS YOU'RE IN LOVE WITH HAYATA-KUN.
HA HA HA! ISN'T THAT A *SCREAM?*
THINKING YOU'VE GOT A GIANT CRUSH ON... ER...

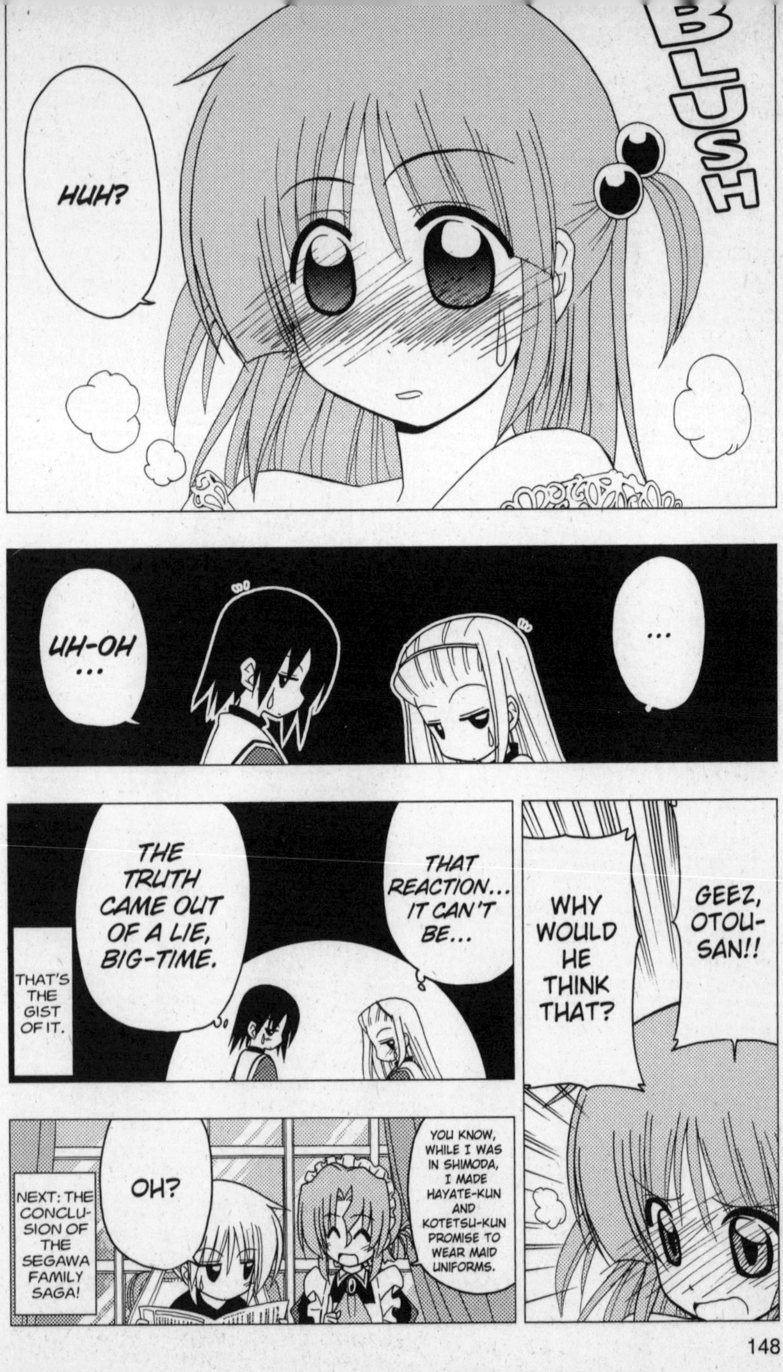
BLUSH
HUH?
...
UH-OH ...
GEEZ, OTOU-SAN!!
WHY WOULD HE THINK THAT?
THAT REACTION... IT CAN'T BE...
THE TRUTH CAME OUT OF A LIE, BIG-TIME.
THAT'S THE GIST OF IT.
YOU KNOW, WHILE I WAS IN SHIMODA, I MADE HAYATE-KUN AND KOTETSU-KUN PROMISE TO WEAR MAID UNIFORMS.
OH?
NEXT: THE CONCLUSION OF THE SEGAWA FAMILY SAGA!

Episode 10: "No Definite Plans"

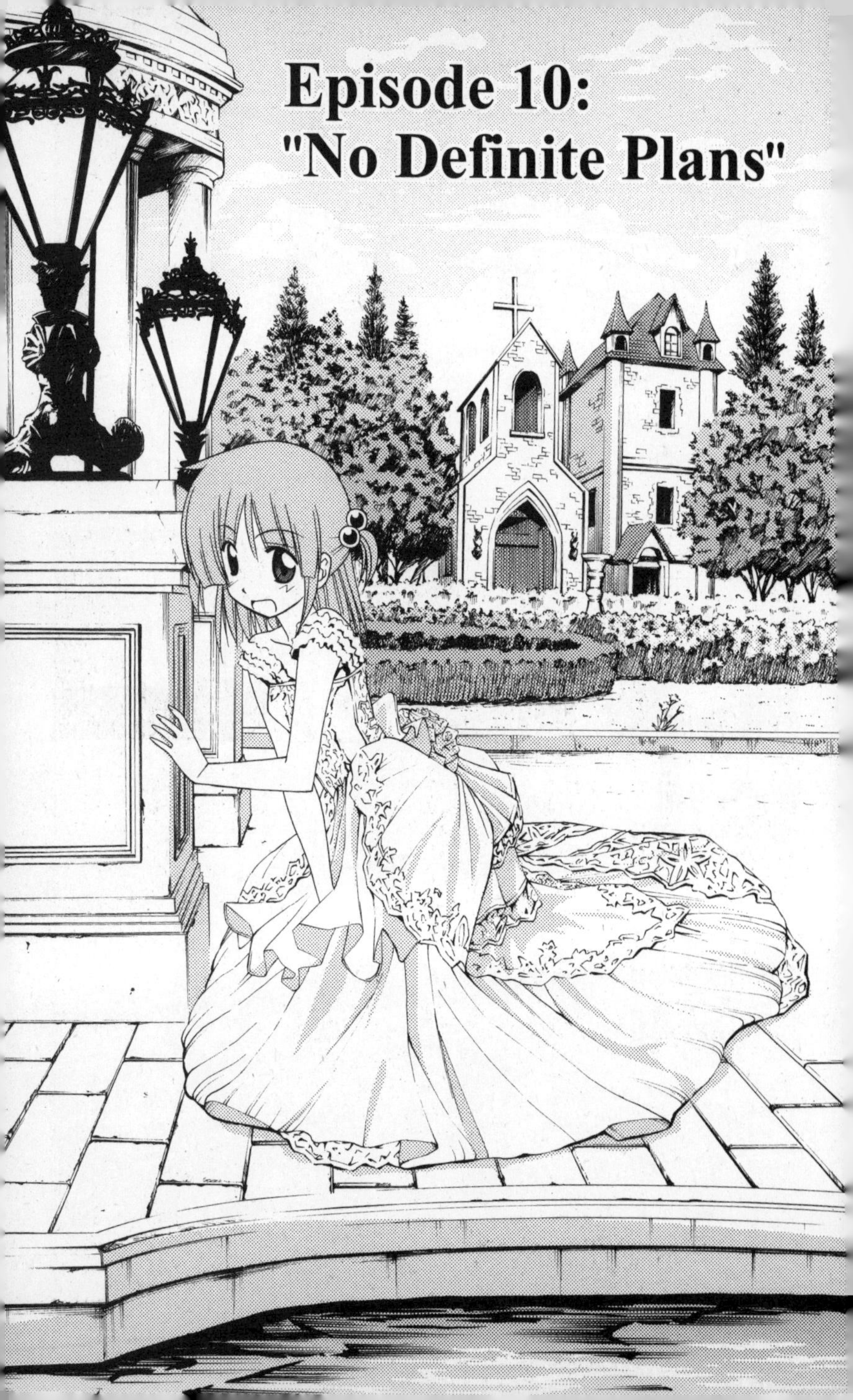

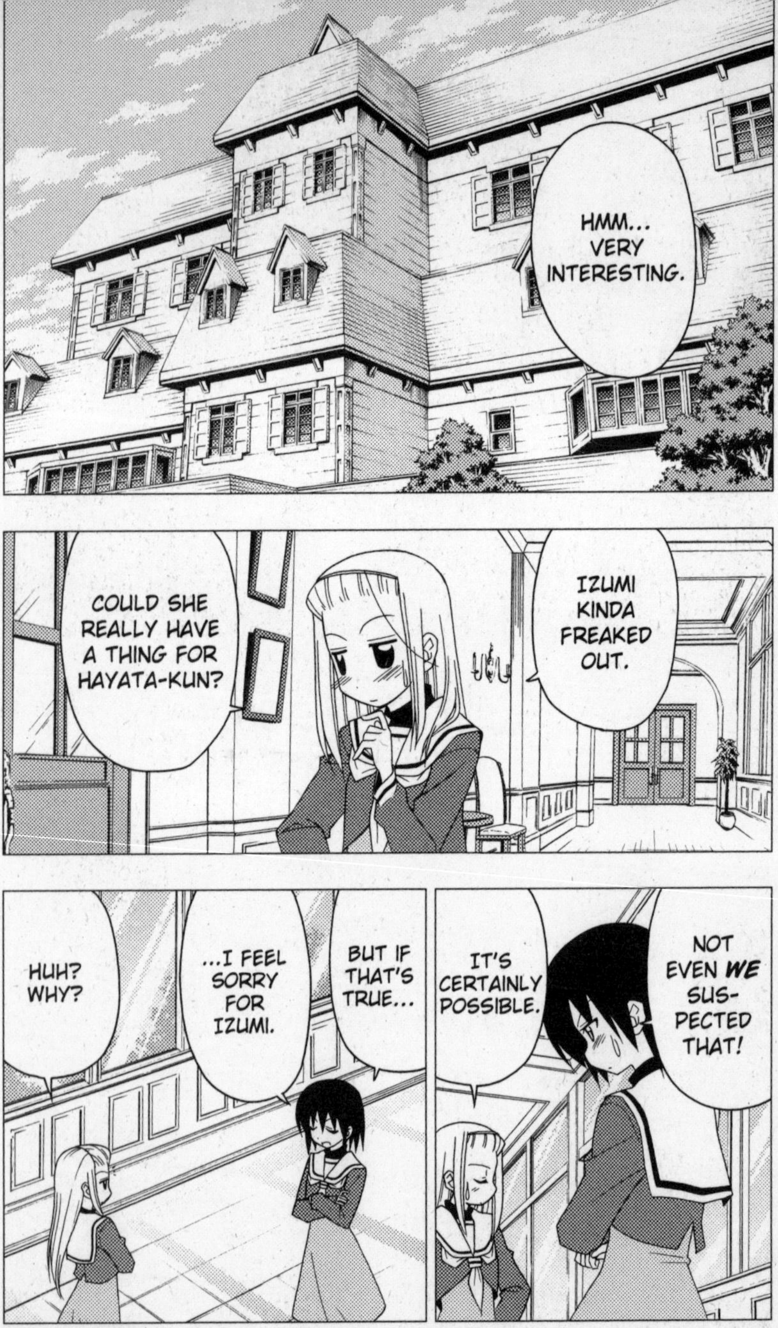
HMM... VERY INTERESTING.
IZUMI KINDA FREAKED OUT.
COULD SHE REALLY HAVE A THING FOR HAYATA-KUN?
NOT EVEN *WE* SUS-PECTED THAT!
IT'S CERTAINLY POSSIBLE.
BUT IF THAT'S TRUE...
...I FEEL SORRY FOR IZUMI.
HUH? WHY?

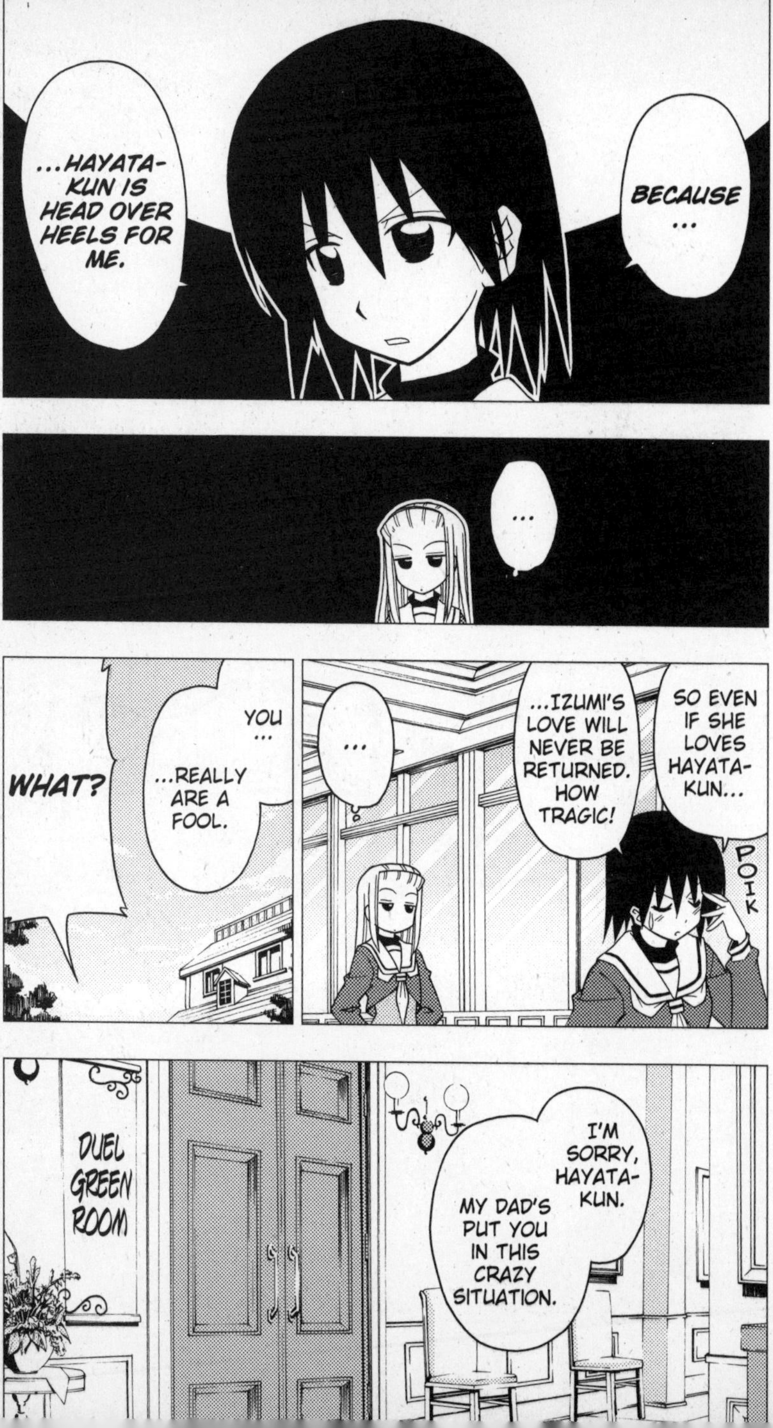
BECAUSE ...
...HAYATA-KUN IS HEAD OVER HEELS FOR ME.
...
SO EVEN IF SHE LOVES HAYATA-KUN...
POIK
...IZUMI'S LOVE WILL NEVER BE RETURNED. HOW TRAGIC!
...
YOU ...
...REALLY ARE A FOOL.
WHAT?
I'M SORRY, HAYATA-KUN.
MY DAD'S PUT YOU IN THIS CRAZY SITUATION.
DUEL GREEN ROOM

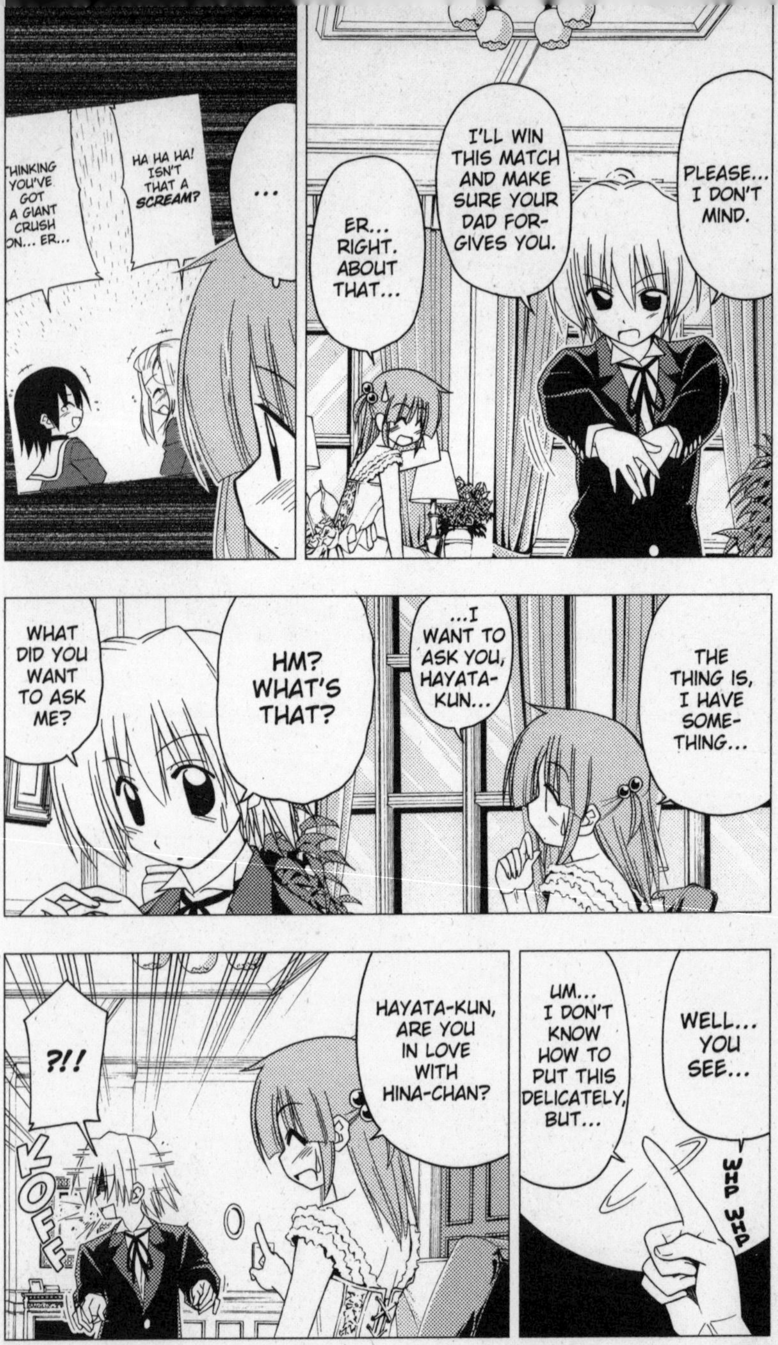
PLEASE... I DON'T MIND.
I'LL WIN THIS MATCH AND MAKE SURE YOUR DAD FORGIVES YOU.
ER... RIGHT. ABOUT THAT...
...
HA HA HA! ISN'T THAT A SCREAM?
THINKING YOU'VE GOT A GIANT CRUSH ON... ER...
THE THING IS, I HAVE SOMETHING...
...I WANT TO ASK YOU, HAYATA-KUN...
HM? WHAT'S THAT?
WHAT DID YOU WANT TO ASK ME?
WELL... YOU SEE...
WHP WHP
UM... I DON'T KNOW HOW TO PUT THIS DELICATELY, BUT...
HAYATA-KUN, ARE YOU IN LOVE WITH HINA-CHAN?
?!!
KOFF

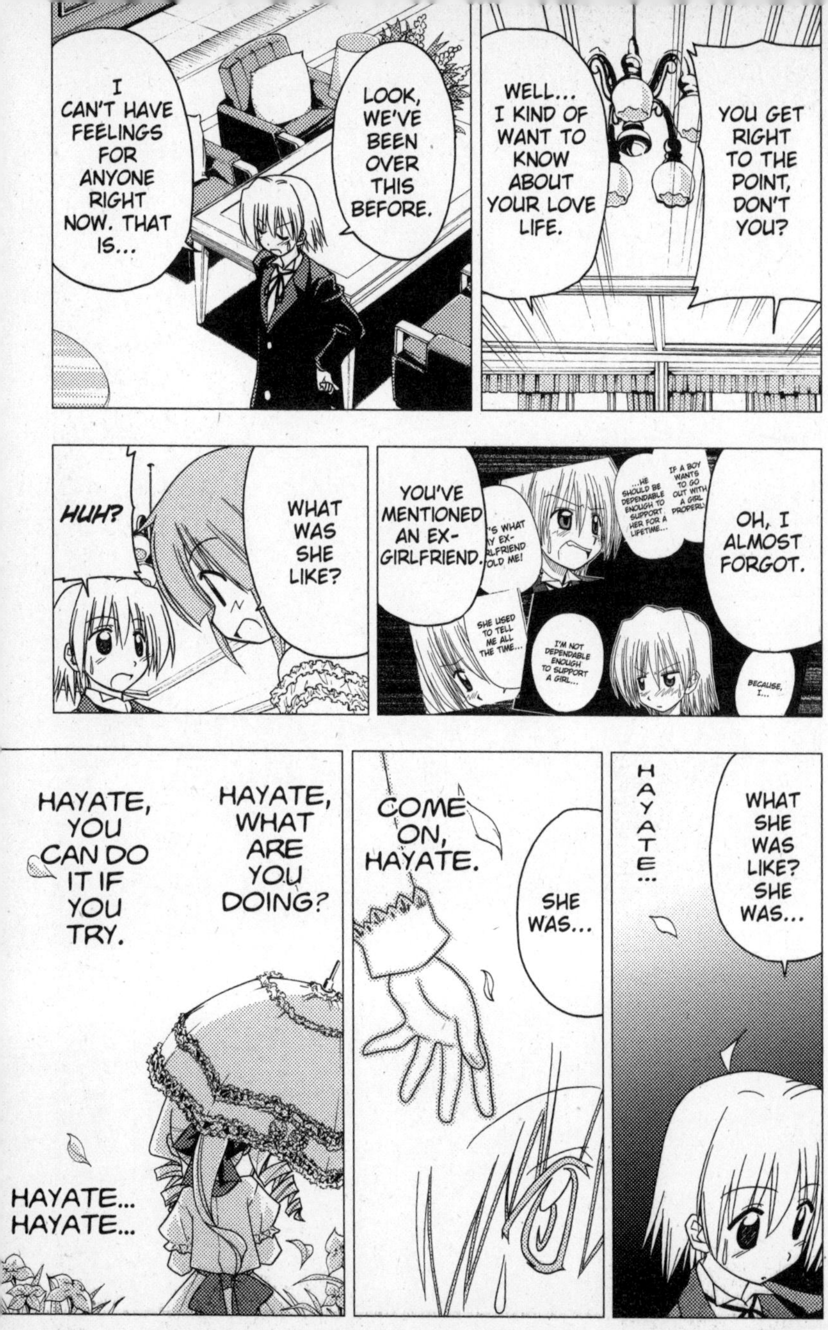
YOU GET RIGHT TO THE POINT, DON'T YOU?
WELL... I KIND OF WANT TO KNOW ABOUT YOUR LOVE LIFE.
LOOK, WE'VE BEEN OVER THIS BEFORE.
I CAN'T HAVE FEELINGS FOR ANYONE RIGHT NOW. THAT IS...
OH, I ALMOST FORGOT.
IF A BOY WANTS TO GO OUT WITH A GIRL PROPERLY
...HE SHOULD BE DEPENDABLE ENOUGH TO SUPPORT HER FOR A LIFETIME...
SHE USED TO TELL ME ALL THE TIME...
I'M NOT DEPENDABLE ENOUGH TO SUPPORT A GIRL...
BECAUSE, I...
YOU'VE MENTIONED AN EX-GIRLFRIEND.
WHAT WAS SHE LIKE?
HUH?
WHAT SHE WAS LIKE? SHE WAS...
HAYATE...
SHE WAS...
COME ON, HAYATE.
HAYATE, WHAT ARE YOU DOING?
HAYATE, YOU CAN DO IT IF YOU TRY.
HAYATE... HAYATE...

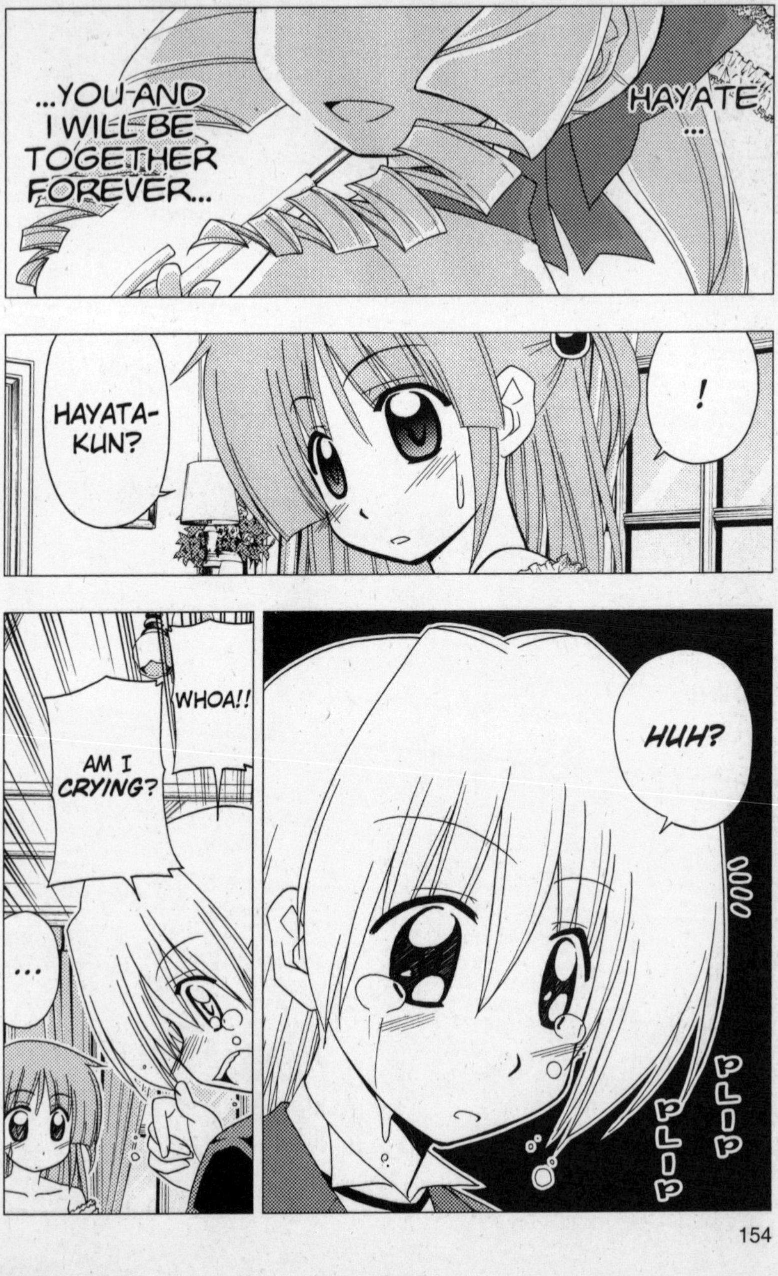
HAYATE ...
...YOU AND I WILL BE TOGETHER FOREVER...
!
HAYATA-KUN?
HUH?
drip drip
WHOA!!
AM I CRYING?
...

HOW STRANGE!
WHY WOULD I DO THAT?
...
NOW I UNDER-STAND.
HUH?
I FINALLY GET IT.
BACK THEN...
I'VE HAD ENOUGH OF YOU!!
ENOUGH, HAYATE!!
...SHE WAS RIGHT.
THE ONE WHO WAS WRONG...

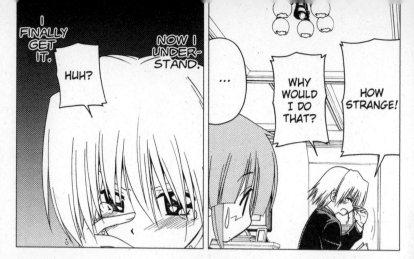

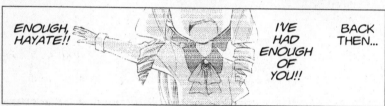

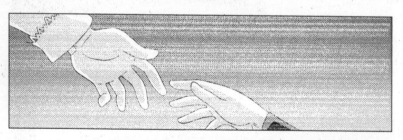

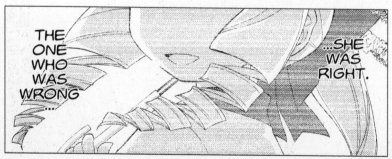

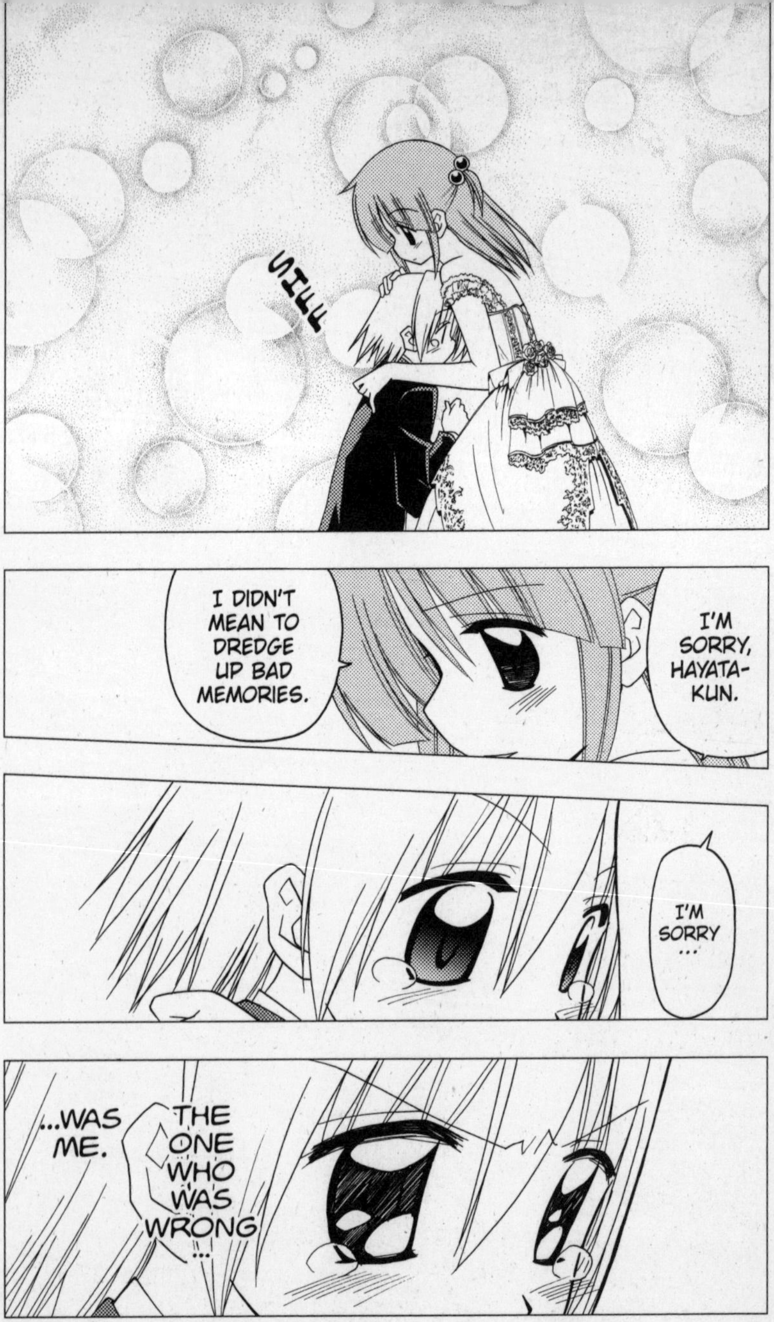
STILL
I'M SORRY, HAYATA-KUN.
I DIDN'T MEAN TO DREDGE UP BAD MEMORIES.
I'M SORRY...
THE ONE WHO WAS WRONG...
...WAS ME.

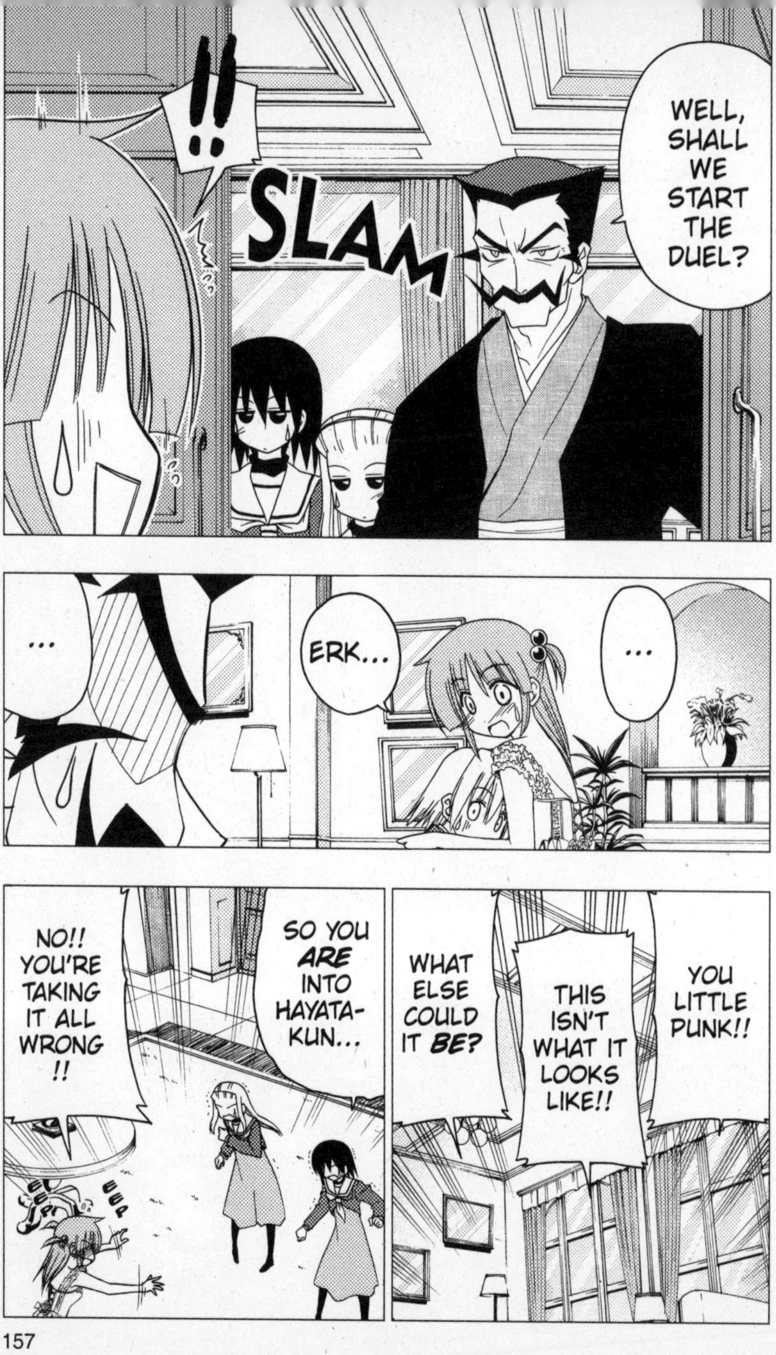
WELL, SHALL WE START THE DUEL?
SLAM
!!
...
ERK...
...
YOU LITTLE PUNK!!
THIS ISN'T WHAT IT LOOKS LIKE!!
WHAT ELSE COULD IT *BE*?
SO YOU *ARE* INTO HAYATA-KUN...
NO!! YOU'RE TAKING IT ALL WRONG!!
EEP

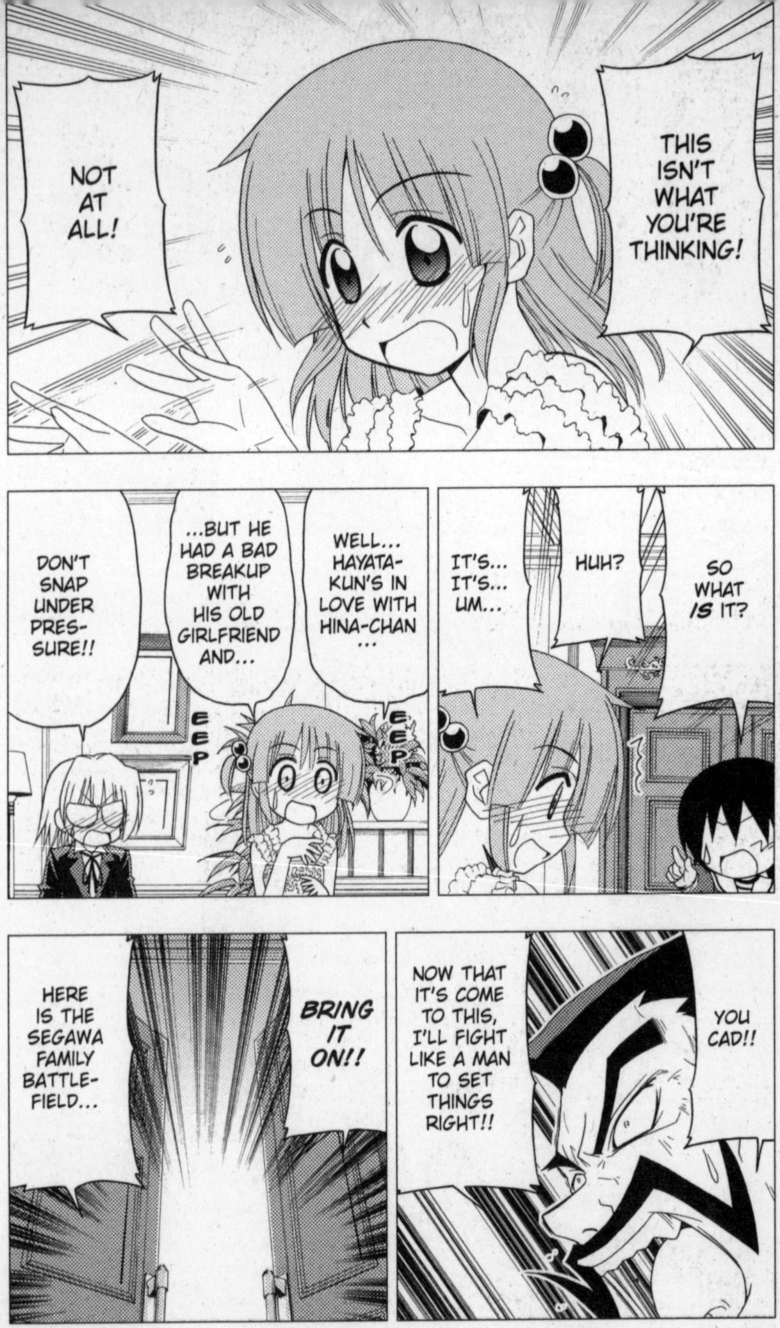
THIS ISN'T WHAT YOU'RE THINKING!
NOT AT ALL!
SO WHAT *IS* IT?
HUH?
IT'S... IT'S... UM...
WELL... HAYATA-KUN'S IN LOVE WITH HINA-CHAN...
EEP
...BUT HE HAD A BAD BREAKUP WITH HIS OLD GIRLFRIEND AND...
EEP
DON'T SNAP UNDER PRES-SURE!!
YOU CAD!!
NOW THAT IT'S COME TO THIS, I'LL FIGHT LIKE A MAN TO SET THINGS RIGHT!!
BRING IT ON!!
HERE IS THE SEGAWA FAMILY BATTLE-FIELD...

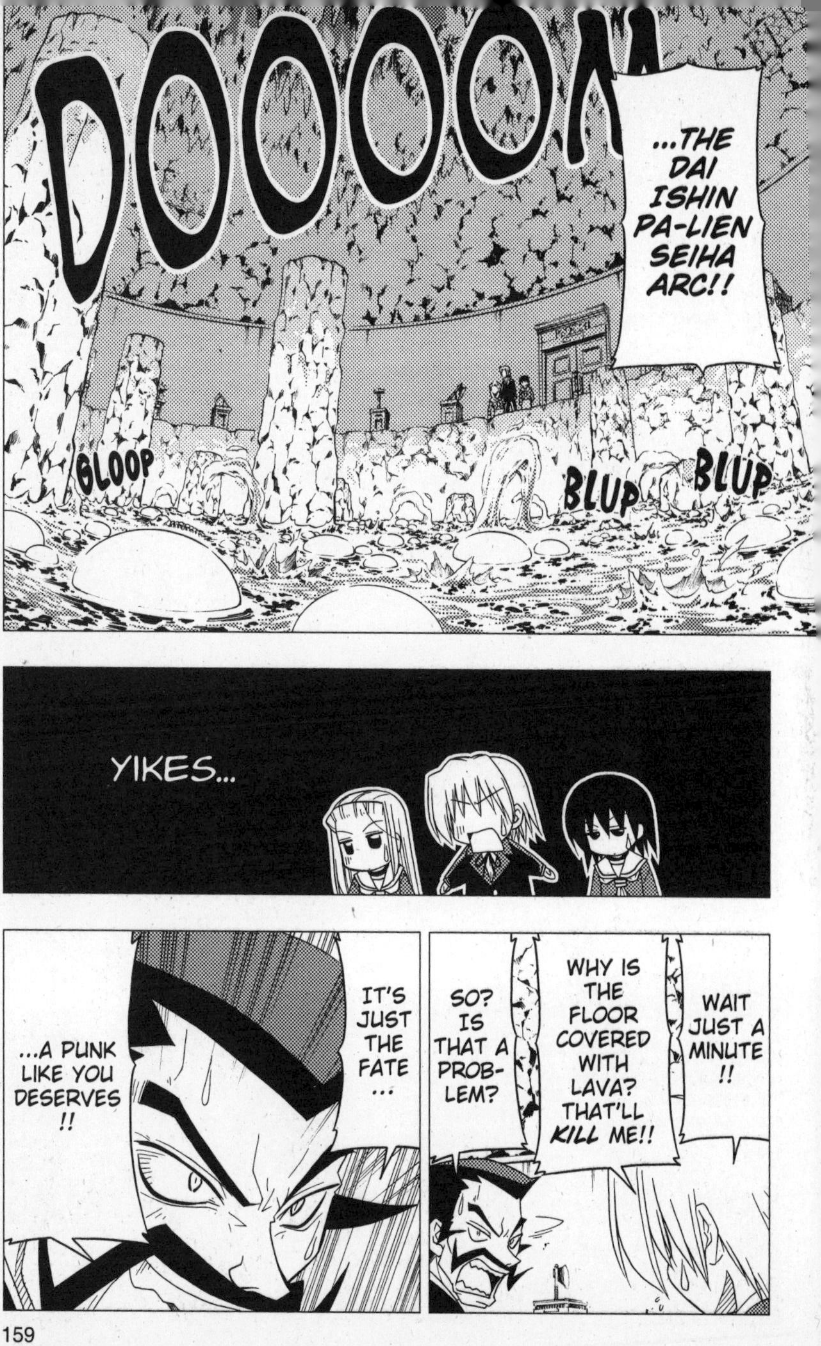
...THE DAI ISHIN PA-LIEN SEIHA ARC!!
DOOOOM
BLUP
BLUP
GLOOP
YIKES...
WAIT JUST A MINUTE!!
WHY IS THE FLOOR COVERED WITH LAVA? THAT'LL *KILL* ME!!
SO? IS THAT A PROB-LEM?
IT'S JUST THE FATE...
...A PUNK LIKE YOU DESERVES!!

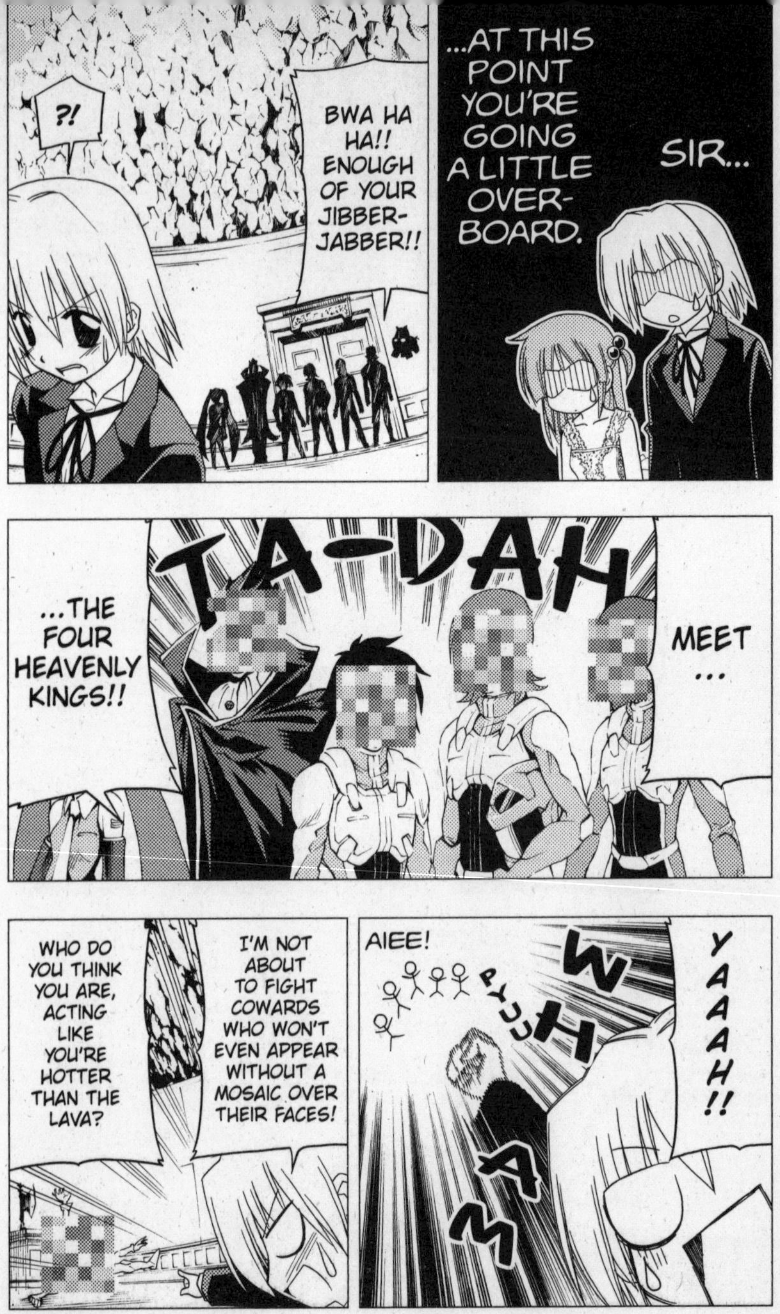
SIR...
...AT THIS POINT YOU'RE GOING A LITTLE OVER-BOARD.
BWA HA HA!! ENOUGH OF YOUR JIBBER-JABBER!!
?!
TA-DAH
MEET...
...THE FOUR HEAVENLY KINGS!!
YAAAAH!!
WHAM
PYUU
AIEE!
I'M NOT ABOUT TO FIGHT COWARDS WHO WON'T EVEN APPEAR WITHOUT A MOSAIC OVER THEIR FACES!
WHO DO YOU THINK YOU ARE, ACTING LIKE YOU'RE HOTTER THAN THE LAVA?

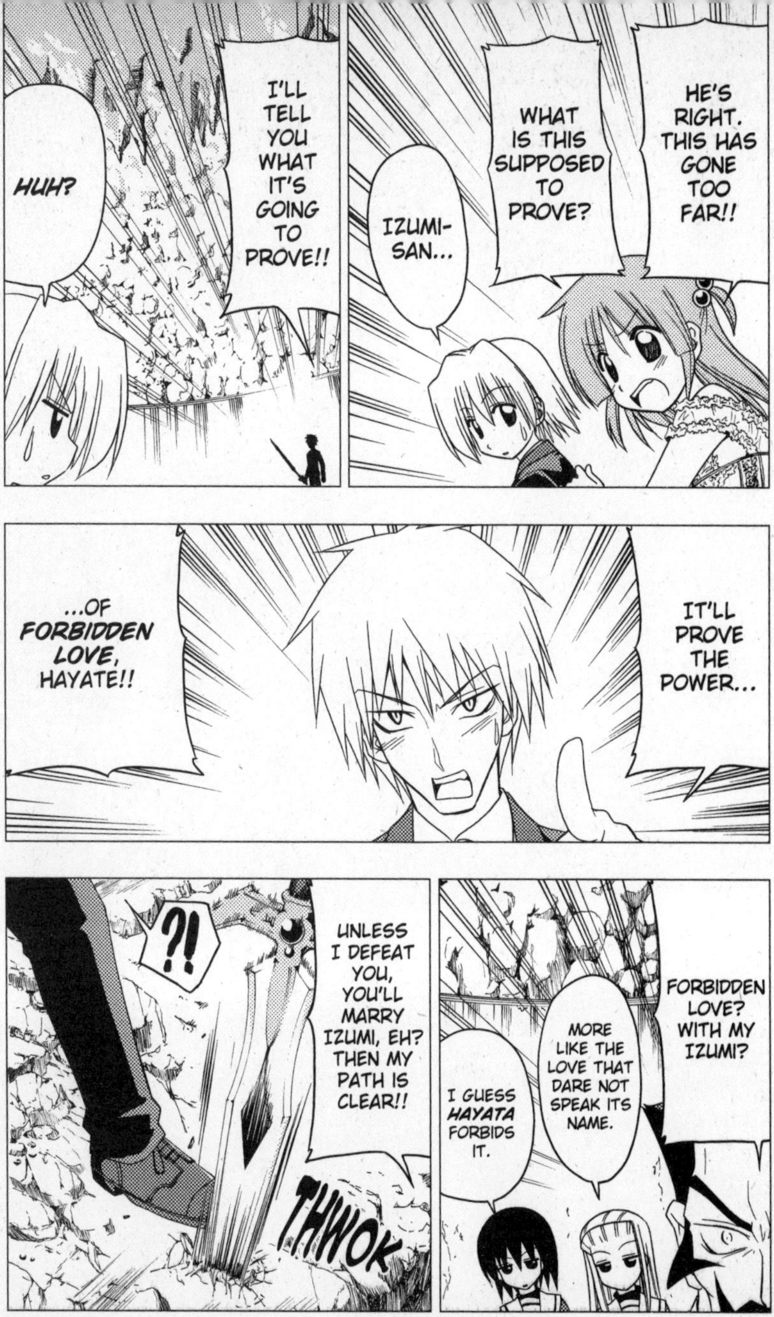
HE'S RIGHT. THIS HAS GONE TOO FAR!!
WHAT IS THIS SUPPOSED TO PROVE?
IZUMI-SAN...
I'LL TELL YOU WHAT IT'S GOING TO PROVE!!
HUH?
IT'LL PROVE THE POWER...
...OF *FORBIDDEN LOVE*, HAYATE!!
FORBIDDEN LOVE? WITH MY IZUMI?
MORE LIKE THE LOVE THAT DARE NOT SPEAK ITS NAME.
I GUESS *HAYATA* FORBIDS IT.
UNLESS I DEFEAT YOU, YOU'LL MARRY IZUMI, EH? THEN MY PATH IS CLEAR!!
?!
THWOK

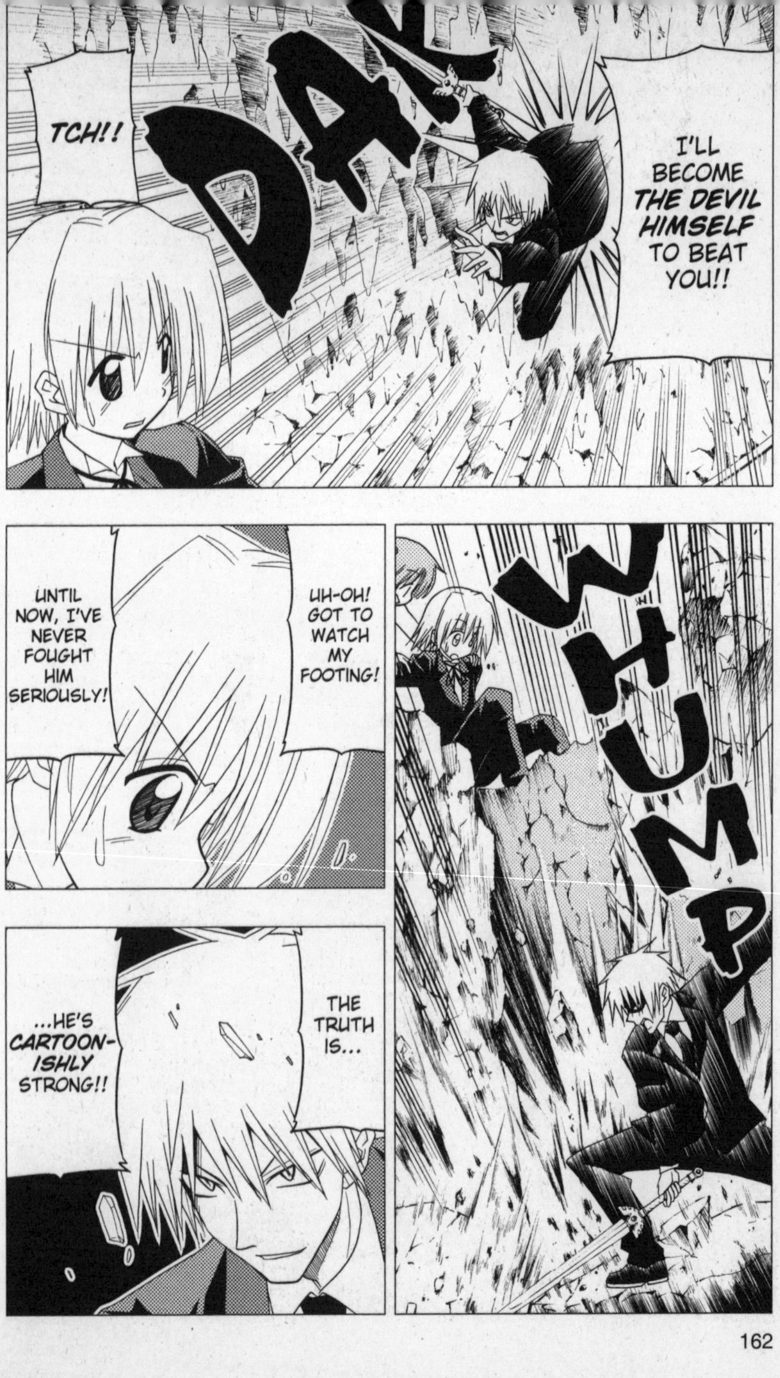
I'LL BECOME THE DEVIL HIMSELF TO BEAT YOU!!
DA
TCH!!
WHUMP
UH-OH! GOT TO WATCH MY FOOTING!
UNTIL NOW, I'VE NEVER FOUGHT HIM SERIOUSLY!
THE TRUTH IS...
...HE'S CARTOON-ISHLY STRONG!!

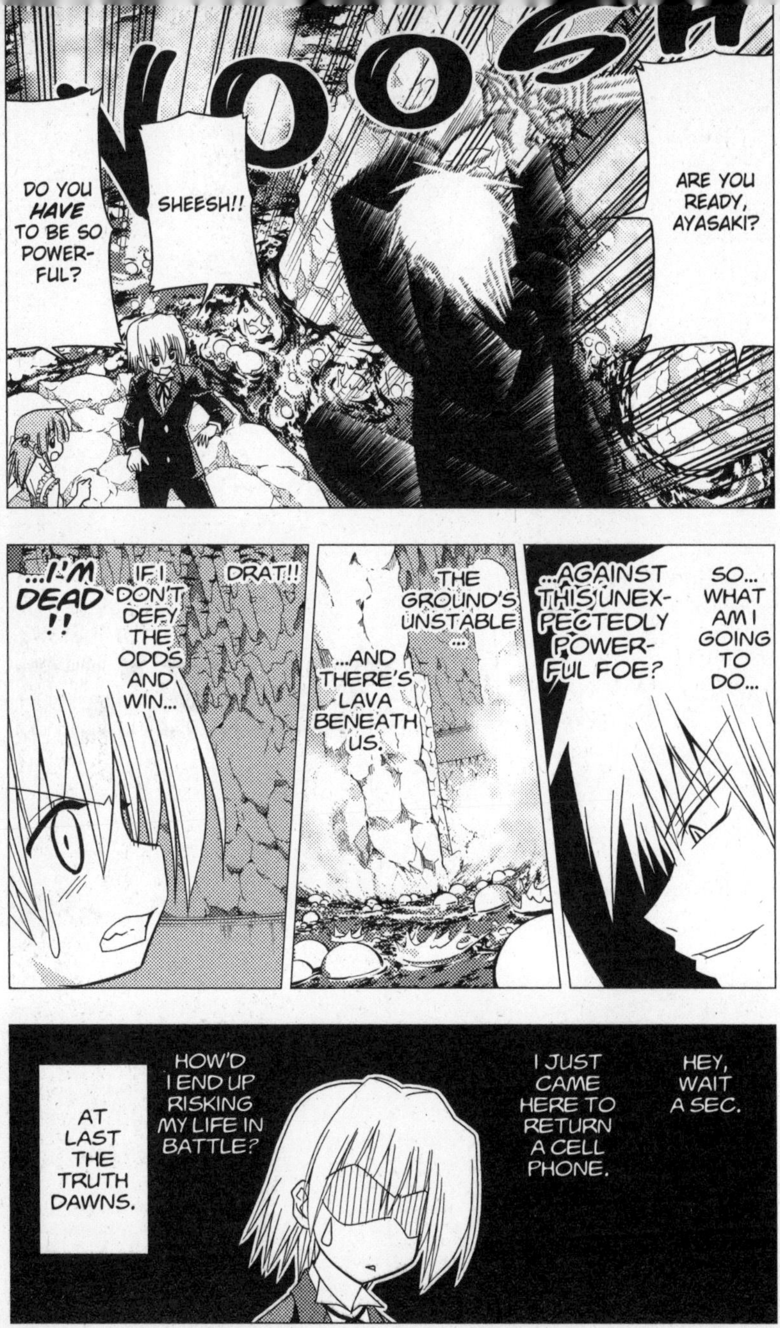
WOOSH
ARE YOU READY, AYASAKI?
SHEESH!!
DO YOU HAVE TO BE SO POWER-FUL?
SO... WHAT AM I GOING TO DO...
...AGAINST THIS UNEX-PECTEDLY POWER-FUL FOE?
THE GROUND'S UNSTABLE...
...AND THERE'S LAVA BENEATH US.
DRAT!!
IF I DON'T DEFY THE ODDS AND WIN...
...I'M DEAD!!
HEY, WAIT A SEC.
I JUST CAME HERE TO RETURN A CELL PHONE.
HOW'D I END UP RISKING MY LIFE IN BATTLE?
AT LAST THE TRUTH DAWNS.

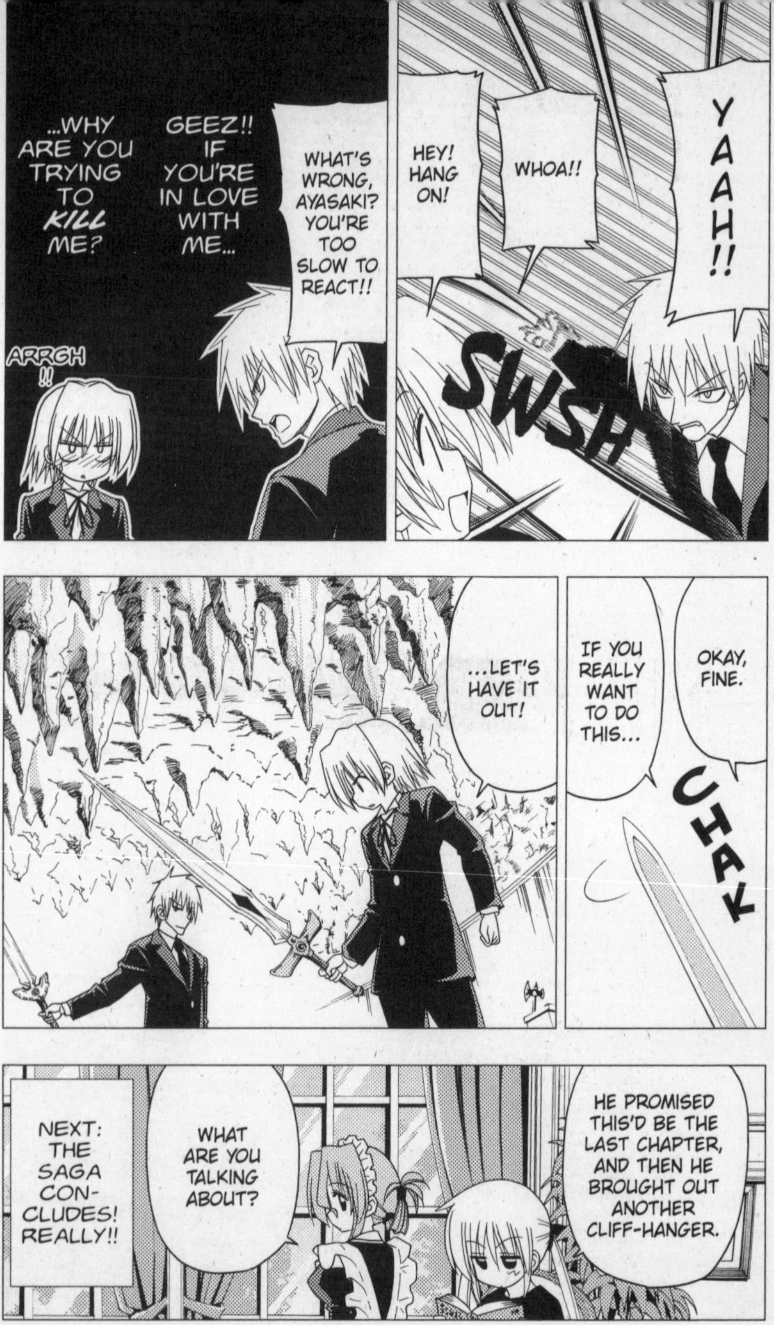
YAAH!!
WHOA!!
HEY! HANG ON!
SWSH
WHAT'S WRONG, AYASAKI? YOU'RE TOO SLOW TO REACT!!
GEEZ!! IF YOU'RE IN LOVE WITH ME...
...WHY ARE YOU TRYING TO KILL ME?
ARRGH!!
OKAY, FINE.
IF YOU REALLY WANT TO DO THIS...
CHAK
...LET'S HAVE IT OUT!
HE PROMISED THIS'D BE THE LAST CHAPTER, AND THEN HE BROUGHT OUT ANOTHER CLIFF-HANGER.
WHAT ARE YOU TALKING ABOUT?
NEXT: THE SAGA CON-CLUDES! REALLY!!

Episode 11: "For Now, Try Discussing It with Body Language"

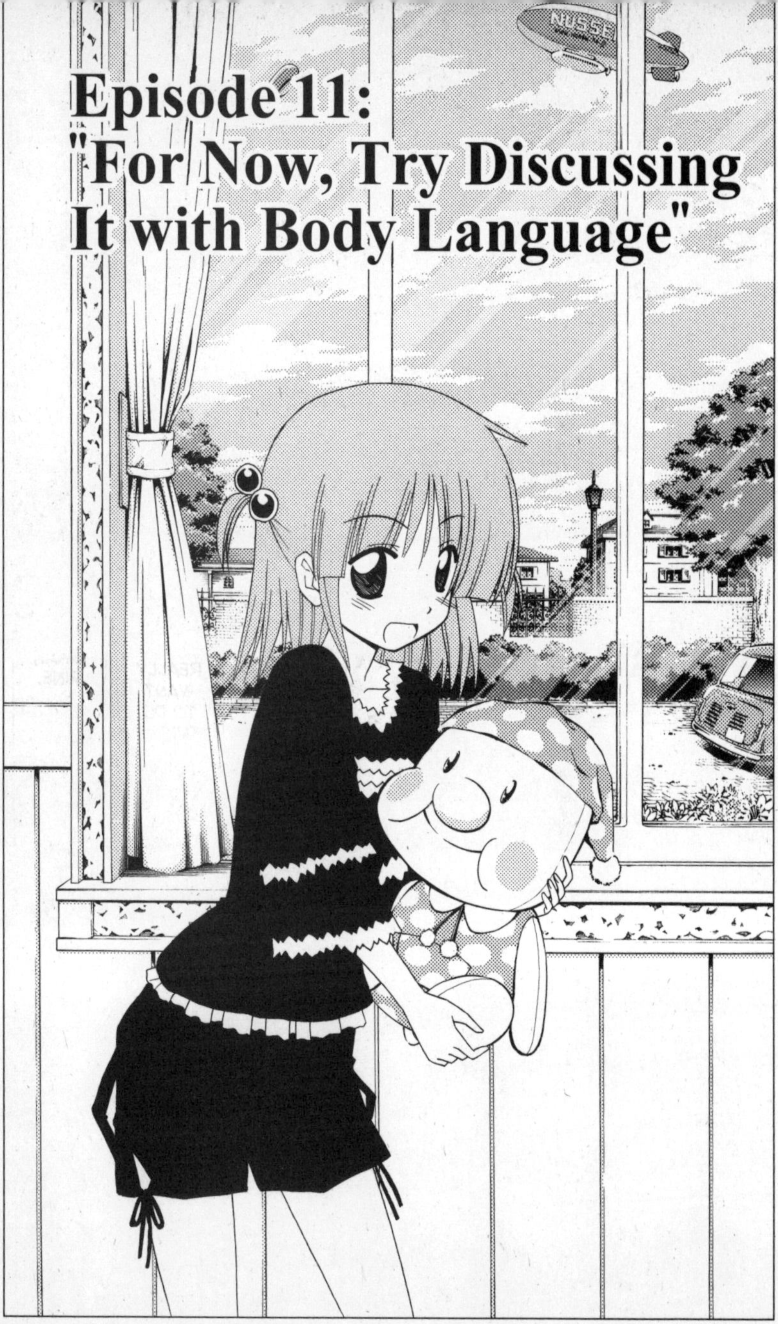

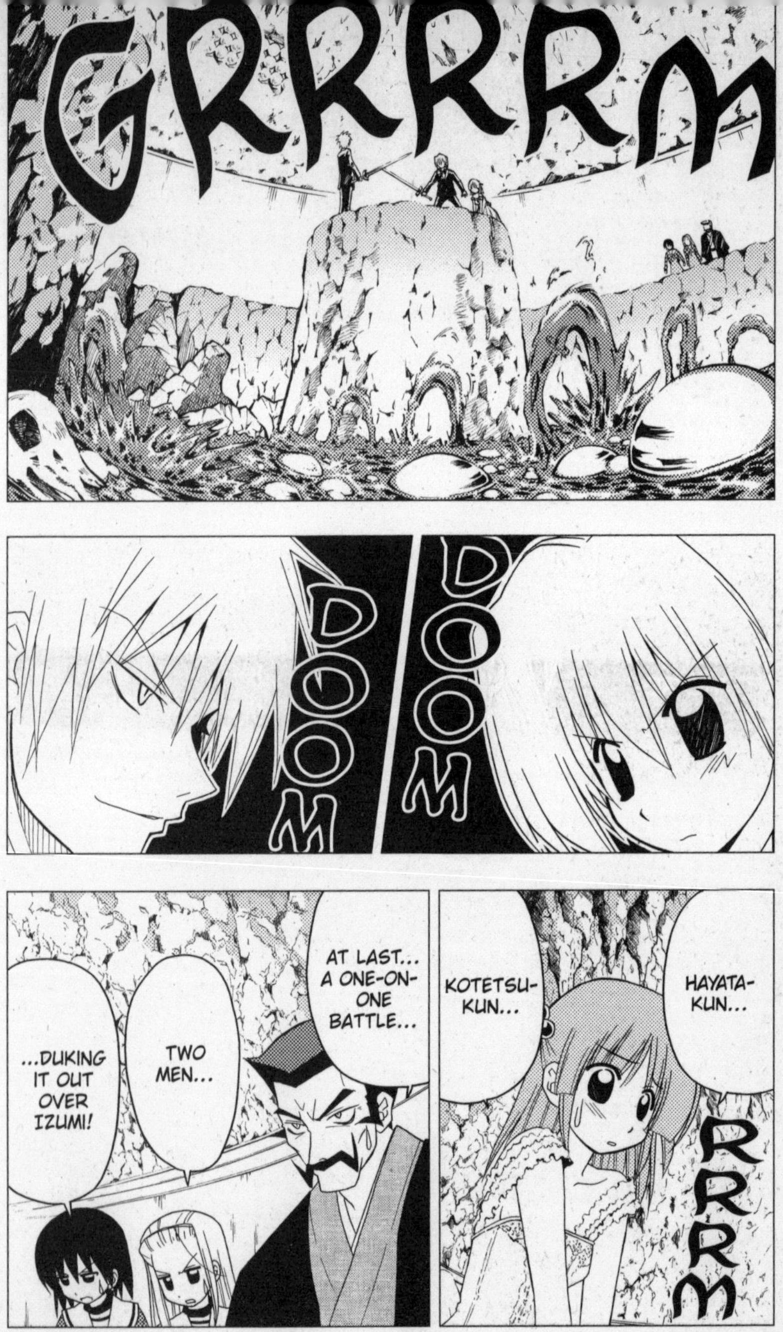
GRRRRM
DOOM
DOOM
HAYATA-KUN...
KOTETSU-KUN...
RRRM
AT LAST... A ONE-ON-ONE BATTLE...
TWO MEN...
...DUKING IT OUT OVER IZUMI!

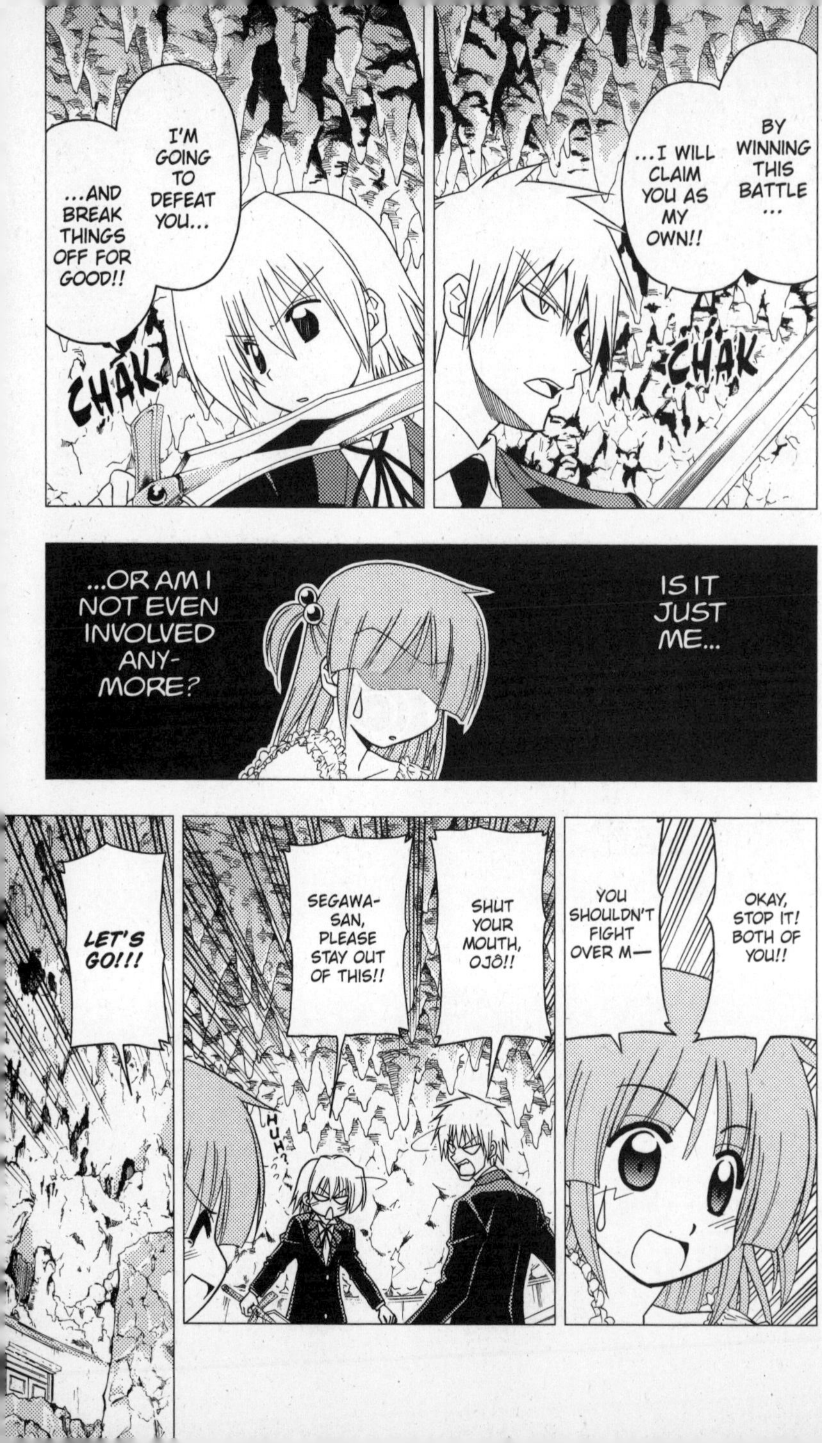
BY WINNING THIS BATTLE...
...I WILL CLAIM YOU AS MY OWN!!
CHAK
I'M GOING TO DEFEAT YOU...
...AND BREAK THINGS OFF FOR GOOD!!
CHAK
IS IT JUST ME...
...OR AM I NOT EVEN INVOLVED ANY-MORE?
OKAY, STOP IT! BOTH OF YOU!!
YOU SHOULDN'T FIGHT OVER M—
SHUT YOUR MOUTH, OJÔ!!
SEGAWA-SAN, PLEASE STAY OUT OF THIS!!
HUH?
LET'S GO!!!

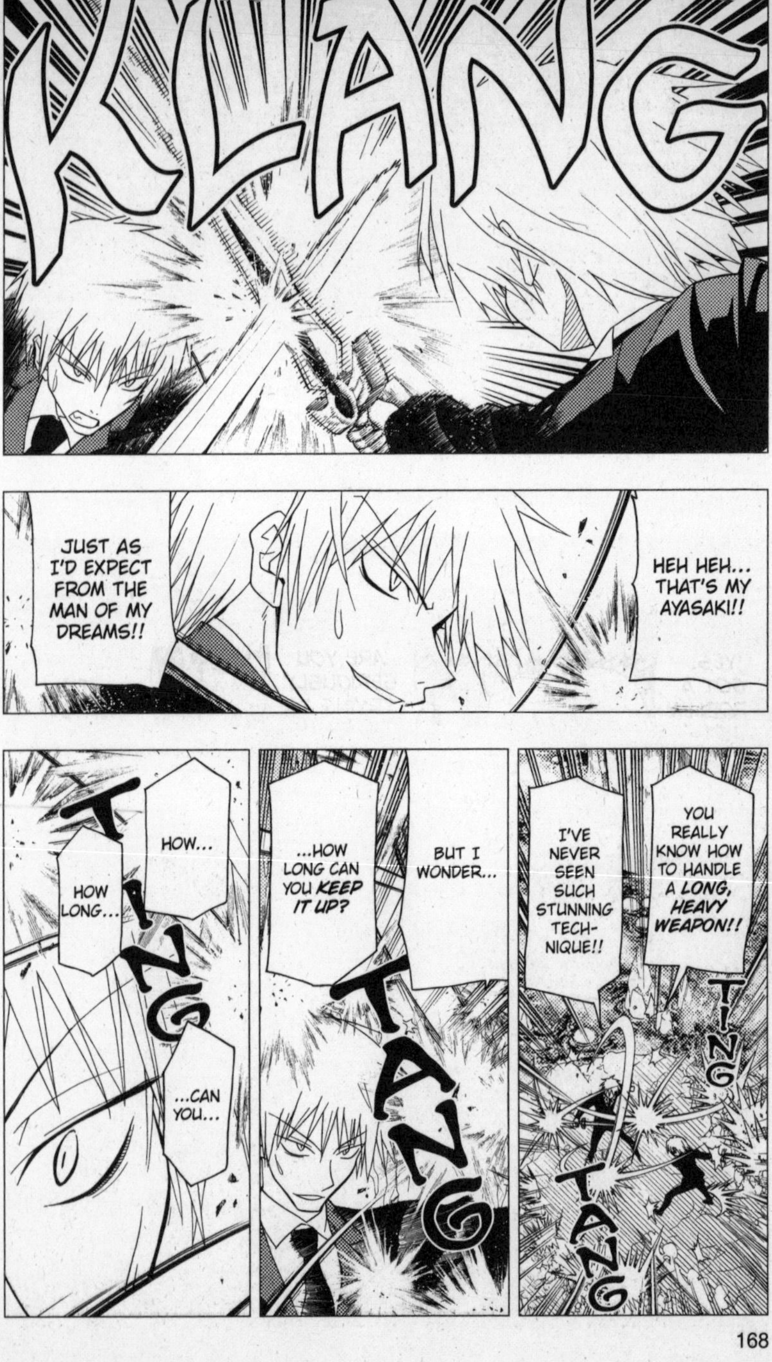
KLANG
HEH HEH... THAT'S MY AYASAKI!!
JUST AS I'D EXPECT FROM THE MAN OF MY DREAMS!!
YOU REALLY KNOW HOW TO HANDLE A *LONG, HEAVY WEAPON!!*
I'VE NEVER SEEN SUCH STUNNING TECH-NIQUE!!
TING
TANG
BUT I WONDER...
...HOW LONG CAN YOU *KEEP IT UP?*
TANG
HOW...
HOW LONG...
TING
...CAN YOU...

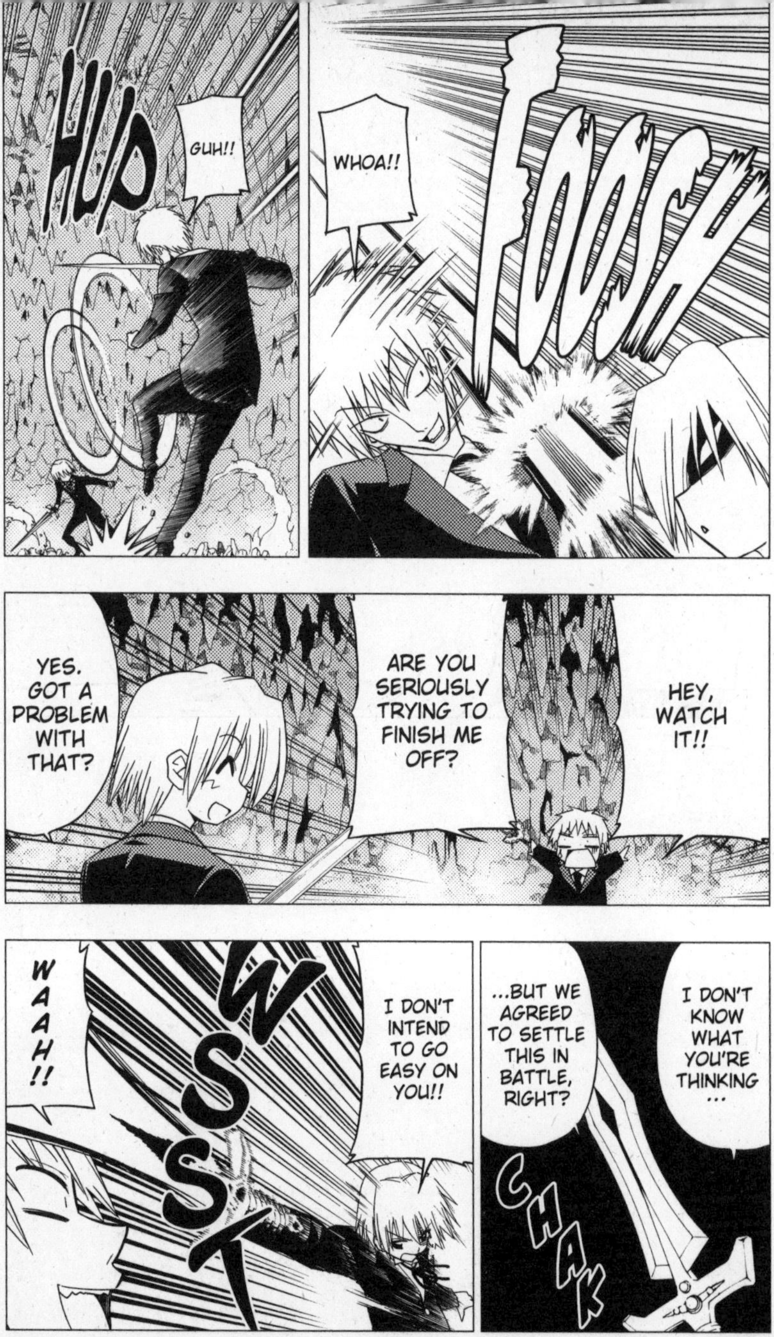
WHOA!!
FOOSH
GUH!!
HUP
HEY, WATCH IT!!
ARE YOU SERIOUSLY TRYING TO FINISH ME OFF?
YES. GOT A PROBLEM WITH THAT?
I DON'T KNOW WHAT YOU'RE THINKING...
...BUT WE AGREED TO SETTLE THIS IN BATTLE, RIGHT?
CHAK
I DON'T INTEND TO GO EASY ON YOU!!
WSSST
WAAAH!!

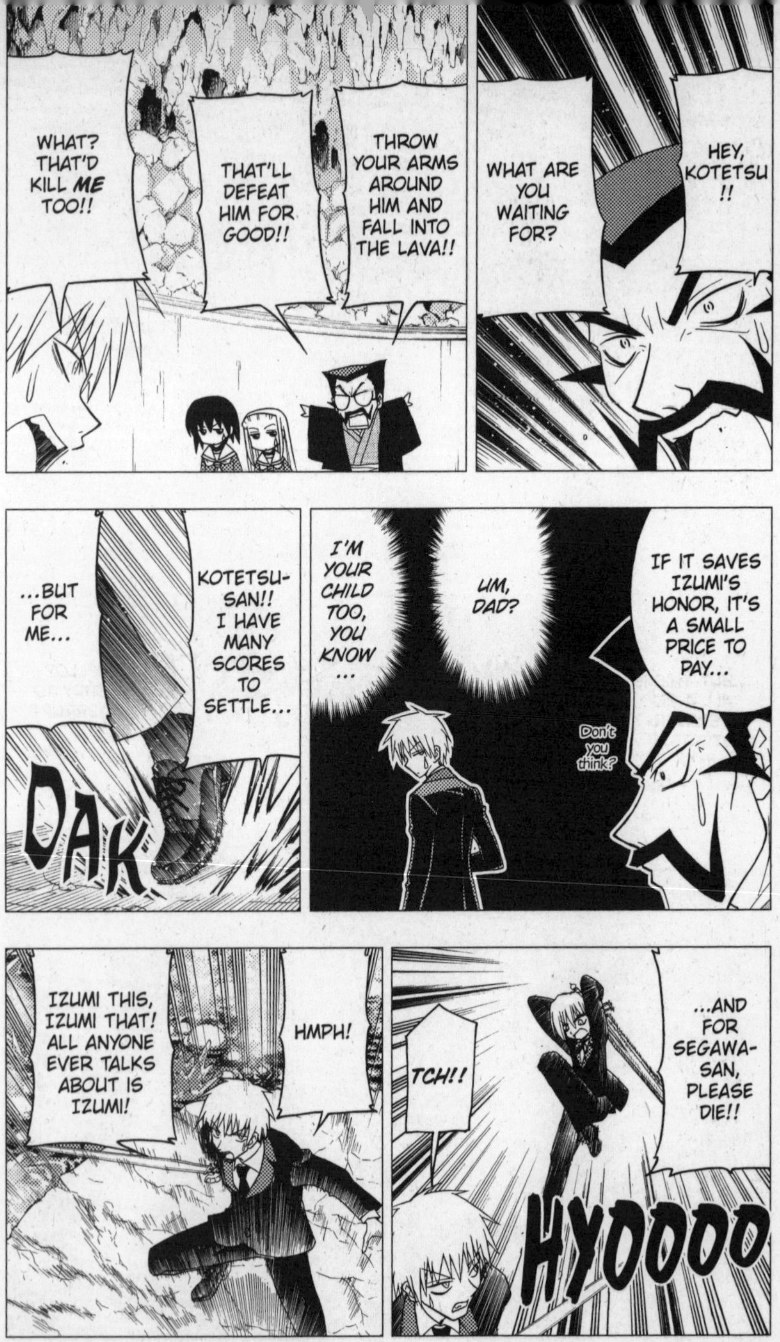
HEY, KOTETSU!!
WHAT ARE YOU WAITING FOR?
THROW YOUR ARMS AROUND HIM AND FALL INTO THE LAVA!!
THAT'LL DEFEAT HIM FOR GOOD!!
WHAT? THAT'D KILL *ME* TOO!!
IF IT SAVES IZUMI'S HONOR, IT'S A SMALL PRICE TO PAY...
Don't you think?
UM, DAD?
I'M YOUR CHILD TOO, YOU KNOW...
KOTETSU-SAN!! I HAVE MANY SCORES TO SETTLE...
...BUT FOR ME...
DAK
...AND FOR SEGAWA-SAN, PLEASE DIE!!
TCH!!
HYOOOOO
HMPH!
IZUMI THIS, IZUMI THAT! ALL ANYONE EVER TALKS ABOUT IS IZUMI!

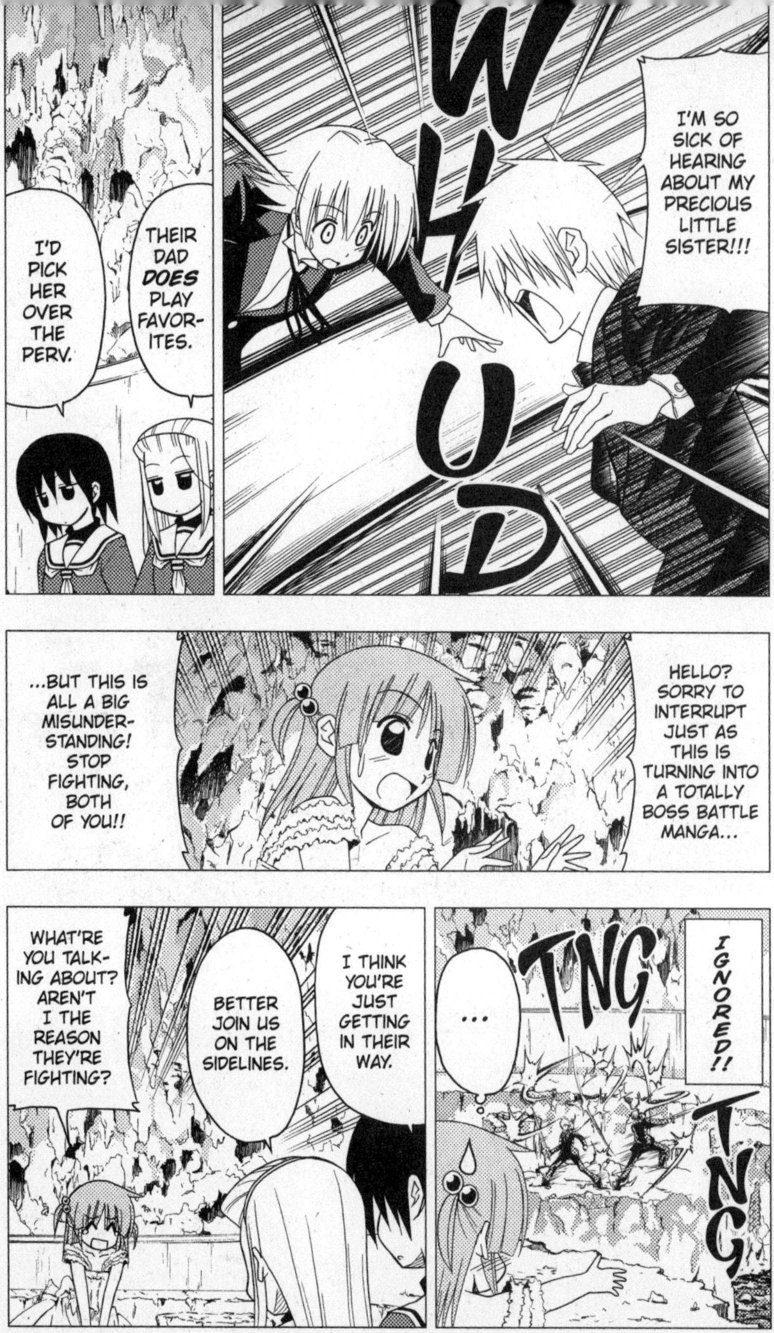
WHUD
I'M SO SICK OF HEARING ABOUT MY PRECIOUS LITTLE SISTER!!!
THEIR DAD **DOES** PLAY FAVORITES.
I'D PICK HER OVER THE PERV.
HELLO? SORRY TO INTERRUPT JUST AS THIS IS TURNING INTO A TOTALLY BOSS BATTLE MANGA...
...BUT THIS IS ALL A BIG MISUNDERSTANDING! STOP FIGHTING, BOTH OF YOU!!
IGNORED!!
TNG
...
TNG
I THINK YOU'RE JUST GETTING IN THEIR WAY.
BETTER JOIN US ON THE SIDELINES.
WHAT'RE YOU TALKING ABOUT? AREN'T I THE REASON THEY'RE FIGHTING?

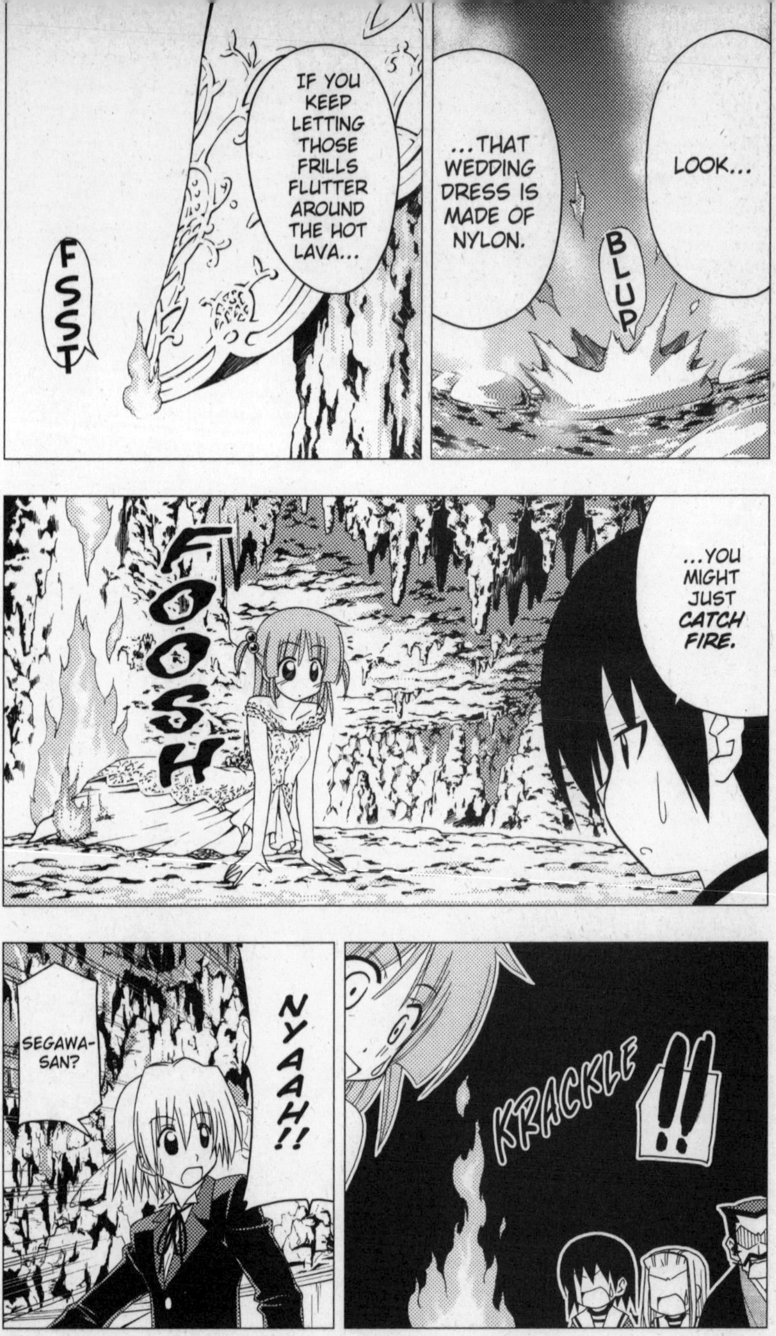
LOOK...
...THAT WEDDING DRESS IS MADE OF NYLON.
BLUP
IF YOU KEEP LETTING THOSE FRILLS FLUTTER AROUND THE HOT LAVA...
FSST
...YOU MIGHT JUST CATCH FIRE.
FOOSH
KRACKLE
!!
NYAAH!!
SEGAWA-SAN?

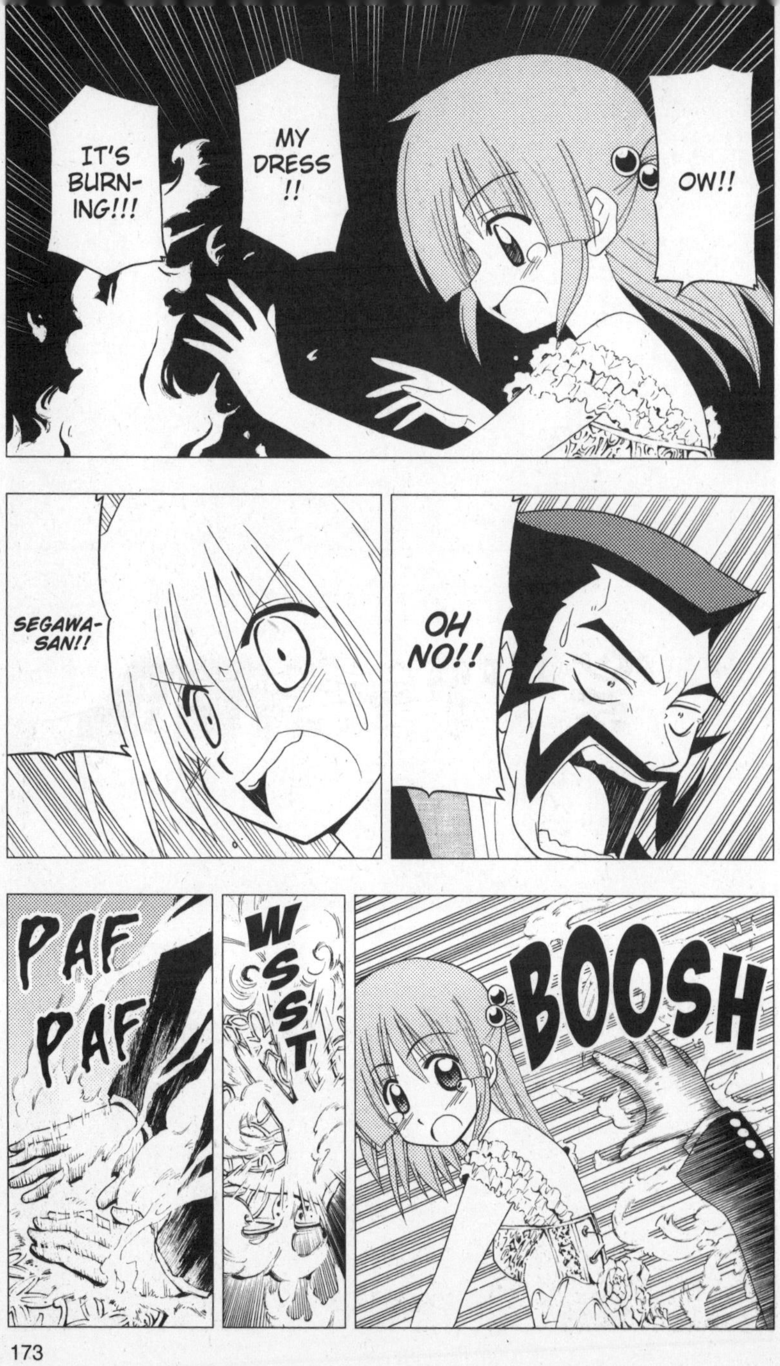
OW!!
MY DRESS!!
IT'S BURNING!!!
OH NO!!
SEGAWA-SAN!!
BOOSH
WSSST
PAF PAF

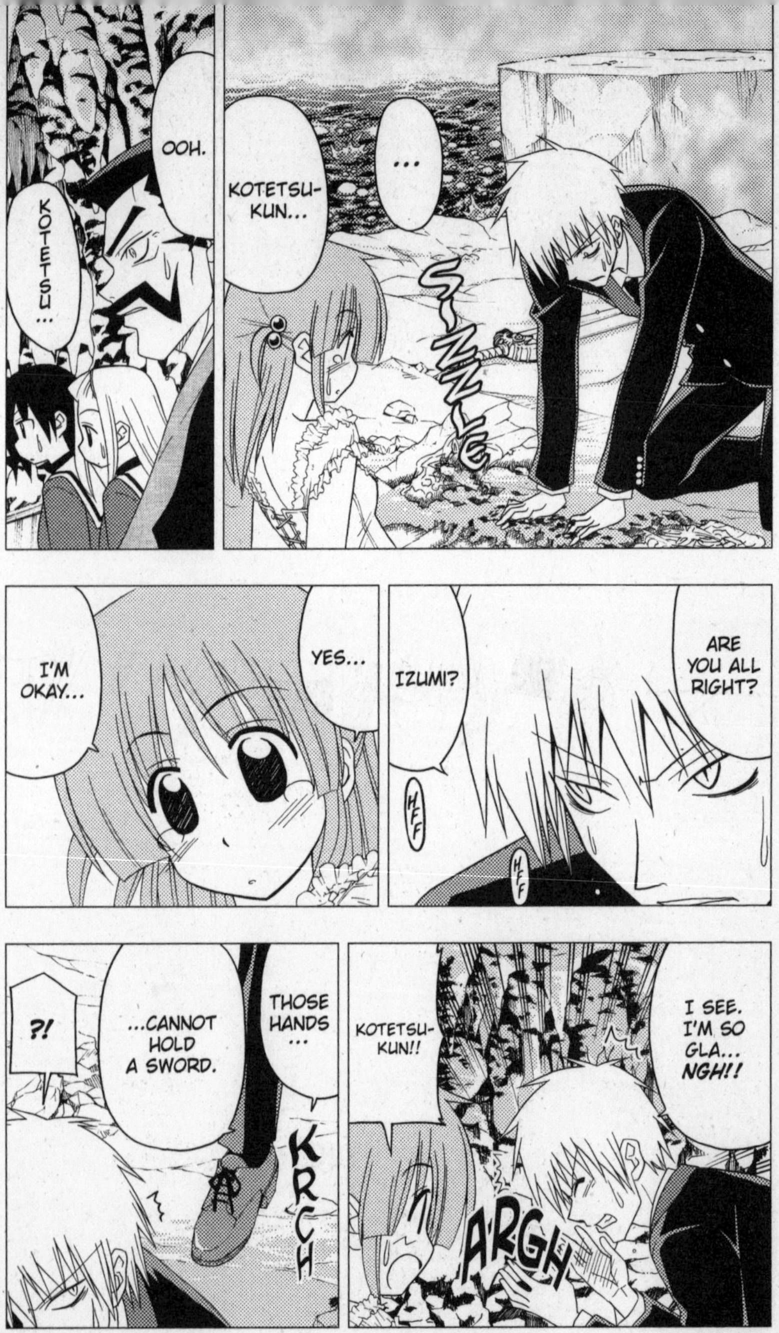
...
KOTETSU-KUN...
SIZZLE
OOH.
KOTETSU...
ARE YOU ALL RIGHT?
IZUMI?
HFF
HFF
YES...
I'M OKAY...
I SEE. I'M SO GLA... NGH!!
KOTETSU-KUN!!
ARGH
THOSE HANDS...
...CANNOT HOLD A SWORD.
KRCH
?!

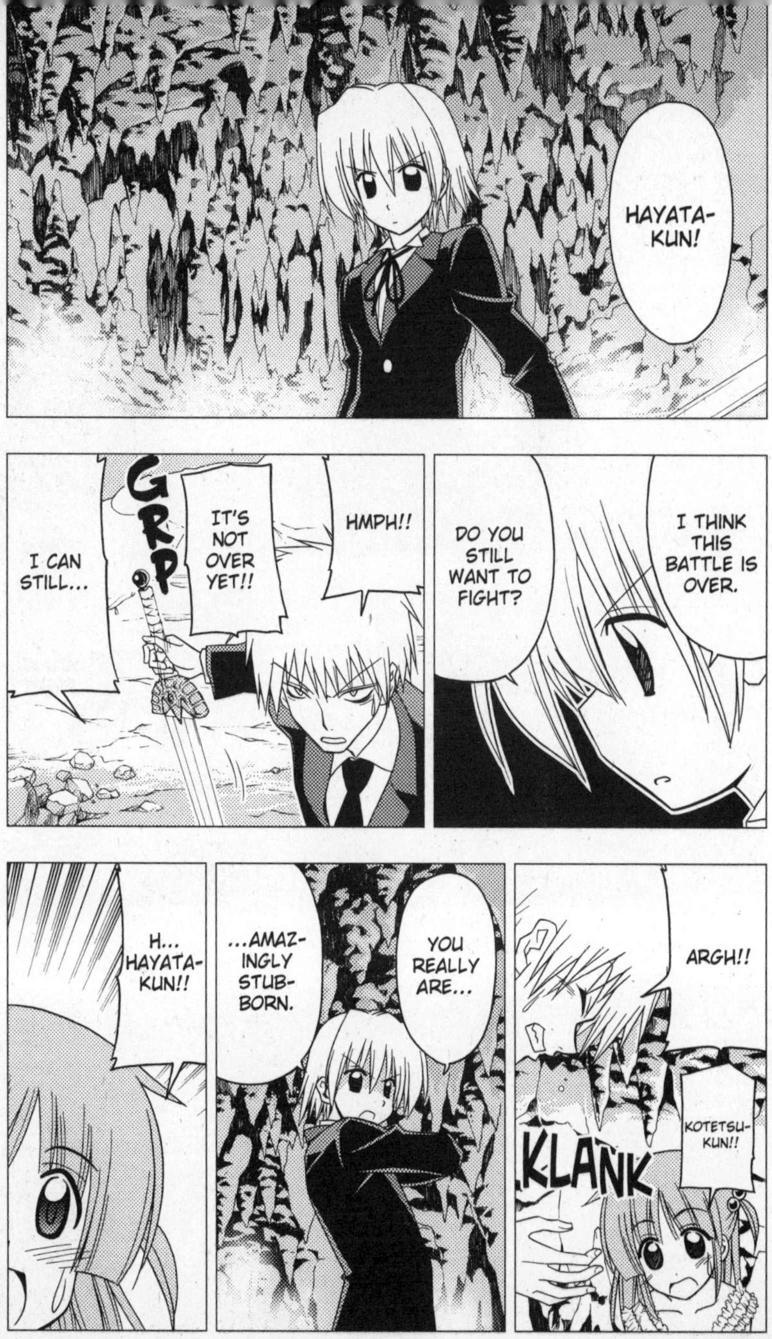
HAYATA-KUN!
I THINK THIS BATTLE IS OVER.
DO YOU STILL WANT TO FIGHT?
HMPH!!
IT'S NOT OVER YET!!
GRP
I CAN STILL...
ARGH!!
KOTETSU-KUN!!
KLANK
YOU REALLY ARE...
...AMAZINGLY STUBBORN.
H... HAYATA-KUN!!

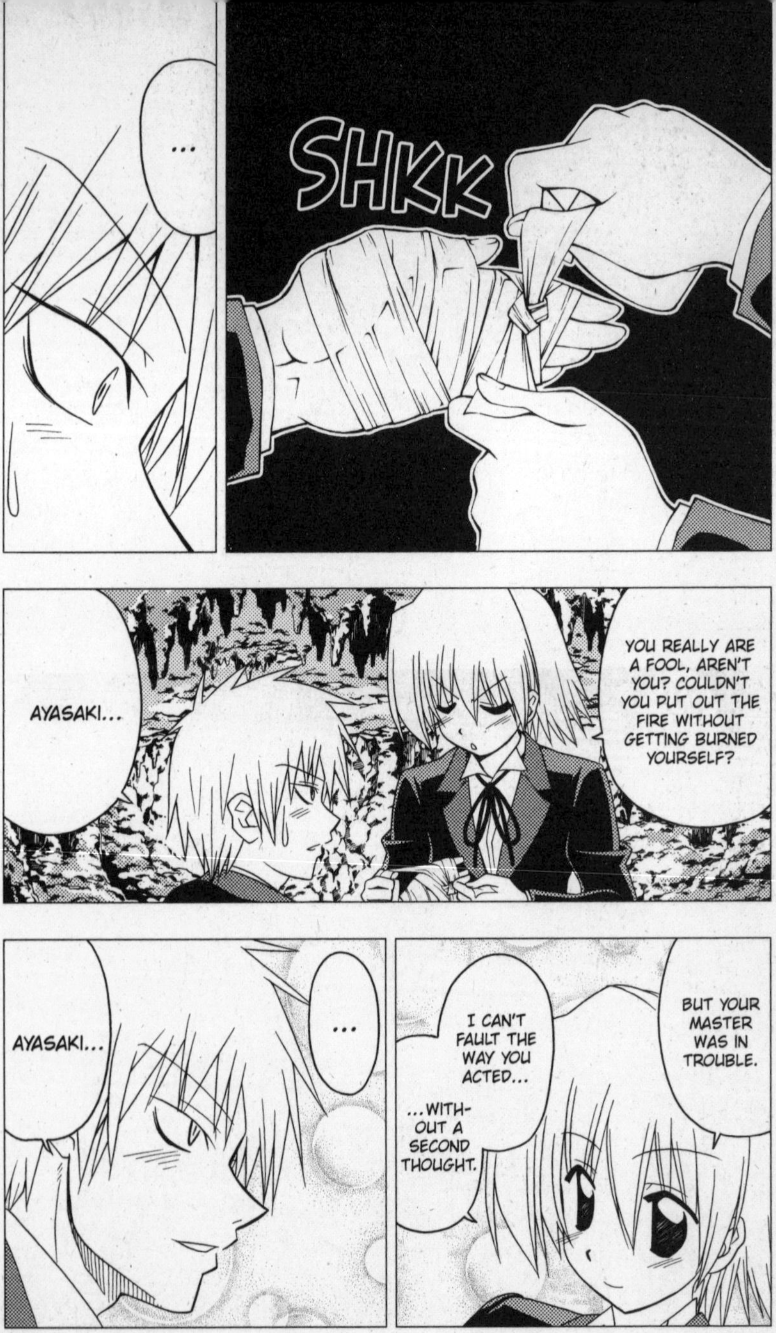
SHKK
...
YOU REALLY ARE A FOOL, AREN'T YOU? COULDN'T YOU PUT OUT THE FIRE WITHOUT GETTING BURNED YOURSELF?
AYASAKI...
BUT YOUR MASTER WAS IN TROUBLE.
I CAN'T FAULT THE WAY YOU ACTED...
...WITH-OUT A SECOND THOUGHT.
...
AYASAKI...

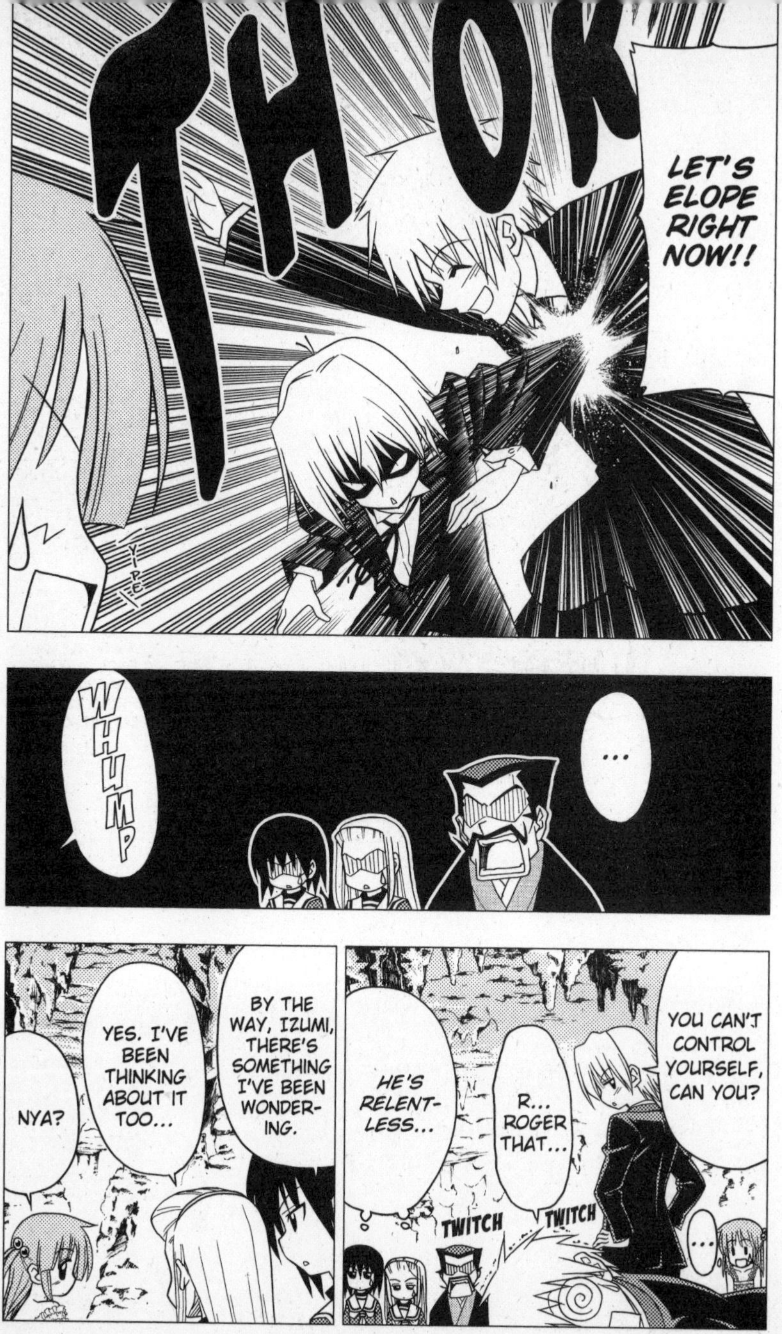
LET'S ELOPE RIGHT NOW!!
THOK
YIPE
...
WHUMP
YOU CAN'T CONTROL YOURSELF, CAN YOU?
...
R... ROGER THAT...
TWITCH
TWITCH
HE'S RELENT-LESS...
BY THE WAY, IZUMI, THERE'S SOMETHING I'VE BEEN WONDER-ING.
YES. I'VE BEEN THINKING ABOUT IT TOO...
NYA?

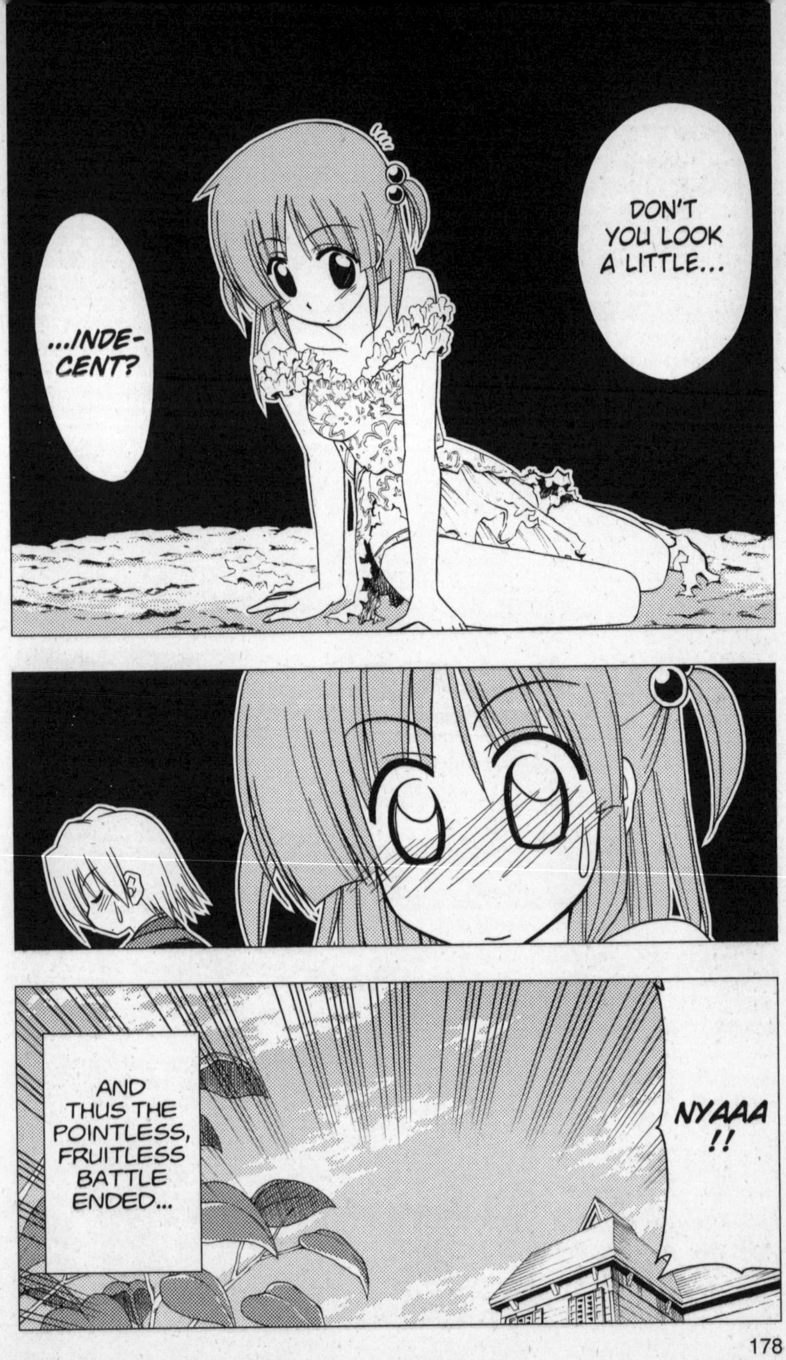
DON'T YOU LOOK A LITTLE...
...INDE-CENT?
NYAAA !!
AND THUS THE POINTLESS, FRUITLESS BATTLE ENDED...

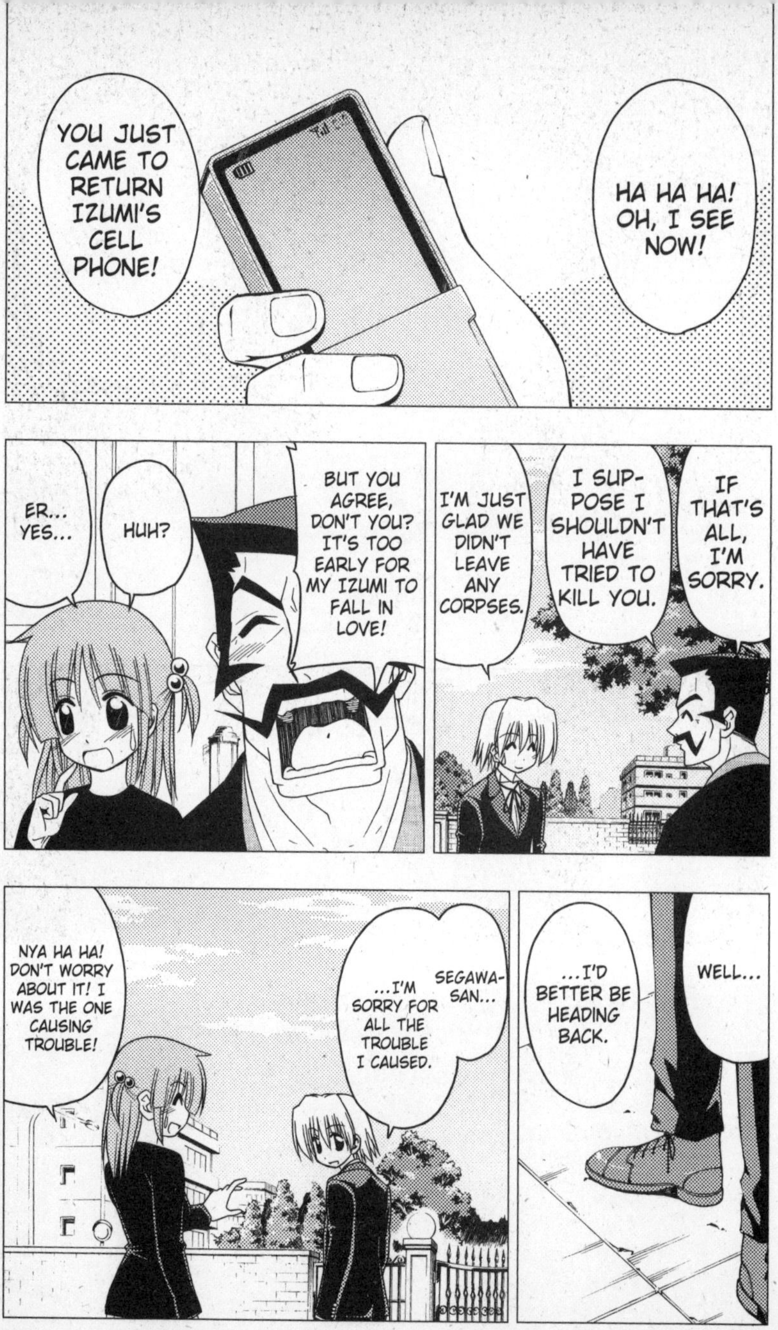
HA HA HA! OH, I SEE NOW!
YOU JUST CAME TO RETURN IZUMI'S CELL PHONE!
IF THAT'S ALL, I'M SORRY.
I SUPPOSE I SHOULDN'T HAVE TRIED TO KILL YOU.
I'M JUST GLAD WE DIDN'T LEAVE ANY CORPSES.
BUT YOU AGREE, DON'T YOU? IT'S TOO EARLY FOR MY IZUMI TO FALL IN LOVE!
HUH?
ER... YES...
WELL...
...I'D BETTER BE HEADING BACK.
SEGAWA-SAN...
...I'M SORRY FOR ALL THE TROUBLE I CAUSED.
NYA HA HA! DON'T WORRY ABOUT IT! I WAS THE ONE CAUSING TROUBLE!

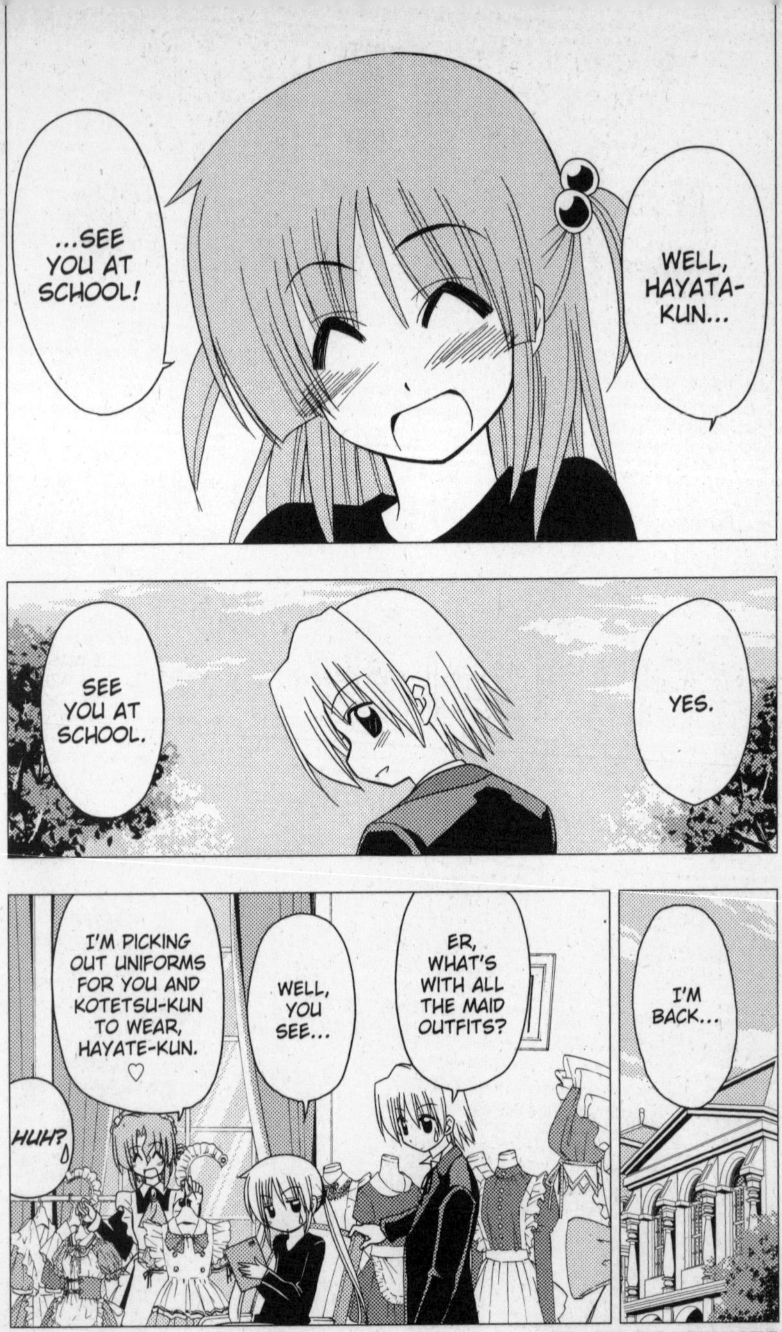
WELL, HAYATA-KUN...
...SEE YOU AT SCHOOL!
YES.
SEE YOU AT SCHOOL.
I'M BACK...
ER, WHAT'S WITH ALL THE MAID OUTFITS?
WELL, YOU SEE...
I'M PICKING OUT UNIFORMS FOR YOU AND KOTETSU-KUN TO WEAR, HAYATE-KUN. ♡
HUH?

TO BE CONTINUED

HAYATE THE COMBAT BUTLER

BONUS PAGE

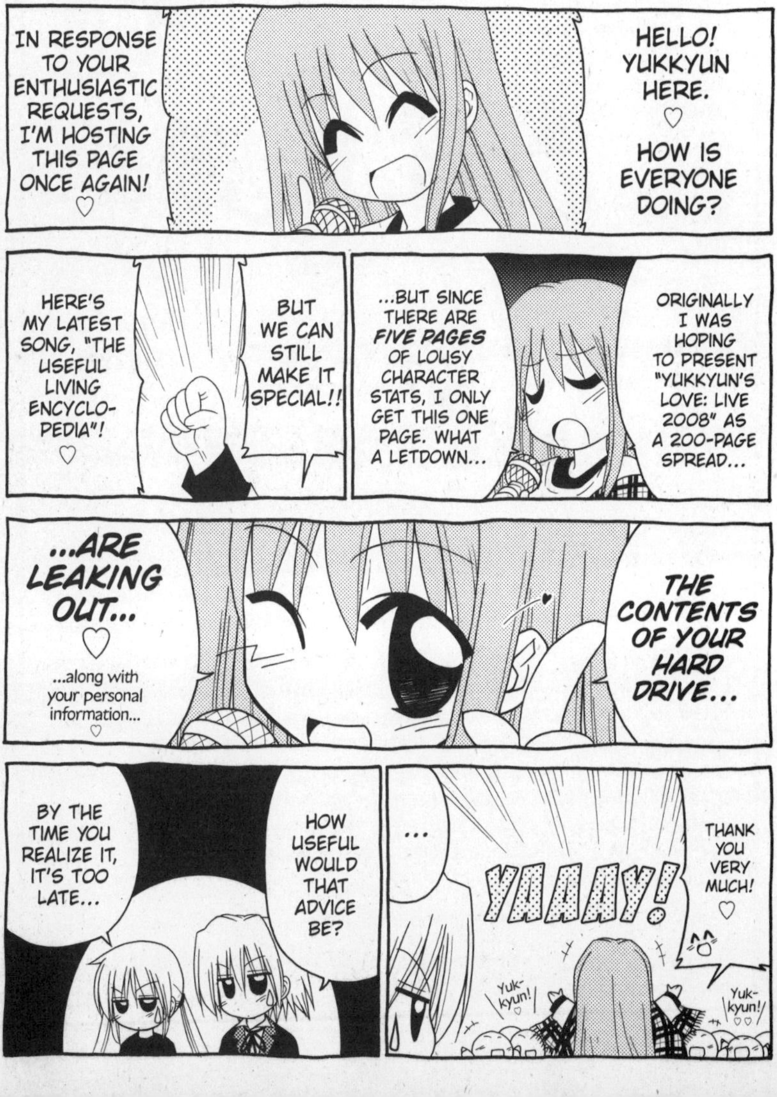

HELLO! YUKKYUN HERE. ♡
HOW IS EVERYONE DOING?
IN RESPONSE TO YOUR ENTHUSIASTIC REQUESTS, I'M HOSTING THIS PAGE ONCE AGAIN! ♡
ORIGINALLY I WAS HOPING TO PRESENT "YUKKYUN'S LOVE: LIVE 2008" AS A 200-PAGE SPREAD...
...BUT SINCE THERE ARE *FIVE PAGES* OF LOUSY CHARACTER STATS, I ONLY GET THIS ONE PAGE. WHAT A LETDOWN...
BUT WE CAN STILL MAKE IT SPECIAL!!
HERE'S MY LATEST SONG, "THE USEFUL LIVING ENCYCLOPEDIA"! ♡
THE CONTENTS OF YOUR HARD DRIVE...
...ARE LEAKING OUT... ♡
...along with your personal information... ♡
THANK YOU VERY MUCH! ♡
YAAAY!
Yuk-kyun! ♡♡
Yuk-kyun! ♡
...
HOW USEFUL WOULD THAT ADVICE BE?
BY THE TIME YOU REALIZE IT, IT'S TOO LATE...

PROFILE

[Age]
28

[Birthday]
December 23

[Blood Type]
AB

[Family Structure]
Father (Mikado Sanzenin)
Mother (Deceased)
Husband (Deceased)
Daughter (Nagi Sanzenin)

[Height]
152 cm

[Weight]
40 kg

[Strengths/Likes]
Family, songs

[Weaknesses/Dislikes]
Everything else

YUKARIKO SANZENIN

She started out as the mother of the heroine in an unreleased manga I drew a long time ago. Maya, the alien at the hot spring, is sort of a reincarnation of the same character.

In *Hayate*, she has a similar role. She's just like she is in the bonus manga: bright, cheerful and a natural goofball. Above all, she's vulnerable.

She's also totally incompetent. If you asked people who knew her when she was alive, they'd all answer in chorus, "She couldn't do anything by herself." She was so clueless that even little Nagi thought her mother couldn't survive on her own. Nagi's personality is a byproduct of the negative example set by her mom. Still, everyone found her endearing. In a sense, she embodied the very definition of an ojô-sama, even though she probably never saw real money in her life.

I plan to write something about her husband in the future.

By the way, her cause of death was not an illness. Maybe I'll get into greater detail someday… Maybe.

PROFILE

[Age]
15

[Birthday]
December 30

[Blood Type]
O

[Family Structure]
Father, Mother,
Brother

[Height]
149 cm

[Weight]
39 kg

[Strengths/Likes]
Mathematics

[Weaknesses/Dislikes]
Everything else

FUMI HIBINO

She's the future Hakuou Gakuin Student Council President (at least, that's the plan).

I made up her character on the spot in volume 15, so she doesn't have a complicated backstory or anything. I guess I'd been thinking about the sick daughter of the woman Hayate helped in volume 8, and I thought I'd like to have that girl appear later in the story. But I didn't expect her to turn out like this.

I was surprised. I think Fumi's mother is a goofball just like her daughter, so maybe there was never really anything to worry about back in volume 8. That's why she returned the money she borrowed so quickly.

Fumi is a flexible character, so I plan to work her into the story here and there. By the way, I had a hard time with her appearance; I wanted her to look different from the existing characters, so I put a lot of effort into designing her. What do you think? Speaking as the artist, I'd say she turned out pretty well…

PROFILE

[Age]
15

[Birthday]
February 10

[Blood Type]
B

[Family Structure]
Father
Mother
Grandfathers (many)
Grandmothers (many)
Brothers and sisters (many)

[Height]
154 cm

[Weight]
42 kg

[Strengths/Likes]
Travel, airplanes

[Weaknesses/Dislikes]
Spicy food, puns

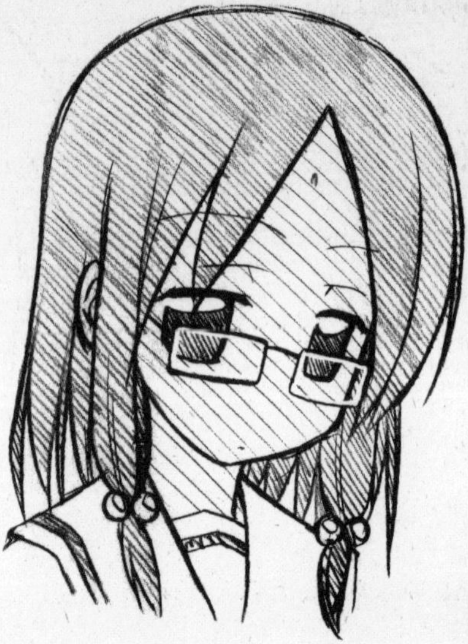

SHARNA ALAMGIR

Sharna is a foreign exchange student from India. She was created to play the straight man to Fumi's goofball character. She basically exists to provide snappy comebacks, so in a way she shares a heart and mind with Fumi.

I don't have a specific background story for her. I chose her surname just now as I was writing these character stats.

She probably doesn't like spicy curry.

Since she's attending Hakuou, I think she's a member of a royal family in India. It's probably a big family. As for why she's from India… Honestly, I don't know. Heh. When I was thinking about the character who would play the straight man to Fumi, for some reason I had the idea that she ought to be Indian, so I made her a foreign exchange student and went from there.

I think her partnership with Fumi has gone quite well, even though I made it up on the spot. I want to do more with them down the line. Her skin tone on the back cover of volume 15 didn't turn out the way I wanted, so I'd like to do a better version sometime.

PROFILE

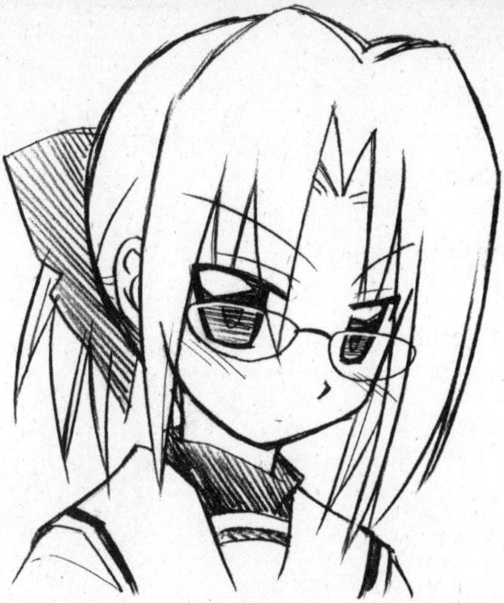

[Age]
16

[Birthday]
August 30

[Blood Type]
A

[Family Structure]
Father, Mother, Grandmother

[Height]
158 cm

[Weight]
45 kg

[Strengths/Likes]
Games, reading, theater, Sakuya-san

[Weaknesses/Dislikes]
Aika-san, ramen

CHIHARU HARUKAZE

Chiharu is the third maid-san to appear in this manga. If you don't know how she became a maid-san, please check out volume 14. ☆

So far we've only seen her as the secretary of the Hakuou Gakuin Student Council and as a maid, but she's actually quite the chameleon. I chose her name, Chiharu, because the kanji *chi* means "one thousand." She's the girl of a thousand faces. Her "cool" persona is what you see when she's not playing a role.

In the future I think she'll reveal other personas in addition to her maid character, like in *Glass Mask*, so please keep an eye out for her. I also want to explore her relationship with Nagi at some point.

PROFILE

[Age]
17

[Birthday]
October 9

[Blood Type]
B

[Family Structure]
Father, Mother, Fiancé

[Height]
160 cm

[Weight]
43 kg

[Strengths/Likes]
Information collection, tea

[Weaknesses/Dislikes]
Physical exercise

AIKA KASUMI

Aika is the student council vice president. If she were physically stronger, she'd be the president right now. She was the one who recommended Hinagiku as president. She had to repeat a year because of illness, so she's a year older than Hayate and his classmates.

In addition to her poor health, she has very slow reflexes. So even if she were stronger, she still wouldn't be any good at physical activities—not even catch. She can't keep up with the speed of the ball, and she has no upper-body strength.

But she rules the school with an iron fist thanks to her sadistic personality.

She's the wealthiest ojô-sama at Hakuou Gakuin. Her relationship to the Sanzenin family and the reason Mikado gave her that stone will soon become clear… At least, that's my plan.

I've come up with another character who will appear with her in an upcoming story line, but for now she's not doing very much.

As her artist, I like her a lot. She's very easy to draw.

HATA HERE. I JUST REALIZED WE'VE MADE IT ALL THE WAY TO VOLUME 16. HOW HAVE YOU ALL BEEN DOING?

TIME PASSES QUICKLY, DOESN'T IT? BY OCTOBER, THIS MANGA WILL HAVE BEEN RUNNING FOR FOUR YEARS. AT THIS POINT I CAN CALL IT A LONG-RUNNING SERIES, RIGHT? PERSONALLY, THOUGH, I FEEL LIKE IT'S JUST GETTING STARTED.

BY THE TIME THIS VOLUME HITS SHELVES, EVERYONE READING THE MONTHLY INSTALLMENTS IN *SHONEN SUNDAY* WILL KNOW THIS, BUT IN THE NEXT VOLUME *HAYATE* WILL HIT A MAJOR TURNING POINT.

NOW THAT THE FIRST SEASON OF THE ANIME HAS WRAPPED UP, I THINK I CAN GO AHEAD AND MAKE SOME BIG CHANGES IN THE DIRECTION OF THE MANGA. I'M NOT SURE HOW MUCH YOU READERS WANT THIS TO HAPPEN, BUT I'VE COME TOO FAR TO TURN BACK NOW. I'M GOING TO FOCUS ON MY BIG PLANS AS I DRAW!

EVEN THOUGH I'M A LITTLE NERVOUS ABOUT HOW THE UPCOMING DEVELOPMENTS WILL GO OVER, I HOPE YOU KEEP READING.☆

OKAY, CATCH YOU LATER IN VOLUME 17!!
SEE YA!☆

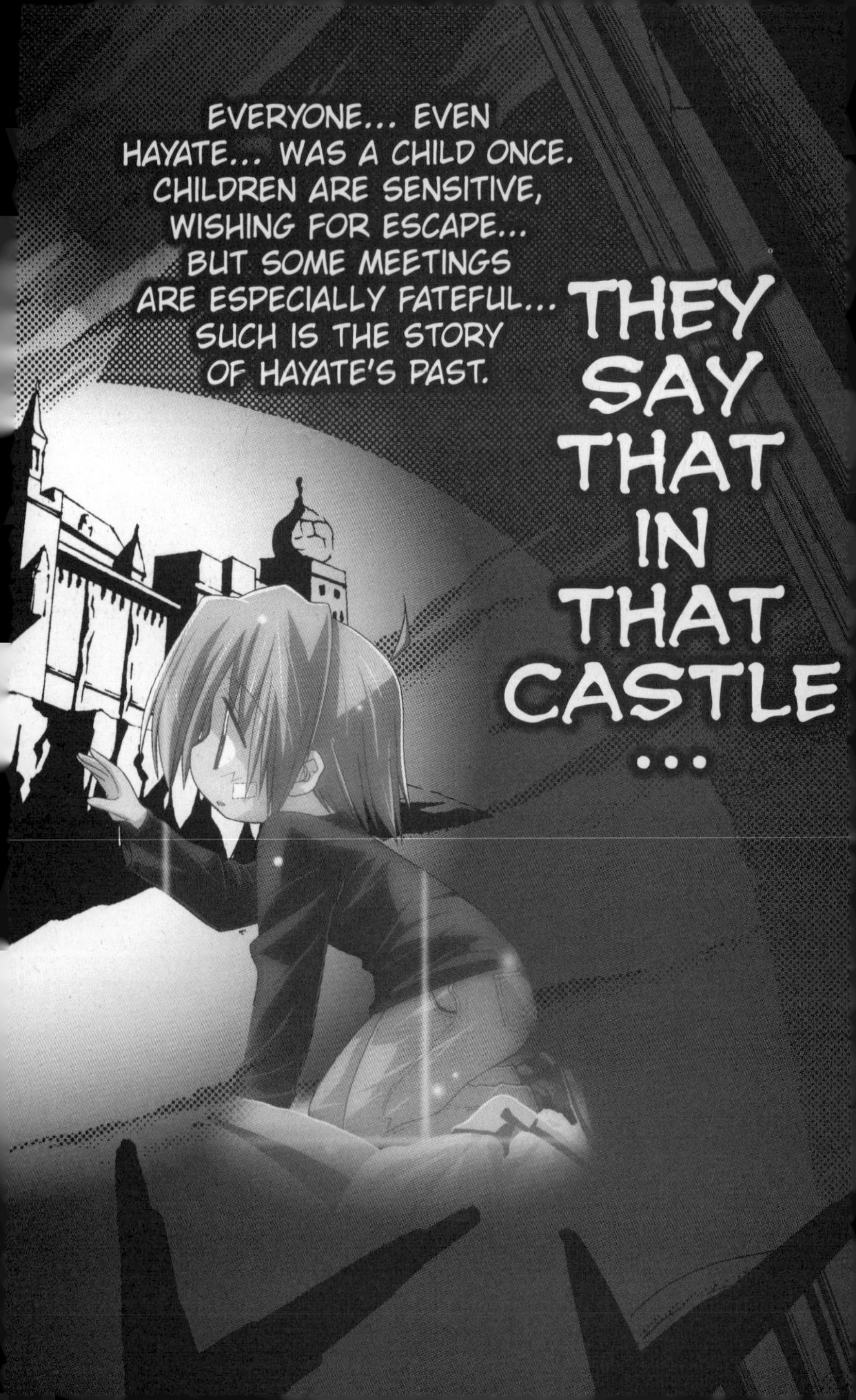
EVERYONE... EVEN HAYATE... WAS A CHILD ONCE. CHILDREN ARE SENSITIVE, WISHING FOR ESCAPE... BUT SOME MEETINGS ARE ESPECIALLY FATEFUL... SUCH IS THE STORY OF HAYATE'S PAST.
THEY SAY THAT IN THAT CASTLE...

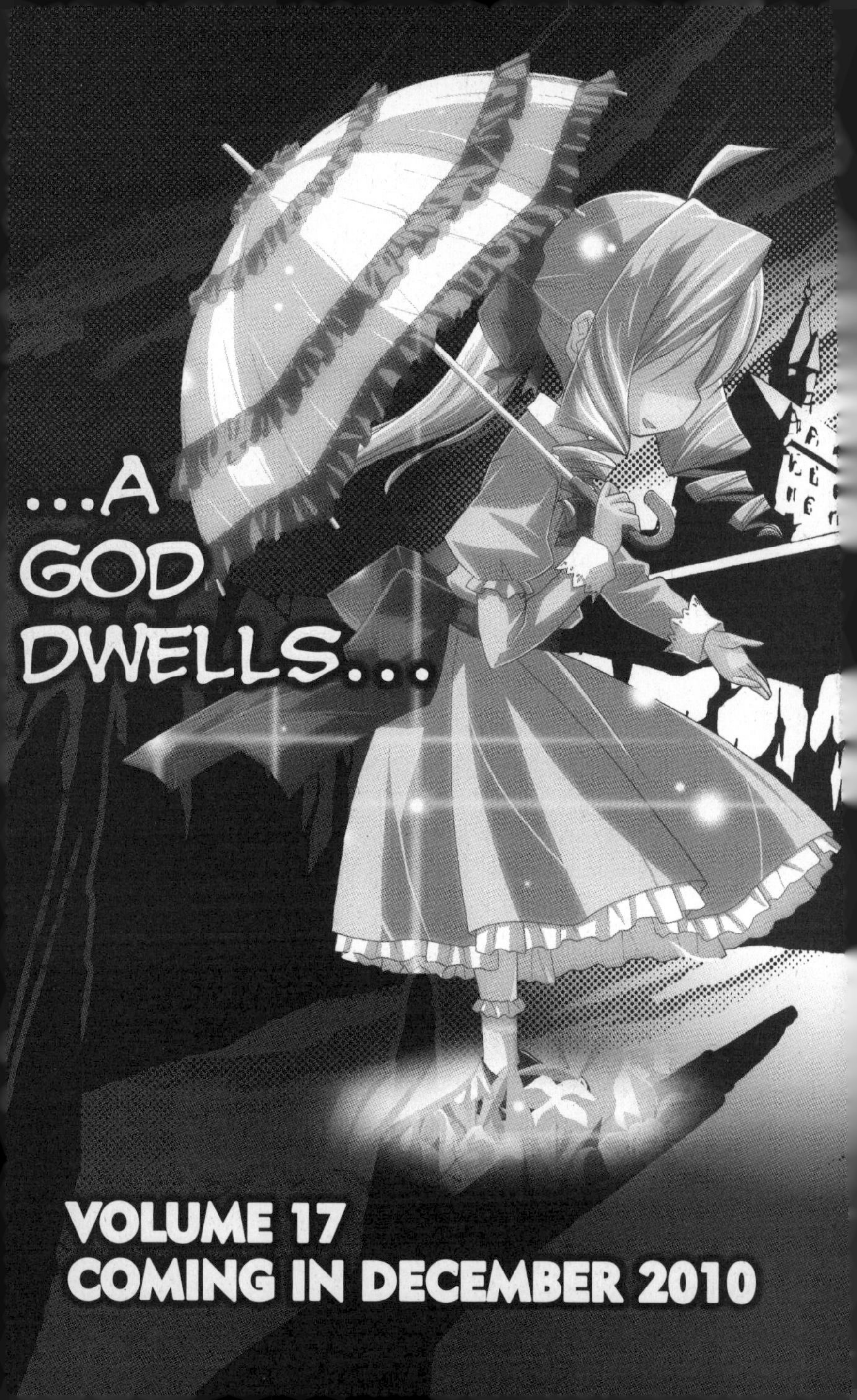
...A
GOD
DWELLS...
VOLUME 17
COMING IN DECEMBER 2010

The East Indian Is Surprised Too

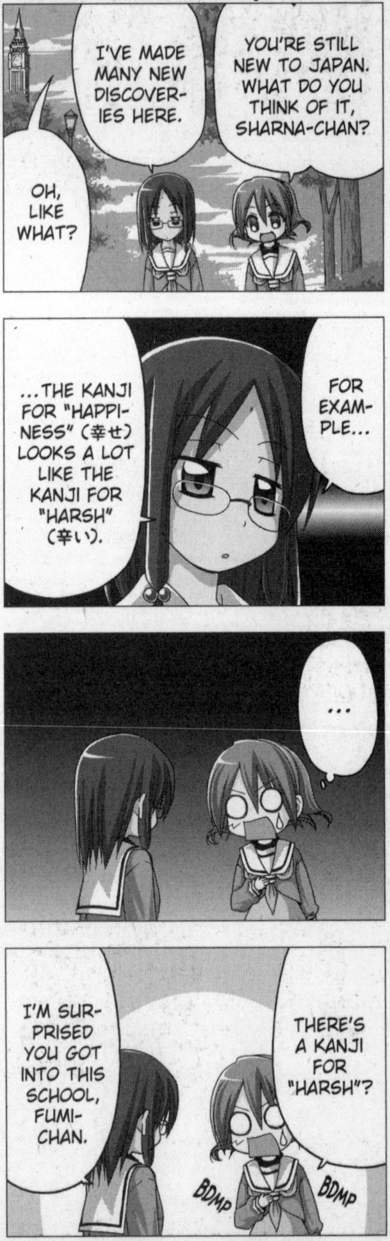
YOU'RE STILL NEW TO JAPAN. WHAT DO YOU THINK OF IT, SHARNA-CHAN?
I'VE MADE MANY NEW DISCOVERIES HERE.
OH, LIKE WHAT?
FOR EXAMPLE...
...THE KANJI FOR "HAPPINESS" (幸せ) LOOKS A LOT LIKE THE KANJI FOR "HARSH" (辛い).
...
THERE'S A KANJI FOR "HARSH"?
I'M SURPRISED YOU GOT INTO THIS SCHOOL, FUMI-CHAN.
BDMP
BDMP

The Japanese Is Surprised Too

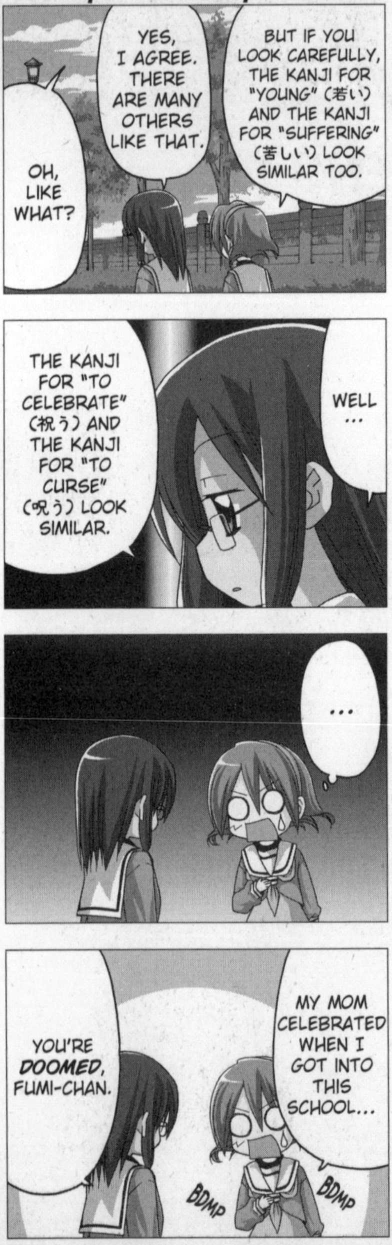
BUT IF YOU LOOK CAREFULLY, THE KANJI FOR "YOUNG" (若い) AND THE KANJI FOR "SUFFERING" (苦しい) LOOK SIMILAR TOO.
YES, I AGREE. THERE ARE MANY OTHERS LIKE THAT.
OH, LIKE WHAT?
WELL...
THE KANJI FOR "TO CELEBRATE" (祝う) AND THE KANJI FOR "TO CURSE" (呪う) LOOK SIMILAR.
...
MY MOM CELEBRATED WHEN I GOT INTO THIS SCHOOL...
YOU'RE *DOOMED*, FUMI-CHAN.
BDMP
BDMP

HAYATE THE COMBAT BUTLER

BAD END (8)

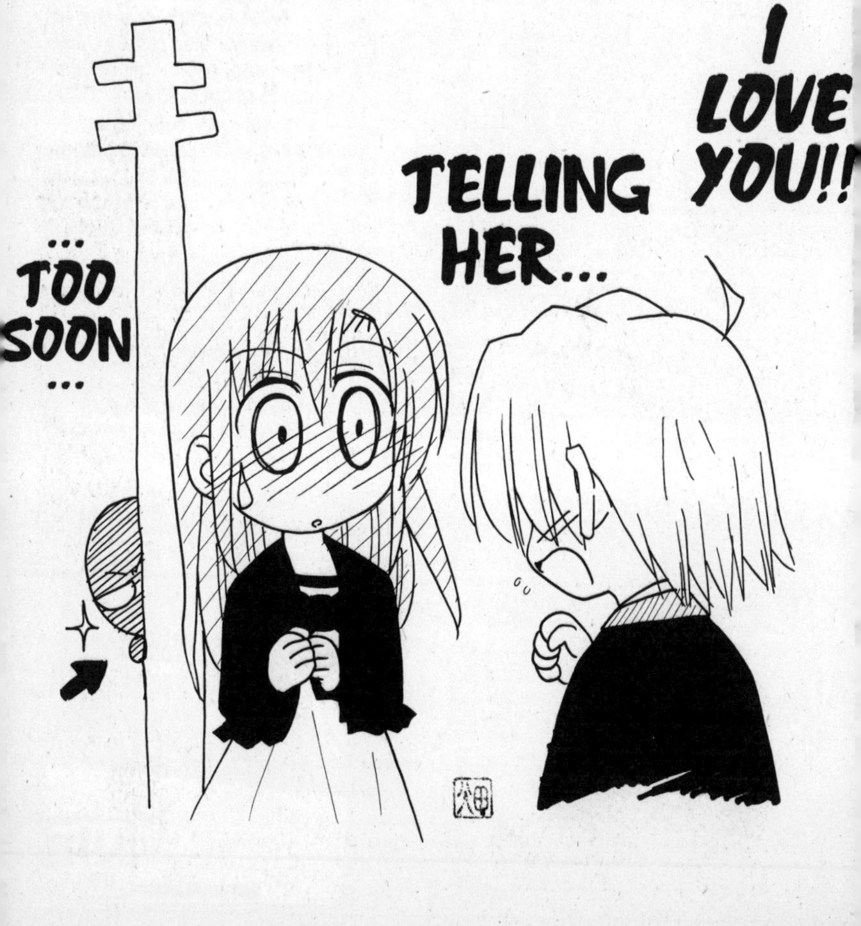
I LOVE YOU!!
TELLING HER...
...TOO SOON...

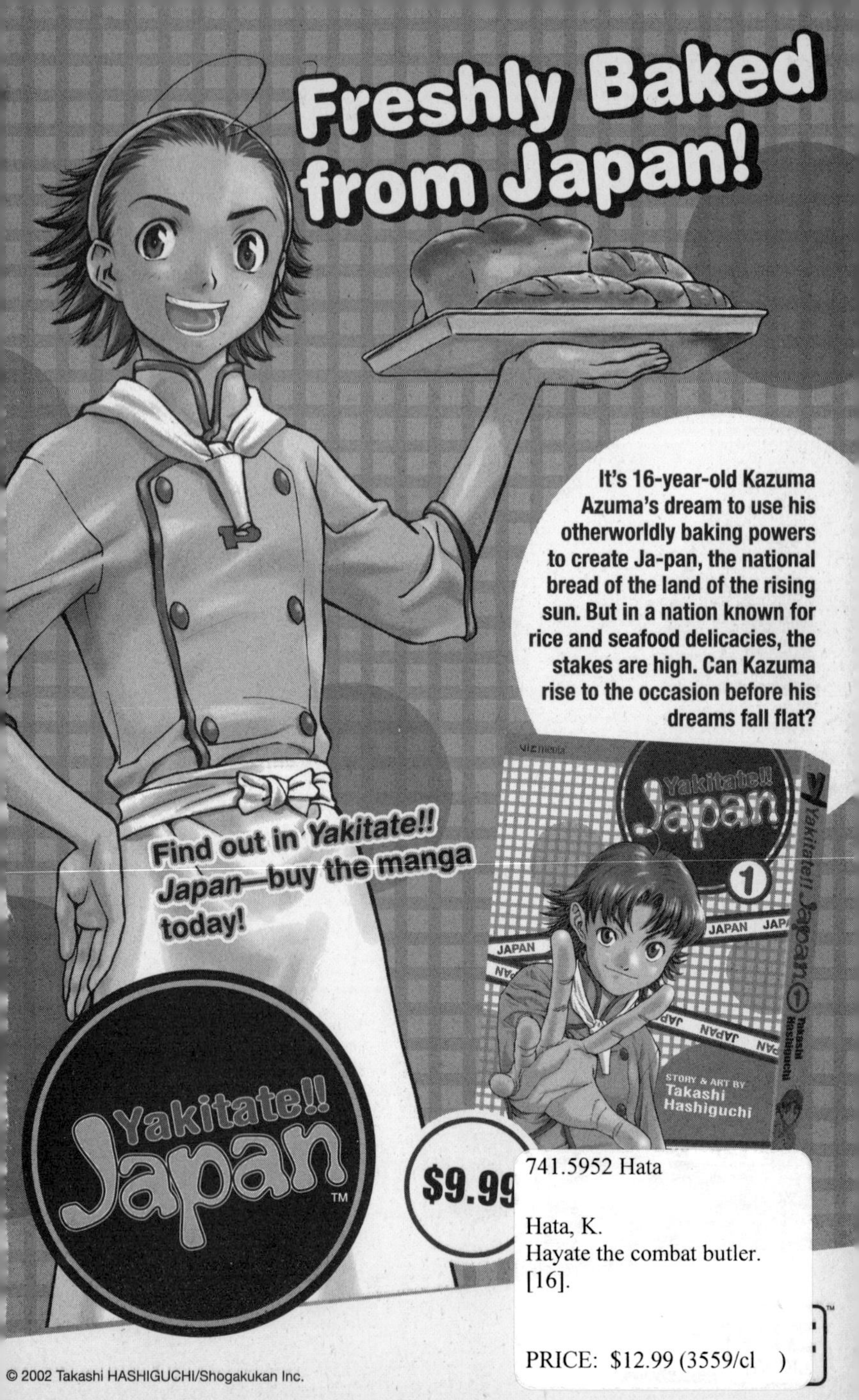

Freshly Baked from Japan!
It's 16-year-old Kazuma Azuma's dream to use his otherworldly baking powers to create Ja-pan, the national bread of the land of the rising sun. But in a nation known for rice and seafood delicacies, the stakes are high. Can Kazuma rise to the occasion before his dreams fall flat?
Find out in Yakitate!! Japan—buy the manga today!
Yakitate!! Japan 1
STORY & ART BY Takashi Hashiguchi
Yakitate!! Japan
$9.99